CARRYING ON

THE CARRY ONS AND FILMS OF PETER ROGERS AND GERALD THOMAS

IAN FRYER

FONTHILL

Fonthill Media Language Policy

Fonthill Media publishes in the international English language market. One language edition is published worldwide. As there are minor differences in spelling and presentation, especially with regard to American English and British English, a policy is necessary to define which form of English to use. The Fonthill Policy is to use the form of English native to the author. Ian Fryer was born in Blackpool and educated in Leeds; therefore, British English has been adopted in this publication.

Fonthill Media Limited
Fonthill Media LLC
www.fonthill.media
books@fonthill.media

First published in the United Kingdom and the United States of America 2023

British Library Cataloguing in Publication Data:
A catalogue record for this book is available from the British Library

ISBN 978-1-78155-906-2

Typeset in 10pt on 13pt Sabon
Printed and bound in England

Contents

Introduction: Carrying On, Regardless

The Carry On films have become such a huge edifice in the landscape of British comedy history that, whether they love them or loathe them, everybody seems to have an opinion about what they are and what they represent. The films were, however, made over such a long period that it is a lot harder to tie them down than one might think. The Carry Ons are many things, evolving over the years from their beginnings as a series of ensemble comedies set in the sorts of bureaucratic institutions that ordinary people found themselves having to negotiate in the post-war period. National Service, the comprehensive education system, or National Health Service hospitals were great social levellers, and the early Carry Ons found humour in people from widely different backgrounds placed in situations where they were forced to work together and discover what they had in common.

Eventually, the writing of the series passed on from Norman Hudis to Talbot Rothwell, and the scripts became more gag-based. The series expanded into a series of historical mini-epics, each one satirising a Hollywood film genre, but the audience was still able to recognise itself in the characters. The wonderfully diverse ensemble cast of the films represented a cross-section of British society—performers such as Sidney James, Kenneth Williams, and Hattie Jacques spanned the entire social spectrum; if you did not see yourself in any of the cast members, you might recognise instead your neighbour or your boss. Only at the sad, sorry dog-end of the series did the Carry On films lose their special, organic link with its audience and become some of the things they are often accused of being.

It has been one of the absolute pleasures of my writing career to present the stories of these wonderful actors and comic performers; it is a terrible cliché, but we really will never see their like again. The conditions in the British entertainment industry that produced not only the main Carry On cast members, but also such wonderful character actors as Richard Wattis and Patrick Cargill who only pop up occasionally in the films, no longer exist. Actors, writers, and directors could gain experience in forms of theatre such as of variety, cabaret, revue and repertory theatre, which have today almost completely disappeared. British cinema once produced screen comedies on an industrial scale, which allowed performers and technicians to hone their craft, while BBC Radio comedies were able to make talented artists into national stars virtually overnight with the right exposure on *ITMA*, *Ray's A Laugh*, or *Educating Archie*. Today, the British entertainment scene produces barely a handful of television sitcoms—potential talent has a lot fewer outlets.

Perhaps a relevant question is 'should Carry On carry on?' Does a movie series so steeped in both the comedy scene and wider society of the 1950s to the '70s have a place in the very different world of the twenty-first century? In reality, perhaps things are not so different today as they were fifty years ago—people have similar hopes and dreams and, no matter what their background is, they still find the same things funny. In many ways, we all have a piece of Carry On in our hearts; we recognise something of ourselves in regular cast members such as Sidney James, Kenneth Williams, Joan Sims, and Barbara Windsor, and in the situations they were put into by the two main screenwriters of the series, Norman Hudis and Talbot Rothwell.

This means that, despite the 1990s failure of *Carry On Columbus*, there is no reason why new Carry On productions should not be made. The keeper of the Carry On flame today is the indefatigable Brian Baker, to whom the rights of the Carry On brand were passed by Peter Rogers himself. Brian is filled with ideas on how to continue the series, which look very likely to reach fruition with a stage musical adaptation of *Carry On Girls*, featuring songs from the era in which the original film was made. Although there have been stage versions of Carry On in the past, most notably *Carry On London*, a major West End hit during the 1970s heyday of the original series, the new *Carry On Girls* woud sidestep comparisons with the original cast by putting its new cast in a different context.

The book you are reading expanded during its writing from being about the Carry On movies into something of a love letter to the filmmaking partnership of Peter Rogers and Gerald Thomas. Despite the huge audiences their films attracted, the Rogers and Thomas films have attracted little of the serious critical attention of other staples of the British comedy film, such as films of the Boulting brothers or the beloved Ealing Studios comedies. One could be forgiven for thinking that the pair only made Carry On films, whereas in fact the huge and lasting success of the Carry Ons has somewhat overshadowed the formidable contribution Rogers and Thomas made during a career spent at the very centre of British popular filmmaking. Peter Rogers, in particular, produced a huge range of films beyond his famous comedies, taking in thrillers, crime movies, and even a particularly lovely science fiction time-travel romance. Perhaps this book will go some way to redressing the balance and giving some of these films the attention they deserve.

Time and taste moves on, but even though the Carry Ons are products of their time, this does not mean that they cannot be enjoyed today—their near-constant presence on British television proves this to be the case. The Carry On pictures have become part of the background of British life—as British as fish and chips and beer served at room temperature, and we often take them for granted. Read on and discover a series of films that are often a lot more thoughtful, clever, and revealing about British life and attitudes than they are given credit for. Hopefully, we will all have a good laugh along the way!

1

Before the Carry Ons: The Early Peter Rogers and Gerald Thomas Films

Circus Friends (1956)

Gerald Thomas completed his last film as a film editor, the Second World War submarine drama *Above Us the Waves,* for his brother Ralph Thomas, released in late March 1955. This proved a great attraction and was the sixth most popular film at the British box office in 1955. With a big success under his belt, Gerald Thomas began life as a film director for producer Peter Rogers at that traditional training ground for new directors, the Children's Film Foundation. Peter Rogers both wrote and produced their first film together, *Circus Friends.* Rogers created a story about the efforts of two circus children and their Alsatian dog to retrieve a circus pony given to a farmer in lieu of a debt. Peter Rogers had experience making films for the foundation, his previous Children's Film Foundation production, *The Dog and the Diamond,* having won an award at the Venice Film Festival.

The special needs of the Children's Film Foundation made them perfect for directors learning their craft. They had to be structurally very simple with no flashbacks, so that even the youngest of audience members could understand what was going on. Everything needed to run in a consecutive sequence of events, with simple dialogue. As an experienced film editor, Gerald Thomas would have had no difficulty in handling a more complex narrative than the one here, but the restrictions placed upon him allowed Thomas to concentrate on the more unfamiliar tasks of dealing with a film crew and actors.

The four children who were the main cast members—Alan Coleshill, David Gilley, Pat Belcher and an eleven-year-old Carol White—were recruited from the Corona Academy, a famous theatre school which at this point operated from Chiswick in West London. Carol White must have impressed Rogers and Thomas, as she would be cast by them again a few years later in *Carry On*

Teacher. The youthful members of the cast were backed up by a large number of very experienced British character players. These included John Horsley as Mr Marlow, the circus owner and ringmaster; Meredith Edwards as the farmer who takes ownership of Pinto the Pony; the ubiquitous Sam Kydd as his farm hand; plus Harry Towb, Mona Washbourne, Conrad Philips and a future regular Carry On presence in the shape of Frank Forsyth.

Location shooting took place at Harefield, Hertfordshire, in April 1956 as part of a five-week filming schedule. The church hall was converted into a police station for the filming, while other scenes featuring the circus took place at nearby Batchworth Heath. Production was typically swift, and *Circus Friends* was submitted to the British Board of Film Censorship for classification on 8 August 1956. The film received its world premiere (though it was hardly treated as a gala occasion) at the Saturday Morning ABC Minors film show at The Ritz cinema, Richmond, Surrey, on 20 October 1956 at 11 a.m.

Circus Friends went on to become an absolute staple of the Children's Film Foundation and Saturday morning picture shows for decades to come, which is pretty good going for the work of a first-time director. After its initial 1956 screening, the film was still turning up as a strange window into an imagined past for movie-going youngsters in late 1978, marking an incredible twenty-two-year run.

The Passionate Stranger (1957)

Peter Rogers and Gerald Thomas' next project after *Circus Friends* saw Rogers as producer once more, with his new directorial prospect this time acting as associate producer on a project entitled *A Novel Affair*. This made a lot of sense as Gerald Thomas would have already learned a lot about the construction of a film story from his experience as a film editor, and had gotten his feet wet as a director on *Circus Friends*. On both this and the forthcoming *After the Ball*, he would learn about the other aspects of running a film production. The film was shot at Shepperton Studios in June and July 1956 by director Muriel Box (who was Peter Rogers' sister-in-law), from a script by Muriel and her husband Sidney Box, based on a story by Muriel written in 1949, which had been previously optioned by Rank.

The idea behind the film was extremely clever, involving an extended 'story within a story' sequence. The framing device involved Carlo, a well-built and handsome, but good-mannered young Italian man, being hired as chauffeur to Roger and Judith Wynter. Roger is wheelchair-bound with polio, while Judith is an author of popular romantic fiction. Judith is struggling with her latest novel and unsatisfied with what she has produced so far. Her publisher suggests that she seeks inspiration from real events happening around her, which sparks an idea. Struck with inspiration, Judith spends the following weeks writing a new story, entitled *The Passionate Stranger*.

The novel begins with the arrival of Mario, a handsome, virile Italian man, as chauffeur to Lord and Lady Hathaway. Lord Hathaway is an international diplomat, crippled, haughty, and embittered, while Lady Hathaway is a renowned concert pianist, frustrated in her artistic career by her husband's insistence on keeping her close. Mario and Lady Hathaway are thrown together when their Rolls-Royce breaks down near a small country village, and a passionate affair ensues. Back in the real world, Carlo reads the manuscript of *The Passionate Stranger* and picks up on the similarities between the story and real life. He gains the mistaken impression that Judith Wynter is in real life romantically interested in him. Carlo attempts to recreate the circumstances of the novel, only to discover the huge difference between romantic fiction and reality.

The project retained the working title *A Novel Affair* during its production and was extremely well cast: Ralph Richardson and Margaret Leighton portrayed Roger and Judith Wynter/Lord and Lady Hathaway, Carlo Justini played Carlo the chauffeur, and Patricia Dainton the maid, who was called Emily in the framing story and Betty in the novel sequence. Muriel Box also has some good directorial ideas, with the framing story being shot by cinematographer Otto Heller in monochrome, while the novel scenes are in lush Eastmancolor. In these scenes, Margaret Leighton is glamorous in the extreme, dressed in a series of gowns by the queen's dressmaker Norman Hartnell—Leighton was blessed with the sort of tall, willowy figure that fashion designers dream of, and she looks stunningly attractive in many scenes, while in others she was deliberately overdressed to the point of absurdity.

Unfortunately, the film, which by the time it had been publicised to the cinema trade and submitted to the BBFC in December 1956 had been retitled *The Passionate Stranger*, does not work at all. The attempts at showing the story of the novel as being analogous to the 'real' lives of the characters, only with hugely elevated levels of melodrama, are largely misjudged. The whole thing is played too straight, with opportunities for satirical comedy frustratingly passed up. Some of the performers enter into the proper spirit of the thing, with Margaret Leighton overplaying marvellously in the colour scenes. In the monochrome framing sequence, she looks at Carlo as if he has gone mad when he pledges his love to her after reading the novel. Patricia Dainton, as the maid in both stories, demonstrates her range—mousey and using her natural Scottish accent in the black and white scenes, transforming herself to sassy, sexy and English when the film moves to colour.

The idea cried out for a broader comedic approach, which it eventually would receive when Peter Rogers and Gerald Thomas returned to the same basic idea to great effect three years later in *Please Turn Over*. As it was, *The Passionate Stranger* fell crashingly between the two stools of romantic comedy and romantic drama. If Muriel Box did not seem to know what kind of film she was making, the publicity department at distributors British Lion had no chance. Bizarrely, advertising for the film went to great lengths to keep the central idea of the film secret, which meant that the posters and trailers all gave the impression that *The Passionate Stranger* was just an absurdly clichéd romantic drama. For most of its length, that is exactly how the film turned out, so perhaps that was fair enough. It did not make any great waves when it toured British cinemas from February 1957, with the Western *Thunder over Arizona* in support, and soon fell into obscurity.

After the Ball (1957)

After the Ball began shooting at Beaconsfield in October 1956 on a six-week schedule under director Bob Compton Bennett, who generally dropped his first name on his film credits to become simply Compton Bennett. Bennett had scored a huge success in 1947 with the psychological drama *The Seventh Veil* and three years later helmed a big budget version of *King Solomon's Mines* for MGM, starring Deborah Kerr and Stewart Granger. His career had declined somewhat in the years that followed to the extent that he was available to direct co-features at Beaconsfield.

This would be Gerald Thomas' last film credited as associate producer under Peter Rogers before he became a full-time film director, and indeed Thomas would go straight to work on his next directorial assignment when *After the Ball* wrapped, with shooting on *Time Lock* commencing in December 1956. It should be added that some sources list Gerald Thomas and Compton Bennett as co-directing 'The Sickness of Kilimanjaro', an episode of the filmed television series *White Hunter* released the following year, but the episode is unavailable for viewing and this cannot be confirmed.

After the Ball would be one of a run of Peter Rogers pictures inspired by a television production. Singer and actress Pat Kirkwood had been seen as a very hot prospect and had crossed the Atlantic to try her luck in Hollywood. This did not go well, with Kirkwood appearing in only one film before returning home in the midst of a suicide attempt. She remained very popular in Britain, however, especially for her performances as legendary music hall stars Marie Lloyd and Vesta Tilley. These were made available to a wider audience when Pat Kirkwood starred in a series of four television specials for BBC Television in 1955 and 1956. The third of these was *The Great Little Tilley*, written by Kirkwood's husband Hubert Gregg, who was an interesting figure in his own right. The multitalented Gregg was an actor, writer, playwright, and songwriter, in the latter capacity having written the all-time classic 'Maybe It's Because I'm a Londoner'.

The Great Little Tilley gained extra publicity when its original broadcast date of Thursday, 16 February 1956 was cancelled due to Musicians' Union strike action. As it happened, Pat Kirkwood was in bed on the planned production date with a sore throat, so perhaps it was for the best. The show eventually took place on 15 March 1956 and garnered excellent reviews for Kirkwood's lead performance. Peter Rogers was always on the lookout for television properties to adapt for the big screen, and this story offered something a little different. A musical drama shot in Eastmancolor would stretch the facilities of the relatively small Beaconsfield Studios to their limits, and hopefully change a few minds as to what the studio was capable of. In the aftermath of *After the Ball*'s successful production, Rogers announced to the trade ambitious plans to upgrade Beaconsfield's facilities and add a third soundstage to the site. As events transpired, Peter Rogers' spell in charge at Beaconsfield did not have much longer to run as Julian Wintle and Leslie Parkin's enterprising film and television production outfit Independent Artists leased the entire studio from February 1958.

After the Ball was the story of the professional career of music hall male impersonator Vesta Tilley, who was a huge star in the Edwardian era and famously convinced many young men to enlist in the army during the First World War. The production quality of the film was quite decent within the limitations of its budget, and Pat Kirkwood really threw herself into the musical numbers, but dramatically, *After the Ball* had some problems. The script by Hubert Gregg and Peter Blackmore was hopelessly old-fashioned, assailing audiences with the sort of stilted dialogue only found in historical biographies, such as 'Got to move with the times, after all, this is 1882'. The two main characters, meanwhile, age not a day in a time span of twenty-five years, though Laurence Harvey is eventually kitted out with a moustache and joke shop wig to denote the ravages of the years.

In a review of the original BBC TV production, Patrick Campbell put his finger on the film's central problem: 'Drama needs conflict, and there was little in the career of Miss Tilley that did not move smoothly on oiled wheels'. Thus for the film adaptation, the life of Tilley's future husband Walter de Frese had to be mined for family conflict. Laurence Harvey was cast in this role, complete with his vertiginous quiff, which stayed in place for all his roles, no matter how unhistorical the actor's signature hairstyle might be. There was a move afoot in the British film industry to build Harvey up into a big star at this point, and on one level, it was something of a coup for producer Peter Rogers to secure the services of British cinema's potential new star. Harvey had by this time been very good in Lewis Gilbert's 1954 film noir *The Good Die Young* and made a decent enough fist of playing author Christopher Isherwood in

I Am A Camera. Playing a romantic lead was never in his range, however, and from the evidence of *After the Ball*, it was well beyond his capabilities at this point in his career. True movie stardom was coming for Harvey, who was catapulted into the big time when *Room at the Top* was released in January 1959.

After the Ball, meanwhile, went out on a double bill with Gerald Thomas' next film as director, *Time Lock*, from August 1957. Laurence Harvey was top billed, both on promotional materials and on the credits seen on screen. It must have been galling for Pat Kirkwood to cede top billing to the conspicuously less talented Harvey, particularly in a production where she clearly had the starring role. The unnamed reviewer of the *West London Observer* amusingly described the character of Walter de Frese as being 'played with agonising charm by Laurence Harvey' in a review that found *After the Ball* distinctly old-fashioned compared with its partner in its waltz around Britain's cinemas, *Time Lock*.[1]

Time Lock (1957)

Peter Rogers and Gerald Thomas had two films released in September 1957, both based on television plays. *The Vicious Circle* had originally been a BBC serial written by the corporation's star suspense writer Francis Durbridge and suffered from the fact that much of the potential audience had watched the original. For *Time Lock*, however, Rogers came up with the bright idea of adapting an American television play. He wrote the script himself, based on an original work by Arthur Hailey that had been broadcast on 28 November 1956 on America's NBC network as part of the *Kraft Theatre* anthology series. Hailey was an Anglo-Canadian writer who became a popular TV writer in the mid-1950s and would become a best-selling novelist in the mid-60s with titles such as *Hotel* and *Airport*. A story written around the restrictions of being performed in a small television studio in New York proved perfect for a low-budget British film adaptation and had the added advantage that very few British moviegoers would be familiar with the story.

Time Lock was shot at Beaconsfield Studios in December 1956 and was awarded its BBFC certificate on 31 January 1957. Distributors Lion International publicised the film along with its slate of releases at that year's Cannes Film Festival in April, and *Time Lock* was screened to the London cinema trade on 27 June. It was booked on the Gaumont cinema circuit and went on release on 11 August at the bottom half of a double bill with the previously mentioned Beaconsfield production, *After the Ball*, though *Time Lock* tended to garner better reviews.

The film's story involves the child of an accountant in a bank who wanders into the bank's main vault as the staff are about to close up for the weekend and is locked in. By the time the child's disappearance is discovered, the vault's time lock has been activated, and a desperate race against time begins to somehow get into the sealed vault before the air supply runs out. Rogers made a few changes in his adaptation, most notably changing the location from the US to Toronto, which allowed the English Home Counties to double in outdoor scenes for rural Canada and gave the production a little more leeway in terms of accents. While the *Kraft Theatre* version had featured former Hollywood B-picture star Chester Morris and future A-list movie director Sidney Pollack, Rogers and Thomas called in pretty much every British-based North American actor of the era. *Time Lock* can be regarded as being of some level of historical importance just for getting Robert Beatty, Robert Ayers, Alan Gifford, Lee Patterson, and Gordon Tanner into the same film—that other ever-present Yank in 1950s British cinema Paul Carpenter must have been busy that week.

Lee Patterson had carved a niche for himself as the bequiffed American bad-boy of British B-pictures, playing a succession of surly leather-jacketed petty criminals. *Time Lock* is something of a change of pace for him, donning a suit in order to play Colin Walker, the accountant whose young son is trapped in the vault. Betty McDowall, who was Australian but generally played English roles, co-stars as Colin's wife Lucille, and the pair understandably spend most of the film worrying about the fate of their son. The bank's safe expert Dawson (Robert Beatty) is called in and hatches a plan to use the physical strength of manual workers among the crowd gathered outside the bank to break into the uncrackable safe. Among the would-be rescuers is none other than a young Sean Connery, who plays one of a welding team trying to gain access to the safe.

Time Lock works very well indeed, the economy of the enclosed setting allowing Rogers and Thomas to employ a large cast and add a few other frills, such as a location-shot sequence in which Robert Beatty is picked up by helicopter to take him to the bank. Stanley Black's music is very good, especially his opening theme with a suspense-building 'tick tock' motif. Gerald Thomas turns out to be quite a decent dramatic director here, maintaining the suspense right to the end. In typical Thomas fashion, he does an efficient, unfussy job, letting the better-than-average script do the hard work for him.

The Vicious Circle (1957)

The Vicious Circle might just be the best of the Rogers-Thomas thrillers. It was based on a six-part Francis Durbridge-written serial that was screened by BBC TV from 10 March 1956 with the unprepossessing title of *My Friend Charles*. The film features a screenplay by Durbridge himself that attempts to simplify one of his typically labyrinthine stories. The plots of his TV and radio serials were legendary for being almost impossible to follow, but his work was nevertheless extremely popular for many years in both Britain and Germany.

This factor made Peter Rogers' decision to adapt a Durbridge serial a good bet for export sales, with the film being seen across Europe and Scandinavia as well as in the traditional English-speaking markets for British pictures. In Germany, where local producers made their own version of Durbridge's serials, along with works adapted from other English thriller writers such as Edgar Wallace, the film was retitled *Interpol Ruft Berlin* (Interpol Calls Berlin).

Time Lock had established Gerald Thomas as a dramatic director, and as a result, his next film was able to attract the services of a *bona fide* movie star in the form of John Mills. By 1957, Mills was close to reaching the peak of his stardom, following *The Vicious Circle* with hits such as *Dunkirk*, *Ice Cold in Alex*, *I Was Monty's Double*, and *Tiger Bay*. The presence of Mills was probably a factor in the producers' ability to attract a very good supporting cast, including Roland Culver, Wilfrid Hyde-White, and Derek Farr.

The Vicious Circle also both looks and sounds terrific, with lovely, shadowy film noir photography by Otto Heller which adds to the film's atmosphere enormously; this might actually be the best-looking film that Peter Rogers and Gerald Thomas ever made together. Stanley Black provides a very suspenseful score, which gives an added sense of scale to what is already a very well-carpentered film. As for the plotline, John Mills plays Dr Howard Latimer, suspected of murder when a German actress he has been asked to meet when she arrives at the airport is found dead in his apartment. Any further explanation of the plot would take up the rest of the chapter, so labyrinthine is the story—some things never change in the world of Francis Durbridge.

Reflecting on *The Vicious Circle* in a *Times* interview a couple of years later, Peter Rogers was rueful about the decision to adapt a serial that had been screened on prime time BBC Television at 8 p.m. on Saturday nights only a year before the film was shot:

> Audiences don't ask for films and television to be at opposite poles, provided that they *are* different. They like to see television favourites in films, so long as they are not doing exactly the same thing, since then why should they go out and pay money to see something they can stay at home and see for nothing? We ran into this trouble a few years ago with *Vicious Circle*, based on a Francis Durbridge television serial: it had a new name and a new cast, but as soon as people heard its hero was called Dr Latimer they instantly said: 'Oh, that must be *The Brass Candlestick*. We saw it on television'.[2]

Why anyone might have thought *My Friend Charles* was called *The Brass Candlestick* remains unrecorded.

The Vicious Circle was reported in *Kinematograph Weekly*'s 23 May 1957 edition as being ready for release, but it was not screened for the cinema trade until 27 August. The film was released early the following month and made its way around the United Kingdom's cinemas for the next couple of months. It was accompanied on its travels by *The Wayward Girl*, a 1957 drama about a young woman who gets trapped in a parole racket. This was produced in 'Naturama', which makes the film sound like a nudist movie, but was actually the name of Republic Pictures' anamorphic widescreen process (one might describe it as the poor man's CinemaScope, except that in some ways it worked better). *The Wayward Girl* was one of Republic's last productions, studio head Herbert J Yates announcing the end of motion picture production at the company's 1958 annual general meeting.

The Duke Wore Jeans (1958)

The previous two Rogers and Thomas productions had stuck pretty closely to the standard British B-picture thriller tropes of the era, and Gerald Thomas had proved himself as a capable dramatic director. *The Duke Wore Jeans* saw Thomas adapting to more comedic fare, which proved to be much closer to the sort of material that suited him. This featured Tommy Steele in the dual role of an ordinary young bloke who likes a good sing-along with his trusty guitar, and his double, the son of a duke. The young cockney takes the place of the young aristocrat during a trip to a Ruritania-esque country (in which, naturally, everyone is portrayed as English, with the exception of the Austrian Eric Pohlmann). The duke's son is there to discuss cattle-breeding, but the royal family are more interested in marrying off their daughter to him, this idea being a non-starter as he is already secretly married.

Naturally, the chirpy young doppelgänger, with his occasional bursts of lightweight rock 'n' roll, is seen as a breath of fresh air and goes down a storm, particularly with the young princess (played by June Laverick). As you might gather from the plot description, it is all very silly, but actually works pretty well. Norman Hudis wrote a decent script, while Rogers and Thomas hired a solid cast capable of handling this type of material with ease. Tommy Steele is personable and fun—one can see how he later became a star of stage musicals—and some excellent character players were hired, particularly Alan Wheatley as the king and the aforementioned Eric Pohlmann as a sneaky prime minister.

Naturally, *The Duke Wore Jeans* is a musical and, in that regard, has a decent pedigree, featuring songs by Tommy Steele's regular writing team of Lionel Bart and Michael Pratt, both of whom would become much better known after Tommy Steele's hit-making era—Bart as the composer of the smash hit musical *Oliver!* and Pratt in his other career as an actor, most famously in the 1969 ghostly television detective series *Randall and Hopkirk (Deceased)*.

Tommy Steele was a Bermondsey-born former seaman (then known as Tommy Hicks) who was catapulted to fame as Britain's first home-grown rock 'n' roll star with his number thirteen hit single *Rock With the Caveman* in 1956. After following that up with his number one hit *Singing the Blues* in 1957, an attempt was made to capitalise on Steele's success with a film of his life story, imaginatively titled *The Tommy Steele Story*. Incredibly to modern sensibilities, the film was put into production by the executive producer, Peter Rogers, with a script by Norman Hudis, only four months after Steele first hit the charts. It has to be remembered, however, that not only did no one know whether Steele's entire career was going to be a flash in the pan, but for all anyone knew, the entire phenomenon of rock 'n' roll might be over in six months' time. With speed being of the essence, Steele, Bart, and Pratt wrote twelve songs in seven days, and other acts were brought in to help pad out the film's eighty-one-minute length, including Humphrey Littleton, the Chas McDevitt Skiffle Group, and Calypso performer Tommy Eytle.

The Tommy Steele Story packed in the teenagers to their local ABC cinema, and *The Duke Wore Jeans* was on the studio floor at British National Studios, Elstree, on 21 October 1959, beginning a six-week filming schedule. By now a proven cinema attraction, Steele got a much better financial deal than the £3,000 he was paid for *The Tommy Steele Story*, and an article in the magazine *Truth* revealed that his salary for the new film was £20,000 plus 10 per cent of the takings.[3] Gerald Thomas was drafted in to direct the new film, and in an interview for trade magazine *Kinematograph Weekly*, he revealed something of what was at stake with the new film: 'Of one thing we are sure. This film will have to be a lot better than the first Steele picture. If it isn't, we won't have an audience for a third'.[4] The audience for a third film was certainly there, but Steele's next prodution, *Tommy the Toreador*, would be made by other hands.

For the present, however, *The Duke Wore Jeans* fitted in nicely with ambitious plans by Anglo-Amalgamated to release more expensively produced, teenage-oriented product during 1958. To this end, the company also released a film adaptation of the BBC's teen music television show *6.5 Special* and a slew of American imports originally made for the drive-in market, including *Reform School Girl*, *Motor-Cycle Gang*, and the future cult classic *I Was A Teenage Frankenstein*.

The Duke Wore Jeans began playing around the country on the ABC circuit at the end of March 1958 in a 'U' certificate double bill with *Blood Arrow*, a low-budget Western from 1958 starring Scott Brady and written by future *Star Trek* and *Space: 1999* producer Fred Freiberger. If nothing else, this illustrates the random nature of B-picture choices in British 1950s cinemas.

Chain of Events (1958)

We now reach an interesting turn in the screen partnership of Peter Rogers and Gerald Thomas. Thomas has proved himself as a dramatic director with *Time Lock* and graduated to the slicker, more expensive *The Vicious Circle* and *The Duke Wore Jeans*. From here, one might have expected Rogers and Thomas to try their hands at even more expensive fare, but instead, they made a pair of supporting features back-to-back. The future course of Rogers and Thomas' filmmaking career can be detected in the production of these two films, *Chain of Events* and *The Solitary Child*: the best possible ensemble casts gathered together in films made with maximum speed and efficiency.

Chain of Events was shot at Beaconsfield by Gerald Thomas as director for his producer Peter Rogers back-to-back with *The Solitary Child*, each film having a three-week shooting schedule. It was made by Beaconsfield Films for distributors British Lion, with a screenplay by Patrick Brawn, an actor who turned to writing with some success, later becoming story editor of the first season of the TV series *The Avengers*. His script was based on a radio play called *London Story*, which had been written by another actor turning his hand to writing, Leo McKern. Publicity for *Chain of Events* claimed that this made Gerald Thomas the first director in history to shoot two feature films in six weeks. As these were not feature films, but actually B-pictures of only about an hour each in length, this translated to about the standard length of a low-budget feature film shoot. It was still an impressive achievement, however.

Chain of Events was the first of the two films to begin shooting, in June 1957, with studio work at Beaconsfield and location filming in Uxbridge, where the crew shot scenes outside the post office, the railway station, and on the high street. For the filming, Thomas used what was later described as a mobile film studio, which was in reality a double-decker bus hired from London Transport containing the company's camera equipment. This caused problems when members of the public tried to board the bus, taking some convincing that the vehicle was not a regular bus service.[5]

The script is an unusual one showing how one, seemingly minor, transgression causes a ripple effect—or even a chain of events—which ends in blackmail and death. Bank clerk Kenneth Griffith (whose character is called Clarke and works in a bank) tries to dodge paying his bus fare because he does not have any change. He is caught by bus conductor Cyril Chamberlain and makes such a fuss about it that he ends up being prosecuted. He gives the name and address of a bumptious, irritating bank customer (played by Ballard Berkeley), who is subsequently so furious at being called into court that he insults the judge instead of defending himself properly, and as a result is fined £5. So far, so relatively minor, but cheerful newspaper reporter Dermot Walsh is in court, so the story of a prominent businessman being fined for fare-dodging is splashed on the front page of the newspaper. Unfortunately for Walsh, once the businessman has calmed down, he is able to establish an alibi. Also, he is about to invest in Walsh's newspaper, so his editor is forced to give Walsh the sack. As a result, Walsh heads for his local pub, where he drunkenly blurts out that the paper's owner is keeping a mistress. This is within earshot of gossip writer Jack Watling, who takes the information to a professional blackmailer. After that, things start to get really complicated.

As you can tell from the above partial story synopsis, *Chain of Events* packs a lot of story into its sixty-two-minute running time. The film zips along in entertaining fashion, boosted by a very well-chosen cast that includes several future Carry On regulars. Besides the aforementioned Cyril Chamberlain, Joan Hickson plays Elsie, the barmaid at Dermot Walsh's local pub; Anthony Sagar is a comedy drunk on Kenneth Griffith's fateful bus journey; while Freddie Mills is great fun as the incredibly dim thug Tiny. One can certainly see how Peter Rogers and Gerald Thomas detected comedic possibilities in the boxing champion, casting him in *Carry On Constable* and *Carry On Regardless*. Susan Shaw, playing Dermot Walsh's plucky girlfriend, would soon turn up in *Carry On Nurse*, while Frank Forsyth was in no fewer than eight Carry Ons over the years.

Special mention should go to two cast members who were excellent here: Martin Wyldeck is smoothly menacing as the blackmailer, and Harold Lang, here playing rival crook Jimmy Boy, was an absolute master in playing cheerful, oddly likeable creeps in British B-pictures throughout the 1950s and '60s until his untimely death in 1970.

Ironically, considering the efforts made to make the film as quickly and economically as possible, *Chain of Events* stayed on the shelf for over a year before being released. It finally ran on the Odeon circuit from early October 1958 as the B-picture to the psychological drama *The Man Upstairs*, which starred Richard Attenborough as a mentally disturbed man involved in an armed siege.

The Solitary Child (1957)

Going into production at Beaconsfield Studios in July 1957, immediately after filming on *Chain of Events* wrapped, *The Solitary Child* was written by Robert Dunbar from a novel by Nina Bawden. Philip Friend plays wealthy farmer James Random, who was acquitted of the shotgun murder of his first wife and had recently remarried to the much younger Harriet, played by Barbara Shelley. The household soon degenerates into an atmosphere of paranoia and fear, which Harriet can only escape if she discovers who really murdered the first Mrs Random. Was it really Robert after all? He seems to hate his sixteen-year-old daughter Maggie, who has mental health issues and obsessively makes drawings of the murder. Also acting suspiciously are Robert's sister (played by Sarah Lawson), her veterinarian boyfriend Jack Watling, and neighbour Rona Anderson.

Two performances really stand out here: first, the luminously beautiful Barbara Shelley as Harriet, seeing peril at every turn. Stealing the show, however, is Julia Lockwood, daughter of the famous Gainsborough Studios star Margaret Lockwood, giving a marvellously naturalistic performance as Maggie. Like her character, Lockwood was aged sixteen at the time of filming and plays to perfection the key role of a disturbed child on the cusp of womanhood, who may well have committed a horrific murder. Lockwood worked steadily for the next decade and in 1959 would be cast by Gerald Thomas and Peter Rogers in their comedy *Please Turn Over*. She never quite had the career her obvious talents deserved however, eventually marrying the actor Ernest Clark—best known for playing the irascible surgeon Sir Geoffrey Loftus in the sitcom *Doctor in the House* and its various follow-on series—and retired from acting in 1976.

The Solitary Child is a very effective piece of work, given its budget and time constraints. With its increasingly isolated and paranoid heroine, it plays like a precursor to the string of psychological thrillers such as *Taste of Fear* that Jimmy Sangster wrote for Hammer Films in the sixties. The only factor hampering the film is that it runs out of time to tell its story in a running time of only sixty-three minutes, resulting in a rushed and disappointing ending. Perhaps it was better that audiences got a film that was well-paced for most of its length than if Thomas had rushed the whole thing in order to make room for a big scene to end the film with.

The Solitary Child was certified by the BBFC for exhibition on 13 November 1957, the same day as *Chain of Events*. Despite the speedy and economical production of the film, it was not shown to the cinema trade until December 1958 and remained unreleased until February 1961, when it was placed on the bottom half of the bill with Ralph Thomas's *No Love For Johnnie*, an X-rated political drama starring Peter Finch made for Rank and produced by Peter Rogers' wife Betty E. Box. Ironically, this film could not be shown at Rank's own Odeon chain of cinemas, as that circuit had a long-standing policy of not screening X-rated pictures, so the rival ABC cinema chain showed the film instead. It also played some dates in support of the Kenneth More drama *The Greengage Summer* and the Dennis Price comedy *Watch It, Sailor*. Cinema audiences in the Republic of Ireland got a chance to see *The Solitary Child* from July 1962 and through most of 1963 in support of the British movies *13 West Street* and *Jigsaw*.

2

Carry On Sergeant (1958)

Filming Dates: 24 March 1958–2 May 1958
Original Certificate: U (Classified by BBFC 7 July 1958)
Running Time: 83 minutes 23 seconds

Release Details

London release: 18 September 1958 (Plaza Cinema, London, following a run of *The Revenge of Frankenstein*).

Carry On Sergeant had its first trade screening on Friday, 1 August 1958 and received its general release three weeks later, on 21 August, after two weeks of highly successful pre-release screenings. It was sent out on the road with several B-pictures: on the ABC circuit, it was often seen with the 1955 Western *Man With The Gun* as support feature. This was a Western starring Robert Mitchum that had originally been released in the UK in October 1955 under the title *The Trouble Shooter*. Elsewhere, *Carry On Sergeant* was paired with two different thrillers directed by Montgomery Tully at Merton Park Studios for Anglo-Amalgamated—in some areas, it was seen with Tully's *The Long Knife*, starring Joan Rice, while elsewhere cinemagoers saw *Man with a Gun*, featuring Lee Patterson.

It is interesting to note that there was rarely any effort made to put the Carry On films into comedy double-bills, although this often happened when the films were re-released. The tendency for Carry Ons during their first release was instead to create a contrasting pair of films, perhaps so that a few extra patrons might be attracted who wanted to see a Western or crime picture even if they did not fancy a Carry On.

What's Carrying On?

Sgt Grimshawe (William Hartnell) is about to retire from his position training new recruits and makes a large bet that with his final batch of National Service recruits he will finally win the coveted Star Squad prize for best platoon. Unfortunately, he is landed with the biggest set of misfits ever to wear an army uniform, including Charlie Sage (Bob Monkhouse), who receives his call-up papers on his wedding day and is desperate to somehow finally have a wedding night with his bride (Shirley Eaton).

Who's Carrying On?

A Peter Rogers Production
Director: Gerald Thomas
Screenplay by Norman Hudis with additional material by John Antrobus
Based on *The Bull Boys* by R. F. Delderfield
Music: Bruce Montgomery
Photography: Peter Hennessey
Art Director: Alex Vetchinshky
Editor: Peter Boita

William Hartnell: Sergeant Grimshawe, the frustrated drill sergeant trying against his instincts to train his new charges with kindness instead of by shouting.

Bob Monkhouse: Charlie Sage, the new conscript whose wedding is interrupted by the call to duty.

Eric Barker: Captain Potts, the officious officer in charge of the army training camp.

Shirley Eaton: Mary Sage, Charlie's new bride, so desperate to spend some time with her husband that she sneaks into the camp as a NAAFI cook.

Dora Bryan: Norah, Mary's friend in the NAAFI who shows her the ropes and takes a shine to nervous new conscript Horace Strong.

Kenneth Connor: Horace Strong, hypochondriac new conscript who is convinced he suffers from every disease and ailment imaginable, but who nonetheless attracts the amorous attentions of NAAFI cook Norah.

Charles Hawtrey: Peter Golightly, incredibly camp and physically uncoordinated conscript who struggles to achieve even the most basic military task.

Kenneth Williams: James Bailey, an intellectual snob who regards the army and its regulations as inefficient and absurd until his attitude is thawed by the plight of Herbert Brown.

Terence Longdon: Miles Heywood, who looks and talks like an officer but has absolutely no interest in military matters and refuses a chance to go to officer training school.

Norman Rossington: Herbert Brown, a misfit who has spent his entire National Service in the training camp as the army has been unable to teach him anything at all and has given up on him.

Hattie Jacques: Captain Clark, medical officer at the camp who is faced with a barrage of imagined ailments from Horace Strong; her strategy to get to the bottom of Horace's problems changes his life.

Carry On Critics

Although R. F. Delderfield only retains a small credit on the final film and his original storyline was changed almost out of recognition, his name being attached to the film gave *Carry On Sergeant* some added publicity. His name recognition was not as high in 1958 as it became in the 1960s and '70s in the wake of his popular trilogy of novels *A Horseman Riding By*, but he was an established novelist as well as a screenwriter. This certainly seems to have impressed the anonymous film critic of *The Times* in their review of Monday 22 September 1958: 'Mr R.F. Delderfield, from whose *The Bull Boys*, *Carry On, Sergeant* [*The Times* adding a comma to the film's title] at the Plaza Cinema, is adapted, has shown a shrewd sense of that the public wants.' Despite this basic misunderstanding of the authorship details of the film, the paper's reviewer still seemed mildly positive about the end result: 'every now and again a line or a situation is genuinely funny'. This sounds fair enough, though the film's advertising was, as one might imagine, rather more effusive. Newspaper listings for *Carry On Sergeant* described Rogers and Thomas's efforts as 'The Funniest Film of the Year!'

The British Film Institute's magazine *Monthly Film Bulletin* was as unconvinced as to the merits of the film in its September 1958 edition as had been *The Times*' reviewer:

> The professional skill of William Hartnell and Dora Bryan lends some reality and humour to this conventional farce, in which all the characters come from stock. Charles Hawtrey, as a weedy incompetent, and Kenneth Williams, as a condescending intellectual, provide some genuine laughs. The rest of the humour is either overdone or half-baked.

One comment is interestingly typical of the reviews the film series as a whole would receive over the years: '*Carry On Sergeant* is a traditionally English mixture of old farcical situations, well-worn jokes, and comic postcard characters.'

The Guardian's 'W.J.W' was snootily disapproving in a round-up of films screening at Manchester's cinemas on 2 September: '*Carry On Sergeant*, the

British bore, is another helping of lumpish fun about an awkward squad of National Service men, as boldly imaginative as a recruiting poster'. Thankfully, Penelope Houston in *The Observer* (many decades before that venerable newspaper merged with and became the Sunday version of *The Guardian*) was able to be both brief and briskly positive: '*Carry On Sergeant* provides for any appetites not yet sated with army farce in a film commendably brisk and played with great determination'.

By the time the film returned to West End cinemas for a run at the Ritz Cinema from 26 January 1959, its achievements, at least according to the film's advertising, had apparently become even more impressive: 'The laughter hit of the century! Returns by Demand to the W. End'.

Meanwhile, *Carry On Sergeant* was exported to the States, receiving a relatively positive reception from *The New York Times*' film critic Howard Thompson, as the film opened at the Baronet Theatre on Third Avenue and Fifty-Eighth Street:

> Without being the least bit original or inspired, *Carry On Sergeant* manages to be a fast and friendly little import that should cause no pain ... As produced by Peter Rogers, the picture retains a blandly impish air as it ticks off one familiar incident after another, with a goodly air of amusing dialogue.

If he ever saw the review, Charles Hawtrey would have been tickled pink that he was singled out for praise: 'The funniest "inmate" by far is Charles Hawtrey, as a wispy chap who can hardly stand up'.

Variety, the American showbusiness newspaper, gave its plaudits to another member of the cast: 'Kenneth Connor steals most of the honors as the hypochondriac being chased by a love-starved army waitress, played characteristically by Dora Bryan. He has a shade too much to do, but never misses a trick.' *Variety*'s reviewer was generally quite positive about this British import: '*Carry On Sergeant* is an army farce exploiting practically every army gag, but while some of the writing is careless and there is no attempt to develop a reasonable story, it is by no means sloppily produced.'

By the end of 1959, Peter Rogers film activities had begun to attract attention, and he explained his production philosophy in an interview with *The Times* on 5 November of that year:

> Our Carry On films ... are known as 'modest budget films', which means in practice that they cost about £70,000 each. This compares on the one hand with around £125,000 or more for the average Rank comedy (which is usually in colour and has one or two established stars), and on the other with about £15,000 (or often more) for the normal run of second features, shot in about three weeks.

> This means that they are designed to earn their cost and a reasonable profit just from showings in this country ... I should not like to work on a precarious balance by which some of the cost and all the profit had to be sought from doubtful international markets ... The exhibitors feel that they should pay half as much rental for a £100,000 film as for a £500,000 film even of the cheaper film takes twice as much at the box office. So if you do make a cheap film you have to keep it quiet and pretend it cost more than it did.[1]

Carry On Comments

Norman Hudis came up with the script format that formed the bedrock of the Carry On format in an act of happy necessity forced upon him by the state of the working script he had been presented with:

> The script had been left hanging in mid-air. I retained the first part, wherein a newly married conscript wants to consummate his marriage with his new wife ... Looking for the rest of the script I thought, why concentrate on one conscript? Dozens come in with every intake, so I'll invent a few.[2]

Despite occasionally casting performers better known for their work as solo comedians, such as Frankie Howerd, Jimmy Logan and, to an extent, Phil Silvers, Peter Rogers was generally in favour of developing a cast of comedy actors, as Bob Monkhouse was to discover; he commented about his core Carry On cast:

> They weren't comics ... they were actors playing comedy, and comics, you see, like Phil [Silvers], stick out like a sore thumb amongst these people. That's one of the secrets of casting that sort of film, not to have comics. We did have Bob Monkhouse on the first one. It didn't work.

That does sound a little unfair on Monkhouse, who was quite a capable comedy actor, deliberately putting himself in the mould of his comedic hero Bob Hope. Indeed, as he matured, Monkhouse even proved that he had the range to take on serious acting roles.

It certainly would have come as a surprise to Bob Monkhouse had anyone told him that Peter Rogers did not think his casting was working, though possibly less so in the aftermath of *Carry On Sergeant*'s success, as he revealed in his 1993 autobiography *Crying With Laughter*:

> [Peter Rogers] came out of the projection room where he had just been watching me in that morning's rushes. 'I'm more than delighted with you,

> my lad', he said, slapping me on the back. 'You're going to be my golden boy'. He never hired me again.[2]

Indeed, the bright personality and reactive comedic style of Monkhouse—he was a master of the double-take and comically quizzical reaction to whatever lunacy was happening in front of him—makes him the ideal performer to introduce us to the film's storyline. More than just a straight-man, he is an exaggerated everyman figure who represents us, the audience, as we are introduced to the more extreme comic characters he meets.

Some of these are introduced by director Gerald Thomas in interesting ways, demonstrating a degree of care in his work that, to be frank, is not always apparent in his pre-Carry On work. Charles Hawtrey is clearly seen as a great asset to the production, as he is given a really big entrance, crashing into the scene through a pair of double doors. In many of his future Carry On appearances, he would similarly be given an impactful introduction—his opening scene in *Carry On Constable*, bird cage in hand, springs immediately to mind. Kenneth Williams, on the other hand, was known to most audiences as a radio performer at this stage of his career, so is introduced by the sound of his voice before we actually see him.

Williams' character is written to use only part of the range of voices and character types he had displayed in his radio career. We do not get the sudden lapses into the 'snide' voice that betrayed the actor's working-class roots that he would deploy to great effect in future films, even when playing the Indian khasi of Kalabar in *Carry On Up the Khyber*. By dint of his superior education, Williams' character James Bailey (it is even rather a surprise to see him playing a character with such a commonplace name) becomes the *de facto* leader of the conscripts, convincing them to try their hardest in the film's latter part for the sake of Sergeant Grimshawe.

But why did *Carry On Sergeant* hit the spot quite so accurately in 1958? Bearing in mind the legendary rule of cinema coined by screenwriter William Goldman—'Nobody knows anything'—there are a few clues to be found in the times in which the film was made. When Peter Rogers happened upon R. F. Delderfield's well-thumbed treatment for *The Bull Boys*, it was unusual for the subject matter of National Service to be covered in a British film.

National Service was a holdover from the Second World War, a period of compulsory military service brought into being by the National Service Act 1948. This meant that male civilians who were able to pass the medical and were not employed in an 'essential service' (coal mining, farming and the merchant navy) would be called up for eighteen months of service in one of Britain's armed forces. At this point, the country was finally at peace after enduring six years of total war. By 1950, British forces were once again in harm's way, seeing action in the Korean War and anti-colonial uprisings in

Cyprus, Kenya, and Malaya. As a result, the period of National Service was increased to two years, making the prospect of military service even less popular among young men just starting careers or discovering the worlds of girls and alcohol.

The important point from the perspective of cinema is just how militarised a society Britain was by the end of the 1950s. A huge percentage of the movie audience—itself still very large at this stage, before the spread of commercial television encouraged many to stay at home—had served in the military, either during the war or for their National Service. During the 1950s, military matters became an abiding concern for British film studios, which turned out large numbers of war movies. These served a few different purposes: first, war movies became a sort of British equivalent to the Western or gangster movies made in America, providing a film genre in which British actors could run around firing guns; secondly, as it became clear that the British Empire was in terminal decline, the war movie served as a method by which Britain could polish its increasingly fragile self-image; and finally, perhaps most importantly, the military represented a shared national experience, to which it was only natural that filmmakers would attempt to appeal.

Thus in 1958, when *Carry On Sergeant* reached cinemas, it was fighting for attention among a platoon of home-produced war pictures, such as *Dunkirk, Carve Her Name with Pride, Ice Cold in Alex, Sea of Sand, The Silent Enemy*, and Hammer's gruesome hit drama set in a Japanese concentration camp, *The Camp on Blood Island*. Interestingly, Hammer also scored a big hit with *Up the Creek*, a comedy featuring Peter Sellers in his first starring role in a feature film. This was a comedy set on board a Royal Navy ship with little to do in peacetime whose bosun (Sellers with an Irish accent) is a Bilko-esque figure who uses the vessel to run multiple businesses at the port where it is semi-permanently berthed.

This breezy service comedy was so successful that a sequel was rushed into production by Hammer, keen not to be typecast into making only their internationally successful horror pictures. *Further Up The Creek* was made so quickly that it made it into cinemas a mere six months after the original. In this time however, Peter Sellers was already on his way to becoming a major film star and was at Shepperton Studios filming *The Mouse that Roared* for major Hollywood producer Carl Foreman. In his place, Hammer Films hired none other than Frankie Howerd, who was undergoing something of a career slump at the time and was more than happy to take the role at short notice. Hammer even had their own National Service comedy released in 1958 in the form of *I Only Arsked!*. This was the movie version of Granada Television's popular sitcom *The Army Game*, which was beaten to the screens by over two months by *Carry On Sergeant*, which featured a large contingent of former *Army Game* stars.

It is significant that the two National Service-based movies released within months of each other in late 1958 were both comedies. British cinema of the 1950s was still quite heavily censored, not just on the more obvious level of violence and nudity, but also in terms of what themes were permissible in a film that was to receive a 'U' or 'A' certificate and thus be acceptable for release through one of the major national cinema chains.

The major previous example of a large-budget British movie aimed at a popular audience using National Service as its theme was *These Dangerous Years*, a 1957 semi-musical drama starring popular singer Frankie Vaughan. Here, Vaughan plays a rough Scouse gang leader and singer who is called up and, after a series of dramas involving the camp bully, straightened out. Being from the rather staid cinematic stable of Herbert Wilcox and Anna Neagle, *These Dangerous Years* was never going to be a searing look at the problems of teenage Britain. It does, however, give an interesting look at the officially sanctioned view of National Service on screen: National Service was portrayed as beyond doubt a very good thing that helped keep the young men of Britain on the right path. It was at this point in time, however, that the government began to phase out National Service, the last conscripts being called up at the end of 1960.

What this meant was that there was a window of opportunity in which there was a large population very receptive to films that satirised military institutions, however gently, and a more relaxed censorship environment in which it was possible to make such comedies. On television, *The Army Game* was quick off the mark, debuting in June 1957 on the still-new ITV network and running for great success for four years. On radio the BBC eventually joined in with *The Navy Lark*—though it should be noted that the corporation's cult hit *The Goon Show* was at heart based around service comedy—which ran from 1959 until early 1976 before a final episode wrapping the series up to celebrate the queen's silver jubilee in 1977.

In 1958, the time was ripe for Britain to take a National Service film comedy to its heart, and by a combination of happy accident, sharp scriptwriting, and perfect casting, *Carry On Sergeant* was that film.

3

Carry On Nurse (1959)

Filming Dates: 3 November 1958–12 December 1958
Original Certificate: U (Classified by BBFC 30 January 1959)
Running Time: 85 minutes 3 seconds

Release Details

London release: 5 March 1959 (Carlton Cinema, following a run of Paul Newman and Joanne Woodward in *Rally Round the Flag Boys*).

Before the film's London public debut, *Carry On Nurse* was screened for employees of Anglo-Amalgamated from all over Britain at a special convention to celebrate the company's tenth anniversary, held from 27 February to 2 March at *Les Ambassadeurs* club in London's Mayfair, which later became famous as the location in which Sean Connery's James Bond was introduced to audiences in *Dr. No*.

Carry On Nurse went on general release from 15 March, paired with a tight little sixty-two-minute British crime drama entitled *Breakout*. This was produced by Independent Artists at Beaconsfield Studios, which was run by Peter Rogers and directed by Peter Graham Scott. The film starred Lee Patterson (the bequiffed Canadian king of the British B-picture, who had featured in *Carry On Sergeant*'s B-picture *Man with a Gun* and would later appear in *Carry On Regardless*), Hazel Court, and Terence Alexander in a tale of a local government official who has a sideline in organising prison breakouts.

What's Carrying On?

Life among the nurses on a hospital ward as a disparate group of patients come and go, including a snooty academic, a boxer with a broken hand, a radio addict, and a newspaper reporter. The patients at first spend their time arguing and then form a bond as a new patient, Jack Bell (Leslie Phillips), arrives with a bunion that threatens to derail a tryst with his girlfriend Meg (June Whitfield).

Who's Carrying On?

A Peter Rogers Production
Director: Gerald Thomas
Screenplay by Norman Hudis, based on the play *Ring For Catty* by Patrick Cargill and Jack Beale
Music: Bruce Montgomery
Photography: Reginald Wyer
Art Director: Alex Vetchinshky
Editor: John Shirley
Kenneth Connor: Bernie Bishop, a professional boxer admitted to hospital with a broken hand; he is a family man and an all-around friendly chap outside of the ring.
Shirley Eaton: Staff Nurse Dorothy Denton, a very glamorous but highly efficient nurse who occasionally has to fight off the attentions of her patients, but whose heart might be melted by Ted York.
Kenneth Williams: Oliver Reckit, highly educated and convinced that he would be able to organise the entire hospital more efficiently; his frosty demeanour is unexpectedly thawed by the arrival of romantic interest.
Charles Hawtrey: Humphrey Hinton, a flamboyant enthusiast of the hospital's radio service who spends most of his day with his headphones on.
Hattie Jacques: Matron, the central point around which the efficient running of the ward runs; the nurses are in a state of mild terror during her daily ward inspection.
Bill Owen: Percy Hickson seems permanently exasperated, particularly when he is stranded in the ward with a broken leg and no access to a bedpan.
Terence Longden: Ted York, admitted with appendicitis, is a journalist who is subsequently convinced by his editor to write a series of articles about his stay; however, he is more interested in Staff Nurse Denton.
Leslie Phillips: Jack Bell, admitted to hospital with a bunion, which is a potential disaster for Bell as it threatens to delay a romantic weekend with his girlfriend Meg (June Whitfield).

Joan Sims: Student Nurse Stella Dawson, a good-hearted, but extremely accident-prone young nurse.

Wilfrid Hyde-White: The Colonel, a fearsome old military man ensconced in a private room who spends his days having hospital orderly Mick (Harry Locke) place horse racing bets for him.

Carry On Critics

The *Monthly Film Bulletin*'s reviewer in its April 1959 edition was less than impressed, describing *Carry On Nurse* as 'A somewhat stale farce, mixing slapstick, caricature and crudely anatomical humour, puts life in a public hospital ward in the same cheerlessly rollicking category as the barrack room.'

The Times' reviewer of Monday, 9 March 1959, was even less impressed: 'A series of broad music-hall jokes set in a hospital, and anything less edifying is difficult to imagine'. Even that paper's anonymous reviewer had some words of praise, however: 'Once or twice, out of the blue, in more than once sense of the phrase, there emerges a moment of shrewd observation'. Hattie Jacques was singled out for particular praise: 'Miss Hattie Jacques, as Matron, steam-rolls her way through script and ward with majestic authority'.

If these reviews were less than enthusiastic, Paul Dehn (who would later co-write the screenplay for *Goldfinger*) was downright damning in the 4 March edition of the *News Chronicle*, railing against the use of sexual innuendo in a film bearing a 'U' certificate:

> There is surely something wrong with a Board of Censors who will permit such stuff to be passed as fit entertainment for an uninstructed child ... I found its unsmutty sketches so tedious and its final joke so hoary that I would sooner be certified than see it again myself.

Classified advertising for the film contained probably the first instance of the phrase 'Carry on Laughing' attached to the films, the Carlton Cinema's screenings being heralded with 'Carry on Laughing at CARRY ON NURSE'.

The New York Times' influential movie critic Bosley Crowther was moved to comment about the film in that paper's 10 September 1960 edition. *Carry On Nurse* had gained an unusual amount of attention for a low-budget British comedy, not to mention box office receipts: 'If you want to know what the British have been howling at lately (don't ask us why!), take a look at the new film at the Little Carnegie'. Crowther was decidedly unimpressed, as no doubt was Leslie Phillips, whom the critic misidentified as Cyril Chamberlain.

> All they do is run through their routines ... and hackneyed routines they are, tending mostly towards roughhouse antics and intimate hospital gags. The script by Norman Hudis is pure Roquefort, the direction of Gerald Thomas is vaudeville-times. Yet this film has been a vast success in Britain.
>
> As we said above, don't ask us why.

Variety, which tended to be more concerned with box office potential than art, was rather more positive, in a review that lapses into that paper's trademark slang:

> *Carry On Nurse* does for hospitals what its predecessor (*Carry On, Sergeant*) did for military life. The yocks come thick and fast. The humour tends to be repetitious, flirting with sex and dealing with such typical hospital subjects as bedpans, enemas, preparing patients for operations and so on.

Carry On Comments

Like most sequels, *Carry On Nurse* tries to be the same as its predecessor, but different enough for audiences to want to pay for their cinema tickets a second time. Screenwriter Norman Hudis here cleverly manages to replicate the structure of *Carry On Sergeant* while changing the setting. While the structure of *Sergeant* came together piecemeal in an attempt to create a useable script out of R. F. Delderfield's original screen treatment, here it would seem quite a lot of thought went into working out what the appeal of the film was in an attempt to make the new film not only similar to the first one, but better.

Carry On Nurse's hospital setting, like the military establishment of *Sergeant*, allows a tension to be set up between the permanent staff of the organisation (the regular army personnel and the doctors and nurses respectively) and the more transient people within. The latter, conscripted soldiers and hospital patients, have been pulled out of their normal lives unwillingly for a limited period and many rail against the authority this imposes on them.

This allows Hudis to have some of the actors play basically the same character as before. Kenneth Williams in both films plays a snobbish intellectual whose objections to the often illogical restrictions of the organisation he finds himself in are softened by an emotional attachment. In *Sergeant*, he befriends a fellow soldier (Norman Rossington) who he is able to teach better than the army can; in *Nurse*, he is in the unfamiliar position of being the film's romantic lead, falling in love with Jill Ireland, who brings him academic books to read.

Terence Longden returned to the cold of November and December in Iver Heath, home of Pinewood Studios after having spent the previous six months at Rome's Cinecittà Studios appearing in *Ben Hur*. For his trouble (and a considerably smaller salary than Metro-Goldwyn-Meyer provided), he was given, like Kenneth Williams, a very similar character to that which he played in *Carry On Sergeant*, though his character arc was better written and constructed in *Sergeant*. There, his character was clearly of the officer class (Sergeant Grimshawe assumes he is actually is an officer and gives him a lift) and we learn during the film that despite coming from a family of senior officers, he does not have a military bone in his body. In *Carry On Nurse*, he plays a newspaper reporter who is genuinely hospitalised, then hired by his editor to write an exposé of hospital life. Curiously, this promising plotline is never mentioned again and one wonders if some material was cut to keep the film down to an acceptable length.

Charles Hawtrey also returns, though curiously his interaction with the other characters is strictly limited. He plays Humphrey Hinton, who is every bit as flamboyantly effeminate as his Private Golightly had been in *Sergeant*, but here has the added restriction of spending almost the entire film in bed. In a triumph of facial and physical pantomime, Hinton is addicted to the hospital radio service, which he flicks between the various BBC radio services available at the time, always through headphones so we never hear what he does. Thus, for example, he bursts into tears at the daily soap opera *Mrs Dale's Diary* and falls out of bed conducting the orchestra while listening to (presumably) the *BBC Third Programme*.

Kenneth Connor was a real highlight in *Carry On Sergeant*, playing virtually a dual role of as a hypochondriac who becomes a physical superman. Although his part in *Nurse* is not as flamboyant, Connor shows his versatility as Bernie Bishop, a part that also showcases the actor's physicality—it is hard to believe that he celebrated his fortieth birthday during the filming of *Carry On Nurse*. Bernie is also given some of the best lines in the film, which he delivers with great aplomb.

Curiously, one of the most memorable performers in the film is Hattie Jacques in the comparatively small role of Matron. The actress had impressed during *Carry On Sergeant* in the running gag of the medical officer presented with endless visits from a hypochondriac Kenneth Connor, and Rogers and Thomas were keen to have her return. Unfortunately, Jacques was recovering from stomach surgery at the time of filming, so a smaller role was written especially for her. While Joan Hickson's Ward Sister is in day-to-day control of the ward, the entire running of the place appears to revolve around Matron's daily inspections. If Jacques is not on screen, then the other characters are anticipating her visits and potential wrath. Hattie is in full dragon mode here, in contrast to the more sympathetic side she displayed in *Sergeant*, bolstered by a memorable musical theme composed for Matron by Bruce Montgomery.

Some new actors were introduced, notably Leslie Phillips in a career-defining role as Jack Bell, in hospital to have a bunion removed, which threatens to ruin a weekend away with his girlfriend June Whitfield (the latter being a natural Carry On performer who would not return to the series until the 1970s). This acts as another mirror image of a *Carry On Sergeant* plotline, a variation on Bob Monkhouse's attempts to consummate his interrupted marriage to Shirley Eaton. It is also a pointer to the type of humour the series was aiming at—for an unmarried couple to attempt to go away on a 'dirty weekend' was quite a thing in 1959, especially such a well-spoken pair as Jack and Meg.

As Jack Bell, Phillips gained a catchphrase, 'ding dong', which would stick with him for the rest of his career, and what could have been a permanent place in the Carry On team. While Phillips decided that he did not want to be typecast as a Carry On actor—at least not for the money Peter Rogers was offering—he remained an important part of the series for the next few films. It is possible that this came at the expense of Terence Longden, who proved unavailable for most of the shooting of *Carry On Constable*, but was a very similar type of actor to Leslie Philips. Even at this early stage, the Carry Ons represented working class comedy, both in the writing and the casting—the Doctor film series could have accommodated both actors, but not the Carry Ons.

With Dora Bryan otherwise engaged, Rogers and Thomas found another, ostensibly similar performer to fill the role of accident-prone Nurse Dawson. In the process, one of the bedrocks of the Carry On regular cast was discovered in the form of Joan Sims. Although Sims was here playing the role of clumsy newcomer, over the course of the next few films, she proved just as able to play the glamorous love interest, but with a comedic edge. This is possibly one of the reasons why Shirley Eaton's roles in the series were to become shorter and eventually disappear altogether. Eaton is an absolutely luminous screen presence and it requires no great leap of imagination from the viewer to work out why Bob Monkhouse and Terence Longden's characters in *Sergeant* and *Nurse* are head-over-heels in love with her. Eaton's statuesque presence only presented a limited number of comedic possibilities however, and in essence, she was playing the role of the straight woman in a series that increasingly did not need one. Stunning though the sight of Shirley Eaton in a nurse's uniform is, it is Sims that one remembers when looking back on *Carry On Nurse*.

For *Carry On Nurse*, the series attracted its first big name guest star in the form of Wilfrid Hyde-White. Hyde-White was one of those character actors who only seemed 'right' as he got older. He was aged fifty-five when he filmed his scenes for *Carry On Nurse* but to modern audiences looks at least ten years older as the Colonel, a crusty, roguish old devil who spends his time shouting at the nurses and getting Harry Locke's hospital orderly to put horse racing bets on for him. One wonders if the role was written expressly with Hyde-White in mind, as the actor was one of the most notorious (and unsuccessful) gamblers in the British acting profession, a habit which at one point led to an appearance in the bankruptcy court.[1]

Masters as ever at getting value for their money, Peter Rogers and Gerald Thomas had the Colonel put into a private room, enabling them to film the relatively expensive guest star Hyde-White's scenes in the shortest possible time. In retrospect, attracting Wilfrid Hyde-White would appear even more miraculous for an as-ever low budget Carry On production when he became an international star character actor after his role as Colonel Pickering in George Cukor's 1964 film musical *My Fair Lady.*

Although *Carry On Nurse* is bigger and better in most ways than its predecessor, it does not have quite so satisfying a plot as *Carry On Sergeant*. The platoon at the centre of *Carry On Sergeant*'s story has a well-defined story arc in which, after a series of misadventures, they bond as a cohesive unit for the sake of their retiring sergeant and become efficient soldiers. By necessity forced upon the film by its hospital setting, *Carry On Nurse* is more a collection of individual stories about each patient. The script does create a common cause for the patients to work together to solve, in the form of Jack Bell's bunion, which threatens to ruin its owner's love life. The patients get drunk and band together to perform the delayed operation themselves. This remains a rather unlikely development, to say the least, but it is undoubtedly the comedic highlight of the film, giving each of the participants their own chance to shine.

Performing a drunk act for comedy is not so easy as one might think—do not think too badly of me for putting forward this opinion, but Sid James had a tendency to overplay when called upon to be drunk for a scene. For *Carry On Nurse*, our collection of patients pitch their performances at just the right level, even if the amount of champagne consumed hardly seems sufficient to make that many people as drunk as all that. The communal act of getting drunk together and trying to solve a problem breaks down the social barriers between the group and they decide to perform the operation on Bell's bunion themselves in an empty operating theatre. Charles Hawtrey and Bill Owen are especially good despite not even being a part of the main scene. Hawtrey gets the chance to perform in drag for the first time in a Carry On, a speciality of the actor in his stage career, and pitches his performance at just the right level. The slightly built actor is just convincing enough when disguised as a nurse—he is not what one might call convincingly female (a trick he was able to pull off as a younger actor) but not ridiculous, so the character retains his dignity. Owen's character Percy Hickson, immobilised by a leg in plaster, is the subject of an effective running gag in which he is desperate for the toilet but had nobody to help him. It is as basic as humour gets, but Owen's range of pained expressions pulls it off beautifully.

After having to perform drunk scenes, the cast members that make it to the operating theatre then have to pull off an even harder challenge than the drunk scene: laughing uncontrollably. The two Kenneths—Connor and

Williams—are the stars of the show here, as Connor's would-be anaesthetist Bernie Bishop accidentally lets laughing gas loose. Connor sells the early part of the scene, moving gradually and seamlessly from drunken seriousness to giggling wreck. Even better is Kenneth Williams, in a scene which the actor was born to play and which may be seen as pivotal in the actor's development as a screen actor.

Williams' laugh was legendary, both on screen and off, and in this scene the more out-of-control he becomes the funnier he is. In *Sergeant* and for most of *Carry On Nurse*, the actor gives quite a controlled, even low-key performance but here the brakes are slowly removed and he goes gloriously over the top. For Kenneth Williams and for the Carry On series as a whole, the lesson was clear: subtlety was for other movies—Carry On pictures only got funnier the more over the top they were written and played.

4

Carry On Teacher (1959)

Filming Dates: 15 March 1959–24 April 1959
Original Certificate: U (Classified by BBFC 20 May 1959)
Running Time: 88 minutes 52 seconds

Release Details

London release: 3 September 1959 (Plaza Cinema, London—following a run of *Last Train from Gun Hill*).

With *Carry On Teacher* having been completed as early as May, there was plenty of scope for pre-release screenings. The film was premiered at The Forum, Jersey, on 6 August, at an event attended by Kenneth Connor, Peter Rogers, and Gerald Thomas, plus Anglo-Amalgamated's Stuart Levy. *Kinematograph Weekly* reported that *Teacher* went on to play to packed houses.[1] *Carry On Teacher* made its highly profitable way around the nation's cinemas from 21 August alongside another Independent Artists B-feature produced at Beaconsfield—*The White Trap*, directed by Sidney Hayers, once again featured Lee Patterson, this time alongside a strong cast of British performers including Conrad Phillips and Michael Goodliffe. This time, Patterson is trying to escape from prison in order to clear his name and get back to his pregnant wife.

What's Carrying On

William Wakefield (Ted Ray), headmaster of inner-city school Maudlin Street Secondary Modern, wants to move on to a big, newly built school close to his hometown. This is a great opportunity for Wakefield, but to stand a chance, Maudlin Street must impress child psychologist Alistair Grigg (Leslie Phillips), who has been sent to the school to research modern methods of education. Grigg is instantly smitten with Maudlin Street's PE teacher Miss Allcock (Joan Sims), but their happiness is short-lived as a wave of coordinated bad behaviour and practical jokes causes chaos. But what is the reason behind this sudden outbreak of anarchy in the classrooms of Maudlin Street?

Who's Carrying On?

A Peter Rogers Production
Director: Gerald Thomas
Screenplay by Norman Hudis
Music composed and directed by Bruce Montgomery
Photography: Richard Wyer BSC
Art Director: Lionel Couch
Editor: John Shirley

Ted Ray: William Wakefield, headmaster of Maudlin Street Secondary Modern School, a father figure who rejects the use of the cane in favour of kindness and understanding.

Kenneth Connor: Gregory Adams, school science teacher whose head is usually in the clouds and who is, appropriately, building a rocket as a class project.

Charles Hawtrey: Michael Bean, a music teacher attempting to instil some culture into his pupils via his beloved grand piano and the cacophonous school orchestra.

Leslie Phillips: Alistair Grigg, a child psychologist who finds that his fancy theories, which sounded fine when he was being trained in Vienna, are not so effective among the recalcitrant kids of Maudlin Street.

Edwin Milton: Kenneth Williams, Maudlin Street's English teacher who is attempting to put on the school's performance of *Romeo and Juliet*, while desperately trying to hide the more salacious details of Shakespeare's play from the children.

Hattie Jacques: Grace Short, the school's maths teacher who thinks that the avalanche of bad behaviour at the school can be stemmed by using the cane as much as possible.

Joan Sims: Sarah Allcock, Maudlin Street's PE teacher. She immediately falls for Alistair Grigg, but their relationship is endangered when she disapproves of his theories of how children should be raised.

Richard O'Sullivan: Robin Stevens, leader of the gang of underage terrors causing chaos at Maudlin Street, but for a surprising reason.

Carry On Critics

The Times film reviewer of 5 September 1959 was reminded irresistibly of the Will Hay school comedies:

> Mr. Ted Ray is somewhat subdued as the headmaster—the memory of Will Hay in tattered cap and gown, seediness incarnate, engaged in a desperate battle to hold on to the little authority he possesses, will not be banished.

The reviewer seems determined to damn the film with the faintest of praise, with compliments followed with a swift smack around the face with a critical wet fish:

> Miss Hattie Jacques makes, in all senses of the phrase, a stalwart champion of the principle of corporal punishment, and the film seems funnier—or, to put it another way, less painfully unfunny—when she is on the set.

Even three films into the series, *The Times* sees the films hardening into a set formula (little did they know how much the Carry Ons would change and develop over the years): 'The formula, which reaches back in spirit to the custard pie and the atmosphere of the old music hall, has now set into well-defined lines, and it is a formula that pays.'

The *Monthly Film Bulletin* was a little more pleased with the latest efforts of Rogers, Thomas, and company:

> Another slapstick farce in the 'Carry On' series which, although predictable and occasionally pressed too hard. Still manages to register some adroitly timed humour. The cast attacks its material—largely a string of familiar practical jokes—with verve and evident enjoyment, but is severely limited by stock characterisation and a television style of presentation.

The Guardian's 'W.J.W' was brief but approving, describing *Carry On Teacher* as 'a hearty slapstick affair with the humour of a radio serial.'

Variety was very enthusiastic in their review of *Carry On Teacher*, using its occasionally hard to penetrate argot:

> Third entry in Peter Rogers' socko Carry On series combines virtually the same team to use the same yock-raising formula, this time in the scholastic field, and the laughs come readily. This time Norman Hudis has developed a slightly stronger story line and made the characters more credible. [The *Variety* reviewer appears not to have realised that *Teacher* has basically the same plot as *Carry On Sergeant* relocated to an inner-city comprehensive.]

Some of the gags are telegraphed but the cheerful impudence with which they are dropped into the script is completely disarming.

Carry On Comments

The Carry On films were riding high, and their success helped the National Film Finance Corporation, the government body set up in 1949 by Harold Wilson, which allowed producers to access finance from a levy placed on cinema ticket sales, make a profit in 1960–61 for the first time in five years. Among the top eight contributors to the NFFC's coffers were three Carry Ons: *Nurse*, *Teacher*, and *Constable*, and the very Carry On-influenced *Dentist in the Chair*, which starred familiar faces Bob Monkhouse, Kenneth Connor, and Eric Barker.[1]

The box-office success of the series was not something that Peter Rogers took for granted, and although *Carry On Teacher* continued the tradition of putting the same cast members into different professions, here a new factor was added. It was thought that a central figure was needed for the established cast to revolve around, serving the same purpose as William Hartnell's Sergeant Grimshawe in *Carry On Sergeant*. Popular radio comedian Ted Ray was recruited for the task, a seasoned comic who immediately fitted in to the established cast and, at the age of fifty-four, was twenty years older than many of the Carry On ensemble.

Interestingly, despite being a natural laugh-getter, Ray generally acts as the straight man here: he is a kind and ultimately serious father figure around whom the story revolves. In this context, his performance works very well, giving the cast a central figure to react both to and against. Ray was so successful as William Wakefield that he was immediately recast in the next Peter Rogers production, the excellent *Please Turn Over*. Unfortunately, Ted Ray's association with the Carry On team was to end in a somewhat unexpected manner at this point. The actor's services were being loaned to Peter Rogers Productions by Associated British Picture Corporation, who had Ray under an exclusive film contract, but had never actually cast him in anything. The fact that a rival company had cast Ray in two successful pictures was a source of some embarrassment within ABPC and, despite the fact that these films were packing audiences into the company's ABC cinema chain, Anglo-Amalgamated were told in no uncertain terms no longer to use Ted Ray in its films. Anglo was in no position to endanger its relationship with the company that distributed its films, so Peter Rogers was given the order to drop its popular new actor. ABPC subsequently never did put Ted Ray into any of its films, and his career as a screen actor ended here.

To join the new star, most of the existing Carry On cast members from the first two films were retained with a few exceptions. The plot of *Carry On*

Teacher meant that there were fewer adult roles than previously, as many of the parts were written for children, thus Bill Owen, Terence Longden, and Michael Medwin were missing this time around, as was Eric Barker. The only part in Norman Hudis' script that might have been suitable for Barker was that of headmaster William Wakefield, which was earmarked for Ted Ray. In fact, *Carry On Teacher* reunited Ray with two of the cast of his popular radio series *Ray's a Laugh*, in the form of Rosalind Knight and the multi-voiced Kenneth Connor. Other cast members were also employed elsewhere during the filming of *Teacher*: Joan Sims was appearing in the West End theatre production *Breath of Spring*, while Kenneth Williams was both playing one of the ugly sisters in Cinderella at the Colosseum Theatre and appearing on the BBC radio series *Beyond Our Ken*.

The schoolchildren, described in the credits as The Saboteurs, included a few names that would go on to greater fame: Richard O'Sullivan was already an experienced actor at the age of fifiteen, but *Carry On Teacher* represented his first major comedy role, a genre in which he would become a major television star of the 1970s and '80s. Carol White also developed a solid acting career before being propelled to stardom in the epochal television production *Cathy Come Home* in 1965 and opposite Terence Stamp the following year in the feature film *Poor Cow*, both for director Ken Loach. Larry Dann, meanwhile, made his Carry On debut here and continued acting in the years that followed, including touring the world with Joan Littlewood's Theatre Workshop, until a chance meeting with Gerald Thomas saw his return to the series after sixteen years in *Carry On Behind*. Also visible in a few sequences is a fourteen-year-old Francesca Annis, uncredited in her first feature film role. Earlier in 1959, she had appeared in the fifty-minute Children's Film Foundation production *The Cat Gang*, which also featured Jeremy Bulloch, who also turns up in *Carry On Teacher*. Many of the child actors recruited for the film were being taught acting at the Corona Academy in Chiswick.

As with the previous two films, a suitable location was found for the film's setting, Maudlin Street Secondary Modern, a choice of name that in 1988 would inspire that noted Charles Hawtrey fan Morrissey to write the song *Late Night, Maudlin Street*, not his greatest achievement but nonetheless worthy of note here. With Hattie Jacques' role in *Carry On Nurse* being smaller than intended due to health issues, here she was back to playing a full part in proceedings as part of a group of teachers designed by scriptwriter Norman Hudis to represent a full range of character types and approaches to the teaching profession.

Thus Hattie's maths teacher is a forceful proponent of caning, which headmaster Wakefield is against on principle, a stance which allows Hudis to repeat the 'softly, softly' approach of Sergeant Grimshawe in *Carry On Sergeant*. Kenneth Williams' English teacher is also generally against corporal punishment, but his major scene is a fascinating sequence in which he attempts to teach the class Shakespeare's *Romeo and Juliet*, the subject of the forthcoming end of term school play. With Leslie Phillips' educational psychologist present, the pupils attempt once more attempt to disrupt the class, but in this case they have a point. The play is being taught to the children in a version edited for children, but Williams is unable or unwilling to explain exactly what has been taken out. Of course, the kids know full well what has been removed from a play about a love affair between two fourteen-year-olds, and have great fun talking about it in front of a spluttering Williams.

Kenneth Connor is excellent as the school physics teacher preoccupied with his pet project of launching a miniature rocket and, appropriately, has his head in the clouds, lapsing into a series of spoonerisms at times of stress. Hudis also has fun giving his character a mutual attraction to School Inspector Rosalind Knight, who returns in a rather larger role after a very effective cameo in *Carry On Nurse*. In *Carry On Sergeant*, Connor's Horace Strong was terrified of the attentions of Dora Bryan, and here the same idea is repeated, with Connor turning into a nervous wreck as soon as he tries to express his feelings. The trick that the pupils play on him does seem rather cruel though—they add a fuel pellet to his beloved rocket, which causes it to go off in the classroom when he demonstrates it.

Also rather cruel is the trick played on Charles Hawtrey's Mr Bean, the music teacher. The character clearly loves his subject and especially his grand piano, so is distraught when the children saw through its legs, causing it to collapse during a music lesson. A fascinating relationship is set up between Hawtrey and Kenneth Williams here, as the two teachers work on the performance and music of the aforementioned school play. Hudis at last abandons his attempts to turn Williams into a romantic leading man and instead has him and Charles Hawtrey fighting like cat and dog in a very camp manner indeed. In the film's climax, an overcome Williams even kisses Hawtrey, getting his face slapped for his trouble.

The big finish of *Carry On Teacher* is Hawtrey and Williams' aforementioned school play, which is ruined in spectacular fashion by the gang of saboteurs. Beyond the visual gags involved with the deliberate torpedoing of the play is a well-observed display of terrible acting and an unlistenably awful orchestra, which would be very familiar to anyone who has actually sat through a school play. It is this underlying realism that makes the scene really work.

The central romantic pairing of *Carry On Teacher*, however, is not Hawtrey and Williams, or even Kenneth Connor and Rosalind Knight, but instead Leslie Phillips' highfalutin' child psychologist, full of fancy ideas from his Austrian tutor about letting children be free to discover themselves (or something like that), and Joan Sims' games teacher Miss Allcock. There are few more satisfying sights in British comedy than Leslie Phillips when a pretty girl has caught his eye, and here he and Sims fall for each other hook, line, and sinker at first sight. The instantly smitten Phillips even gets to repeat his 'ding-dong' catchphrase from *Carry On Nurse*, proving that it worked even away from the context of his character's name in that film of Bell.

Joan Sims is here a world away from the daffy nurse she played in the previous film, and is very effective as an attractive, sporty games mistress. The only problem came when Phillips came to say her character's name in the most adoring manner. He was under strict instructions from the British Board of Film Censors (which operated a service to filmmakers to examine their scripts to ensure the finished result was likely to get the certificate the producers desired) to say the name 'Allcock' without putting a stress on either syllable.[2] The uniquely fruity upper-class vowels of Phillips made any pronunciation of the name appear suggestive, but the actor played the lines with the straightest face possible and just about got away with it. The jokes written for Sims and Phillips here are several shades more suggestive than Norman Hudis had written for previous films in the series, with dialogue such as: 'Do you favour the Swedish method?' 'Well I say it's the same the whole world over.'

One of the jokes the classroom saboteurs play on Miss Allcock is to substitute her shorts for a pair several sizes too small. This results in a short-splitting scene that is an interesting precursor to *Carry On Camping*'s famous bra-removal scene ten years later. An interesting coda to the Allcock and Griggs romance is that as a child psychologist, Alistair Griggs turns out to be something of a charlatan, having realised long ago that 'free expression is just the thing for other people's children'.

Some of the jokes are very effective, such as a sequence in which the teachers are dosed with itching powder during a staff meeting. This is played very well by the cast, who attempt to preserve their dignity and ignore their increasing discomfort as they grow ever itchier until the meeting dissolves into a mass orgy of back-scratching set to music. There is something very English about the scene, as all concerned refuse to admit to the others that anything is wrong and carrying on (as it were), which allows the scene to build to heights of absurdity.

Other scenes strengthen the impression that Norman Hudis was starting to repeat himself, especially one in which the teachers' tea is spiked with alcohol. This plays very much as a repeat of the *Carry On Nurse* scene in which the patients are overcome by laughing gas, only here the idea is somewhat less effective.

Carry On Teacher proved to be another big box office success for Peter Rogers Productions and its distributor Anglo Amaglamated, aided by a clever trailer showing a scroll of text and heavy music, which gave the impression that audiences were in for a serious documentary before it becomes clear that a comedy is being advertised, a format which was repeated for several future

Carry On trailers. The trailer was also the first to give a Carry On movie a subtitle, a feature that would become common in later films in the series written by Talbot Rothwell. In this case, potential audiences were promised '*Carry On Teacher*—or how to become a delinquent in ten easy lessons'.

While *Carry On Teacher* kept the series running along in very profitable fashion, it does not belong in the front rank of Carry On pictures. Despite it possessing plenty of charm and the good nature which are the hallmark of Norman Hudis' Carry On scripts, there are just too many repeated elements from the first two films. It all works acceptably well, however, and points Kenneth Williams' screen character in the direction it would head in years to come. Some new ideas were clearly needed as the Carry On team geared up for their next adventure—this time, they were joining the police.

5

Carry On Constable (1960)

Filming Dates: 9 September 1959–18 December 1959
Original Certificate: U (Classified by BBFC 3 February 1960)
Running Time: 87 minutes 44 seconds

Release Details

London Release: 25 February 1960 (Plaza Cinema, London—following a run of *A Touch of Larceny*).

With *Carry On Teacher*, Anglo-Amalgamated were determined to strike while the iron was hot, and the film was trade screened on 18 February, only a couple of weeks after it was passed by the British Board of Film Censors. *Teacher* was sent out on its general release on 28 February, the Sunday following its West End debut.

This time, instead of a homegrown support feature, *Carry On Constable* was released along with *Road Racers*, a motor racing drama that had been released in the USA the previous March by American International Pictures. The largely unknown cast was headed by Joel Lawrence, Marian Collier, and Skip Ward.

What's Carrying On?

With Britain suffering under an influenza epidemic, Police Sergeant Frank Wilkins finds his local station chronically understaffed. As a result, he is sent four new recruits, the dedicated and efficient WPC Passworthy and three bumbling new constables who came bottom of the class at police school—

Stanley Benson, Tom Potter, and Charlie Constable. Completing the new intake is a special constable brought on to the force to boost the numbers during the emergency, the fay and effete Timothy Gorse. Wilkins is under pressure from his superior, the bumbling Inspector Mills, to improve his station's efficiency or be transferred elsewhere, but his four new male constables prove disastrous in their early cases. If they don't shape up, Wilkins will be out.

Who's Carrying On?

A Peter Rogers Production
Director: Gerald Thomas
Screenplay by Norman Hudis, based on an idea by Brock Williams
Music composed and directed by Bruce Montgomery
Photography: Ted Scaife
Art Director: Carmen Dillon
Editor: John Shirley

Sidney James: Sergeant Frank Wilkins, who is not so old that he cannot remember when his days as a green young constable, so tries to show his inexperienced new charges some patience.

Eric Barker: Inspector Mills, who talks a lot about discipline and efficiency but often seems more interested in his Shubunkin than in doing any work.

Kenneth Connor: Charlie Constable, who, on passing out from police school, is now Constable Constable. He has two abiding obsessions: superstitions of all types and WPC Passworthy.

Charles Hawtrey: Timothy Gorse, promoted from part-time special constable to the full-time force during the emergency. Overwhelmingly fey, Gorse takes an almost childlike joy in all aspects of life and is impossible to dislike.

Kenneth Williams: PC Stanley Benson, who thinks he is destined for much better things, despite what he regards as the terrible injustice that he came bottom of his class in police school.

Leslie Phillips: PC Tom Potter, formerly of the 'syphon squirting and waiter de-bagging' classes, now so badly in need of a regular income that he has joined the police force. He has retained his eye for the ladies, however—'Tom Potter, none hotter'.

Joan Sims: WPC Gloria Passworthy, the most efficient of the new recruits by quite some distance, and with absolutely no intention of fraternising with policemen.

Hattie Jacques: Sergeant Laura Moon, in charge of the station's WPCs, who does not quite realise how much she likes Sgt Wilkins until he is about to be transferred out of the station.

Carry On Critics

The *Monthly Film Bulletin* reviewer sounds downright weary, even as they acknowledge that the Carry Ons were developing into a series with some potential longevity:

> The Carry On series looks like becoming an anthology of all the slap-and-tickle music-hall jokes that have ever been cracked ... Out of this frayed material a little comedy is coaxed by the familiar cast as they grapple with the random situations that pass for a plot. Eric Barker's disorganised Inspector and Sidney James' infinitely weary Sergeant come nearest to real humour; the rest are only too obviously playing for the stalest of comic effects.

The Times' reviewer of 29 February 1960 was downright scathing in his opinion of *Carry On Constable*, finding that the film 'has little to recommend it except its pace, and even this is not achieved by the flow of the narrative or by skilled direction, but by a rapid succession of irrelevant incidents and the use of a large number of contrasted characters.' One very acute observation is made, however: 'The cast is a large one, and the players far too many to mention. There are some amusing performances, but all these comedians are of the same weight, and there is an urgent need for one outstanding performer to carry the rest along with him'. Although as we now know this would be a role that Sid James would run with for years to come, as *The Times* reviewer notes here, he plays 'a surprisingly subdued sergeant'. On the evidence of his debut Carry On performance, one would not necessarily realise that a cinematic era was beginning.

Variety was a little more impressed with the senior (*i.e.* older) members of the *Carry On Constable* cast: 'Eric Barker is excellent as the inefficient inspector in charge of the station while Sidney James, a newcomer to the team, is in his usual first-class form as the sergeant who is annoyed with the recruits.'

Carry On Comments

The writing process for *Carry On Constable* took a considerable length of time, which perhaps indicates that Peter Rogers still had doubts as to the direction in which the Carry On films were to go. Despite Norman Hudis appearing to be comfortably established in the role of writer on the film series, other writers were still being engaged to work on the films. In this case, both John Antrobus and Brock Williams worked on early drafts of the script. Antrobus, the Associated London Scripts writer who had worked on drafts of *Carry On Sergeant*, saw little of his work make it to the final shooting script of *Carry On Constable* but he was rewarded (on top of his writer's fee) with a small role in the film.

Brock Williams was then approached to work on the projects, and although his efforts were no more successful than those of Antrobus, he ultimately received a 'based on an idea by' credit onscreen. It is possible that this was because Williams' name still carried a degree of cachet within the industry. The prolific Cornwall-born writer had a career which stretched back to the beginning of sound films of England, spending fifteen years at Teddington Studios working for Warner Brothers' British arm making 'quota quickies'. Although these were, by definition, cheap, quickly produced entertainments that received little attention from either critics or audiences, they did see him working with Michael Powell, who went on to be Britain's most skilled and feted director. By the end of the 1930s, this saw Williams working on more prestigious assignments such as *Q Planes* and *Contraband* for Powell and his directing partner Emeric Pressberger. After landing a couple of directing assignments himself, by the 1950s Williams was back to working on B-pictures and filmed television series for the new ITV commercial television service. This included episodes of *The Gay Cavalier*, a now-lost series made for ITV's original London contractor Associated-Rediffusion.

Ultimately, the *Carry On Constable* baton was passed back to Norman Hudis, who produced a storyline similar to that of *Carry On Sergeant*. Both films feature a disparate set of new recruits learning their trade under an authority figure who is under time pressure. The casting process for the part of Sergeant Wilkins was vital, and with Ted Ray ruled out for the part by the executives at Associated British, a new face to the series was brought in, who would go on to become the single actor most associated in the public mind with the Carry On films—enter Sidney James. Sid fitted in to the series perfectly right from the beginning, with his natural flair for comedy and vast screen experience. As Frank Wilkins, the actor gives a performance slightly different to his future Carry On roles, being rather more serious than he would he would later become—the famous Sid James cackle had yet to appear.

Faced with three new recruits and a reservist pressed into front-line service due to a flu epidemic, as with other Norman Hudis authority figures created for *Carry On Sergeant* and *Carry On Teacher*, Sergeant Wilkins tries to show understanding rather than harsh discipline. In this case, Wilkins is put into opposition to Eric Barker's Inspector Mills. Mills is a development of the Captain Potts character that Barker played in *Carry On Sergeant*, here professing to be a stern disciplinarian while actually having little idea as to what is going on and being more worried about his fish tank than the day-to-day running of his police station. He blames Wilkins for the problems the station is having, and if the new intake of constables do not shape up, he will have him transferred. As it transpired, not only would Mills be transferred out of the station at the end of the film, Barker himself would leave the Carry Ons for the next eighteen years, returning only for a cameo role in *Carry On Emmannuelle* in 1978. By this point, sadly, Barker's career had for many years consisted of mere wordless cameos after a serious stroke in 1967 left him almost paralysed down the left side.

The four male recruits to Sergeant Wilkins' force are clearly written for the actors cast to play them, taking on as they do the characteristics that proved so successful in previous Carry On films, but in some cases with interesting, subtle differences. Kenneth Williams' PC Benson is clearly modelled on the highly educated, self-regarding characters he portrayed in *Sergeant* and *Nurse*. Williams' characters were given humanising touches by Norman Hudis in these films—in *Sergeant* by the bond he forms with Norman Rossington's Herbert Brown when trying to educate him, and in *Nurse* by his romance with Jill Ireland's hospital visitor. PC Benson is humanised in a different way, with his experiences on the beat teaching him that he is not the genius of the police force that he thinks he is. In previous Carry Ons, Williams' characters were genuinely highly educated people, but here we see little real evidence that Benson is as clever as he thinks he is. In fact, he is convinced that he can divine whether someone is a criminal type via the long-discredited pseudoscience of phrenology. Not surprisingly, his attempts to put his theories into practice do not go well, resulting in his braces being stolen and him almost being conned out of his savings by a trickster (played by Terence Longdon, returning for a brief cameo).

Continuing a theme begun in *Carry On Teacher*, Williams is paired up with Charles Hawtrey for key scenes, during which he camped up his performance considerably—the days were over when Kenneth Williams was a viable romantic male lead in a Carry On movie. Hawtrey in *Carry On Constable* is the absolute dictionary definition of camp and is given one of his greatest entrances: Gerald Thomas in effect repeats Hawtrey's introduction from *Carry On Sergeant* in which he crashes through the door and knocks over Bill Owen. Here, Hawtrey's Constable Gorse enters in a cloud of campness, giving effusive greetings to everyone while carrying his caged budgerigar and a huge bunch of flowers. Gorse is a lovely character, absolutely impossible to dislike and displaying an innocent, childlike joy at all of life. The key scene that explains his character occurs when Gorse finds a scooter in the street belonging to Irene Handl's errant child. Even though he is on duty patrolling his beat, Gorse cannot resist having a ride on the scooter and sets off down the street with an expression of pure, innocent enjoyment on his face. Such fun, of course, cannot last, and before long, he runs into Kenneth Williams' PC Benson being dragged along by Lady, the station's German Shepherd, and falls down a flight of stairs.

After being paired up in *Carry On Teacher* as what amounts to a catfighting gay couple, Williams and Hawtrey here don drag when going undercover as

'Agatha' and 'Ethel' in an attempt to apprehend a shoplifter at Brian Oulton's department store. Both Gorse and Benson are clearly having a great time in drag, only spoiled by the fact that the shop staff think they are a pair of lunatics and have them arrested by the store detectives.

Kenneth Connor, whose roles in the Carry On films thus far had demonstrated the actor's range, is here given a role which is a virtual rerun of his Horace Strong from *Carry On Sergeant*. Instead of Strong's crippling hypochondria, PC Charlie Constable (and some obvious, but genuine fun is had with his new rank of Constable Constable) is superstitious to an absurd extent, which he has to overcome in order to find love. This time, the object of his affections is Joan Sims' WPC Gloria Passworthy, which shows how effective she was as love interest opposite Leslie Phillips in *Carry On Teacher*. Sims' role within the Carry On films had changed considerably since she joined the cast in *Carry On Nurse* as a clumsy, daffy student nurse, basically replacing Dora Bryan when that actress decided not to continue with the series. Next she was sporty and lusty in *Carry On Teacher*, and here Sims is super-efficient and professional WPC Passworthy, but still with a sparkle in her eye and clearly not completely resistant to the clumsy, nervous advances of Charlie Constable.

Leslie Phillips returns as his signature lothario character, having by now basically replaced Terence Longdon as the posh chap placed in a situation where he is out of his element. His opportunities to be a romantic lead in *Carry On Constable* are strictly limited: his Constable Potter fancies Constable Jill Adams as soon as he sets eyes on her, but she then gets the flu and is not seen again until the end of the film. He does get a lovely scene with Shirley Eaton, returning (like Terence Longdon) for a cameo role that exposes Tom Potter's sensitive side, his people skills giving the young Constable a rare success. Potter's life as a policeman begins inauspiciously when he accidentally helps jewel shop thieves headed by Freddie Mills, who was very famous at the time as a boxing champion. Potter bursts into Eaton's bathroom thinking she is a burglar—we hear what might well be the first flushing toilet ever heard in a British film—only to find the lovely young woman in the buff. Instead of the expected lascivious reaction we might expect given Phillips' screen image, he ends up giving Eaton, who has argued with her fiancée, marriage advice.

This was to prove Eaton's final Carry On role, and truth be told, the series had developed in directions which did not suit the actress's wholesome charms. While there was still a need for an object of desire in the films, so central a role required a comedic performer, and the part was here filled extremely well by Joan Sims. Although she appeared in no more Carry On films, over the next few years Eaton did appear in a run of comedies heavily influenced by the series. These were *A Weekend with Lulu* (opposite Bob Monkhouse and Leslie Phillips), *Nearly A Nasty Accident* (with Kenneth Connor and Eric

Barker), *Dentist On The Job* (Monkhouse and Connor starring along with Eric Barker and Charles Hawtrey), and *What A Carve Up* (starring Sid James and Kenneth Connor).

Sid James gives an interesting performance, playing a more reserved authority figure than he would in future films, which suits the material perfectly. He is also given a putative romance with Hattie Jacques' Sergeant Moon, and the two actors have a great chemistry together which works extremely well on screen and would be developed in future films. Joan Hickson returns, playing a role far removed from her ward sister in *Carry On Nurse*. This time, she plays the permanently drunk Mrs May, who finds herself in the police cells after an especially raucous night on the sauce. As a result, she witnesses the first nude scene in Carry On history, and it is the male cast members (as it were) who are exposed as the four new recruits run screaming from the station's freezing cold showers. This was clearly viewed as a major sequence in the film as it featured on the film's poster artwork.

One advantage of using the police as a background to a Carry On film is that the material suits an episodic structure, which allows Norman Hudis to write material for each of the leading cast members to showcase their strengths. A basic plot structure around which the other stories revolve is provided by the constant pressure Inspector Mills put Sergeant Wilkins under. This eventually brings the story, in a very natural way, to its climax in the last fifteen minutes as Wilkins is put on notice that he will be transferred out of the station. The bumbling new recruits are sent out on patrol in pairs to minimise the chance of them causing disasters, and they realise that they need a big success to save their jobs. Sergeant Wilkins and Constable Potter are on the scene for a wage snatch, which results in a car chase and the villains escaping. Proving that he really is an intelligent policeman once he drops the phrenology nonsense, Benson deduces that the villains have probably stayed in the area rather than leaving the country. He and Potter spot the villain's car near a derelict old house and call in Constable and Gorse so they can make the arrests themselves.

The three robbers (Michael Balfour, Jack Taylor, and Eric Boon) are getting ready to escape wearing police uniforms, resulting in an enormous fight which acts as the film's climax. Interestingly, this starts out as a Laurel and Hardy-style slapstick comedy before turning into what is genuinely quite a violet punch-up. It is of especial note that Charles Hawtrey really gets stuck in during this scene, performing quite a high fall from a staircase—between this scene and his fall from the scooter earlier in the film, *Carry On Constable* is probably the most physically demanding film Hawtrey ever made. The only problem with this scene is that it was shot on location in the actual derelict house, which looks genuinely grungy and dangerous and gives the film a cheap look at an important stage of proceedings. Unfortunately, Gerald Thomas did not have the budget available to make the location look atmospheric, so instead, these scenes look rather stark and underfunded.

Ultimately, *Carry On Constable* is a good-hearted film. The nearest we get to a villain (apart from the wage-snatchers) is Inspector Mills, and even he is pretty well impossible to dislike. The film ends on a note of irony as Mills is seen to be so good at encouraging the new recruits he has berated for the entire film that he is promoted to run the police training college. As a result, instead of being transferred away from the station by Mills, Sergeant Wilkins is promoted and given Mills' old job. We also see that no less than three budding love affairs are beginning by the end of the film: Wilkins and Moon, Constable and Passworthy and Potter and WPC Harrison. It is a nice note to end the movie on.

Interestingly, *Carry On Constable* was the first of a run of nine Peter Rogers Productions films released between 1960 and 1963 officially co-produced with GHW Productions. With Peter Rogers Productions operating at its peak of productivity, it is very possible that this was a co-production deal on paper only, which presented Rogers and/or Anglo-Amalgamated with tax advantages—Hammer Films would occasionally produce films under a similar flag of convenience in this same period. GHW Productions had previously been a production company set up by Bolton-born producer George Walker, which operated under the wing of the Rank Organisation from 1938 until Walker's retirement in 1959. Somewhat bizarrely, Walker's last film, the religious drama *The Crowning Gift*, was released four years after his 1962 death.

Carry On Constable proved an extremely popular box office draw, being in the top three pictures in the United Kingdom of a year when all three major money-earners were, unusually, British productions. The top moneymaker of 1960 was another British comedy, *Doctor In Love*, while the other was Lewis Gilbert's war movie *Sink the Bismark!* It is somewhat remarkable in retrospect that it would be over a year until the release of the next Carry On picture, but also a tribute to the care that Peter Rogers put into getting the script just right before putting the next film in the series into production.

What would eventually become the next Carry On picture, the deliberately episodic and sketch-based *Carry On Regardless*, had its roots in an idea Norman Hudis had been working on some years previously. This had been shelved before Hudis able to satisfactorily develop a linking theme, but was not the only potential Carry On that the writer was working on in this period. With *Carry On Sergeant* having proved enduringly popular and military comedies remaining audience favourites, it was a sound idea to look at another of the armed services for inspiration. Thus Norman Hudis was assigned *Carry On Flying* to work into a shooting script, with the regular cast members finding themselves in the RAF. Work on the project was halted when it occurred to Peter Rogers that the film would be a hostage to fortune, since a plane crash close to or during the film's release would prove disastrous to its box office prospects. Writer Michael Pertwee, the brother of occasional Carry On actor and future Doctor Who Jon Pertwee, submitted an idea entitled *Carry On Smoking*, which was not about hijinks in the tobacco industry but instead set in a fire station. Since this would have similarly been a major conflagration away from box office disaster, *Carry On Smoking* proceeded no further than the idea stage.

Despite Anglo-Amalgamated (and the ABC cinema chain that screened their films) being desperate for the guaranteed box-office draw of a new Carry On picture, Peter Rogers held out until he had one that he was happy to proceed with. In the interim, Peter Rogers and Gerald Thomas kept busy with comedies outside of the series, making *Watch Your Stern* and *No Kidding*, both of which featured a host of Carry On regulars, before finally putting another Carry On film onto the Pinewood studio floor.

6

Carry On Regardless (1961)

Filming Dates: 28 November 1960–17 January 1961
Original Certificate: U (Classified by BBFC 1 March 1961)
Running Time: 89 minutes 39 seconds

Release Details

London Release: 17 March 1961 (Odeon, Marble Arch—following a run of *Five Golden Hours*).

A second, charity premiere of *Carry On Regardless* took place at the Forum Cinema, Birmingham, on 28 March 1961 in aid of the Royal Commonwealth Society for the Blind. While the charitable nature of the event was commendable, it was in no way a premiere, as not only had the film opened eleven days earlier, but also *Carry On Regardless* had gone on general release on Sunday 26 March.

Carry On Regardless was released in the United Kingdom via the ABC circuit paired with one of two Anglo-Amalgamated productions, depending on where you lived. The first was *The Malpas Mystery*, directed by Sidney Hayers at Beaconsfield Studios for Julian Wintle and Leslie Parkin's Independent Artists as part of the popular Edgar Wallace film series. Most of the Edgar Wallace films were produced by Jack Greenwood at Merton Park Studios but a few came from other hands. In some areas, *Carry On Regardless* was instead supported by another breezy little Anglo-Amalgamated crime drama which itself was rebranded as part of the Edgar Wallace series when the films were shown on television. This was *Crossroads to Crime*, about dirty dealings in the road haulage business which has a minor place in history as the first cinema film to be directed by Gerry Anderson, the future producer of the Supermarionation puppet films including *Thunderbirds*.

What's Carrying On?

Bert Handy is due to open his new Helping Hands employment agency, but his advert in *The Times* for people seeking varied, exciting work has received no responses. At the last moment, a varied group of people at the local Labour Exchange—including the bored exchange clerk—see the advert and turn up *en masse*. Bert hires them and we see the new employees on their assignments, which range from babysitting to a chimp's tea party to being seconds at a boxing match. Meanwhile, Bert keeps being visited by a mysterious potential client who speaks in a strange gobbledegook language which neither he nor his secretary Miss Cooling can decipher.

Who's Carrying On?

A Peter Rogers Production
Director: Gerald Thomas
Screenplay by Norman Hudis
Music composed and directed by Bruce Montgomery
Photography: Alan Hume BSC
Art Director: Lionel Couch
Editor: John Shirley

Sidney James: Bert Handy, proprietor of the Helping Hands agency where people can hire staff to perform unusual tasks.

Kenneth Connor: Sam Twist, bored Labour Exchange clerk who leaps at the chance of doing something more interesting, and possibly even fulfilling his dreams of becoming a fearless secret agent.

Charles Hawtrey: Gabriel Dimple, weedy-looking and bespectacled, but with the heart of a lion; he is willing to take on a heavyweight boxer and act as bouncer in a strip club.

Joan Sims: Lily Duveen, who wants to have just as much adventure as the men, though she proves to have absolutely no head for wine.

Kenneth Williams: Francis Courtenay, who speaks sixteen languages fluently, is convinced he has what it takes to be a model and proves much better with chimpanzees than he is with children.

Bill Owen: Mike Weston, who proves very disappointed when he is sent to be a strip club bouncer and instead is confronted with a very different group of birds.

Liz Fraser: Delia King, who brings glamour to the agency and is willing to do anything, from trying on a lady's wardrobe to wrestling with an over-powered floor cleaner to almost getting married due to a clerical error.

Terence Longdon: Montgomery Infield-Hopping, who had been turning up to the Labour Exchange in a chauffeur-driven car. In his search for workplace excitement, he demonstrates the ideal bachelor pad and has a mud bath.

Esma Cannon: Miss Cooling, Bert Handy's secretary, who assures her boss that he will eventually 'get staffed' and organises an incredibly complex system so that the staff get the right assignments.

Carry On Critics

The Times' reviewer of 20 March 1961 was surprisingly positive about *Regardless*, and the ongoing popularity of the series in general:

> This is the latest offering in the 'Carry On' series, and that, for those who know the kind of farcical, cheerful vulgarity in which it specializes, is description and criticism enough. Here is British humour at its most awe-inspiring.

The *Monthly Film Bulletin* reviewer also, even this early in the series' history, seemed rather wearily (and warily) admiring of the Carry On's status as a critic-proof factory of comedy:

> By now there's a sort of ritual charm about the antics of the regulars, Kenneth Connor, Kenneth Williams, Charles Hawtrey, so steeped in double meanings that even the most innocent incident becomes automatically suspect.

Although *Carry On Regardless* can be seen in hindsight as the series just about to hit its stride, the comments of the unnamed reviewer remain quite acute:

> This comedy seems staler, less yeasty than, say, *Carry On Nurse*. But the series has worked up such popular appeal it can probably coast along on that momentum very nicely for some time, before the public finally calls its bluff.

Penelope Gilliatt, in *The Observer* on Sunday 19 March 1961, was also very perceptive in summing up the appeal of the Carry Ons in the era that Norman Hudis wrote them:

> If this film, too, is a colossal success, it will not be too surprising. Apart from having a completely undisturbing sense of humour, and apart from drawing off the best-loved stars of revue, TV screen and radio ... it also expresses many of our deepest popular assumptions. Class distinctions are recognised

as firm and right; dignity is felt to be tainted if mixed with ambition; decent behaviour is kind, staunch and thrives in crisis.

Variety admitted defeat when writing about the film: 'Any serious criticism of *Carry On Regardless* is futile ... Ingenuity of scriptwriter Norman Hudis is sometimes a bit strained, but he has come up with some sound comedy situations'.

Carry On Comments

The idea of a Carry On movie made up of a series of sketches had been around for some time. Norman Hudis had originally set to work on a project entitled *What A Carry On*, but the idea was set aside at an early stage before a structure for the film could be worked out.[1]

The motivation behind the making of a sketch film under the Carry On banner came in part from Peter Rogers' mailbag, which was filled with suggestions for Carry On situations. Looking back, it might seem odd that the producers would deliberately set up a project which would use up a huge amount of material. Of course at this point, the idea of a film series running for over twenty years was unprecedented and no one knew at what point the game would be up for the Carry Ons. In 1960, no doubt the idea of using up a glut of ideas seemed like a splendid one.

With Sidney James back in the cast after the success of his *Carry On Constable* debut, it was clear that Norman Hudis' script had to have him at its centre. Thus the notion of an employment agency was formulated and for the first time we get to see the characterisation that James would use for the rest of the series. *Carry On Constable*'s Sergeant Wilkins was written as a relatively stern authority figure and indeed was not originally written for Sid at all. This time, Norman Hudis was clearly writing specifically for Sid, which results in a characterisation which fits like a comfortable overcoat and a far more relaxed performance from the actor. Hudis even slips in a gag referencing Sid's love of betting on the horses during a scene in which he is mistaken for a hospital inspector, which turned into one of the film's best jokes. Not that Sid had an entirely smooth time on *Carry On Regardless*, as the actor was knocked unconscious after he slipped and fell down a flight of stairs, not that this delayed production in any way—as Sid had delivered his lines perfectly well before falling, the production (in typically efficient Gerald Thomas fashion) simply moved on to the next, Sid-free scene while James recovered.[2]

Joan Sims returned and was unexpectedly reteamed with Liz Fraser, the latter making her Carry On debut, shortly after they had been an effectively glamourous double act in Ralph Thomas' *Doctor in Love*. Although Fraser was new to the Carry Ons, the thirty-year-old actress was already a comedy veteran, among her credits being eight episodes of the *Hancock's Half Hour* TV series and the Peter Sellers films *The Smallest Show on Earth* (1957), *I'm Alright Jack* (1959), and *Two Way Stretch* (1960). During the filming of *Carry On Regardless*, Fraser even appeared with Sid James as a part of the BBC's *Christmas Night with the Stars* show on Christmas Day 1960. Liz Fraser had been cast at a late stage of production, as Hattie Jacques had originally been cast as Delia King, but then underwent exploratory surgery for a stomach complaint in the autumn of 1960. When it became clear that Jacques would not recover in time for her to play such a major role, the part of Delia was recast and somewhat reduced. Whatever the size of the role, a new Carry On regular had been found. Hattie was well enough to spend a day filming a cameo appearance as a hospital ward sister opposite Joan Sims' Matron for a much-reduced fee of £100.[3]

Terence Longdon also returned for his final appearance in the Carry Ons. He was also a second choice, replacing Leslie Phillips, who surprised Peter Rogers by leaving the Carry On series without so much as a backward glance, not wanting to be tied down in the public mind to a long-running film series, especially one that paid so little as the Carry Ons.[4] Terence Longdon, who was basically the same physical and social type as Phillips, fitted the part like a glove and had been a member of the Carry On team since *Carry On Sergeant*. Nevertheless, the part of Montgomery Infield-Hopping was reduced in size due to the recasting—even by 1961, Phillips was a far bigger box office draw than Terence Longdon. In fact after the opening scene which brings the characters together, we barely see him again until an hour into the film.

Charles Hawtrey is also conspicuously absent for much of the film, much to the actor's displeasure. He reportedly asked for top billing, a recurring theme in his professional career, and felt that there was a lack of comedic material for him.[5] To be fair, the fact that audiences do not get to see Hawtrey in action until forty-five minutes into the film was not the fault of Norman Hudis or the producers. A sequence in which Hawtrey hid in a bedroom wardrobe writing down everything Eleanor Summerfield said in her sleep was cut due to BBFC objections. Nevertheless, this was an ominous sign in the relationship between Peter Rogers and Hawtrey, who had an unfortunate and recurring habit of sabotaging his relationships with employers with demands for top billing or more money. Positive outcomes for such negotiations were exceedingly rare, and it would not be long before Hawtrey would miss a Carry On film as a result.

The sketch format of the film provided, at script stage at least, plenty of opportunities to cast Hawtrey against type and his two major scenes are actually quite effective, putting the actor into scenes in which his skinny build and fey manner made him seem unsuited. In the first of the two, he takes over in a boxing match from a terrified Dynamite Dan, who backs out, claiming a broken little finger. Dan was played by 'Tiger' Joe Robinson, who was in real life a legendary Judo expert who went on to appear in everything from Italian muscleman epics to the James Bond film *Diamonds Are Forever*. Robinson's opponent, Massive Mickey McGee, was played by burly former professional boxer Tom Clegg, who became something of a regular in the in the series, turning up in *Spying, Cleo, Cowboy, Screaming* (probably his best-known part, as Oddbod), and *Loving*. For the record, our Charlie wins by an accidental headbutt. This sequence also features the return of Freddie Mills as Dynamite Dan's manager, Bert Handy's old friend Lefty, who had previously appeared in *Carry On Constable*. Mills had been Britain's most famous boxer and turned his fame into a film acting career, with varying results, before dying in mysterious and violent circumstances in 1965. For what it is worth, *Carry On Regardless* features one of Freddie Mills' most enthusiastic and natural performances, playing nicely off Sid James. This is perhaps not surprising as Sid was a generous actor who would always help an inexperienced performer give their best.

Hawtrey's second scene is a very odd sequence during part of the film in which the Helping Hands staff members are all sent out on the wrong assignments. Hawtrey's Gabriel Dimple is sent in place of Bill Owen to be a bouncer at Sidney Tafler's Soho strip club. This has all the makings of a lengthy and memorable scene, as the ever-game Dimple decides to take the job anyway. At this point, however, the scene just ends, which is a terrible waste of a good set-up.

While the sketch format provided, at script stage at least, plenty of opportunities for Charles Hawtrey, it was an even better showcase for the wide-ranging talents of Kenneth Connor. Connor is probably the actor who gets the most to do over the course of *Carry On Regardless*, his first assignment being to act as a babysitter for honey-voiced cutie Fenella Fielding's Penny Panting, the latter vamping like crazy in what amounts to a dry run for her turn five years later as Valeria in *Carry On Screaming*. She does not really want a babysitter, just an excuse to make her neglectful husband Ed Devereaux jealous.

Connor's major scene comes when a mysterious foreign client phones on a bad line to hire someone to go to the Forth Bridge. The foreign client is played by none other than Eric Pohlmann, who would soon find employment in the James Bond films as the voice of supervillain Ernst Stavro Blofeld. This assignment appeals to the adventurous nature of Connor's character Sam Twist, who sets off by train as if on a spy mission, complete with Humphrey Bogart-style trench coat and hat; this was before the James Bond gave cinematic secret agents a considerable wardrobe upgrade. The mystery client actually wants a fourth at bridge, so the people he tries to make contact with on the train are mystified. Among these is a leopardskin-clad Mata Hari-type played by none other than Betty Marsden. Since the summer of 1958, she had starred alongside Kenneth Williams in the BBC Light Programme comedy show *Beyond Our Ken*, led by the urbane, velvet-voiced Kenneth Horne. Marsden would go on to play a much more prominent role in 1969's *Carry On Camping* as Terry Scott's wife with the foghorn laugh, Harriet Potter.

The spy sequence is quite a complex scene, whereas a much simpler sequence works even better for Connor's abilities; he is hired as a replacement waiter at a gentlemen's club in which silence must be observed at all times. Within minutes, the absurd old duffers who make up the club's membership reduce Connor to uncontrollable fits of laughter. It is an utterly simple idea that works superbly well and highlights the great strength of *Carry On Regardless*: the film gives opportunities for scenes that a longer-form narrative would never have afforded.

A particularly good example of this is a short sequence that is not even connected to the linking device of the Helping Hands agency in which Kenneth Connor attempts to give up smoking with the support of Joan Sims, who wants to give up eating sweets. The whole sketch leads up to a verbal joke so complicated and barely amusing that it is not worth repeating here, but the joy the two actors display in performing together is so palpable that it makes Norman Hudis' dialogue play far better on screen than it reads on the page.

Kenneth Williams also does rather well out of *Carry On Regardless'* patchwork format. Williams still retained vestiges of his fresh-faced youth at this stage and benefits from Norman Hudis' habit of writing for him somewhat more likeable characters than Talbot Rothwell would later in the series. His character of Francis Courtenay retains the vanity of the pompous authority figures he would go on to play for the Carry Ons, but Courtenay is adventurous (he did volunteer for Helping Hands, after all) and eager to please. In the course of the film, he proves perfectly willing to take a chimpanzee for a walk—more than that, in the course of his assignment, he becomes the monkey's protector against a hostile world and takes him to the zoo for a chimp's tea party so the animal can be among his own kind. There is not much by way of a punchline to the scene, but that is okay. It is just a pleasure to see Williams operating at the peak of his abilities in such unusual circumstances, and even looking like he is enjoying himself.

Even better is a sequence in which Courtenay acts as a translator to Terence Alexander and his German wife Julia Arnall (both actors making their only Carry On appearances). Alexander needs a translator as his wife will only argue with him in German, which means he has no idea why she is so violently annoyed with him. The scene takes an interesting left turn when Courtenay bursts into tears and begs them to reconcile because he is from a broken home. This, naturally, gives Williams an opportunity to overact shamelessly as only he could, which is, as the old expression goes, enough to make a cat laugh.

Norman Hudis also cleverly seeds a running gag through part of the film, which has the effect of setting up a short scene with a very effective payoff. An assignment is available as a photographic model, which immediately appeals to the Courtenay/Williams vanity. He preens and boasts about his suitability for the job until, finally, he is given the assignment. On turning up at Michael Ward's photographic studio, it turns out that his client (Ian Wilson) is advertising bee-keepers' masks.

Not everyone does as well out of *Carry On Regardless* as the two Kenneths. Bill Owen is landed with the rather thankless role of Mike Weston (and there never was an actor who looked less like a Mike Weston than Owen) who, until the finale, only has one scene, a throwaway bit in which he is mistakenly sent to look after Molly Weir's houseful of caged birds rather than Sidney Tafler's strip club. Perhaps, like Terence Longden, Owen's small role here prefigured his future in the Carry On series—one more role, if anything even smaller, in *Carry On Cabby*, ended his run on the series.

Liz Fraser does not get a huge amount to do as a late replacement for Hattie Jacques playing Delia King. It is clear immediately how talented she is however, and that the Carry Ons had happened on an actress who mixed the sex appeal of Shirley Eaton with a keen sense of comedy. In her big scene, Fraser is hired to try on a wardrobe of clothes bought by Jimmy Thompson as a wedding present for his wife. Liz is extremely decorous in the role (to say the very least—producers at the time had a habit of putting her into underwear or bikinis) but her performance does not rely on her physicality and gives the performance of an expert farceur.

The film's other major actress, Joan Sims, grabs the opportunities that the film affords her with both hands, not only in the aforementioned smoking scene with Kenneth Connor, but also in a scene which benefits from her ability to play a really great drunk scene. She is collecting invitations for a wine-tasting held by Howard Marion-Crawford, one of the great character actors of the post-war era and himself no stranger to the pleasures of the grape. Having finished her appointed task, Joan is invited to join the wine-tasting and, not realising that the point of the exercise is to taste a small sample of each drink, proceeds to very quickly get steaming drunk. Joan plays the scene to freewheeling perfection, but the scene is also of interest for a couple of its other cast members: Michael Nightingale makes his first appearance in a Carry On film as one of the wine-tasters and would go on to become possibly the ultimate Carry On small part actor. Spotting Nightingale's often uncredited appearances, which last right up to the end of the series with *Carry On Laughing* and *Carry On Emmannuelle*, is one of the entertaining pleasures of the regular Carry On watcher. Rather more prominent in the wine-tasting scene is Nicholas Parsons in his only Carry On role, playing a wolfish wine-taster who likes the look of the sloshed Joan Sims rather too much. Even drunk, Joan is no pushover and Parsons gets knocked over for his trouble.

This being a Norman Hudis script, the whole thing has to be wrapped up in the end with the characters working together for a common end. This time, the thread that binds the extremely disparate plot elements together is the appearances of an increasingly exasperated Stanley Unwin, who cannot make Sid and his secretary Esma Cannon understand what he is saying. For the uninitiated, this is because the former BBC sound engineer Unwin made an entire career out of a type of double-talk known as Unwinese, which sounded enough like English that the listener could catch a vague gist of his meaning without really understanding a word of what was being said. Eventually, it turns out that he is the landlord of Helping Hands' offices and is serving them notice to quit. They get a stay of execution if they can clean up a ramshackle old house Unwin has bought.

While many of the cast feature in an earlier sequence as demonstrators at the Ideal House Exhibition (which also features a tiny, non-speaking role for a very young Sally Geeson), here at last the whole cast is brought together in a major physical comedy sequence. As well as the pleasure in finally seeing the cast working together, the ending is a welcome change of pace, with a series of destructive visual gags as the Helping Hands crew inadvertently wreck the house they are supposed to be tidying up. Of course everything ends happily, which is only appropriate for what is a very happy, likeable film in the Carry On catalogue. Very few people would describe *Carry On Regardless* as their favourite in the series, but the format of the film means that there is something for everyone—if you do not like a scene, something different will be along in a few minutes.

7

Carry On Cruising (1962)

Filming Dates: 8 January 1962–16 February 1962
Original Certificate: U (Classified by BBFC 13 March 1962)
Running Time: 89 minutes 57 seconds

Release Details

Carry On Cruising appears not to have had a London West End screening, going instead straight into general release from Sunday, 15 April 1962.

The full-colour *Carry On Cruising* found itself paired with a choice of monochrome support features from Anglo-Amalgamated's Edgar Wallace series. *The Share Out*, directed by Gerald Glaister at Merton Park Studios, concerns a gang of crooks blackmailing people into selling property at knock-down prices. Bernard Lee, about to become world-famous as M in the James Bond films, investigates while Alexander Knox, Moira Redmond, and William Russell (himself about to ascend to fame as part of the original cast of *Doctor Who*) also feature. In other parts of Britain, *Cruising* was paired with *Flat Two*, directed by Alan Cooke, in which two men are framed for the murder of a blackmailer. A strong cast is headed by John Le Mesurier, Jack Watling, and Bernard Archard.

What's Carrying On?

Wellington Crowther has worked his way up from nothing to become captain of the cruise ship SS *Happy Wanderer*, no mean feat for an old cockney sea dog. The *Happy Wanderer* is the most efficiently run ship in the fleet, and after ten years in charge, Captain Crowther now has the chance of being made captain of a new transatlantic liner. Crowther puts the ship's success down to having a settled crew who he has worked with for years, thus he is disconcerted to learn that there are five newcomers on his latest voyage, vital for his chances of landing the new job. With a new first officer, ship's doctor, head cook, captain's steward, and barman, Crowther's chances of landing a prestigious new berth might be lost at sea.

Who's Carrying On?

A Peter Rogers Production
Director: Gerald Thomas
Screenplay by Norman Hudis, from a story by Eric Barker
Music composed by Bruce Montgomery and Douglas Gamley
Photography by Alan Hume BSC
Art Director: Carmen Dillon
Editor: John Shirley

Sidney James: Captain Wellington Crowther, a tough old seadog who has worked his way to a captainship, despite his working-class roots. He knows there are people on the board of the cruise line who think he is too low class to be a ship's captain, so if anything goes wrong on this trip, his chances of being made captain of the new transatlantic liner might be scuppered.

Kenneth Williams: First Officer Leonard Marjoribanks (pronounced Marchbanks) has been made first officer of the *Happy Wanderer* at short notice after the previous office holder got six draws on the football pools.

Kenneth Connor: Doctor Arthur Binn, who diagnosed himself as needing a sea voyage, so swapped his job as medical officer at Consolidated Marmalade with the SS *Happy Wanderer*'s Dr Jepson. He soon finds himself in love and tongue-tied around passenger Florence Castle.

Liz Fraser: Gladys Trimble, on this cruise around the Mediterranean to get away from men and help her friend Flo find a husband—until she claps eyes on the ship's hunky PT instructor (Vincent Ball).

Dilys Laye: Florence 'Flo' Castle, on the cruise with her best friend Gladys in order to find a husband. After a disastrous attempt to impress the ship's PT instructor, she loses hope, but her future spouse might be closer than she thinks.

Esma Cannon: Bridget Madderley, an elderly lady setting sail on her own on the Happy Wanderer, but game for anything and able to sink almost as much alcohol as permanently drunk barfly Ronnie Stevens.

Lance Percival: Ship's Cook Wilfred Haines, from an old seafaring family, but hiding a terrible secret: if he cannot see the sea and the sky, he gets dreadfully seasick. He is the maker of the world's strangest celebration cake and the revolutionary Haines method of breaking mass quantities of eggs.

Jimmy Thompson: Ship's Barman Sam Turner, on a quest to recreate the captain's favourite drink, the Aberdeen Angus, the recipe for which is only known to Angus, his predecessor. Also kept busy refuelling a drunken passenger who never gets off at any port, just drinks whatever they do in that country.

Cyril Chamberlain: Captain's Steward Tom Tree, the new steward to Captain Crowther, despite having only served on three voyages before, and they were on the Margate ferry.

Carry On Critics

The *Monthly Film Bulletin*'s reviewer recognised that *Carry On Cruising* was, at heart, a glossier, rather more relaxed reworking of the themes and structure of *Carry On Sergeant*:

> The style is if anything even more easy-going, achieving a kind of comedy shorthand which often relies on the familiar screen eccentricities of such regulars as Sid James, Kenneth Connor and Kenneth Williams to raise a laugh without the strain of developing a given situation to its illogical conclusion.

Variety was also less than impressed with the work of the scriptwriter: 'Maybe Norman Hudis, who has so skilfully scribed this run of hits, should have a sabbatical'. The paper's critic even gives an instant sketch of the regular contribution of each of the regulars:

> Jumping, familiarly, through their well-placed circus hoops are Sidney James (he glowers), Kenneth Williams (he plays archly), Kenneth Connor (he dithers), Liz Fraser (she flaunts a shapely figure) and Esma Cannon (she twitters).

Carry On Comments

First, a slight digression: It was clearly quite a feather in Peter Rogers' cap for Nat Cohen and Stuart Levy to allow his low-budget Carry On film series to make the leap to colour photography with *Carry On Cruising*, while also indicating the status the films had achieved within the Anglo-Amalgamated release schedule.

Of the twenty-five British pictures released by Anglo-Amalgamated in 1962, only two were in colour. The first of these was *Carry On Cruising* on 13 April, followed in July by *Some People*, a drama released in July to promote the duke of Edinburgh's award scheme. This represented something of a comeback for its star, Kenneth More, who had lost his Rank film contract and found himself virtually blackballed from the movie industry after falling foul of Rank's notorious managing director, John Davis. During the year, Anglo also had Peter Rogers produce another colour feature, *The Iron Maiden*, which was premiered in London on 3 January 1963.

That Levy and Cohen were entrusting comedy films with expensive colour photography was in itself quite a development, one which had begun with the release of the Peter Rogers production *Raising the Wind* in September 1961. This indicated an increasing confidence on behalf of Anglo-Amalgamated that what had previously been almost exclusively a B-picture studio could start to compete on level terms with the more polished products of Rank such as the Doctor series. The few previous British-produced Anglo-Amalgamated films to have been in colour had largely been in the horror and SF genres, in which colour had been *de rigueur* since the huge success of Hammer Films' *The Curse of Frankenstein* and *Dracula* the previous decade. Thus *Horrors of the Black Museum* (1959), *Peeping Tom* (1960), and *Konga* (1961) had all been released in blazing Eastman Colour. There had, however, been an earlier British Anglo-Amalgamated release, the first in the company's history. This was *Nudist Paradise*, first released on 26 January 1959 on a double bill with *Liane, Jungle Goddess*. The latter was a 1956 West German production in which the title character, a sort of junior female Tarzan, was played by the sixteen-year old Marion Michael. This was an ideal pairing for the flesh-filled main feature as the pubescent heroine plays the first half of the film topless, not especially covered up by her long blond hair.

If the title *Nudist Paradise* rings a bell, it has another Carry On connection: future Carry On writer Talbot Rothwell clearly remembered the film when he was writing his script for *Carry On Camping* in 1969, borrowing its title for the film that Sid and Bernie take an unsuspecting Joan Sims and Dilys Laye to at the beginning of the story.

Meanwhile, back in 1962, Peter Rogers and Gerald Thomas set about assembling the strongest script and cast for *Carry On Cruising*, the story of which originated with former Carry On star and occasional writer Eric Barker. Barker had submitted an idea about a European coach holiday. This was passed to Norman Hudis, who retooled the idea into a script about a Mediterranean cruise. This he did by reaching for his much-used storyline about newcomers to an organisation eventually coming good to aid an authority figure. Freshness was added to the mixture by the nature of the setting, the SS *Happy Wanderer*, travelling to various locations in Southern Europe and North Africa. This also adds an episodic feel to the storyline, making *Carry On Cruising* more similar to the sketch-based *Carry On Regardless* than might first appear.

It was vital that the right cast be assembled for this major step up for the Carry On films, and naturally Sidney James was at the head of the cast as Captain Wellington Crowther. While his predecessor as the father figure of the Carry On cast, Ted Ray, had a certain natural gravitas—unusual for a stand-up comedian—which would have made him ideal casting as a ship's captain, Sid was somewhat cast against type. This gave Norman Hudis the key to the film's plot, as we learn that Captain Crowther has worked his way up from nothing to spend ten years as the most efficient captain in the fleet. If he is going to progress to the next stage, however, he is going to have to overcome class barriers erected due to his working-class origins:

> There are some copper-bottomed gentlemen on the board who still think it's dead-wrong for an h-dropper like me to be a ship's captain, and they would scuttle me if they had half a chance. And that is why I have built this whole crew round me so that they don't get the chance. That is also why I get nervous when I see new faces. Your faces are new, so I'm nervous. To me you look like disaster on six legs. Prove me wrong, that's all I ask.

In one short piece of dialogue, Norman Hudis sets up the film's key plot element: Captain Crowther's settled crew is upset by no fewer than five new arrivals in key positions on a voyage, the success of which could see Crowther promoted to a plumb new role captaining a transatlantic liner. In the role of the new first officer, Kenneth Williams was cast, his status as a comedy star outside the Carry On series by now enhanced by his radio success on the BBC Light Programme alongside Kenneth Horne. This was even played up in the film's trailer, which featured the scene in which the two Carry On Kenneths, Connor and Williams, dress up in Spanish-style: 'Fancy dressing up like this is beyond our ken,' exclaims the narrator. Although Williams has been an ever-present feature in the Carry On films to this point, he was a star of some magnitude by now and, perhaps understandably, asked Peter Rogers for a pay rise. No more money was offered, but an added incentive for the actor to sign on to the production was the promise of location shooting in Gibraltar.[1] As events transpired, the production never left the land-locked confines of Pinewood Studios in Iver Heath, Buckinghamshire, save for a day's second unit work at Southampton docks.

Williams is written for slightly differently here by Hudis than in previous Carry On films. The standard Williams character had been an intellectual type with an over-inflated sense of his own superiority, whereas here Williams is presented as ultimately being a good-hearted and efficient first officer. Like his fellow new shipmates, he comes good when he stops trying to impress his captain and instead simply tries to help the passengers to the best of his abilities.

Kenneth Connor also had a new characterisation of a sort as Doctor Binn, allowing him to display confidence and professional competence in his medical capacity while also succumbing at times to the attacks of nerves that Norman Hudis would generally write for his characters. In a very similar manner to his Gregory Adams in *Carry On Teacher*, what turns Connor's character here into a gibbering wreck is the possibility of love. His potential partner here was played by Dilys Laye, a newcomer to the Carry On crew who was cast at a late stage. Her role of Flo Castle was originally to have been played by Joan Sims, who at this stage was the reining female romantic lead among the Carry On regulars. One theory that has done the rounds is that Sims had begun a romance with one of the studio carpenters during production on *Carry On Regardless*, which Peter Rogers so disapproved of that he dropped her from the cast of *Carry On Cruising*, also leaving her out of *Jack*, *Cabby*, and *Spying*. Doubt has been cast on this theory, most notably in Andrew Ross' authorised biography of Joan Sims, *Too Happy a Face*, which prefers the official explanation that Sims fell ill.[2] Although this does not explain her absence from the subsequent three films in the series, Joan Sims was at this point at the peak of her popularity as an actress, with offers coming in from stage, screen, radio, and television. It is perfectly possible that she simply was not available for these films, and in the absence of any corroborative evidence of the existence of an amorous carpenter (which sounds for all the world like the star of a seventies sex comedy), there is no reason to believe other than that Sims was simply ill when *Carry On Cruising* went before the cameras.

Dilys Laye proved an inspired piece of casting, handling the comedic aspects of her role with practiced ease and grace, while looking extremely fetching in a selection of swimwear. She also forms a believable and fun double act with Liz Fraser as Gladys Trimble—the pair make very believable best friends, with Dilys on the cruise to find a husband, while Liz is trying to get away from the attentions of men. Despite this, they end up squabbling over the attentions of hunky PT instructor Vincent Ball (who performs a very creditable double front flip). Eventually, Gladys works out that Flo is actually in love with the hapless Doctor Binn (on very little evidence) and works with Kenneth Williams to bring the two together via a bizarre plan that involves Gladys snogging the doctor until he realises he loves Flo.

Liz Fraser, it must be said, is absolutely smoking hot as Gladys Trimble, looking ravishing without really trying in a pair of trousers and a red jumper. The only reason she could not have played the more substantial role of Flo is that it would have been impossible to believe that she could not find a husband—as it stands, it is stretching credulity slightly that the lovely Dilys Laye might have problems in that department. Laye was certainly a success in *Carry On Cruising* by any standards, being cast by Peter Rogers and Gerald Thomas for three further Carry Ons: *Spying*, *Doctor*, and *Camping*.

One actor who did not return for *Carry On Cruising* was Charles Hawtrey who, emboldened by a flattering newspaper review, embarked on a doomed quest for more money (which even Kenneth Williams, whose public popularity was far greater, had not been able to negotiate) and better billing. 'His agent', claimed Peter Rogers later, 'wanted ten times the money he had before, a star on the dressing room door, and one thing and another'.[3] This did not go down well with Rogers, and Hawtrey was not in a mood to back down, so the producer recast his role as Wilfred Haines, ship's cook. Fortunately, a replacement was readily to hand in the form of Lance Percival, catching the actor and occasional singer before his star rose considerably as a singer of topical calypso songs on the sensationally popular BBC satirical television show *That Was The Week That Was*, which debuted in November 1962. Percival was tall and thin, his prominent ears, crooked nose, and drawling speaking voice giving him a naturally comedic air—he did not have to strain for comedic effect, he just *was* funny. He had also recently appeared with Kenneth Williams in the Peter Rogers and Gerald Thomas production *Twice Around the Daffodils*, which was eventually released almost simultaneously with Carry On Cruising.

Percival was a known quantity and fitted in so well that it's difficult to imagine anyone else playing the role of Haines. Although this would ultimately be his only Carry On role, he clearly found the approval of both the film's producer and its star, as he appeared in two episodes of Sid James' BBC sitcom *Citizen James* a few months later, and in 1965 was cast in a major role in a further Rogers/Thomas comedy, *The Big Job*. Charles Hawtrey, however, would breeze back into the Carry On cast as if nothing had happened for the next film in the series.

Esma Cannon returned as Bridget Madderley, an elderly lady determined to make the most of her cruise, and it is clear that Norman Hudis enjoyed writing for the actress, giving her some key scenes. Jimmy Thompson gets the best of his three Carry On roles here as Sam the barman, sharing a running gag with Ronnie Stevens as a drunken passenger who never leaves the ship, simply getting enthusiastically hammered on whatever the local drink happens to be where the *Happy Wanderer* is berthed. Amazingly for such a fixture on the British comedy acting scene, his unnamed drunken passenger here is Ronnie Stevens' only Carry On role. He is such a familiar face to fans of 1960s comedy and so effective here that one sort of assumes he could pop up at any moment in other films in the series, but his busy career led him elsewhere. One actor who did pop up all the time in Carry On films of this period was Cyril Chamberlain, who was genuinely a series regular but never one of its stars. His role here as Tom Tree, the captain's new steward, is one of his more substantial, and he is a cheerful presence.

One change that would prove to be far-reaching was in the music department. Bruce Montgomery's jaunty, big-band Carry On theme had become a talisman for the series since its first appearance in the opening moments of *Carry On Sergeant* and the composer became a key member of Peter Rogers' production team. With *Carry On Cruising*, however, for the first time a new name appeared alongside that of Montgomery, that of Douglas Gamley. The thirty-seven-year-old Australian composer had worked on some high-profile pictures over the previous few years, including *Fire Down Below* (1957), *The Admirable Crichton* (1957), *Gideon's Day* (1958), and *Tarzan's Greatest Adventure* (1959). Gamley was a solid, experienced composer and conductor, and most importantly of all, he was reliable. This was an increasingly important factor as Bruce Montgomery succumbed to the alcoholism that blighted his music career and limited his other profession as a talented writer and critic of crime fiction. Montgomery would only compose the music for one more film, the 1966 crime thriller *The Brides of Fu Manchu*.

As a viewing experience, *Carry On Cruising* is remarkably pleasant. It is a well-carpentered film in more ways than one: not only is Norman Hudis' script very well-constructed—episodic by necessity of its subject matter but with a strong through-line tying the incidents together—but the production itself is quite impressive. Despite the film being almost entirely studio-bound, Art Director Carmen Dillon's SS *Happy Wanderer* sets are on a large scale and are convincing on the screen, belying the fact that the film was produced on a relatively low budget. *Cruising* cost some £40,000 more than the previous film in the series, *Carry On Regardless*, but the production was hardly awash with cash, making the sleek look of this latest film something of an achievement. The tatty old house location that made the ending of *Carry On Constable* look so dowdy and cheap was, only two years later, a distant memory.

It goes without saying that the cast work extremely well together—the interplay of ensemble casts are at the core of the continuing appeal of the Carry Ons—but this cast in particular represents an unusual combination, giving *Carry On Cruising* a different feel to other films in the series. Not only do we have Lance Percival's lugubrious charm, but also good roles for Jimmy Thompson and Cyril Chamberlain, which adds something new to the mixture. The two Kenneths—Williams and Connor—also interact nicely in this film; it is a genuine pleasure to see them have scenes together where they joke around and have fun in each other's company.

There really is a feeling here that, despite Norman Hudis recycling the plotline of *Carry On Sergeant* once again, the films are developing and avoiding falling into the trap of repeating themselves. The films in the series from this period are a particularly interesting and varied batch: *Cruising*, *Cabby*, *Jack*, and *Spying* each have a different look and feel to them. It does not matter that two of these were only added to the Carry On roster at a late stage of production—what it was possible for a Carry On film to be was expanding in interesting ways.

8

Carry On Cabby (1963)

Filming Dates: 25 March 1963–7 May 1963
Original Certificate: U (Classified by BBFC 31 May 1963—the first film in the series to be passed uncut)
Running Time: 93 minutes 37 seconds

Release Details

Carry On Cabby needed a passenger as it travelled around Britain's cinema circuit from 29 September 1963. It was assigned one by Anglo-Amalgamated in the shape of *The Partner*, another Edgar Wallace B-picture from Jack Greenwood's Merton Park Studios. Gerald Glaister directs Guy Doleman and Yoko Tani in the story of a film studio head and an Asian actress mixed up in a tax avoidance scheme that leads to theft and murder.

What's Carrying On?

Charlie Hawkins runs Speedee Taxis, the biggest and most successful cab company in town, living in an apartment over the firm's offices with his wife, Peg. The firm is a big success, employing largely ex-servicemen, but Charlie is a workaholic, neglecting the increasingly fed-up Peg. The final straw comes when Charlie misses their wedding anniversary meal out after his taxi is flagged down by an expectant father. In revenge, Peg secretly sets up Glamcabs, an all-female taxi company staffed by mini-skirted young women in brand new saloon cars. The new company quickly takes most of Speedee Taxis' custom and threatens to put Charlie's firm out of business, until a gang of robbers forces the Speedee Taxis crew to save their new competitors.

Who's Carrying On?

A Peter Rogers Production
Director: Gerald Thomas
Screenplay by Talbot Rothwell, based on an original story by S. C. Green and R. M. Hills
Music composed and conducted by Eric Rogers
Photography: Alan Hume BSC
Art Director: Jack Stephens
Editor: Archie Ludski
Sidney James: Charlie Hawkins, the taxi-mad boss of Speedee Taxis who is driven first to sabotage, then to drink when he discovers his own wife is running his main competitor.
Hattie Jacques: Peggy Hawkins, neglected wife of Charlie, who declares war on her taxi-mad husband when picking up a fare takes precedence over their wedding anniversary.
Kenneth Connor: Ted Watson, Charlie's mechanic and second-in-command at Speedee Taxis, who is in danger of neglecting his girlfriend Sally as much as Charlie does Peggy.
Charles Hawtrey: Terry Tankard, nicknamed 'Pintpot' by his old army pals ('are you sure they said "Pintpot"?'), is a former bulldozer driver who drives a taxi in the same way as he did his former vehicle, terrifying anyone brave enough to venture into his cab.
Esma Cannon: Flo Sims, wife of Smiley Sims who is prevented by union shop steward Allbright from taking the place of her husband when he falls ill. Instead she becomes Glamcabs' office manager.
Liz Fraser: Sally, who works at the local cab drivers' café and is the girlfriend of Ted Watson. A friend of Peggy's, she acts undercover for Glamcabs in their battle of the sexes.

Carry On Critics

Carry On Cabby was ignored, for once, by the film reviewer of *The Times*, though *Monthly Film Bulletin*, which reviewed every film released in Britain, was cautiously positive about the new film:

> The plot is more solidly constructed than usual but leaves ample room for jokes about busts, beds, pregnancy and female impersonation. Every now and then the results are very funny, though one might wish that the final chase had been briefer and more inventively scripted.

Variety ran their critical eye over *Cabby* in the paper's 31 December 1962 edition: 'Not at first intended to be one of the series, the film has a rather stronger storyline than usual.' Various cast members were singled out for special praise:

> Hattie Jacques extracts fun from the role of James' wife. Kenneth Connor, Esma Cannon, Charles Hawtey, as an accident-prone nitwit, and Liz Fraser, as Sally the glamorous waitress-Mata Hari, are old students of the Carry On technique, and effortlessly milk the laughter. So, too, are some of the cameo players often used for one gag.

Carry On Comments

With Norman Hudis struggling with the task of producing a script for *Carry On Spying* that met the approval of Peter Rogers and, as it would soon transpire, about to emigrate to Hollywood, it was becoming clear that a new scriptwriter was needed. Talbot Rothwell's submission on spec of his script *Poop-Decker RN* came at a perfect time and greatly impressed the producer (this will be covered more fully in the chapter on *Carry On Jack*), but before it could be progressed further, Peter Rogers had another project which required urgent attention.

The comedy writing duo of S. C. Green and R. M. Hills had provided a treatment for a comedy set in the world of taxi driving which Peter Rogers and Gerald Thomas were keen to make their next production. Green and Hills, who were of the habit of using their initials to add a touch of class to their screen credits, were better known in the business as Sid Green and Dick Hills and even better known to the general public as the unlikely TV stars 'Sid and Dick'. Green and Hills were two school friends who reached the very top tier of British comedy scriptwriting, even cracking the fiercely competitive American market. They initially came to prominence writing for Dave King, a comedian who became a big star of the early days of British commercial television in the 1950s before changing tack and becoming a character actor. Green and Hills then became scriptwriters for the comedy double act Morecambe and Wise, becoming vital in the revival of Eric and Ernie's television career after the dismal failure of their small-screen debut *Running Wild* on BBC Television in 1954.

In 1962, Morecambe and Wise were finally given another slot at television stardom for Lew Grade's ATV, the biggest provider of popular entertainment on the ITV network. Unlike in 1954, when they were shoehorned into unsuitable material, Morecambe and Wise insisted on using their own writers, Sid Green and Dick Hills. The new series, entitled *Two of a Kind*, quickly became a major hit, but was almost scuppered immediately due to a major strike by the actor's union Equity, which lasted from November 1961 to April 1962, crippling much television production. *Coronation Street*, one of the very few drama programmes to continue through the strike, did so with a core cast of only fourteen actors who were on long-term contracts. Morecambe and Wise got around the problem of being unable to hire actors to appear in their sketches by having Green and Hills play all the parts. This wheeze proved popular, the practice continuing after the strike ended, and so was born the acting careers of 'Sid and Dick', as Green and Hills were popularly known.

Green and Hills were hot properties and had other work outside of their writing for Eric and Ernie, including writing twenty-six episodes of Sid James' post-Hancock sitcom *Citizen James*. This meant, however, that the pair were too busy to work their screen treatment for a comedy set in the world of taxi cabs into a full script. The project was put into the hands of Peter Rogers' new star writer Talbot Rothwell, who needed to turn out a completed script in double-quick time. He turned for help to an old friend and colleague in the form of Sid Colin, who had created *The Army Game*, for which Rothwell had also written. Colin had an unproduced script, *The Streets of Town*, which was to provide the climax for eventual Rothwell's script. Although he was not credited for his contribution, Rothwell gave his friend a percentage of his fee.

The final script was at this stage entitled *Call Me A Cab*, which was the name the film was produced under and retained until shortly before its release. The script appears not to have met the approval of one of the core Carry On cast members, as revealed by Kenneth Williams in his diaries: 'Read script of the Peter Rogers film *Call Me A Cab* and hated it. Wrote and said I didn't want to do it.'[1]

Williams either could not or would not be convinced to change his mind. As the film was not at this stage envisaged as being part of the Carry On series, it is possible that Williams' presence was not regarded as being vital and some experimentation in casting was possible. Williams' biographer Christopher Stevens gives quite a different view of event, claiming that the actor's agent, Peter Eade, was holding out for a fee for his client of over £5,000, far in excess of what Peter Rogers was willing to pay.[2] On the other hand, Charles Hawtrey, who had dropped out of the role of the ship's cook in *Carry On Cruising* due to similar issues, was more than happy to take on the part of accident-prone trainee cabbie 'Pintpot' Tankard, breezing back as if nothing had happened. Williams had been pencilled in to play officious union shop steward Allbright, a role which remained in the film in reduced form played by Norman Chappell, many of Allbright's lines being given to Charles Hawtrey.

The rest of the cast was lavishly sprinkled with familiar Carry On names, Sid James and Hattie Jacques continuing their romantic partnership which had worked so well in *Carry On Constable*, but this time playing husband and very annoyed wife. Kenneth Connor plays Sid's mechanic and second-in-command Ted Watson, this time in a romantic pairing with Liz Fraser, while Bill Owen, as the constantly miserable 'Smiley' Sims, plays the last of his Carry On roles. Cyril Chamberlain turns up in his final Carry On part of any import as Sarge, the radio operator of Sid's taxi firm—he has a tiny, blink-and-you-miss-it part in *Carry On Spying*, but his Carry On career really ends here.

Some notable Carry On performers made their first appearance in the series here: Amanda Barrie, who would soon achieve immortality in the title role of *Carry On Cleo*, is magnificent as Anthea, who gets the biggest role of any of the Glamcabs girls and whose leggy portrait also made up the lead image on the film's posters. After appearing in three previous Peter Rogers/Gerald Thomas productions, Jim Dale made his Carry On debut here as Jeremy, whose wife's phantom pregnancy is responsible for Sid missing his own wedding anniversary night out. Peter Gilmore makes a good impression as Dancy, head of the gang that tries to rob the Glamcabs payroll and would go on to appear in a further ten Carry Ons.

Norman Chappell has the major role of officious union shop steward Allbright and is actually very good in the part. Chappell was such a ubiquitous presence in British comedies from the sixties to his early death at the age of fifty-seven in 1983 that it is something of a surprise to learn that he did not return to the Carry On films for seven years, when he was finally cast as a plotter against the king in 1970's *Carry On Henry*. In the same year, he filmed scenes for *Carry On Loving* that were cut from the finished film. Chappell's stock-in-trade of bug-eyed, harried officiousness finally found a regular Carry On berth in the *Carry On Laughing* TV series of 1975, in which he appeared seven times.

The film was shot at Pinewood stages A and C and on location on the streets of Windsor, Berkshire, from 25 March to 7 May 1963, where the Norman Wisdom comedy *On the Beat* had been filmed the previous year. Filming on *Carry On Cabby* was completed on 7 May 1963 and is a great example of how Gerald Thomas' practice of editing his films in the camera shortened the post-production process, as the film was ready to be screened for the British Board of Film Censorship by the end of the month. This remarkable turnaround was matched the following year by the rush-release of *Carry On Jack*, another film which began life outside the Carry On series.

The new film not only had a new writer but also a new composer, with Bruce Montgomery's ongoing issues with alcohol causing him to be dropped from future Peter Rogers productions, to be replaced by Eric Rogers, who had made uncredited contributions to previous films. Whereas Eric Rogers would go on to provide the scores to every subsequent Carry On film up to 1975's *Carry On Behind* and returned in 1978 for *Carry On Emmannuelle*, Bruce

Montgomery would only score one more film, the 1966 thriller *The Brides of Fu Manchu*.

As *Carry On Cabby* is such a car-centred production, it is worthwhile to spend a little time discussing the various motor vehicles featured in the film. The London taxis used by Sid's firm were hired for the duration of the filming from the London General Cab Company. PEG 1, the aged vehicle assigned to Pintpot, was a 1937 Austin 12/4 Taxi with a body manufactured specially for the London General Cab Company, which had owned the car since it was new. The car, which is still in existence today, made another film appearance in 1975 when it briefly appeared in the London-shot Walt Disney production *One of our Dinosaurs is Missing*. Pintpot's other form of transport is Douglas Vespa Sportique scooter. Sid's character Charlie Hawkins drives a newer model of London taxi, a 1954 Austin FX3. For some reason, the car is decked out with false number plates, a fact which film-buffs only know for certain because precisely the same set of plates were used three years earlier on a removal van in the 1960 thriller *The League of Gentlemen*.

The most notable vehicles used in *Carry On Cabby* are the fleet of fifteen Ford Consul Cortinas used by Glamcabs. Ford of Britain, an offshoot of the American Ford Motor Company, was particularly keen to promote the Consul Cortina as the model had only been launched some six months before the filming of *Carry On Cabby* began, shortly before the London Motor Show of October 1962. With its rear fins and distinctive rear light cluster (nicknamed 'Ban the Bomb lights' due to their resemblance to the symbol used by the Campaign for Nuclear Disarmament), the new model continued Ford's policy of taking styling cues from American car design. The Consul part of the Cortina's name was dropped in 1964, but the model was a roaring success, selling over a million cars before being replaced by a heavily redesigned Mark 2 version in 1966.

Another notable car seen in *Carry On Cabby* would be very easy to miss: the Wolseley 6/99 police car which arrives to cart off the villains at the end of the film. The 6/99 was only produced between 1959 and 1961, before being replaced by the very similar-looking 6/110. The model seen in *Cabby*, bearing the number-plate 716 TDP, became a familiar sight on both the big and small screens during the early to mid-1960s, seemingly being used whenever a British production needed a police car. It was first seen in the 1962 Stanley Baxter comedy *The Fast Lady* before being hired by Peter Rogers Productions for *Carry On Cabby*. During 1963, the Wolseley saw service as transport for the boys in blue in the Peter Sellers comedy *The Wrong Arm of the Law* and the Miss Marple mystery *Murder at the Gallop*. The car was used again for the next film in the series, *Murder Ahoy* (1964) and was then hired during 1965 for use in the ITC filmed police series *Gideon's Way*. The car made one final appearance that is known of, in the Anglo-German crime thriller *Circus of Fear*, which was released in West Germany in April 1966 ahead of its US release in May 1967 and British release in November of that year.

A further bit of product placement was Sid's tipple of choice when he turns to drink at the prospect of his collapsing marriage and company. It transpires he has a safe full of Johnnie Walker Red Label, the Scotch of choice for boozers in low-budget 1960s British movies. Earlier in the film Hattie and Liz Fraser get plastered on Booth's Dry Gin, a name from the past which one wishes would return to off-licence shelves in these gin-sodden times.

Despite being made in black and white, *Carry On Cabby* cost an estimated £10,000 more to make than its Eastmancolor predecessor *Carry On Cruising*. This demonstrates just how expensive location filming was in 1963 compared to working in the studio, as Cruising hardly ventured out of Pinewood. With production costs being a little on the high side for a Peter Rogers production, it would seem that distributors Anglo-Amalgamated suffered slightly from cold feet, suggesting at a very late stage that the film's title be changed from *Call Me a Cab* (a very old joke indeed which I am sure everyone reading this book knows the punchline to) to *Carry On Cabby*. In the process, Peter Rogers and Gerald Thomas' film was transformed from a quirky little comedy which might have struggled to be noticed into a sure-fire success. Eric Rogers' score had clearly been completed before the title change occurred, as its central melody quotes the film's original title, a common practice among film composers which left available the possibility for a theme song.

It would be going a bit far to describe *Carry On Cabby* as grittily realistic. For that, audiences would have to go to another production featuring Sid James driving a cab, which happened to debut on BBC Television (which only had one channel at the time) while *Carry On Cabby* was still on release in British cinemas. This was *Taxi!*, which ran for two series of 13 episodes each, starting from 10 July 1963. The BBC's previous solo vehicle for Sid, Citizen James, was a sitcom created for the actor by Ray Galton and Alan Simpson in the aftermath of his ejection from *Hancock's Half Hour*. In contrast to this, *Taxi!* was created by Ted Willis, best known for *Dixon of Dock Green*, and for the first series was largely scripted by dramatic writers such as N. J. Crisp, a regular contributor to *Dixon*, and Irish novelist Lee Dunne. The second run of thirteen episodes was written in its entirety by sitcom writer Harry Driver and Jack Rosenthal, who started out in sitcoms but became better known for filmed comedy-dramas.

Carry On Cabby is an interesting anomaly in the Carry On canon, partly born of the fact that it was never planned to be part of the series and partly because it sees the films in a state of transition. Working from Sid Green and Dick Hills' story, this is a decidedly atypical example of Talbot Rothwell's work for the Carry Ons. Rothwell was a natural-born gag writer whose best work presented situations that were pegs on which to hang a series of verbal and visual jokes. *Carry On Cabby* is similar in many ways to Norman Hudis' scripts for the series, being a variation on the standard Hudis plot of having a group of misfits thrown into an unfamiliar situation and coming good in the end.

At the core of the film is a domestic comedy-drama about a wife being neglected by her workaholic husband and getting her own back. This is helped enormously by the reteaming of Hattie Jacques and Sid James, who had displayed great chemistry together in *Carry On Constable*. Hattie is at her most glamorous here and is given some lovely dresses to wear. In real life, Hattie, who was married to John Le Mesurier at the time, was in the midst of a very serious extra-marital affair, had lost a great deal of weight, and gained a lot of confidence.[3] Perhaps not surprisingly, *Carry On Cabby* was Hattie's favourite of the Carry Ons, as besides her physical transformation, this represents probably her most prominent role in any feature film. Although she is second-billed behind Sid James, who was already at this point the acknowledged head of the Carry On cast, Hattie's role really is equal to that of Sid and she carries it off wonderfully well. Peg Hawkins is a far more three-dimensional role than was normally asked of Hattie, allowing her to be sad, happy, angry, and steaming drunk.

Charles Hawtrey rides back into Carry On action on his Vespa motor scooter in jeans and a black leather biker jacket, looking for all the world like a camp, emaciated version of Marlon Brando in *The Wild One*. 'Pintpot' Tankard represents one of Hawtrey's most lovable characterisations—always happy and desperate to please, like an accident-prone puppy who is liable to break the crockery at any moment. Kenneth Connor gets a good role, too, as Ted Watson, the garage mechanic. Not only is he in a fairly stable relationship this time (with Liz Fraser's Sally, the lucky dog!), but he also gets to appear in drag as the advance guard of Charlie Hawkins' aborted raid on Glamcabs. It is interesting that Connor got to do this instead of Charles Hawtrey, who had specialised in drag earlier in his career. Hawtrey would have been perhaps a shade too convincing for the gag to have worked properly—as with later films in the series in which Bernard Bresslaw and Kenneth Cope were put into female clothing, the point was that he looked just ridiculous enough.

Liz Fraser gives dependable support in the role of Sally, but it is less interesting than some of her previous parts and rather overshadowed by Amanda Barrie, who is marvellous as Anthea, the most prominent of the Glamcabs drivers. In her Carry On debut, Barrie gives roughly the same performance as the one which would later make her a comedy legend in *Carry On Cleo*: a very sharp cookie indeed who hides her brains behind her looks and a slightly vague upper-middle class manner. Barrie clearly impressed the producers as an artwork reproduction of her leggy figure in Glamcabs mini-skirted uniform was the main image used *Carry On Cabby*'s advertising, pushing the more established Carry On stars to one side.

Among Amanda Barrie's fellow Glamcabs drivers were Valerie Van Ost, who went on to appear in rather larger roles in *Carry On Doctor* and *Carry on Again Doctor*. These were part of an interesting career that included roles in the Hammer film *The Satanic Rites of Dracula* and in the pilot episode of *Space: 1999*, both in 1973, before she changed career and became a casting director. Carole Shelley, who had previously been seen in *Carry On Regardless*, also featured in a small role. The actress would soon move to America, where she became a mainstay of the Broadway stage for decades.

Two other performers get unusually good roles here: Esma Cannon gets such a big part that here name even appears on the poster. Normally specialising in dotty old ladies rather older than her true age, here she plays Flo, wife of an ill taxi driver who wants to take his place in order to earn some money but is prevented due to union rules. She gets to play the part in her natural Australian accent, which is lovely to hear and gives her performance a much more confident, strident tone than Cannon was normally allowed to display and it is no surprise when she becomes Peg's second-in-command at Glamcabs. Given that she retired from acting after *Carry On Cabby*, it is nice to see Esma finishing on a high note in a role that gave her something more interesting to do than her normal typecasting allowed. Norman Chappell also shines as Allbright, bringing a very different performance to the role than would have Kenneth Williams, for whom a larger version of the same role was originally written. The character is, in effect, an early version of Kenneth Cope's Vic Spanner from *Carry On At Your Convenience*: a silly, ineffectual man given undeserved power.

The story also takes a fun new turn in its final half hour, as the male cabbies of Charlie's company, who all have military backgrounds (as, to be fair, most of the adult male population of Britain did in 1963), use their tactical experience to track down the villains who have kidnapped Peg and Sally—they even refer to the robbers as 'the enemy'. This all could have been a little routine, since we know perfectly well that the baddies are going to get caught, but Peter Gilmore as Dancy, leader of the villains, really understands what acting this sort of part in a Carry On film requires. We know he is a villain—after all, he is wearing the standard 1960s villain uniform of dark suit and shirt paired with a light-coloured tie—but as the situation begins to turn against him in unexpected ways Gilmore plays comedic befuddlement to absolute perfection. Gilmore sells the scene to the audience and without him the climax to the film would not have worked half as well as it does. This was clearly not lost on Rogers and Thomas, as the actor would have a long career in the Carry Ons until he finally achieved leading man status in 1971 with the BBC TV series *The Onedin Line*.

9

Carry On Jack (1964)

Filming Dates: 2 September 1963–26 October 1963
Original Certificate: A (Classified by BBFC 5 December 1963 [cut])
Running Time: 91 minutes

Release Details

London Release: Screenings at the New Victoria cinema from 23 February 1964.

Carry On Jack played in the UK on the ABC circuit from 15 March 1964 along with with *The Verdict* as its support feature. This was another in the ongoing Edgar Wallace series of B-crime thrillers being made at Merton Park Studios for Anglo-Amalgamated. Cec Linder, in the same year that he played James Bond's CIA ally Felix Leiter in *Goldfinger*, features as an American gangster deported to England thanks to his use of another man's passport. He then finds that the now-dead man is suspected of a murder committed many years previously. Zena Marshall and Paul Stassino, who also made notable appearances in 1960s Bond films, also appear.

What's Carrying On?

Midshipman Albert Poop-Decker, newly qualified after eight and a half years at naval college, so desperate is the Royal Navy for manpower due to the war with Spain, is sent to serve on the frigate *Venus*. Before he arrives at the ship, however, he is taken to Dirty Dick's, a house of ill-repute, where he is knocked unconscious and his clothes and papers taken by Sally, who works there. Poop-Decker is pressganged onto the *Venus* by the ship's brutal First Officer

Howett and Bosun Angel, while Sally has taken his place and identity onboard the ship. The *Venus* is led by the incompetent and cowardly Captain Fearless, whom Howett and Angel plot to get rid of so they can fight the Spanish more effectively. Albert, meanwhile, joins Sally in her quest to find her lost love, Roger, who used to lodge at their house.

Who's Carrying On?

A Peter Rogers Production
Director: Gerald Thomas
Screenplay by Talbot Rothwell
Music composed and conducted by Eric Rogers
Photography: Alan Hume BSC
Art Director: Jack Shampan
Editor: Archie Ludski
Kenneth Williams: Captain Fearless, whose attempts to live up to his name are hampered by his being seasick, squeamish, and cowardly.
Bernard Cribbins: Midshipman Albert Poop-Decker, newly qualified after eight and a half years at naval college, and possibly the least competent naval officer ever to have sailed the seven seas.
Juliet Mills: Sally, who works at the local house of ill-repute but who yearns to go to sea in order to rescue her intended, Roger, who she thinks is being held prisoner in Spain.
Charles Hawtrey: Walter Sweetly, a cesspit cleaner pressganged into service on the *Venus* along with Albert, who follows him on his adventures.
Donald Houston: Jonathan Howett, brutal first officer of the *Venus*, desperate to get rid of Captain Fearless so he can fight the Spanish properly.
Percy Herbert: Mr Angel, bosun of the *Venus* and sidekick to Howett who proves to be less than competent in dealing out punishment with the dreaded cat.
Jim Dale: the younger of two Sedan carriers, offering a weird sort of taxi service at the dockside where his fairs end up walking.

Carry On Critics

The Times reviewer of 20 February 1964 was less than keen on the excursion into historical territory:

> The notion of introducing costume and parody into an essentially unsophisticated framework does not help, compelling the scriptwriter to

> put in too many flat passages of exposition. A handful of the jokes are very funny, but the feeling remains that the series should return to form when it returns to the twentieth century.

One may feel that this is not a review to which time has been kind. Richard Roud in *The Guardian* the following day was brief and dismissive about the film: 'There is very little to be said about *Carry On Jack*: if you like this sort of thing, then this is the sort of thing you like—but it's not one of the best of the series.' In the same paper, the semi-anonymous reviewer 'B.N.' , in a round-up of films playing in *The Guardian*'s ancestral home of Manchester, gave a not-dissimilar verdict: 'There are plenty of laughs for the undemanding: others may see in it a goonish attempt to parody *Billy Budd*.' Is anyone else reading this book reading this getting fed-up of reading journalists describing Carry On fans as 'undemanding' at this point?

The *Monthly Film Bulletin* was a little more pleased with the Carry On team's imperfect, but creditable introduction to historical comedy:

> Opening with a skit on Nelson's famous death-bed scene, this addition to the 'Carry On' series has some richly comic scenes worthy of the best of its predecessors. But once at sea, its invention falters, and the remainder of the film is extremely variable.

Interestingly, the reviewer recognises just how good Jim Dale's regrettably brief contribution to *Carry On Jack* is: 'The early scene involving the two "carriers" (Jim Dale and Ian Wilson) is probably as good as anything the series had yet produced'.

Films and Filming, for that magazine's April 1964 edition, sent Jack Cutts to review *Carry On Jack* and he rather liked what he saw: 'Critical heresy maybe, but I quite enjoyed *Carry On Jack*. Nothing new in the Carry On line perhaps ... but for what it sets out to do, it does very well. To say more would be unfair, to say less would be uncharitable'.

Variety was impressed with the physical quality of the production: 'Only two of the "resident" company—Charles Hawtrey and Kenneth Williams—are on parade. This one, however, has an added credit in its very okay costuming and art work'. In *Variety*-speak, this is high praise indeed.

Carry On Comments

With *Call Me a Cab* safely in the can and rechristened to become part of the Carry On series, Peter Rogers returned to the *Poop-Decker RN* script that first brought Talbot Rothwell to his attention. The script went through several different working titles on its way to the screen, a tale of some interest in itself. The original title was thought to be not quite right, and after a period as *Steady, Boys, Steady*, Rothwell suggested *Up the Armada*. This was felt to be perfect by Peter Rogers and Gerald Thomas, but this was felt by the British Board of Film Censorship, at this point led by its secretary, John Trevelyan, to be an unacceptable *double entendre*. This decision demonstrates in miniature the random and quickly changing nature of censorship; some five years later, the title *Carry On Up The Khyber*, which utilises exactly the same joke in an even more obvious manner to anyone with a passing familiarity with rhyming slang, was passed by the BBFC with nary a murmur.

Thus by the time scripts were being sent out to the actors that Rogers and Thomas hoped to cast, the title had changed once more and the production was known as *Carry On Sailor*. This change was made after Peter Rogers had sought the permission of the writer himself, which was certainly not a contractual obligation, but Rogers had another consideration in mind: the producer was keen to maintain a working relationship with his new star writer but it was looking like Rothwell's first two projects for Peter Rogers Productions would be retrofitted into the Carry On series. Would Talbot Rothwell object to becoming known as a writer of Carry On films, often derided both within the industry and by the critics? I think we all know the answer to that.[1] Of course, the film underwent one more change of title before finally reaching cinemas, as *Carry On Sailor* was felt to be too similar to *Carry On Cruising* and did not convey the radical difference between the two films. Drawing on earlier navel terminology, *Carry On Jack* was eventually decided on.

It cannot be underestimated how major a decision it was to include both *Cabby* and *Jack* into the Carry On series. Both are very different in tone and content to the previous films in the series with *Jack* essentially being a large-scale historical adventure. Today, the historical Carry Ons are the cornerstone of the series' popularity, but when the film was being shot in the spring of 1963, hitching the script to the Carry On bandwagon represented not only something of a risk, but a considerable expansion of what a Carry On film could be.

Casting the film held some challenges. The nature of the script meant that there were fewer opportunities to cast regular Carry On cast members, so character actors of the calibre of Donald Houston, Percy Herbert, and Cecil Parker were called upon, well known for their roles in straight dramas but with a solid history of working in comedy—Houston, you may recall, back in 1954 had been one of the main cast members in Ralph Thomas' *Doctor in the House*.

A young male lead was required for the part of Poop-Decker, originally the film's title role and still the central point of identification for audiences. Fortunately, Britain had a new comedy star who fitted the bill perfectly—

Bernard Cribbins was a skilled performer who had been propelled into the top rank of British comedic talent by a run of three top ten comedy records during 1962. He also happened to be a burly ex-paratrooper who was more than capable of handling any action scenes this new film may require.

One regular Carry On performer Rogers and Thomas were very keen to attract back to the series was Kenneth Williams, who had been missing from the cast of *Carry On Cabby*. In order to attract Williams back, Rogers made the actor an interesting offer—sending him the script, he offered Williams the choice of playing either Captain Fearless or Albert Poop-Decker.[2] Rogers clearly realised that the role of Fearless was tailormade for Williams' talents and seems to have made a calculated gamble that he could both appeal to the actor's vanity and rely on him to realise which part was by far the most suitable for him.

For the female lead of Sally, Liz Fraser—by this point established as the glamorous female lead of the Carry Ons—was pencilled in, but matters were taken out of the producer's hands when Stuart Levy phoned and specifically told him not to use her. Levy was the joint head, along with Nat Cohen, of Anglo-Amalgamated, distributor of the Carry On films, so arguing would have been damaging to Peter Rogers' most important business relationship. This highly unusual situation arose out of a conversation between Fraser and Levy in which the actress made comments about the marketing and promotion of the film series, which upset the latter. In contrast to the 'dumb blonde' image she portrayed in the Carry Ons, Liz Fraser was very intelligent and in the world of 1960s filmmaking, the advice of a 'mere' actress was unwelcome, to say the least.

Instead, Juliet Mills was sought for the part, an actress who was very much a known quantity. Mills had already starred in *Twice Around the Daffodils* for Peter Rogers and Gerald Thomas in 1962 and had recently completed *Nurse on Wheels* as a late replacement in the lead role for Joan Sims. Mills proved a very strong female lead in *Carry On Jack*, though in some ways might be seen as a little demure for the part of Sally, whose precise role at Dirty Dick's is somewhat unclear. It must be said that she is at least a hair's breadth more convincing in male attire posing as Midshipman Poop-Decker than one can imagine the blonde bombshell Liz Fraser being.

Surprisingly, *Carry On Jack* came in at an estimated cost of £152,000, a mere £2,000 more than *Carry On Cabbie* had cost, and £4,000 more than the film that followed, the considerably cheaper-looking *Carry On Spying*. One reason why the Eastmancolor mini-epic that was *Carry On Jack* could be made without pushing the boat out was that sets ideal for the film's HMS *Venus* were available for comparatively little cost, having been designed by Art Director Arthur Lawson and constructed at great expense for director Lewis Gilbert's *HMS Defiant*, which had been shot over at Shepperton Studios.

HMS Defiant, the filming of which two of the film's stars, Alec Guinness and Anthony Quayle, fitted in during a break in the shooting of David Lean's *Lawrence of Arabia*, is worthy of our attention.

Carry On Jack took more than just its sets from director Lewis Gilbert's film; the film's story also resembles that of *HMS Defiant* in many respects. Written by Nigel Kneale and Edmund H. North from the novel *Mutiny* by Frank Tilsley, *HMS Defiant*, set during the Napoleonic Wars, is concerned with the clash between the kindly, highly experienced Captain Crawford (Alec Guinness) and his new first officer, the sadistic martinet Lt. Scott-Padgett (Dirk Bogarde, taking an almost sexual delight in having occasional Carry On actor Johnny Briggs flogged half to death). The film revolves around the power struggle between the two men as Scott-Padgett attempts to undermine Crawford's position, while the ordinary seamen, led by Anthony Quayle and Tom Bell, plot a mutiny against their inhuman conditions.

Watching *HMS Defiant* is a decidedly strange experience for the Carry On fan, as in several cases, the film presents scenes that would be replayed for comedic effect in *Carry On Jack* on exactly the same sets. Murray Melvin plays a well-spoken young gentleman, press-ganged into naval service after Scott-Padgett's men raid a dockside inn—sound familiar? We even get a scene in which the captain is operated on while in a delirious state, though here he loses an arm rather than a leg. *HMS Defiant*, however, was not the only seafaring historical adventure in cinemas while *Carry On Jack* was being planned.

What really made Jack a dead-on comedic pastiche that grabbed the attention of audiences was the fact that MGM's vast, three-hour-long remake of *Mutiny on the Bounty* had finally staggered into cinemas in Britain and America in November 1962. The running time was not the only thing about the film that was bloated, with interference from producer, studio, and star causing original director Carol Reed to walk off the film, while star Marlon Brando's self-indulgent behaviour on set became the stuff of legend. While MGM's elephantine, badly reviewed, $19 million production did not have a hope of making its budget back, both the production and release of the film were ballyhooed to the skies by the world's press. When Talbot Rothwell's deadly accurate spoof of the biggest publicity bonanza of the age dropped onto the doormat of a delighted Peter Rogers, it became clear that least one film producer was going to make money out of *Mutiny on the Bounty*.

Carry On Jack sits on its own among the series, quite different in tone and scope to the films that came both before and after. This has led to the film to be perennially underrated over the years, since it lacks both the 'band of misfits coming good' theme of the Norman Hudis-scripted films (in fact, it could be argued that Rothwell's script actively subverts this theme), or the full-blooded seaside postcard rudeness that would come a few films later.

Had *Carry On Jack* been written by Norman Hudis, there is a fair chance that the plot would have involved a group of incompetent sailors who band together in the end to defeat the Spanish Armada. As this is a Talbot Rothwell script, any such preconceptions are turned on their heads—our hero Albert Poop-Decker is a hopeless nincompoop who is no better a sailor at the end of the film than at the beginning. Villains Howett and Angel, meanwhile, are brutal—it is hard to warm to a pair of characters who essentially kidnap the film's hero and try to whip him to death—but have no other aim than to run an efficient warship and defeat their country's enemy. Howett is clearly a better sailor and ship's captain than Captain Fearless; the crew love him, and under his guidance, they almost defeat the Spanish Armada, stopped only by the film's blundering heroes.

The film is considerably buoyed by its performances, Bernard Cribbins rising to the challenge of his first leading role superbly. His natural comedy instincts and the athleticism of a former paratrooper make him the ideal leading man for this particular example of Carry On—more than normal, the narrative of the film rests on one set of shoulders and Cribbins does a marvellous job. The casting of *Carry On Jack*, while lacking many of the regular series cast, is finely balanced in a way that helps the film enormously. *Jack* has three major comedic roles; Cribbins' Albert Poop-Decker, Kenneth Williams' Captain Fearless, and Charles Hawtrey as Walter Sweetley. The rest of the cast is largely made up of solid, experienced character actors, playing roughly the same roles as they often did in in serious historical dramas.

In a film which has a fair amount of narrative to get through compared to the average Carry On—*Constable* and *Regardless* had almost no plot at all, to speak of—this is extremely helpful, with the comedy actors getting to bounce off the character performers to great effect. This can be seen right from Cribbins' first scene, when he is finally given his midshipman's orders after eight and a half years at naval college by a wonderfully splenetic Cecil Parker, here given 'special guest star' billing.

The scope of *Jack* is clear right from the beginning, when Gerald Thomas stages what is probably the most elaborate joke in the history of Carry Ons, a live-action recreation of Arthur William Devis' 1807 painting *The Death of Nelson, 21 October 1805*. Thomas pulls Alan Hume's camera in to the central action of the scene, which produces a very effective three-dimensional effect and sets up Rothwell's gag, a riff on the legendary 'Kiss Me, Hardy' exchange before Nelson's death. It should also be noted that the scene is very well played by Anton Rogers as Hardy and Jimmy Thompson as Admiral Nelson.

As already noted, the part of Captain Fearless was tailor-made for Kenneth Williams and he plays the role to the hilt—in Carry On mode he knew no other way. Hopelessly out of his depth and a congenital coward, Fearless is an interesting precursor to the part of Caesar that Rothwell would soon create for Williams in *Carry On Cleo*. Fearless creates some of the biggest laughs in the film, especially in Jack's climax when he becomes delirious from gangrene, Williams' skill with voices making the scene leap off the page in a way that it is difficult to imagine any other actor achieving.

Charles Hawtrey, meanwhile, gives what was by this point in time 'The Charles Hawtrey Performance'. This is not meant as a complaint—Hawtrey was the type of actor who had an act: a series of comedic foibles, tics, and looks to camera that were specifically written for and that audiences would be disappointed if they did not get. The plot never revolved around Hawtrey's character in a Carry On film, but the actor made sure audiences noticed him in his own unique way. Rothwell actually writes for Hawtrey very well here, his character Walter Sweetley being at the bottom of the social heap right from his introduction, when we are told he is a cess pit cleaner. He befriends Albert, but as soon as Albert gets his position as midshipman back—more than that, actually takes charge of the ship—Walter is scrubbing the decks.

Although Sally is the only sizeable female role in *Carry On Jack*, it is a good one, and even though Juliet Mills was not the first choice for the part, it is honestly hard to imagine anyone else in the role. Although she had starred in two previous films for Peter Rogers and Gerald Thomas, it is fair to say that Mills was not a comedy performer, but instead an actress who could play comedy. Thus Sally is not given any laughs of her own, instead serving as the straight woman to Cribbins and Williams and as such does an extremely good job to make her performance so memorable.

Also very notable is the contribution of Jim Dale, who turns the small role of a sedan chair carrier into one of the comedic highlights of the film. Already an improvement on his small role in *Carry On Cabby*, Dale was clearly in tune with the direction the Carry On films were headed, giving a full-blooded, broadly comedic turn that led to the actor and singer becoming a regular in the series for the rest of the decade. By the time *Carry On Spying*, the next film in the series arrived, the story included a deliberate showcase for his versatility.

As already noted, Carry On Jack represented a significant upgrade in the scope of the Carry On series—it is a good-looking film with plenty of laughs and excellent sets, taking full advantage of the opportunities presented by the *HMS Defiant* sets the film utilised. *Jack* also began a fruitful run of Carry Ons that spoofed movie genres. Although it is not remembered in the public mind as much as some other films in the series, without *Carry On Jack*'s success, we might not have been treated to *Carry On Screaming, Carry On Cleo, Follow That Camel*, or even the film that was to follow immediately afterward in which Carry On joined the world of James Bond—*Carry On Spying*.

10

Carry On Spying (1964)

Filming Dates: 8 February 1964–13 March 1964
Original Certificate: A (Classified by BBFC 4 June 1964 [cut])
Running Time: 91 minutes

Release Details

London release: 29 June 1964 (ABC Fulham Road).

Carry On Spying's initial UK cinema run saw the film released with the murder mystery *Who Was Maddox?* This was another in Anglo-Amalgamated's Edgar Wallace B-picture series, made at Merton Park Studios, and somewhat appropriately it featured James Bond's boss M, in the shape of Bernard Lee. This time, Lee's Superintendent Meredith investigates a publisher who has been framed for murder while both he and his wife are being blackmailed. Jack Watling and Suzanne Heath played the benighted couple under the direction of Geoffrey Nethercott while the screenplay was by Roger Marshall, one of the main scriptwriters on *The Avengers* and co-creator of the TV series *Public Eye*.

What's Carrying On?

When a secret formula is stolen from a top security laboratory by an undercover agent of the evil supervillain Doctor Crow, the top agents of British Intelligence are called upon. They are all busy however, so Agent Simkins is given the task of retrieving the formula, along with trainee agents Harold Crump, Daphne Honeybutt, and Charlie Bind. The trail leads to Vienna, where they get in the way of Agent Carstairs, master of disguise, and encounter master spy the Fat Man, then to Tangiers before finally entering the secret base of the dreaded Doctor Crow and her criminal organisation STENCH.

Who's Carrying On?

A Peter Rogers Production
Director: Gerald Thomas
Screenplay by Talbot Rothwell and Sid Colin
Music composed and conducted by Eric Rogers
Photography: Alan Hume BSC
Art Director: Alex Vetchinsky
Editor: Archie Ludski
Kenneth Williams: Desmond Simkins, keen but less than competent secret agent who must lead a group of trainee agents into the field thanks to a staffing crisis.
Barbara Windsor: Daphne Honeybutt, trainee agent with a photographic memory and a figure that makes putting on a shoulder holster virtually impossible.
Charles Hawtrey: Charlie Bind, agent Double O—Oh! Licenced to do not very much, but he does look quite fetching in a cycling outfit.
Bernard Cribbins: Harold Crump, trainee agent with a black belt in Ludo and the hots for Daphne Honeybutt.
Jim Dale: Agent Carstairs, our man in Vienna. Master of disguise and trained to kill, but no match for the clumsiness and idiocy of our heroes.
Eric Barker: The Chief, the harried head of the British Secret Service, forced to send our heroes into battle against the dreaded Doctor Crow.

Carry On Critics

The *Monthly Film Bulletin*'s reviewer of September 1964 was decidedly unimpressed, describing the film as 'Straight off the Carry On assembly line' (I cannot imagine what put that imagery into their head). 'A few bright gags are buried in a waste of coy camp, female impersonation and mildly smutty jokes'. They were quite keen on Bernard Cribbins, however, and described Barbara Windsor as 'definitely an asset'.

'A return to form for the "Carry On" team after their last unfortunate tangle with the costume extravaganza,' reported *The Times*, positively raving about the film's qualities on 20 July 1964 after *Carry On Spying* opened its London run at the ABC Fulham Road.

> The verbal humour is as shameless as ever, and often so outrageously childish in its fourth-form *double-entendres* that even the starchiest spectator will have to succumb. Very British, very much a Bank Holiday film and, yes, when all is said and done, very funny.

The Guardian's Richard Roud rather enjoyed *Carry On Spying*, as (he reported in the paper's 31 July edition) did the assembled members of the press: 'Little scandalised gasps of titillation went around the press show of *Carry On Spying*. "Shameless" rose pleasurably to everyone's lips, but it is pretty funny if you're in a really undemanding mood.'

The Observer's Penelope Gilliatt went into some detail about how much she enjoyed the Carry On films, despite their 'badness', claiming 'they seem to be edited with a bacon slicer ... and the comic rhythm jerks along like a car on a cold morning'. One can only imagine how thrilled Peter Rogers and his crew must have been at this backhanded compliment.

> In *Carry On Spying* the characters are not only square enough to wear braces (partly so they can catch on door handles); they are also camp enough to send up the colossal bull of a woman who is the film's heavy parody of Ian Fleming's M, in charge of an organisation called Stench.

Although Gilliatt's heart seems to have been in the right place, this does show that she was perhaps more familiar with the writing of Norman Hudis for the Carry On films than she was with the works of Ian Fleming. The full article is worth seeking out, however, being one of the earliest examinations of the Carry On phenomenon from a 'serious' critical perspective.

The reviewer for *Variety* was equivocal about the wisdom of Kenneth Williams playing such a major role entirely in 'snide' mode:

> Kenneth Williams' brand of camp comedy, while very funny in smallish doses, can pall when he has a lengthy chore as here. But Bernard Cribbins brings some useful virility to his fatuous role, Charles Hawtrey contributes his now familiar performance as the guileless one and Barbara Windsor proves a well-upholstered and perky heroine as the girl spy with a photogenic [*sic.*] memory.

Richard Davis in the August 1964 edition of *Films and Filming* was, considering the magazine's more intellectual readership, sanguine about the quality and prospects of *Carry On Spying*:

> Fashions may come, and new waves may go, but the Carry Ons threaten to stay with us forever. They use material which would make even a seaside

concert party hesitate, and there are always the camp jokes to add to the corn. But this one, like the others, will make lots of money, and that's what the cinema needs so that chaps like you and me can sit back and talk about chaps like Resnais and Antonioni ... Of course what happens is predictable ... but then we're all schoolboys at heart—aren't we?

Carry On Comments

While the SS *Happy Wanderer*'s cruise around Spain, Italy, and North Africa took it no further than the stages of Pinewood Studios during the filming of *Carry On Cruising* in January and February 1962, another Pinewood-based production commenced shooting on 16 January. This, however, was far away from the chilly Hertfordshire countryside as the first James Bond film, *Dr. No,* began filming in sunny Jamaica. Over a year later in March 1963, while Britain struggled to recover from the blizzards of the freezing winter that had caused chaos from mid-December to early March, *Carry On Cabby* began shooting. Gerald Thomas' film was still on the studio floor when the next James Bond film, *From Russia with Love*, began its production elsewhere at Pinewood on 1 April prior to decamping for its Istanbul location shoot later that month.

Such was the momentum that the James Bond films had already generated that writer Richard Maibaum was already working on the script for the next film in the series, *Goldfinger*. Bond was well on the way to becoming a worldwide phenomenon, and the popularity of the series being made on neighbouring stages to the Carry Ons had certainly not escaped the attention of Peter Rogers. The producers had, in fact, registered the *Carry On Spying* title as soon as it had become clear what a huge success *Dr. No* had become. The time was right for Carry On to enter the world of espionage, but production took some time to get going. Norman Hudis delivered a draft script in February 1963, but the writer's original idea of taking on the subject matter of the anti-nuclear movement was seen as being rather too serious in tone for the direction in which the Carry Ons were headed. Talbot Rothwell's more gag-based writing, coupled with the cinematic spoof approach introduced with *Carry On Jack*, meant that the *Carry On Spying* was finally able to make progress. Having worked on *Cabby* and *Jack* in quick succession, however, even the energies and joke supplies of Talbot Rothwell were reaching their limits, and the writer called in his old friend Sid Colin to co-write the script.

Sid Colin had tangential connections with the Carry On series, which helps to demonstrate the small and closely linked world of British post-war comedy writing. Sid had created the hit ITV sitcom *The Army Game*, of which *Carry On Sergeant* became a sort of unofficial spin-off, and had written many of the show's episodes. He also wrote *I Only Arsked!,* the official cinematic adaptation of *The Army Game*, shot at Bray Studios by Hammer Films, kings of the television and radio spin-off and released on 11 November 1958, beaten to the screen by *Carry On Sergeant* by almost two months.

Colin and Rothwell had written together for many years, providing comedy scripts for the BBC's early post-war television service, most of which was broadcast live and is lost to posterity as methods of recording television in the early 1950s were in their infancy. Their work included scripts for *Before Your Very Eyes*, a vehicle for Arthur Askey which ran from 1952 to 1958; *Friends and Neighbours*, a 1954 series featuring the husband and wife team of Janet Brown and Peter Butterworth; and *The Ted Ray Show*, which ran from 1955 to 1958 and also featured Kenneth Connor. Among the other writers for *The Ted Ray Show* was future Carry On scriptwriter Dave Freeman. Colin and Rothwell moved to ITV along with Arthur Askey and his old partner from the radio series *Band Waggon*, Richard Murdoch, for the Associated-Rediffusion series *Living it Up* in 1957. The writers also started branching out into films, writing additional scenes and gags for the 1955 Norman Wisdom film *One Good Turn* and performed similar services for the Tommy Steele musical *Tommy the Toreador*, which also starred Sid James and Bernard Cribbins.

While both writers maintained solo careers during this golden era of British comedy, and Sid was also a professional guitarist, they still teamed up again from time to time despite Rothwell being kept busy writing Carry On scripts. Sid took over the writing of Talbot Rothwell's Frankie Howerd sitcom *Up Pompeii!*, also writing scripts for its sequel, *Whoops Baghdad!* and wrote the screenplays for the show's three movie spinoffs.

While Rothwell and Colin were ready and willing to write a James Bond spoof, the fact was that the Bond movies were only two films into their run and had yet to settle into easily identifiable characteristics audiences would recognise. This was one of the factors that meant Rothwell had to cast his net wider when constructing a Bond spoof, although the film's monochrome photography also had to be taken into account. The Bonds were glossy, colour productions; like the Ian Fleming novels that were their inspiration, a large part of the popular appeal of James Bond movies lay in the sheer luxury that they presented. While *Carry On Spying* is estimated to have cost £148,000 to produce, which was only £4,000 less than *Carry On Jack*, its predecessor saved a considerable amount of money on its impressive sets by renting ones already constructed for *HMS Defiant*.

Despite its black and white photography, *Carry On Spying* was a difficult and complex production to realise on a Carry On budget, designer Alex Vetchinsky having to come up with approximately fifty-four different sets. The savings *Carry On Jack* made on set construction went towards filming in glorious Eastmancolor, whereas *Spying* had to make a virtue of its monochromatic film stock. This meant that at times Gerald Thomas and his cinematographer Alan Hume shot key scenes using the sort of low key lighting effects used in Hollywood film noir productions of the immediate post-war years, with inky blacks and smoky backgrounds. This was especially apparently during the Vienna scenes, which carry deliberate echoes of Carol Reed's famous 1947 drama *The Third Man*.

With the Bond producers' lawyers taking a close interest in the production, it was vital that all aspects of the production resisted straying too close to 007 territory. Thus Eric Rogers provides a heavy, dramatic score but avoids copying guitarist Vic Flick's echo-drenched electric guitar sound from the James Bond Theme, already iconic by 1964. We are, however, treated to a Flemingesque secret criminal organisation which goes by the acronym STENCH, the Society for the Total Extinction of Non-Conforming Humans.

Meanwhile, Austrian character actor Eric Pohlmann—who genuinely was Viennese, having moved to Britain in 1939 to escape the Nazis—is cast in exactly the sort of sinister role that had made him an extremely familiar face in British films and television. In fact, although it was not generally known at the time, Pohlmann had provided the voice of the unseen Ernst Stavro Blofeld in *From Russia With Love*. This tactic of casting straight actors opposite the comedy leads had paid dividends in *Carry On Jack* and was continued here, with Pohlmann playing the Fat Man, a part which bore echoes of the pre-Bond image of espionage, a sort of amalgam of *The Third Man*'s Harry Lime (a part played memorably by Orson Welles) and *Casablanca*'s Signor Ferrari, which had made an unlikely star of the corpulent English actor Sidney Greenstreet.

The cast was led this time by Kenneth Williams as Agent Simkins, for about the only time in a Carry On film taking on the lead role and carrying the weight of the narrative. He gives quite a different performance to normal, the standard Williams persona of highly educated disdain possibly being regarded as too unsympathetic for the task. Instead, the actor adopts a slightly more likeable variation of the 'snide' voice he had developed for the Tony Hancock radio series, which had been the source of his 'stop messing about' catchphrase. As Williams' diaries attest, this was seen as something of a risk, as the 'snide' persona had previously been used as an irritating character for short appearances. Although the experiment was never repeated, here it worked quite well, with Simkins coming across as less self-important than most of Williams' characters in the Carry On series and as a result is far more likeable.

This is, of course, the film in which Barbara Windsor made her Carry On debut, and although she was not to return for a few years, she fits in to the cast beautifully. It is fascinating to note just how much Windsor's presence changes the humour in Rothwell and Colin's script compared to previous Carry Ons. Her physical presence and earthy sexuality immediately result in a slew of boob gags and sex references, which previous Carry On leading ladies such as Joan Sims, Shirley Eaton, and even Liz Fraser could not have pulled off. This affects not just the script, but also Gerald Thomas' direction: he frames her as often as possible in profile, the better to display the impressive effects of her push-up bra (it was often said that Barbara Windsor acted the part of a woman with big boobs, rather than being the actual possessor of them). It is to the film's credit that Windsor's character Daphne Honeybutt is more than just a pretty face, having a photographic memory—demonstrated in an amusingly basic manner as her eyes make the sound of a camera shutter when she memorises things. Daphne also refuses to be cowed by her male counterparts, refusing to comply when the boys order her to stay in the hotel room while they go out on a mission.

Charles Hawtrey's character was originally to be called James Bind, but this was changed to Charles Bind when the Bond producers objected. Bind remains the nearest thing to a comedic James Bond substitute in the film, his attempts at Bondian stylish dressing coming to naught as an expensive double breasted suit on Hawtrey's skinny frame is made to look like a baggy old demob suit. Hawtrey also gets two of the best gags in the film: he gained his Secret Service code name when his assessors saw him and said he was 'double o ... oh'. There is also a marvellous visual gag later in the film when Bind draws his pistol from his shoulder holster and his trousers fall down. It is about as basic as humour gets, but it made me laugh, at least.

Bernard Cribbins as trainee agent Harold Crump does not have so large a role here as he did in *Carry On Jack*, but that was always the nature of the Carry Ons: everyone got their time in the spotlight, and apart from the two established series leads Sid James and Kenneth Williams, the size of their roles would vary from film to film. Again, Cribbins' natural burly athleticism stands him in good stead; his stocky frame and military bearing makes him look like a convincing agent when necessary, while he and Barbara Windsor make a good comedy-romantic pairing. Comedic value is also gained from having the burly Cribbins and emaciated Hawtrey appear in drag as harem dancers in a scene that gives Eric Pohlmann a well-earned chance to play broad comedy. Sadly, Cribbins had nothing like so good a time making *Spying* as he had on *Jack*, culminating in the actor expressing his displeasure on set when a blank-firing gun was fired too close to him. As a result, both Cribbins and the Carry On producers decided they could get along without each other in future.

Fortunately, Rogers and Thomas had an ideal candidate for their next young leading man to hand in the shape of Jim Dale, giving a stand-out performance as Agent Carstairs, who could have solved the case in the first half hour if it were not for our bumbling heroes. Although he is, in effect, a straight man for the main cast members here, the role appears designed to showcase Dale's versatility. He gets two excellent gags, the main one being a running joke in which he turns up in increasingly outlandish disguises, culminating in him being dressed as a lady of the night, in order to swap ever more absurd recognition codes with our heroes and pass on that night's rendezvous:

> 'I'd like a packet of filter-tipped matches, please.'
> 'I'm sorry, I've only got filter-tipped bootlaces.'
> 'I cannot smoke those, they make me deaf.'
> 'Café Mozart, ten o'clock.'

It is a gag that subsequently would be done to death by later spy comedies, but here it is fresh and funny.

Carstairs is also constantly frustrated in his attempts to get the formula back, most memorably getting a toilet door accidentally slammed in his face when he is about to use a *From Russia With Love*-style garrotte watch—a Bond borrowing that the lawyers missed.

Eric Barker returns as the Chief, playing another of his bumbling, ever-frustrated authority figures in what would be the last speaking part he ever played in a Carry On picture. A stroke he suffered in 1967 would severely limit Barker's acting career, but he still popped up on screens both big and small from time to time, even returning for a wordless cameo in *Carry On Emmannuelle* in 1978. In *Carry On Spying*, Barker's appearance is especially enjoyable as he is paired with Richard Wattis, one of the finest British comedy actors ever to raise an eyebrow. Amazingly, considering his ubiquity in British film and television, this was to be Richard Wattis' only Carry On movie role. The actor's trademark air of slightly camp officialdom made what could have been a forgettable sidekick part really stand out. It is a shame he never returned to the series—there are very few films that would not be improved by having Richard Wattis pop up, however briefly. He did film a cameo for the *Carry On Laughing* episode 'Orgy and Bess' in 1974 that was cut from the finished episode. Wattis died suddenly on 25 February 1975, exactly a month after the episode was broadcast.

Dilys Laye is back, this time playing femme fatale Lila, which makes a nice change from the girl-next-door parts she played so well in her other Carry On appearances. We never know until near the end of the film exactly which side Lila is working for, the British or the villainous Doctor Crow. Although the name of *Carry On Spying*'s villain is clearly meant to carry echoes of James Bond's *Dr. No*, this is where the similarity ends for the part is played by none other than Judith Furse. This was not Miss Furse's only Carry On role by any means—she turns up in *Carry On Regardless* and *Carry On Cabby*—but this is her biggest role in the series by some way. It is also a highly unusual role as it is deliberately unclear which gender Doctor Crow is, Furse's lavish physique being flattened out by a dark, unisex costume and her voice overdubbed by John Bluthall, who also appears in the film as the head waiter of Café Mozart. Sadly, despite her career getting an early boost with good roles in Michael Powell and Emeric Pressburger's *A Canterbury Tale* (1944) and *Black Narcissus* (1947), Judith Furse soon found herself terribly typecast by her looks as a neverending series of stereotypical battleaxes. Nevertheless, the actress was still able to pull off the occasional remarkable performance in the most unlikely of circumstances; as Bela Lugosi's assistant Freda in 1952's *Mother Riley Meets the Vampire*, she imbues a fairly thankless role with a palpable sense of sadness and longing.

A fair sprinkling of familiar Carry On faces return in smaller roles: Victor Maddern is back in the quite major role of Doctor Crow's agent Milchmann, who begins the film undercover disguised as a milkman (a joke even I am surprised how much I enjoy). Renee Houston returns from *Carry On Cabby*—not to mention *Twice Around the Daffodils* and *Nurse on Wheels*—but would make her greatest contribution to Carry On in 1971's *Carry On at Your Convenience*. Tom Clegg makes the second of his six Carry On appearances as a doorman, while Gertan Klauber appears in the first of his seven Carry Ons in an amusing cameo as a suspiciously Slavic-looking British Intelligence cypher clark. Also making his Carry On debut is Hugh Futcher as a Tangier native with a bed of nails performing a gag that would be repeated, in all places, in the 1983 James Bond film *Octopussy*. It is also nice to see Patrick Durkin, one of the original National Service conscripts featured in *Carry On Sergeant*, return as a guard.

Somehow, over the years, *Carry On Spying* has tended to slip through the cracks, being probably one of the least-remembered Carry Ons from the series' classic period. This is possibly because it is the last of the black and white films in the series, but whatever the reason, this is a pity as there really is a lot to enjoy about the film.

11

Carry On Cleo (1964)

Filming Dates: 13 July 1964–28 August 1964
Original Certificate: A (Classified by BBFC 30 October 1964 [cut])
Running Time: 92 minutes 5 seconds

Release Details

London release: 10 December 1964 (Warner Cinema, Leicester Square—Replacing John Leyton and Mike Sarne in *Every Day's a Holiday*).

The national release for *Cleo* was somewhat later than its London premiere this time, with the film starting to turn up outside the capital from Sunday 27 December 1964. By this point in time the hour-long British dramatic B-picture was a dying breed, and *Carry On Cleo* was accompanied by *Act of Murder*, which was among the final batch of the Edgar Wallace series produced by Jack Greenwood at Merton Park Studios. Alan Bridges directed stars John Carson, Anthony Bate, and Justine Lord, while Carry On actors Dandy Nichols and Marianne Stone also appear. The story features two couples who arrange to swap houses so each can have a holiday, but one of the couples plans to rob the house of the other.

What's Carrying On?

Julius Caesar, emperor of Rome, is on the latest of his trips abroad, this time to conquer Britain, which is cold, wet, and has given him what the locals call 'a stinking cold'. Accompanied by his close friend and military chief Mark Antony, the pair return to Rome along with a batch of slaves, including busty beauty Gloria, wheelwright Hengist Pod, and neighbour Horsa, who has just moved into the cave next door. When Mark Antony is sent to Egypt to bring the troublesome Queen Cleopatra into line, the Roman general immediately falls in lust with the queen, and the pair plot to get rid of Caesar. Absolutely nothing, however, goes to plan.

Who's Carrying On?

A Peter Rogers Production
Director: Gerald Thomas
Screenplay by Talbot Rothwell (from an original idea by William Shakespeare)
Music composed and conducted by Eric Rogers
Photography: Alan Hume BSC
Art Director: Bert Davey
Editor: Archie Ludski

Sidney James: Mark Antony, right-hand man to Julius Caesar who finds himself in opposition to his old friend the second he sets eyes on the gorgeous Cleopatra.

Kenneth Williams: Julius Caesar, leader of Rome who is popular with everyone except his wife, the senate, and the Roman people.

Kenneth Connor: Hengist Pod, husband of Cenna, who makes an unlikely journey from maker of square wheels to feared bodyguard of Julius Caesar, remaining a total coward the entire time.

Charles Hawtrey: Seneca, father-in-law of Caesar, mystic seer into future events and dirty old devil.

Joan Sims: Calpurnia, wife of Caesar, unhappy with her husband's constant presence abroad conquering other countries and coming back with busty slaves.

Jim Dale: Horsa, Hengist's new neighbour who had a busy time inventing the window frame, then leading a slave revolt with his surprisingly proficient swordplay skills.

Amanda Barrie: Cleopatra, queen of Egypt, all-around hottie and nothing like as dumb as she makes out, who spends her days bathing in asses' milk when not twisting men around her little finger.

Carry On Critics

Carry On Jack can be seen as something of a transitional film between the Hudis and Rothwell styles of writing, and thus *The Times*' lukewarm review was understandable. Their reviewer's antipathy towards *Carry On Cleo* in

The Times' 10 December edition, given its modern status as a classic of British film comedy, makes for puzzling reading:

> The formula does not really lend itself to this particular form, and in addition there are distinct signs of tiredness in the scripting. Corny jokes and even blue jokes are acceptable enough in broad farce, but few of them bear much repetition, and when the same word-plays on phrases like 'at her toilet' are repeated *ad infinitum* even the most farce-oriented spectator will probably find it also *ad nauseum*.

Only Amanda Barrie attracts praise: 'a Cleopatra both funny and alluring'.

The Times' review comes across as positively effusive compared to David Rider's damning words in the February 1965 edition of *Films and Filming*: 'If there's one thing that saddens me when I see a film it's wastage—wastage of ideas, actors, situations, design. *Carry On Cleo* is almost pure wastage from start to finish.' Rider is only warming up in this passage, and soon gets his teeth into a film he appears to have hated on every level:

> Disaster piled upon disaster almost makes this film into an object lesson into how *not* to make a comedy. A pathetically unfunny off-screen narration is delivered by E V H Emmett whose style is fine for newsreel commentary but entirely unsuited to this kind of work.

Rider's list of complaints covers Archie Ludski's editing, Kenneth Williams' overacting (at which point the reader begins to suspect that *Films and Filming*'s correspondent missed the point of *Carry On Cleo* in a very big way), and the size of Amanda Barrie's breasts: 'I could have wished for a more buxom Cleopatra'. Some performers are spared Rider's scorn, especially Sid James, Warren Mitchell, and Jon Pertwee, but overall, it is clear that the Rider funny bone was most certainly not tickled.

The *Monthly Film Bulletin* was a little more accommodating towards the film's qualities when it finally got around to covering the film in its February 1965 edition, though not fully convinced:

> 'Based on an idea by William Shakespeare' runs the legend immediately following the script credit, which suggests a level of wit never quite reached by this latest and pictorially most ambitious of the 'Carry On' series. In fact the film is funny in the usual bludgeoning manner which has made the series so popular.

Riding the coattails of the publicity juggernaut that was *Cleopatra, Carry On Cleo* gained more attention in the USA than the films had since *Nurse*.

It played at two cinemas in central New York alone, the RKO cinemas on 58 Street and 23 Street. *The New York Times*' Bosley Crowther passed his judgement on the film in the paper's 23 October 1965 edition:

> No doubt audiences at Brighton and Blackpool have split their sides at the splurge of low-comedy mugging and the torrent of agonizing puns that constitute *Carry On Cleo* ... But for average American moviegoers and even brainwashed captives of video, this cheap travesty of *Cleopatra*, the Elizabeth Taylor–Richard Burton spectacle film, is not merely likely—it is certain—to be an excruciating bore.

Variety provided a slightly more approving verdict on *Carry On Cleo* from an American perspective:

> This entry from the Carry On stables relies on the bludgeon rather than the rapier, so isn't entirely successful in its purpose ... Talbot Rothwell's dialog is unabashedly corny but this doesn't much matter. But it is also unusually bristling with plodding *double entendres*. Gags, both verbal and visual, suffer from repetition and few are as neat as Julius Caesar's woeful complaint: 'Infamy! Infamy! Everyone's got it in for me'.

The line was misremembered, but remains funny. Also remembered was the actress playing the film's title role:

> Best discovery is Amanda Barrie as the poor man's Cleopatra. Her takeoff of the Queen of the Nile gets nearer to the tongue-in-cheek sense of what filmmakers were aiming at than any of her more experienced colleagues.

Carry On Comments

Since its initial release, *Carry On Cleo* has grown so much in reputation as to be popularly regarded as a the first of the absolutely classic Carry Ons, remembered with glee by fans of the series both young and old. While *Jack* may have been the first of the historical Carry Ons, its origins as a non-series film and unusual cast combination give that film a somewhat semi-detached relationship with the rest of the series. *Carry On Cleo*, on the other hand, is prime Carry On—a cartoonish joke-monster of epic proportions from writer Talbot Rothwell that pointed toward the direction the series would follow until its end.

So fecund was Rothwell's comedic imagination at this point that his jokes extended beyond the bounds of the film itself and into the opening credits;

this included not only a shared screenwriting credit for William Shakespeare, but also the following, which takes the Mickey out of the warnings placed in hopelessly inaccurate historical epics: 'While the characters and events in this story are based on actual characters and events, certain liberties may have been taken with Cleopatra'.

If this was to be the film in which Rothwell finally finds his true *metier* as a Carry On writer, it is worth remembering the pace at which the films were being made at this stage. Incredibly, this was the third Carry On release that year—*Jack, Spying*, and *Cleo* being released in a dizzying seven-month period between April and December 1964. From this distance in time, one can see *Carry On Cleo* as heralding the beginning of Carry Ons' imperial phase—a golden period between 1964 and the end of the decade (ending after either *Carry On Camping* or *Carry On Again Doctor*, depending on your tastes) when every film baring the Carry On name successfully mined comedy gold. For an almost absurdly long period, some six years, everything was just right with the Carry On mix and stayed that way.

The cast had settled into their ideal characterisations and had formed a formidable ensemble, bouncing off each other with comedic glee while Gerald Thomas directed unobtrusively and with great pace, both on the set and on the screen. Writer Talbot Rothwell, meanwhile, had taken the series in a new direction, filling the screen with gags while maintaining strong plotlines. In the process, he virtually created a new film genre, managing to extend to movie length the kind of gag-filled satires on cinematic stereotypes written in much shorter formats for radio by writing teams such as Frank Muir and Dennis Norden (on *Take it From Here*) and Marty Feldman and Barry Took (on *Round the Horne*). A golden age of movie comedy was happening and, as generally happens when such riches are presented, was completely taken for granted by the public at large and the entertainment industry.

But that was all in the future and, back in 1964, Peter Rogers and Gerald Thomas gained inspiration for their latest production from 20th Century Fox's mega-production *Cleopatra*. This had originally been envisaged as a relatively cheap production, and by the time pre-production began at Pinewood in 1960, it was still not an exceptionally expensive production. The film's star, Elizabeth Taylor, was prone to spells of extreme ill-health and production shut down in January 1961 while the actress suffered from an almost fatal bout of pneumonia. With a both a direly ill star and the impossibility of recreating Rome and Egypt in Buckinghamshire in the middle of an English winter militating against continuing, the production decamped to Cinecittà Studios in Rome. There *Cleopatra* became a legendary, elephantine mega-production that caught the imagination of the world not only because of the absurd profligacy of its production but also due to the love affair between the film's two stars, Elizabeth Taylor and Richard Burton, each of whom was married to someone else at the time. The full story of *Cleopatra* is one for another book; suffice to say, that this was material ripe for the broadest possible satirisation, and the Carry On crew were the very people for the job.

It helped matters that the sets for the abandoned production were still available for use at Pinewood, quite a normal practice after a major production has completed shooting (or not, in this case). As has already been noted, *Carry On Jack* made use of sets from the film *HMS Defiant*, and other examples are dotted around the Carry On canon. To pick a less famous example, the street on which Agatha Spanner's boarding house stands in *Carry On At Your Convenience* was actually part of a huge street set left on the Pinewood backlot from the production of Billy Wilder's *The Private Life of Sherlock Holmes*. This was used by many British productions over the next few years before finally being demolished when another production needed the space. The *Cleopatra* sets were supplemented by others rented from the actor Victor Maddern, who played Mark Antony's sergeant major. Maddern had bought the expensively made sets from a stage production of *Caligula* he had appeared in, keeping them in storage before renting them out to Peter Rogers Productions at a handsome profit.

Carry On Cleo starts in quite a different manner to *Cleopatra*, with a wildly unhistorical look at the British tribes that the Roman Empire conquered. They are presented as cave-dwellers, co-existing with dinosaurs (which economically remain safely off-screen) in a sequence that appears to be inspired by the American cartoon series *The Flintstones*, the Hanna-Barbera animated Stone Age sitcom that had been appearing on British screens since the autumn of 1960. This introduces our two heroes, Hengist Pod (Kenneth Connor) and his new neighbour Horsa (Jim Dale), who has just moved in to the cave next door when the Roman legion led by Julius Caesar (Kenneth Williams) and Mark Antony (Sid James)—Julie and Tony to their friends—arrive to haul them off to Rome as slaves.

Rothwell writes both Kenneth Williams and Charles Hawtrey in an interesting way, quite different to how the actors were written by Norman Hudis. This is partly a function of Williams' ever-broader screen characterisations and, one can speculate, likely the result of observing the actors' increasingly extreme on-set behaviour. Williams was a notorious on-set trouser dropper and flasher, a situation made worse on the *Cleo* set when the actor became enamoured of his short-skirted costume.[1] At least this improved his opinion of the film, which had been incredibly downbeat, as his diary entry of 23 July 1964 indicates: 'It's all just like an incredibly tired echo of the beginning of the series. Surely the wheel can't turn much further'.[2]

Williams must have been in a particularly bad mood that day—could there possibly exist a film less like *Carry On Sergeant* than *Carry On Cleo*? Nevertheless, Rothwell has fun with Williams' on-screen image, in effect writing him as both camply gay and heterosexual at the same time. In his very first scene, Julius Caesar, suffering from a stinking cold, is given the opening line 'Ooh, I do feel queer', back when that word had more than one meaning. We soon, however, see him lusting after Julie Stevens' busty slave Gloria, and later in the film, there is a lovely sequence in which Sid's Mark Antony describes to him the charms of Cleopatra:

> Mark Antony: 'You have got to see her. Her hair is black as ebony, her face is like an ivory goddess. Her neck is like a swan.'
>
> Julius Caesar: 'Ooh yes, do go on.'
>
> Mark Antony: 'Her feet are like sculptured marble.'
>
> Julius Caesar: 'Ere, don't leave out the best bits!'

Similarly, the equally camp Charles Hawtrey is written as something of a dirty old man—it s interesting how Hawtrey on-screen seemed to leap immediately from eternal youth to old codger. Also a process began in which Hawtrey's characters were often written as being more than fond of a drink and one cannot imagine that the writer was unaware of his on-set drinking. Plenty of comic material is taken from casting the tiny, bird-like actor as rampantly heterosexual. The sheer unlikelihood of Hawtrey finding any success in his amorous endeavours helps make the character funny, instead of an unpleasant letch. In point of fact, so resolutely likeable was the screen persona Charles Hawtrey adopted for the Carry On films, no matter which character he was playing, that it would have taken an unkind audience indeed to ascribe to him unpleasant motives.

Kenneth Williams' attitude to *Carry On Cleo* must have brightened somewhat when it became clear that he had been gifted the plum line of dialogue in the film. When Julius Caesar is chased through the temple of the vestal virgins by Mark Antony's men, out to kill their supposed leader, Talbot Rothwell needed to give Williams a line which punctuated the scene between Caesar's entrance and the subsequent sword battle with a nice laugh. In search of inspiration, the writer recalled a gag from the radio comedy *Take It From Here* that would be perfect, and contacted that show's writers, Frank Muir and Dennis Norden, for permission to recycle the gag. Permission was duly given and the throwaway line 'Infamy! Infamy! They've all got it in for me!' was added to the script.

The addition of the line not only served the purposes of the scene, but went on to become without doubt the most famous piece of dialogue in the entire Carry On series of films. In 2007, the satellite TV channel Sky Movies ran a poll of comedians, who voted it the greatest one-liner in movie history, and one doubts if it has been topped in the subsequent years. Not only is 'Infamy! Infamy!' a killer line of dialogue, it is also supremely well played by Kenneth

Williams—so much so that one doubts if it would have worked at all had it been performed by any other actor. Could anyone but Williams switch accents from Shakespearean to working class in the middle of a single line? It is Williams' amazing vocal dexterity which really sells the gag, helping lift it to classic status, along with some expert staging: the actor plays the first half of the line to the back row of the theatre, the second almost, but not quite, to the camera. The fourth wall is not quite broken in a Hawtreyesque manner, but it is certainly given a good wobble.

If *Carry On Cleo* was eventually to help assure Kenneth Williams a place in the history of British comedy, the effect on Sid James' career was instant and transformative. His performance as Mark Antony is basically similar to his Sidney Balmoral James characterisation in the Hancock radio series, and noticeably different to the slightly more serious way Sid played his roles in *Constable, Regardless, Cruising*, and even *Cabby*. In those films he was literally in charge of the other regular cast members, while here he is freed from that restriction, which allows Sid to appear more laid back. The film gains doubly from this: the contrast between what Sid does and Kenneth Williams' archly theatrical performance is very effective, as is the playing of a Roman general (a role normally reserved for the Richard Burtons of this world) as a fun-loving cockney. Back in *Carry On Cruising*, the contrast between Sid's working class origins and his holding a high rank was regarded as being so unusual as to be the basis of the entire plot. Here the contrast is never commented on, but played to the absolute hilt in both Sid's performance and Talbot Rothwell's dialogue. The idea works superbly well and Sid James' screen image was set for the next decade.

As Robert Ross points out, Sidney James was transformed by his role in *Carry On Cleo* from a popular comedic character actor into an international leading man, enormously popular in Britain, his original homeland of South Africa and in Australia, the latter responding particularly well to the James rough-hewn charm.[3] Sid's new star status was a double-edged sword, as the smaller roles he happily took for a bit of extra cash soon dried up. However, as the British film industry contracted, far fewer of the bread-and-butter films that had provided him with a day's work were being made, so perhaps the huge success of *Carry On Cleo* came at just the right time. One hesitates to ascribe one individual piece as the masterwork of an actor with such a huge number of credits as Sid James—especially considering what an underrated dramatic actor he was. If, however, one had to point to one role to explain the lasting appeal of Sid, one could certainly do a lot worse than pop them in front of a recording of *Carry On Cleo*. Here they would see the Sid that the British took to their hearts as their roguish best mate.

It helped that Sid got on very well with his leading lady Amanda Barrie, who was nervous at taking on such a large role and much appreciated Sid's support and encouragement. In contrast to his lecherous public image, actresses who worked with Sid invariably found him professional and helpful. This was in contrast to Barrie's relationship with Kenneth Williams; the pair had not got on well in their previous encounter, recording sketches for a Peter Cook TV show, and Williams made sure to cause an argument on the *Carry On Cleo* set between them.[4] Personal relationships notwithstanding, Barrie gives a simply marvellous performance as Cleopatra, playing dumb but clearly being the smartest person in the room. It is a highly effective variation on the much smaller part she played as Anthea in *Carry On Cabby*, and this author doffs his cap to Peter Rogers and Gerald Thomas for having the vision and imagination to go with such offbeat casting.

Carry On Cleo also saw the return of Joan Sims to the series for the first time since 1961's *Carry On Regardless*, though she had worked on three other Rogers/Thomas films in the meantime. This gives us our first chance to see how Talbot Rothwell was to write for the actress, and on this occasion, he lands her with what is basically a nagging wife role. Her character Calpurnia retains the sympathy of the audience as she is stuck with Julius Caesar as her vain, stupid, and probably unfaithful husband, away for years at a time either conquering lands or attending to the far-reaches of his empire. There is more to the part than mere shrewish harridan, especially thanks to the casting of Charles Hawtrey as her psychic father Seneca, but this would be the first of several roles in which Rothwell would write her as a woman trying to hold on to a straying man. In *Carry On Cowboy* as Belle, she would compete with Angela Douglas for the affections of Sid James' Rumpo Kid, while in *Carry On Screaming*, her constantly complaining harpy Emily Bung cannot hope to compete against Fenella Fielding's (literally) smoking hot Valeria. It is certainly good to see Sims back in the Carry On cast however, where she would stay until the very end of the series' original run.

Jim Dale had been moving up the Carry On ranks for a few films now, having in recent years contributed a memorable cameo to *Carry On Jack* and proved a master of disguise in *Carry On Spying*, while still remaining on the periphery of the main cast. From here on, though, there is no doubt that not only is Dale firmly at the centre of the Carry On gang, but that he is almost absurdly talented. Handsome, athletic, and funny, Dale's youthful vigour adds a new dimension to the Carry On cast, which he would remain a central part of for the next five years. In *Cleo*, he forms a great comedic duo with Kenneth Connor, whose Hengist Pod is that classic comedy combination of a stupid man who is convinced of his own cleverness. Talbot Rothwell gives Connor a lot of material to work with here, Hengist's odyssey taking him from maker of square wheels to Julius Caesar's trusted bodyguard. This allows the actor to play several character-types which he was very good at, from cocksure idiot to cringing coward. Kenneth Connor might not be the actor one comes away from *Carry On Cleo* remembering, but it would certainly be a much poorer movie without him.

Carry On Cleo was nothing less than a triumph for the entire Carry On cast and crew, and especially for Talbot Rothwell, who crams so many gags into his script that not only does he keep a large cast of regulars serviced, but he adds still more jokes to the opening credits and to E. V. H. Emmett's narration—Emmett, largely forgotten now, was a radio newsreader and the voice of the Gaumont British company's newsreels, seen at British cinemas for many years. Rothwell had enough comedic invention to spare to write good roles for the likes of Warren Mitchell as slave merchant Spencius (partner of Marcus), Jon Pertwee as a soothsayer, and Carry On semi-regular Tom Clegg as Cleopatra's hulking bodyguard Sosages. Some gags were very much of their time and would be missed by most modern audiences, especially a scene in which Julius Caesar makes a speech to the Roman senate. Kenneth Williams breaks into the rambling, drawling style of Harold MacMillan, British prime minister from 1957 to 1963, before in frustration breaking into MacMillan's 1957 election-winning slogan 'You've never had it so good'.

A degree of unexpected publicity for *Carry On Cleo* was generated when 20th Century Fox, producers of *Cleopatra*, filed a legal suit against the film's producers and distributors, Anglo-Amalgamated and Warner-Pathé. Although *Cleopatra* had opened in British cinemas back in July 1963, with the film being heavily publicised for some six months prior, the film was still doing the rounds of cinemas when *Carry On Cleo* opened in North London on 17 January 1965.

Normally the fact that *Carry On Cleo*'s poster art, by Tom Chantrell, was clearly a close parody of the original Cleopatra poster would not have been too much of a problem and Fox would have had little cause for legal redress. *Cleopatra*'s poster turned out to be quite an unusual case, as Fox based their poster on an existing painting by Howard Terpning, for which they had bought the copyright. Despite Anglo and Warner-Pathé hiring a top legal team, represented in court by Maurice Drake and Quintin Hogg QC (the latter soon to become a prominent politician, better known as Lord Hailsham), the resemblance was rather too strong and a court injunction was granted by Mr Justice Plowman on 21 January, preventing the Chantrell poster from being used. A hastily done, but actually quite clever and attractive photomontage poster was put together by Ray Young in its stead. The attendant publicity certainly cannot have done the box-office prospects of *Carry On Cleo* any harm.

12

Carry On Cowboy (1965)

Filming Dates: 17 July 1965–3 September 1965
Original Certificate: A (Classified by BBFC 21 October 1965 [cut])
Running Time: 92 minutes 5 seconds

Release Details

London release: 24 March 1966 (Carlton Cinema, Haymarket, London—replacing a run of *Our Man Flint*).

The Rotary Club branch at Tonbridge Wells, Kent, had hoped to present the world premiere of *Carry On Cowboy* at the town's Ritz Cinema on 30 March. As events transpired, the screening went ahead, attended by television, stage, and film comedian Richard Hearne, aka 'Mr. Pastry', but it was not the premiere. The Carlton Cinema in London's Haymarket had found that takings for their current offering, the spoof spy thriller *Our Man Flint*, had dropped off so much that they brought forward their run of *Carry On Cowboy* to 24 March.[1]

The general release of *Carry On Cowboy* in the UK began from 1 April, supported by another of the last batch of Edgar Wallace crime movies. This was *Change Partners*, directed by Robert Lynn whose next assignment would be to helm six episodes of the Gerry Anderson puppet SF series *Captain Scarlet and the Mysterons*. In *Change Partners*, an adulterous couple become killers and are subsequently blackmailed by a petty crook. Zena Walker, Kenneth Cope, and Anthony Dawson are featured.

What's Carrying On?

Stodge City is the safest town in the west thanks to the mayorship of Judge Burke, who does not allow either guns or alcohol. The mild west becomes the Wild West when Johnny Finger, the Rumpo Kid, arrives in town, setting up base at Belle's Saloon and shooting dead Sheriff Albert Earp when the lawman tries to kick him out of town. With crime rampant, Judge Burke calls Washington, D.C. for help, but no US marshals are available until Marshal P. Knutt walks through the wrong door and is mistaken for a peace officer rather than his true calling as a sanitary engineer. When he is sent to clean up Stodge City, Knutt does not realise until he arrives that he is not there to sort out the drains. Helped by Albert Earp's daughter Annie Oakley, he must fight the local Indian tribe, the Rumpo Kid and his band of gunslingers, and his own clumsiness to stay alive and clean up Stodge.

Who's Carrying On?

A Peter Rogers Production
Director: Gerald Thomas
Screenplay by Talbot Rothwell
Music composed by Eric Rogers
Songs: 'Carry On Cowboy' and 'This is the Night for Love', music by Eric Rogers, lyrics by Alan Rogers
Photography by Alan Hume BSC
Art Director: Bert Davey
Editor: Rod Keys
Sidney James: Johnny Finger, aka the Rumpo Kid. The toughest, meanest gunslinger in all the West, who descends on Stodge City and turns it from the dullest town in the west to the most dangerous.
Kenneth Williams: Judge Burke, mayor of Stodge City. Strictly speaking, his family name is Wright-Burke, which is pretty appropriate. Under his watch, there is 'No Shootin', No Fightin', No Boozin', No Nothin',' until the Rumpo Kid turns up.
Jim Dale: Marshal P. Knutt, sent by Washington to clean up Stodge City—trouble is, he is not a US marshal, but a sanitation engineer. As a lawman, he is a load of rubbish, but if he does not shape up soon, he will go down the drain.
Charles Hawtrey: Chief Big Heap, the poshest Indian chief in the world, who would not hurt a fly until he starts drinking 'Firewater'. This turns him into a bloodthirsty warrior—until things start getting too dangerous.
Joan Sims: Belle Armitage, who owns the local saloon, keeps a pistol in her cleavage, and immediately falls for the Rumpo Kid—until the Kid's head is turned by the arrival of Annie Oakley.

Angela Douglas: Annie Oakley, gun-toting daughter of recently deceased Stodge City sheriff Albert Earp, out for revenge and not above using her feminine charms to get close to the man who killed him.

Bernard Bresslaw: Little Heap, son of Chief Big Heap, a hulking, fearsome warrior, though perhaps not the brightest member of the Indian nations.

Peter Butterworth: Doc, card-playing crony of Judge Burke and a card-carrying coward.

Carry On Critics

The *Monthly Film Bulletin* gave its usual amused but disapproving verdict on the film in its March 1966 edition:

> There are some quite clever and amusing ideas, but an even heavier than usual reliance on outrageous puns and not particularly subtle *double entendres*. This, in fact, is the nearest-the-knuckle of the series, and some of the gags make the 'A' certificate eminently reasonable.

The Times, reviewing the film on 24 March 1966 on its opening at the Carlton Cinema, was unusually effusive in its praise: 'This latest "Carry On" film is easily the best of their parodies, mainly because the target is larger'. Certain cast members were singled out for special praise: 'Special delights are Charles Hawtrey as a spectacularly unlikely Indian chief and Joan Sims as a bar-room belle'. Jim Dale's talents were also recognised in terms that indicated the future success he would find outside the film series: 'He is really very funny—he has the irresistibly expressive face and body of a born clown.'

'Never have the puns been more outrageous, the off-colour jokes more brazenly delivered. It may not actually be good, but for anyone with a taste for old-style English corn it all feels comfortingly like home,' said Richard Roud in *The Guardian* (Friday 28 March), who also took the film to task for what he viewed as dirty jokes: 'The film is distinguished by the largest number of obscene double-entendres that has ever, I believe, graced the cinema,'

Variety's reviewer was rather more cautious in his praise for *Carry On Cowboy*:

> Story, though familiar nonsense, is less a string of irrelevant situations than usual, giving the team more opportunity for comedy thesping ... Although filmed on a common in Surrey the 'Wild West locations' are adequately authentic, and Alan Hume's color lensing gives an extra touch of class.

Another review of the film from across the Atlantic came from *The Province*, a daily newspaper serving the Canadian province of British Columbia. In the paper's edition of Saturday, 21 May 1966, Lorne Parton was not pleased with this British spin on a very American genre:

> The whole Carry On bit has been done to death, and Cowboy is a suitable epitaph: A good idea gone astray … In essence, *Carry On Cowboy* is an Englishman's cross between *The Three Stooges* and *Destry Rides Again*. Even if it is outrageously tongue-in-cheek, the Brit's version of a western drawl is about as painful as the average American's 'Oh, I sye' version of an English accent. All in all a good movie to stay away from.

Carry On Comments

With *Carry On Cleo* a smash hit both in the UK and abroad, the Carry Ons embarked on a series of historical mini-epics based not so much on actual historical events, but each one instead taking the mickey out of a different movie genre. The next in line for the Carry On treatment was the Hollywood Western, which was by 1965 something of a dying genre, its greatest stars ageing leftovers from the 1940s such as James Stewart and John Wayne. As it happened, the genre remained hugely popular in mainland Europe, and a small production shot in Spain by Italian filmmakers, led by director Sergio Leone, had been making huge waves since its release in September 1964. This film, *A Fistful of Dollars*, would not be released in Britain until June 1967, and by the time *Carry On Cowboy* was released, Clint Eastwood was merely Rowdy Yates, star of the soon-to-be-cancelled TV Western *Rawhide*.

The Western remained a genre ripe for satire, and Peter Rogers, Gerald Thomas, and Talbot Rothwell took aim at their target, both barrels loaded with gags. Rothwell took a similar approach to his subject as he had with *Carry On Cleo*, constructing a plot that allowed each of the main cast members to have plenty to do, while loading the script with a quite incredible number of gags of varying, but surprisingly high, quality. Interestingly, there are occasional, purely accidental similarities between *Carry On Cowboy* and *A Fistful of Dollars*. Both attempt, in very different ways, a deconstruction and blackly comic reworking of beloved Hollywood Western tropes. Both works also feature a comic funeral director character, in the case of *Carry On Cowboy* played by Davy Kaye like a Jewish tailor, overjoyed at the increase in trade since the arrival of the Rumpo Kid.

As ever, Peter Rogers worked to assemble as many of his regular cast members as possible, one of whom was returning to work after a break necessitated by family tragedy. Charles Hawtrey gave a sparkling performance as Chief Big Heap under very difficult circumstances after his eighty-four-year-old mother Alice Hartree died in hospital on 10 March following a fall at home. This was caused by a combination of her advancing dementia, alcohol, and a habit of tottering around on very high heels. Hawtrey was truly heartbroken; as his mother's carer, he blamed himself for not being there to prevent the fatal accident. Very unusually, he backed out of an acting job he had been contracted for—by this point, he worked so seldom outside of the Carry On films that this was a major decision—and *Carry On Cowboy* represented his return to work after the trauma he had undergone. Nobody would have known watching the film that the cheerful sprite they saw on screen was anything other than a happy soul, despite Talbot Rothwell rather pointedly writing Chief Big Heap as being overly fond of 'firewater'. Hawtrey was, indeed, on his best form, forming a very effective double act with Bernard Bresslaw. Most of Bernard was making his Carry On debut, though you will recall that his feet were featured in *Carry On Nurse* back in 1959.

Carry On Cowboy proved a very popular production among the cast, with Sid James regarding it as his favourite of the entire series.[2] Although the film was a broad satire on the Western genre, it still took its basic dramatic structure from those films and gave Sid the opportunity to flex dramatic muscles that had long remained unexercised since the British public took James to its heart as a comedy star. Only Sid James could have played the Rumpo Kid; no one else had the mixture of toughness and comedic skills the role required—before being typecast as a comedy star, Sid was being cast in just this type of rough, outdoorsy part in dramatic films. Although Sid always gave of his best, there is a special relish about his performance in *Carry On Cowboy*.

He also appreciated the hard work put in by Jim Dale as the film's hero, Marshal P. Knutt, sent to clean up the town as a drainage engineer, not as a lawman. Dale's roles in the Carry On films had steadily been getting larger, and since his strong performance in *Carry On Cleo*, it had become clear that here was a handsome young leading man and a hugely talented physical comedian able to carry the load of being the audience's point of identification. Already a highly experienced stage comedian, Dale was perfectly aware that he had to put the work in to make apparently simple gags work while the cameras were rolling. Thus while Sid was practicing his quick draw technique behind the sets, he came across Jim working on being the lousiest draw in the west, a throwaway gag in which his pistol is drawn facing him, taking weeks of practice in order to work on the first take. The hard work paid off, as Dale gets some extremely good/bad jokes on the level of 'You've got to take a posse with you', 'Why, don't they like cats?'

Dale also gets to show off his hard-won physical skills, not only with his trick gunplay sight gags. With his skinny build, flailing arms, and long legs, here Jim Dale has an almost cartoonish physicality worthy of the great silent comedians that suits the material perfectly. It helps that Dale is provided with his perfect leading lady in the shape of Angela Douglas, making the first of her four Carry On film appearances. As Annie Oakley, vengeance-seeking daughter of slain Stodge City sheriff Albert Earp, Douglas has to be part Doris Day in *Calamity Jane*, part English rose, and a tiny bit Marlene Dietrich in *Destry Rides Again*. She outshoots Chief Big Heap's Indian braves, while looking both innocent and sexy at the same time as she emerges from her room at Belle's Saloon in basque and feathers to sing 'This is the night for love'. She hooks Sid immediately, who immediately promises Annie the world: 'I'll buy you diamonds, furs ... I'll even shave every day!'

Joan Sims' Belle is, for a while at least, outshone, leading to a strange but very funny dialogue sequence by Talbot Rothwell as Belle begs Sid to stay with her in increasingly outlandish and flowery terms: 'Don't turn our story into a burning tale of lust, jealousy and passion under a white hot desert sun. Don't make it a saga of sex, vengeance and sudden death in the primitive West.' It is silly and pointless, but almost inexplicably funny.

Joan Sims arrived on the Pinewood Studios set having just finished a West End run in the musical *Instant Marriage*, her role having been taken up by future Carry On star Patsy Rowlands. Featuring music by Laurie Holloway, *Instant Marriage* was written and directed by its star, Bob Grant, who, four years later, would find national fame playing cheeky bus conductor Jacko in the long-running sitcom, *On the Buses*. Grant was something of a theatrical hot property at the time, coming off the back of a prominent role in Lionel Bart's hit musical *Blitz! Instant Marriage* opened at the Piccadilly Theatre on 1 August 1964 and despite some poor reviews ran for a very respectable 366 performances. The cast also included Wallace Eaton, who had already achieved comedic immortality as the regular announcer on *The Goon Show*. For the production, Sims was decked out in some very glamorous dresses, which showed off Sims' legs to their best advantage—these costumes were interestingly similar to the nineteenth century-inspired costumes designed for her by Cynthia Tingley in *Carry On Cowboy*.

Joan Sims was at the height of her career and looking absolutely ravishing. As with Sid James, Joan Sims was also to regard *Carry On Cowboy* her favourite in the series. She loved her costumes and hairstyling in the film so much that she had publicity photographs from the film especially printed, which she gave out to fans for many years.[3]

Kenneth Williams played his role as Judge Burke rather differently to his previous Carry On roles, playing the part rather older than his thirty-nine years with the help of greyed hair, a thick moustache, and a rasping voice. The latter was based on film producer Hal Roach, who had produced the classic Laurel and Hardy comedies in the 1920s and '30s and was still active in the 1960s; he lived to a ripe old age and died in 1992 at the age of 100. Williams was rather worried that the approach he had taken for the role of Burke may have been mistaken, especially after having trouble with the sound recordist on set over his vocalisation.[4] During filming, he began to regret his choice, regarding the voice he was using as being too old for his face, and thinking that he was unfunny and miscast, suggesting that Sidney Bromley (who played cattleman Sam Houston) would have been better in the part.[5]

By the following February, when Williams saw *Carry On Cowboy* in a trade showing, he had warmed considerably to the production and used his diaries to join the chorus of approval from his fellow cast members: 'It was marvellous. It's the first good British comedy in years, the first time a British Western has ever been done, and the first Carry On to be a success on every level'.[6]

On one count, Williams was mistaken, as British Westerns, while hardly being a common sight at cinemas, did actually exist before *Carry On Cowboy*, with at least seven having been made between 1899 and the release of *Carry On Cowboy* in 1966. *Ramsbottom Rides Again* (1956), a comedy vehicle for Arthur Askey, had even featured Sid James as its gun-toting villain, while *The Sheriff of Fractured Jaw*, two years later, featured Kenneth More and Jayne Mansfield in a story very similar to that of *Carry On Cowboy*. Another notable effort was *Savage Guns*, a 1961 British Western directed by Michael Carreras, on a hiatus from his career at Hammer Films, which was headed by his father Sir James Carreras. This latter production was especially important in the history of the genre, as it was the first Western to be shot in the Spanish province of Almeria, which a few years later became the centre of the Spaghetti Western boom.

As if to make up for the lack of Kenneth Connor, both here and in the next few Carry On films, we are treated to the debut of what was to become a new series regular in the form of Peter Butterworth, an actor who would become an absolute bedrock of the series right through to its end in 1979. Here Butterworth plays 'Doc', a town elder and crony of Kenneth Williams' Judge Burke. He and Williams are largely written to play off each other and Butterworth fits in perfectly right from his opening scene. Similarly, as mentioned earlier, Bernard Bresslaw joins the team in *Carry On Cowboy*, and it is like he has been there all along. A burly man (far more so than the beanpole-thin figure he had cut a few years earlier in *The Army Game*) of over 6 feet 7 inches in height, Bresslaw was also presented in his Carry On debut largely as part of a double act. In this case, he cut a fierce and physically imposing figure as Little Heap, son of the tiny, frightfully posh Charles Hawtrey as Chief Big Heap. Their physical disparity was an immediate source of visual humour, and as would become clear in future films, Bresslaw was a talented actor somewhat pigeonholed in the role of the big dope.

While Bernard Bresslaw made a big impression playing it relatively straight, Jon Pertwee played his role as Sheriff Albert Earp absolutely as broadly as possible. Half blind, three-quarters deaf, and crashing into walls, doors, and furniture at every opportunity, Pertwee manages to make Earp even less subtle than his role as the soothsayer in *Carry On Cleo*. In the context of a cameo in a Carry On picture, this was entirely appropriate; Pertwee makes a big impression in a small amount of screen time, being plugged by the Kid and out of the film before he can become annoying.

An interesting factor about *Carry On Cowboy* is its direction by Gerald Thomas. In order for the central conceit of the film to work, it had to really look like a Western rather than a comedy, with dramatic camera-angles and editing at key moments. While Gerald Thomas has directed dramas previously since being promoted to the director's chair by Peter Rogers, these were novice efforts varying wildly in quality and entertainment value. It shows how much Thomas had grown as a director since the Carry On series began some seven years earlier that probably the strongest dramatic direction of his entire career is contained within *Carry On Cowboy*. In one way, the film remained a minor blot on his career, as heavy rain on the first day of filming meant that this was the only production in the series to overrun its shooting schedule. The Carry On production schedules were planned with such military precision in order to keep costs down that there was simply no slack to take up, thus the shooting ran a day over schedule.

As well as being a general satire on the Western genre, in its final section, *Carry On Cowboy* takes specific aim at one of the all-time classic Hollywood Westerns—director Fred Zinnemann's 1952 classic *High Noon*. This was a cinematic reference that almost everyone in *Carry On Cowboy's* 1966 audience would have understood immediately. Although the film's original UK release had been fourteen years earlier, *High Noon* had been screened by BBC Television on Christmas Day 1959 and on 29 October 1961 and its reputation remained high. As the film is now approaching seventy years old and films of the classic Hollywood era are not seen on television so often these days, a few words of explanation would not go amiss.

In *High Noon*, Sheriff Will Kane (Gary Cooper) spends most of the film trying in vain to get the townsfolk of Hadleyville to stand with him against violent criminal Frank Miller, who is due in on the noon train to meet up with his henchmen. Ever efficient, Gerald Thomas deals with this in a single scene in which the people of Stodge City refuse to help Marshall Knutt and run away. As the appointed hour nears, Zinnemann showed us clocks, first as a background detail, eventually in stark close up. This is another detail that Gerald Thomas purposefully copies for comedic effect, at first because the shot was so famous, then because the Stodge City clock was a cuckoo clock, its bird obliterated by the suddenly deadly accurate Knutt. *High Noon* eventually bursts into action with its climactic gunfight, in which we learn just what a tough and wily customer Will Kane is. Instead of walking to his death in a traditional gun duel in the main streets, we see Kane use his knowledge of the backstreets of Hadleyville to outwit and outgun his opponents. In what was a very clever stroke by Talbot Rothwell, sanitary engineer turned gun-toting lawman Knutt uses his knowledge of Stodge City's drains to sneak around underneath the villains and ultimately triumph. At one stroke, Rothwell not only managed to make his main character's weakness into a strength, but also pushes the *High Noon* parallel just a bit further.

Talbot Rothwell may have been an absolute gag machine, but beyond that he was an intelligent writer who, at his peak, wrote scripts of a greater complexity than is generally acknowledged.

13

Carry On Screaming! (1966)

Filming Dates: 10 January 1966–25 February 1966
Original Certificate: A (Classified by BBFC 15 April 1966 [uncut—ironically for a horror comedy])
Running Time: 94 minutes 29 seconds

Release Details

London Release: 18 August 1966 (New Victoria Cinema, Westminster, London).

Carry On Screaming! began to haunt the cinemas of Britain from 24 August, but Anglo-Amalgamated had to decide what to run alongside it after the demise of their Edgar Wallace co-features. It was decided to pair *Screaming* with director William Asher's American stock car racing drama *Fireball 500.* This was an attempt by American International Pictures to place the stars of its light and fluffy Beach Party series of films into a slightly grittier drama. Director William Asher put Frankie Avalon, Annette Funicello, and Fabian through their paces. *Carry On Screaming!* would be the last of the Carry On films to run on the ABC circuit, as the series' subsequent move to The Rank Organisation meant that it moved to that company's Odeon chain of cinemas.

What's Carrying On?

Young women are disappearing from the woods, and when Doris Mann is the latest to be kidnapped, the henpecked Detective Sergeant Sidney Bung and his assistant Slowbotham suspect her boyfriend Albert Potter. Strange deeds are afoot, however, at the Bide-A-Wee rest home, the home of Dr Orlando Watt and his sister Vareria. The Watts' pet monster, Oddbod, is kidnapping the women for Dr Watt to turn into waxen figures, which he sells as shop dummies. With the police's finest on the case, following the trail of bodies, it is only a matter of time before Bung of the Yard gets his man, or possibly his woman, if he can get away from his wife.

Who's Carrying On?

A Peter Rogers Production
Director: Gerald Thomas
Screenplay by Talbot Rothwell
Music composed by Eric Rogers
Photography by Alan Hume BSC
Art Director: Bert Davey
Editor: Rod Keys

Harry H. Corbett: Detective Sergeant Sidney Bung, the second dimmest detective that the police force has to offer, hen-pecked by his wife and swayed by the charms of Valeria Watt.

Kenneth Williams: Doctor Orlando Watt, who does not let the fact that he is dead get in the way of a successful career making wax dummies from live women.

Jim Dale: Albert Potter, prime suspect in the disappearance of a series of young women after Oddbod walks off with his girlfriend, Doris. He exclaims his innocence and claims to have seen her in a shop window.

Charles Hawtrey: Daniel Dann, lavatorial technical operative extraordinary. Possibly the most dapper lavatory attendant in England, until the arrival of Oddbod means his career is about to go down the drain.

Fenella Fielding: Valeria Watt, sister of Orlando and the slinkiest vamp imaginable, poured daily into a red velvet dress. It should be warned that she has a terrible smoking habit.

Joan Sims: Emily Bung, Sidney Bung's harridan-like wife who never seems to leave her bed except to check up on what her husband is up to.

Angela Douglas: Doris Mann, the latest kidnap-victim of the Watts—can Bung and Potter save her from her waxen fate? Probably, to be honest.

Bernard Bresslaw: Sockett, the Watt's hulking, zombified butler who appears to have a very close relationship with Valeria Watt.

Peter Butterworth: Detective Constable Slowbotham, Bung's assistant and absolutely the dimmest detective in the entire police force. Also makes a really unattractive woman!

Carry On Critics

The *Monthly Film Bulletin* reviewer gave *Carry On Screaming!* the bird in no uncertain terms, but whomever the anonymous scribe was appears to have been no fan of the series:

> Apart from an engaging performance by Jim Dale (and some appealing squeaks from monster Odbodd Junior, alias Billy Cornelius), this is glum stuff even by Carry On standards. The regulars, Kenneth Williams in particular, seem too bored to care. Harry H. Corbett overdoes every line, and the horror clichés are rather less amusing than the straight routines in some of Hammer's early epics.

How anyone can accuse the kinetic, hyperactive Williams of appearing bored is, frankly, beyond me, but there you are.

Amusingly, considering the last-minute nature of his casting, Charles Hawtrey was singled out for particular praise: 'Charles Hawtrey is completely winning as a very eager lavatory attendant (come and see me at my convenience). His short appearance is imbued with such concentrated suggestiveness that he manages to steal the picture single-handed'.

Ben Harrison in the March 1967 edition of *Films and Filming* could not have offered a more diametrically opposite opinion:

> The funniest characterisation of the film is not that of the bumbling local detective sergeant [Harry H. Corbett], a role which is bound by its obviousness to be overacted, but that of Dr What who combines his bloodthirsty metier, the mummification of young girls, with such matter-of-fact relish and cozy charm that the resultant contrast is very funny.

Harrison was considerably less amused by the scenes between Sgt Bung and his nagging wife: 'It is less funny and at times embarrassingly so when dealing with the more conventional characters, especially in the terrible scenes between Harry H. Corbett and his wife. These portray the worst British clichés about matrimonial strife'.

The Times reviewed the film on Thursday 18 August, on the opening of *Carry On Screaming*'s London run at the New Victoria cinema; the tone of the paper's review can be judged by the title of the printed article: 'The Farce that Failed'. *The Times*'s critic wrote:

> It is disappointing ... that this new addition to the series is one of the dullest and least spirited of them all ... Even such usually funny fellows as Kenneth Williams and Jim Dale as the innocent at large never manage to hit the right note, while Joan Sims is entirely wasted as a cliché harridan.

One cannot help but agree on that last point, but at least the anonymous *Times* reviewer had some kind words to say about Fenella Fielding: 'When Miss Fielding is around as the Doctor's fiendishly resourceful sister one can see how the film might have worked'.

Penelope Gilliatt in *The Observer*'s Sunday 21 August edition was similarly unenthusiastic, describing *Carry On Screaming!*:

> An instalment that messes about with the conventions of the series and lays an egg ... I'm not sure if it's a good idea for a Carry On picture to do something so deliberate as a send-up of anything, let alone of a form that is already as silly as a horror film. The progress is mostly slothful and worried when it should be cheerfully cavalier and pointless.

Variety reckoned it saw a similar problem with the basic premise of the film:

> Snag is that most horror films themselves teeter on parody and it is rather tough trying to burlesque a parody ... Gerald Thomas' direction as usual is assured, though some of the gags and situations would be helped by speeding up via more ruthless trimming.

Two of *Carry On Screaming*'s actors came in for special praise: 'Corbett mugs a great deal but the role demands it and Fielding as the grisly vamp glitters with an overdone seductiveness which is often funny.'

Carry On Comments

Carry On Screaming! continued the series of movie spoofs that had proved so popular with *Cleo* and *Cowboy*, this time poking fun at the horror films which made the small company Hammer films internationally famous after their huge successes with *The Curse of Frankenstein* in 1957 and *Dracula* in 1958. Such was the nature of the British film industry that there was quite a lot of cross-pollination between the Hammer operation and the regular crew of the Carry On films, for example *Screaming*'s film editor, Rod Keys, was the brother of Anthony Nelson Keys, regular producer of Hammer's gothic horrors. Even more importantly, Alan Hume, cinematographer on the Carry Ons, had been director of photography on Hammer's *Kiss of the Vampire* three years earlier. This, and the fact that Hammer's productions tended to be barely any more expensive to make than the Carry Ons, meant that reproducing the look of Hammer's gothic horrors would be a relatively simple matter.

Talbot Rothwell went further back in horror history for story inspiration, in effect taking his basic plot from the 1933 Warner Brothers classic *The*

Mystery of the Wax Museum, which was very unusual in its day for being a horror picture shot in an early version of the Technicolor process. This was then remade to great success in both colour and 3D as *House of Wax*, starring Vincent Price, while yet another version was in production in Hollywood at about the same time as *Carry On Screaming*, this time as a television pilot film which was eventually released to cinemas in October 1966 under the title *Chamber of Horrors*. Rothwell's twist on the story meant that instead of producing human waxworks for a wax museum, Dr Orlando Watt (whose name seems to have been a joke aimed at the BBC's *Doctor Who*) is making them to sell as shop dummies. The result continued the run of successes for both Rothwell's movie spoofs and for Peter Rogers Productions, who deservedly had another big hit on their hands.

If the filming of *Carry On Cowboy* represented a return to work for Charles Hawtrey after a period of personal trauma, this time the same was true of Kenneth Williams. Williams originally had slight trepidations about taking on the role of Dr Orlando Watt when it was initially offered by Peter Rogers. The character was written, like Judge Burke in *Carry On Cowboy*, as an older man, the father of Valeria Watt, a role that had already been offered to Fenella Fielding. He was not keen to repeat his experience on that film, where Williams was dissatisfied with his own performance and what he saw as the contrast between the raspy, older man's voice he affected and his relatively young face. Rogers was happy to accede, and it was a simple matter to alter the script so that the Watts were brother and sister instead of father and daughter.

Before filming began at Pinewood in January 1966, Williams had another commitment, having agreed to play the lead role of Bernard in Roger Longrigg's stage comedy *The Platinum Cat*. Longrigg was a hugely experienced writer, far more so than most people realised due to the novelist and playwright's habit of writing under a slew of pen names. Despite this, there were worries that Longrigg's script for *Platinum Cat* was not strong enough, and this began to prey on the mind of Williams, along with the inexperience of his co-star Caroline Mortimer. On top of this, personal insecurities brought on by his nerves and fragile mental state caused Williams to adopt an almost starvation diet for weeks on end. The actor's health began to suffer. After falling on stage and suffering a cut under his eye during the previous night's performance, Williams withdrew from the play on 7 December 1965.

Whatever the physical and mental reasons behind Williams' health problems, they were clearly serious: the actor had barely missed a single performance during his entire career to this point. This would have been well-known in the industry, and Kenneth Williams commented in his diaries on the warm and sympathetic welcome he received from both cast and crew on his arrival to the *Carry On Screaming!* set, which represented his return to work after the debacle of *Platinum Cat*.[1] The experience seems to have brought on some form of nervous breakdown that some friends of Williams were later to comment that he never truly recovered from and may even have set him on the road to an eventual suicide.[2]

While Williams was in better spirits by the time the cameras began rolling on *Carry On Screaming!* and was eating normally once again, even under the thick make-up he wore in both films, the effects of his recent health problems can clearly be seen on screen. The actor is much thinner in the face, a phenomenon which perhaps escaped public comment as the resulting emaciated look and make up-induced deathly pallor suited the character of Dr Watt perfectly.

Meanwhile, Charles Hawtrey almost was not in the film at all, not this time because of a contract dispute, but (so the official story went) because Peter Rogers and Gerald Thomas simply could not find a role for him in Talbot Rothwell's script. One might speculate that the actor's increasingly frequent on-set drinking was a major factor. Perhaps this was meant to be a shot across Hawtrey's bows in an attempt to get the actor to clean up his act, or perhaps a permanent demotion from the Carry On ranks was planned.

Either way, when news of the cast list of the latest Carry On production made its way to the industry and its trade reporters, there was some comment on the subject of its missing cast member. A small article by C. H. B. Williamson appeared in *Today's Cinema* decrying the news and wondering if the absence of Hawtrey might have an adverse effect on the box office takings of *Carry On Screaming!*. Bearing in mind that the film was already labouring under the lack of Sidney James (of which more later), it is possible that Williamson might have had a point. The last film in the series to lack a significant number of regular cast members, *Carry On Jack*, was a very well-produced comedy, but somewhat lacked the Carry On feel.

There is considerable irony in the fact that, after all his attempts at improving his position with both Peter Rogers and various long-suffering BBC producers, Charles Hawtrey finally won a victory without even having to try. Stuart Levy of Anglo-Amalgamated appealed to Peter Rogers, nervous of any development which might damage the distributor's most profitable franchise, and suddenly Charles Hawtrey was back in the Carry On fold.[3] This development caused some problems for Rogers and Thomas as it came so late in the production schedule that all the major roles in the film had been filled. Someone had to go, and the unlucky actor was Sidney Bromley, who had impressed Kenneth Williams so much in the role of Sam Houston in *Carry On Cowboy*. He had been cast as the ill-fated toilet attendant Daniel Dann (Dan Dann, the lavatory man), a part that had the advantage of interacting with only a few other cast members in a scene which was to be shot late in the *Screaming* schedule.

In fact, Hawtrey had somewhat taken umbrage at the nature of his role and the way he had been treated by the producers. Professionally, at least, Hawtrey loathed lavatorial humour and viewed the part of Dan Dann as being beneath his standards—though not enough to turn the part down. In the highly unusual position of being in a strong negotiating position, Hawtrey demanded recompense, which he received in the form of an envelope containing £50 in cash.[4] Despite his late casting and the hovering suspicion that he remained in the Carry On cast under sufferance, Hawtrey absolutely sparkles in the role, looking spick and span in a very smart uniform, which helps to remove any suspicion that the role might be beneath him. For the time being, Hawtrey has weathered the storm and the Carry On series remained for the next few years the life raft that kept his career afloat.

As mentioned earlier, one actor who was conspicuous by his absence from *Carry On Screaming!* was Sidney James, whose position as the head of the Carry On cast was undisputed, but complicated by his busy stage and screen career. The scheduling of the Carry On films was always based around the availability of the regular cast members, but this time Sid was simply unavailable and nothing could be done about it. The busy actor had two major items in his diary at this point: a stage success and a television series that would help cement Sid's status as Britain's most popular comedy actor. The first of these was a pantomime which, in retrospect, featured a quite remarkable array of talent. *Babes in the Wood* saw Sid partnered with Kenneth Connor as a pair of bumbling assassins in a cast that also featured Australian singing star Frank Ifield, comedy legend Arthur Askey, and future comedy legend Roy Kinnear, whose star was on the rise after his appearances in the sensationally popular BBC television satire *That Was the Week That Was*. Even the music was star-studded, being supplied by top pop band The Shadows. *Babes in the Wood* proved a big draw, with an extended run at the London Palladium beginning on 21 December 1965 and finally ending on 29 April 1966.

Sid was reaching new heights of popularity; although elevated to the status of comedy star by the Tony Hancock radio series before he had joined the Carry On cast, he had never scored a popular success as a solo star, despite the BBC's attempts with *Citizen James* and *Taxi!* After spending most of his broadcasting career with the BBC, it was to be with the corporation's great rivals ITV that he finally achieved a television success of his own after his painful rejection by Hancock.

Even then, it was not strictly speaking a solo vehicle that finally made a television star of Sidney James (not that Sid cared about such distinctions—no ego-driven actor was he), as *George and the Dragon* was designed to be a comedic clash of personalities between the bloke-ish appeal of Sid and Peggy Mount, Britain's foremost screen battleaxe. It is interesting to note the difference between Sid's screen character in the Carry Ons and his *George and the Dragon* characterisation. The sitcom presented Sid squarely as a (rather over-age) laddish letch, while the Carry Ons had largely presented him as variations on the authority figure over the rest of the cast which he had originally been cast as in *Carry On Constable*. One cannot help but wonder how much this altered Sid's popular image and fed into how Talbot Rothwell wrote for him in future Carry On films. From this point until his next big sitcom hit, *Bless This House*, Sid's dominant screen image was boozy, laddish, and bird-chasing.

Written by Vince Powell and Harry Driver for Associated Television, *George and the Dragon* was a very big success for both Sid and the Lew Grade-headed television company that made it, running for twenty-six episodes over four series. The gruelling recording schedule for the series was not only to make Sid unavailable for *Carry On Screaming!*, but was to prove the straw that broke the camel's back for the health of its hard-working star. That is a tale for another chapter of this book, but it was somewhat fitting that while the demands of a hit television sitcom was to temporarily rob the Carry Ons of its star actor, the ending of another hit television comedy series was to provide *Carry On Screaming* with his replacement.

The BBC's hugely successful *Steptoe and Son* began as a pilot episode, first broadcast on 4 January 1962 as an episode of the series *Comedy Playhouse*. The series proper began on 14 June 1962, running to huge acclaim across four series until the final episode was broadcast on 15 November 1965. This left Harry H. Corbett, one of the two stars of the series, available to take the lead role in *Carry On Screaming*, which began shooting at Pinewood Studios on 10 January 1966.

Steptoe and Son had transformed the careers of its stars. The mixture of a perfectly cast pair of leading men and Ray Galton and Alan Simpson's scripts reaching once again the tragi-comic heights of their final series with Tony Hancock proved the recipe for a genuine television classic. Wilfrid Bramble had been a little-known Irish character actor working on British film, television and the stage, specialising since his forties as old men, and suddenly found himself a national institution. As the rancid old rag and bone man Albert Steptoe, he played opposite Harry H. Corbett as his son Harold—in reality, the two men were only thirteen years apart in age. Corbett (who had added the 'H' to his middle name to avoid confusion with Harry Corbett, the puppeteer behind children's favourite Sooty) had been a serious theatre actor who had worked at the renowned Joan Littlewood Theatre Workshop. His lead role in Littlewood's production of Shakespeare's *Richard II* was feted, and a career as a 'serious' actor appeared to await. This was all blown off course by the overwhelming success of *Steptoe and Son*, after which he was typecast for the rest of his life as a comedy performer.

At this period of British film history, almost any performer who had made a success on television was put on the big screen by studios in search of the next

Norman Wisdom. Thus Corbett joined the likes of Morecambe and Wise and Charlie Drake in pursuit of a film career. He was, however, a very different type of performer to those others, who were pure comedians, and his movie vehicles tended to be, to a greater or lesser extent, comedy-dramas. Films such as *The Bargee* and *The Rattle of a Simple Man* (both from 1964) and *Joey Boy* (made by Frank Launder and Sidney Gilliat for release in 1965) failed to shake off the Harold Steptoe image. The final film in this sequence does have one interesting Carry On connection, being the last movie Freddie Mills appeared in before his mysterious death in July 1965. By the time Corbett accepted the offer to appear in *Carry On Screaming!*, the movie offers had dried up, and this would be his final movie leading role.

By the following year, he was back on television in a sitcom designed especially for him by the ITV company Associated-Rediffusion. This was *Mr. Aitch*, which boasted a stellar writing team including Ray Galton & Alan Simpson, Dick Clement & Ian La Frenais, John Junkin, and future Carry On writer Dave Freeman. The series failed to catch the popular imagination and by 1970 Corbett, resigned to his fate, agreed to the BBC's offer to join Wilfrid Bramble in a revived *Steptoe and Son*. If anything, the series was an even bigger success than before, running to four more seasons and two spin-off feature films, cementing the series' reputation as a landmark in British comedy history.

Carry On Screaming! found Corbett once again as part of a double act, this time with Peter Butterworth, playing Detective Constable Slobotham, a kind of Watson to Corbett's Detective Sergeant Sidney Bung, who represents a sort of dim-witted Sherlock Holmes. Butterworth's role is much larger than in his series debut *Carry On Cowboy*, and it is clear that Talbot Rothwell had gained a much better handle on how to write for the actor. Butterworth's reaction shots are absolutely priceless, his supremely mobile features twitching to hilarious effect. The result is that Corbett and Barkworth represent two old pros thrown together and immediately forming a classic partnership. The pair work in such perfect synchronisation, as though they had been touring the variety circuit together for years.

Corbett is also paired here with Joan Sims, who has a relatively small role here as Emily Bung, Sidney's harridan of a wife. This is certainly quite a change from the glamorous roles Sims was given in earlier Carry On films, as Emily is shown as a screeching nag who appears to never leave her bed except to follow her husband to find out what he is up to. This second part of Sims' return to the Carry On fold is perhaps not the ideal role for her talents, but the actress throws herself into the part with great gusto, and bigger and better roles would follow—and she does get to throw a cheeky wink to the audience at the very end of the picture.

Another great partnership seen here is that between Jim Dale and Angela Douglas, though neither gets as much screen time here as they had in *Carry*

On Cowboy, where they proved themselves as the perfect juvenile leads for the Carry On series. They still manage one great scene together, their characters Albert and Doris courting in the woods before Doris is carried off by Dr Orlando Watt's square-headed scary (actually quite cute) monster Oddbod. Somehow, Douglas manages to make the most unlikely line of dialogue memorably comedic; 'There is something in those ... bushes' is a phrase which fans repeat to Angela Douglas to this day.

While Doris spends most of the film hidden away in Orlando Watt's basement laboratory (or substituted by a plastic dummy in a shop window), Jim Dale's Albert becomes the prime suspect in the disappearance of his girlfriend, helping the police with their enquiries until he eventually expands the Corbett and Butterworth comedy duo into a trio. Possibly the main performer associated in the public mind with *Carry On Screaming* is, however, Fenella Fielding as Valeria Watt, the ultimate British cinematic vamp and the role which the actress would be remembered for to the end of her days.

It almost goes without saying that Fenella Fielding is absolutely perfect as Valeria, a role which sees actress and role in perfect harmony. Of course, this was not Fielding's first Carry On role, as she had turned up in *Carry On Regardless* back in 1961 as Penny Panting, who hired the services of Kenneth Connor's Sam Twist from the Helping Hands Agency in order to make her husband jealous. It also was not the actress's first time performing as a glamorous character in a comedy horror film. Three years earlier, Fielding had appeared in *The Old Dark House*, a remake of James Whale's 1932 horror classic that had originally starred Boris Karloff. The remake brought together the talents of Hammer Films and famed American horror specialist William Castle, the latter having been responsible for a string of low-budget hits including *The House on Haunted Hill* and *Thirteen Ghosts*. Despite a decent cast, including American comic actor Tom Poston and Britain's Robert Morley, *The Old Dark House* proved a complete failure, taking three years to gain a British circuit release even at the height of Hammer's success and subsequently falling for many years into almost total obscurity.

Fenella Fielding also had history with Kenneth Williams. After leaving a violent and unhappy home life in 1952 to pursue her dream of becoming an actress, Fenella Fielding rose to theatrical star status in Sandy Wilson's musical adaptation of *Valmouth* in 1958. Although *Valmouth* gained good reviews, it made nothing like the popular impact of Wilson's previous hit musical *The Boy Friend*, which had transferred to Broadway. This left Fielding free to join the cast of *Pieces of Eight*, a review starring Kenneth Williams which featured material written by both Peter Cook and Harold Pinter. While *Pieces of Eight* proved popular, the ever-insecure Kenneth Williams clashed with his co-star when Fielding began getting laughs as big as the ones he was receiving from audiences. Later in 1959, she had even appeared opposite Sid James in the

Hancock's Half Hour radio episode 'The Poetry Society', though she was very unimpressed by Hancock's drinking, which would go on to engulf the actor's life and career.

Fenella Fielding's movie career never really progressed beyond playing languorously sexy comedy parts, including in three of the Doctor series of comedies. The final one of these had been shot only a short time before *Carry On Screaming!*, playing outrageous Russian prima ballerina Tatiana Rubikov in *Doctor in Clover*. Despite being prodigiously gifted—her work in Ibsen's *Hedda Gabler* and *A Doll's House* was feted—Fielding's stage career faded by the 1970s as her huge personality obscured her acting abilities. As Gyles Brandreth was later to point out, giving Fielding's eulogy, her career path in many ways mirrored that of Kenneth Williams.[5] Both were largely self-taught and self-educated and extremely distinctive in looks, personality, and vocal style—so much so that, despite being much-loved, both by the public and within the acting profession, they became almost impossible to cast in the straight dramatic roles they would have loved to be involved in. The long shadow cast by Fielding's role as Valeria Watt, regularly seen in television screenings of *Carry On Screaming* from the seventies onwards, did little to help matters, helping to crystallise her screen personality in its most extreme form.

Bernard Bresslaw, now firmly established as a member of the Carry On team in only his second credited appearance, here plays the Watt's butler, Sockett. The idea of a deep-voiced, zombified butler played by a 6-foot-7-inch-tall actor carries obvious parallels to modern audiences with the performance of Ted Cassidy as Lurch, the butler in the American TV series *The Addams Family*. This raises an interesting debate, as although the series was screened from 1964 to 1966 in the States, *The Addams Family* took a little longer to make its way to the UK, and still further to journey around the heavily regionalised ITV network. The first British screenings were in early January 1965 on Tyne Tees Television, covering the north-east of England, and it was October before the series reached London via its ITV contractor of the time, Redifussion London. By this time, Talbot Rothwell would have presumably been at an advanced stage in writing the Carry On Screaming script. I think in this case we can give both writer and actor a pass and say that the chances are that neither was aware of the American TV series and any similarities are—as movie credits are wont to say—coincidental.

14

Don't Lose Your Head (1967)

Filming Dates: 12 September 1966–28 October 1966
Original Certificate: A (Classified by BBFC 10 August 1967 [cut])
Running Time: 95 minutes 21 seconds

Release Details

London Release: 2 March 1967 (Leicester Square Theatre, London, replacing Dirk Bogarde and Stanley Baker in *Accident*).

Don't Lose Your Head played in the UK on the Odeon circuit with *The Reluctant Astronaut* as its support feature. This was a 1967 comedy made by Universal Pictures directed by Edward Montague starring Don Knotts as a cowardly janitor at Houston Space Centre who unexpectedly finds himself becoming an astronaut. The film had the misfortune to be premiered two days before the Apollo 1 disaster that killed three astronauts.

Who's Carrying On

A Peter Rogers Production
Director: Gerald Thomas
Screenplay by Talbot Rothwell
Music composed by Eric Rogers
Photography by Alan Hume BSC
Art Director: Lionel Couch
Editor: Rod Keys

Sidney James as Sir Rodney Ffing (pronounced 'Effing'), notorious fop, leader in men's fashion and womaniser who leads a double existence as the Black Fingernail, daring rescuer of French aristocrats from the guillotine.

Kenneth Williams as Citizen Camembert, hatchet-man of French revolutionary leader Robespierre charged with the task of capturing the Black Fingernail at all costs.

Jim Dale as Lord Darcy Pue, trusted friend of Sir Rodney and swashbuckling companion in his French adventures.

Charles Hawtrey as the Duc de Pommfrit, a naughty old aristocrat rescued by the Black Fingernail and spirited to safety in England.

Peter Butterworth as Citizen Bidet, second-in-command to Citizen Camembert who manages the amazing feat of being even more hapless than his boss.

Joan Sims as Désiree Dubarry, Camembert's sister who seeks to avoid the attentions of the Duc de Pommfrit and marry a nice, obscenely wealthy artistocrat.

Dany Robin as Jacqueline, rescued by the Black Fingernail from the French Revolutionary forces, so he can keep her for himself.

What's Carrying On

France, 1789, and with the French Revolution having toppled the power of the former monarch, the aristocracy are losing the heads on the guillotine. When word reaches notorious rake Sir Rodney Ffing via his tailor Henri (played by the decidedly un-French Michael Ward) of the terrible events that are taking place across the channel, he leaps into action with his compatriot Sir Darcy and becomes the swashbuckling adventurer and master of disguise the Black Fingernail. Under this secret identity, Sir Rodney rescues aristocrats and spirits them back with him to England, leaving behind the sign of the Black Fingernail, a drawing of two raised fingers. The leader of the revolution, Citizen Robespierre, is determined to capture the Fingernail and puts his best man on the job, the ruthless Citizen Camembert. It seems that the daring Sir Rodney is in little danger, but then he falls in love with the beautiful Jacqueline.

Carry On Critics

By 1967, one of the more antediluvian strictures of *The Times* had been loosened, and the identity of the paper's film critic was revealed as being that of John Russell Taylor, who had been in that post since 1962. Reviewing *Don't Lose Your Head*, which he correctly identified as being a Carry On film in all but title, he had some rather penetrating insights into the films' continued appeal:

> Some of the jokes are really funny, but a lot of them—the endless patter of surrealistically gratuitous, irrelevant puns, the familiar round of lavatorial and vaguely sexual side-references—make us laugh not so much one by one as by their relentless accumulation, which wears down resistance until we give in to their sheer shamelessness."
>
> 'And soon the Duke de Pommfrit will have had his chips'. If you find that funny right away this is the film for you. If you do not, you will still probably catch yourself giggling shame-facedly by the end of the proceedings.

The *Monthly Film Bulletin* provided a review that was possibly the most hostile that venerable magazine had yet produced for a Carry On film. The safely anonymous reviewer correctly identified *Don't Lose Your Head* as being a part of the series, somewhat in the manner of a government health warning: 'it is identical, taste or style, to any of its predecessors. The prevailing colour of a stream of witless gags is distinctly blue. Carry On enthusiasts will be able to fill in the rest'. One can well imagine the curled lip of the reviewer as they typed their deathless prose, apparently unencumbered by very much previous experience of having actually watched other films in the series.

The Guardian's Richard Roud was similarly dismissive in the few lines he fitted in about the film at the end of his Friday 3 March column:

> As for *Don't Lose Your Head*, what can one say but that this is another in the 'Carry On' series. The scene is the French Revolution, and the printable humour is on the level of: 'My name's Camembert and I'm the big cheese around here'.

Thankfully, Penelope Gilliantt, in *The Observer*'s 12 March edition, was on hand to give probably the most positive critical notice any Carry On film had ever received in the national press: 'The film techniques of the Carry On ensemble have got better in their new film,' she enthused, 'and the jokes, thank heaven, worse ... If you like Blackpool jokes or the double-meanings in Danny La Rue's act, then *Don't Lose Your Head* is 90 minutes of joy'.

Carry On Comments

The Scarlet Pimpernel was created in 1903 by the Baroness Orczy as a stage play, which proved such a hit that, two years later, she turned the story into a novel. A long series of sequels, and even a few prequels, followed, the last of these being published in 1947, while the character also caught the attention of filmmakers. The definitive screen version of the baroness' title character came in 1934, with Leslie Howard's portrayal of Sir Percy Blakeny, aka the

Scarlet Pimpernel. Inadvertently, the countess had also inspired what we now know as the superhero, with her character of a bold avenger and seeker of justice hiding his identity behind a public persona as a harmless, wealthy fop inspiring the Shadow, who expanded from radio to novels and comics, and fellow comic book characters that survive to this day, Superman and Batman.

Also inspired by the adventures of the Pimpernel was a British comedy scriptwriter you may be familiar with by this point named Talbot Rothwell, who had long-harboured a desire to write his own version of the tales. With the Carry On series having turned with great success to spoofing movie genres, in 1966, he saw his opportunity to pitch the notion of satirising the Pimpernel to Peter Rogers, who agreed to the idea.

Everything was running smoothly for Peter Rogers, whose Carry On production schedule was running like a well-oiled machine. *Carry On Screaming* was in the can, post-production complete, cleared by the BBFC, and ready for release at the height of the summer schedule in August. With Rothwell at work on his pet project of a *Scarlet Pimpernel* parody for the next film in the series, it seemed that nothing could possibly go wrong. Yet on 3 June 1966, everything went wrong.

Stuart Levy, half of the duo that ran Anglo-Amalgamated, the company that funded and distributed the Carry On films, died suddenly. Levy was the more reticent of the two Anglo-Amalgamated directors: Nat Cohen was a regular presence at film premieres and had been chief barker at the Variety Club, the international show business social club and charity fundraising organisation that also served as a very useful networking opportunity for film executives. On the other hand, it is a struggle to find even a single photograph of his erstwhile partner. Nonetheless, Levy was an absolutely vital part of Anglo-Amalgamated. The company was not a huge organisation like Rank or Associated-British; it was basically Cohen and Levy and reflected the two men's tastes and desires. With the demise of Stuart Levy, Anglo-Amalgamated became a different company, and that company no longer wanted to finance and distribute Carry On films.

An unsuspecting Peter Rogers was taken out to lunch by Nat Cohen, who announced the news to his friend and long-time colleague. The reasons behind Cohen's decision have never been entirely clear and are worthy of speculation. Peter Rogers stated later that Cohen was suffering from 'a touch of culture up his arse'.[1] He was also being pressured by his own family, who looked down on the Carry Ons, and worried about the image of Anglo-Amalgamated, which was forever looked upon by critics as slightly second rate, thanks to its background in B-pictures and the conveyor-belt releases of two Carry On films per year.

It might seem at first glance unlikely that a tough and experienced operator like Nat Cohen, an increasingly powerful figure in the British film industry, would succumb to such influences, especially regarding a film series that had done much to bankroll Anglo-Amalgamated's operations over the last decade. The idea, however, is not as improbable as it might seem.

Cohen was a clubbable man, a *bon vivant* who craved acceptance from his peers, and was susceptible to pressure. This was demonstrated during the release of aforementioned Michael Powell's *Peeping Tom* in 1960, when pressure within the film industry was put on Cohen to suppress the release of a film that had received horrified reviews from stunned critics. Many a distributor would have plastered the reviews all over the film's posters and ridden the wave of controversy all the way to box-office triumph. Instead, Cohen effectively cancelled the film's British distribution after his business chums at the Variety Club 'put Nat in the doghouse'.[2] Powell, understandably somewhat bitter about actions which destroyed his renowned career in British cinema, later commented that Cohen was 'Scared out his tiny mind'.[3]

There may have been more to Nat Cohen's decision though. The film market was changing and the support features that had built Anglo-Amalgamated were becoming a thing of the past. The *Scotland Yard* series of half-hour films, produced for Anglo-Amalgamated by Merton Park Films and introduced by criminologist and author Edgar Lustgarten, ended in 1961, replaced by *The Scales of Justice*, in which Lustgarten was finally forced out of his book-lined study to show audiences crime in the streets—or at least the leafy lanes of Home Counties England. Even this series was on its last legs by 1966, with the final instalment ready for release the following year. Longer-form B-pictures, such as Anglo and Merton Park's *Edgar Wallace* series, which ended in 1965, were dying out, along with hour-long crime films from smaller studios, such as Butcher's Film Services. Perhaps in this case, Nat Cohen was cannier than he was credited for and saw the need for Anglo-Amalgamated to move upmarket if the company was to continue to prosper.

As events transpired, Anglo-Amalgamated had a very limited future as an independent company. Associated British Picture Corporation had bought a 50 per cent share in the company in 1962, and in 1967, they would increase their share to 74 per cent. As a part of the deal, Nat Cohen took a seat on the board of ABPC, remaining in place when ABPC sold out to EMI and eventually rising to be the most powerful man in British cinema as head of EMI films. From his beginnings as co-producer of short second features, Nat Cohen found himself responsible for approximately 70 per cent of all films produced in the UK in 1973.

All this was in the future, however, and back in 1966, Peter Rogers was in the perilous position of being a producer without a distributor. The obvious place for him to offer his services was Rank, a company that for various reasons immediately welcomed Rogers with open arms. Rank would wind down its film production division over the following decade, a process that had already begun, but a cornerstone of its movie profits had for many years come from comedies. By 1966, Rank's old standbys were reaching the end of their runs and replacements were proving hard to find. The highly successful Norman Wisdom series of comedies would reach their end with the December 1966 release of *Press For Time*, and truth be told, Wisdom was, at the age of fifty-one, getting a little long in the tooth for his loveable, lovelorn fool characterisation.

Meanwhile, and rather closer to home for Peter Rogers, his producer wife Betty Box had recently completed *Doctor in Clover*, which was released in March 1966 and would prove the last in what had been a hugely popular and profitable and popular series until the somewhat regrettable *Doctor in Trouble* four years later. Rank's hopes for a popular new comedy film series rested on the shoulders of comedy duo Morecambe and Wise. Their first two films, *The Intelligence Men* and *That Riviera Touch*, had proved disappointing; the upcoming third film *The Magnificent Two* would make matters worse by being both not funny enough and uncomfortably violent. One can imagine the delighted reactions of Rank's board members when the cheap-to-make and virtually guaranteed profit-producing Carry On films fell into the company's lap.

Rank had another reason to be happy to have a winning series under its auspices. The British film business was awaiting the delivery of a Monopolies Commission report into UK film distribution, which was dominated by the duopoly of Rank's Odeon chain and Associated British's ABC cinemas. The report was expected to by critical of the 'big two', and when it was finally delivered in November 1966, this proved to be the case. No one knew what the recommendations of the report would be, but an insurance policy in the shape of Sid James and the gang could not have come at a better time for Rank. As it transpired, the Monopolies Commission report proved tame stuff, and the Odeon/ABC duopoly carried on almost exactly as before.

Don't Lose Your Head, then, came at a time of change for Peter Rogers that represented both a major opportunity, his Carry On franchise having been accepted into the willing arms of Rank Films, and a huge risk, which, for various reasons, could have sunk the series completely. Rank had accepted Peter Rogers' offer to make films for them, and clearly wanted to release Carry On films, but there was a high degree of uncertainty as to if they had the right to use the Carry On name at all, or at any rate the sole right. Despite Nat Cohen having been the person who had rejected the series in the first place, it was possible that not only did he retain rights over the name, but that if his new direction for the company did not work out, there may have been a financial imperative for him to make further Carry On pictures.

Enter Michael Sullivan, agent not only for Sid James, but also Charles Hawtrey, Jim Dale, and Kenneth Connor. Sullivan realised that if he could sign up some more of the regular Carry On cast, then he would have a very strong negotiating position over Peter Rogers. At the very least, he might be able to get higher fees for his clients who were as a group—despite the oft-voice protestations of Rogers—vital to the continuing success of the series. At the other extreme, Sullivan could have been in a position to take the core cast of the Carry Ons to an alternative series on better terms at Anglo-Amalgamated. As it transpired, Sullivan's idea came to nothing. Kenneth Williams and Joan Sims had been with their agent, Peter Eade, for virtually their entire professional careers and were not about to break strong personal loyalties for the sake of getting a few extra quid out of Peter Rogers.

Rank was fully aware of the situation, which weighed heavily on their decision to drop the Carry On name from their first Peter Rogers production. Not only did the company not want to become embroiled in potential legal action with Anglo-Amalgamated, they also did not want to publicise potential rereleases of Anglo's back catalogue of Carry On films. The fiction that *Don't Lose Your Head* was not a Carry On films was thin indeed, with the film's poster art urging audiences to *'Carry On' laughing until you have hysterics... but DON'T LOSE YOUR HEAD*.

Filming progressed with its usual military precision, despite a few bumps in the road. The first of these occurred when it emerged in the movie trade press that the next Carry On would be a spoof of *The Scarlet Pimpernel*. Representatives of the late Baroness Orczy, who had died in 1947, pointed out that her creation was, in fact, still in copyright. Peter Rogers quickly assured them that his new production was not going to be closely based on *The Scarlet Pimpernel* and, amazingly, they believed him.

Some problems were also caused by Kenneth Williams' ever-outrageous on-set behaviour. He and Joan Sims were on non-speaking terms for a few days after Williams upset some of Joan's guests. In his diaries during this period, Williams expressed 'guilt and remorse' over his general on-set behaviour, describing the contrast between his demeanour at work and his character at home as a 'Jekyll and Hyde existence'. 'I'm loath to relinquish the laughs and the crowd that gathers around me. I need them like other (healthy) people need the affection of a partner'.[4]

On the other hand, despite occasional shortness of temper from Sid James, who loathed performing his drag scenes, and Kenny's self-confessed on-set bad behaviour, rumours of a serious rift between the two were likely overstated. Certainly they were as one when an unexpected appearance was made (by telephone, at least), by a figure from their mutual pasts: Tony Hancock. If Sid James had been upset when Hancock demanded he was dropped from the *Hancock's Half Hour* television series, at which point their pairing had made them the most popular figures in British comedy, Kenneth Williams had been subjected to far greater indignities. Hancock had repeatedly voiced his disapproval of Williams' 'snide' character, which had become wildly popular on the radio series, regarding it as a source of cheap laughs and a cardboard characterisation. The actor was astonished, therefore, to receive a series of urgent on-set phone calls from Hancock, which, in transpired, was a last-minute plea for him to appear in an upcoming concert he had arranged at the Royal Festival Hall in an attempt to boost what was by now a seriously flagging career.

The idea was that the pair would perform Galton and Simpson's classic Test Pilot sketch, an idea which, even if the busy Williams—who was performing in the BBC TV series *International Cabaret* at the same time as filming *Don't Lose Your Head*—had been available, he found distinctly unappealing. He and Sid James spoke about the offer, the latter's reaction being 'You'd be mad to work with him again. The man is a megalomaniac'. The Festival Hall concert took place as planned on 22 September 1966, with singer Marion Montgomery guest starring and musical accompaniment by Tony Hatch and his orchestra, the whole event being recorded for later television broadcast on BBC2. Although the concert was judged to be good enough to be screened, in truth it was grimly unfunny, a dishevelled Hancock appearing only recently introduced to the sub-par script, forgetting his lines, his delivery indistinct and slurred despite a week's 'try-out' of the material having taken place earlier that month at the Bournemouth Winter Gardens. What makes the whole event even sadder is that the packed audience clearly loved Hancock and were willing the show to be better than it is, its star the man he had been five years earlier. Although Kenneth Williams and the Test Pilot sketch would have been the highlight of the show, truth be told, Williams was better off away from the whole thing.

The chances of Kenneth Williams being free to take up the dubious offer from Hancock were small anyway, as the actor was leaving the set early on some days anyway in order to record episodes of his BBC2 television series *International Cabaret*. This was a series compered by Williams at the Talk of the Town nightclub, in which he introduced cabaret acts from all over the world. The format proved surprisingly durable, gaining a loyal audience over its three-year run.

Sid would certainly have been too busy to take up any such offer from Hancock, even had he been inclined to work with his former comedy co-star again. As soon as he finished for the day on the *Don't Lose Your Head* set, he rushed to Bournemouth where he was appearing in *Wedding Fever* at the Pier Theatre. Sid had a particular affinity for the stage farces of Irish playwright Sam Cree, who had originally written the play for the Northern Irish comedian and actor James Young. The combination of Cree and Young was so popular in the province that the 1960 premiere of the play had been attended by the prime minister of Northern Ireland and the lord mayor of Belfast. Sid was so successful in *Wedding Fever* that he toured with it for several years, the Bournemouth run being so popular that he had planned to take the show to Blackpool for the following summer season, but had to drop out following his heart attack and was replaced in the lead role by Freddie Frinton. Sid was back in the play in 1968, this time in Torquay, then in 1969 in played both Great Yarmouth and Blackpool in Cree's sequel to *Wedding Fever, His Favourite Family*. Finally, he returned to Yarmouth in the summer of 1970 with *Wedding Fever* before taking the production on a South African tour, playing Cape Town and Johannesburg. Sid continued playing in Cree's works, which are performed often in Ireland to this day, and was acting in the writer's *The Mating Season* when he suffered his fatal heart attack at Sunderland's Empire Theatre in April 1976.

Music, as ever, came from Eric Rogers, but the composer's suggestion for an opening theme was, for once, rejected in favour of a jaunty theme song written and performed by what turned out to be some of the most important figures in the British music industry. The Song 'Don't Lose Your Head' was written by the writers Bill Martin and Phil Coulter. Martin and Coulter were a combination of a Scottish lyricist and an Irish-born composer who at this point were a new partnership, having teamed up in 1965. The pair went on to have an astonishingly successful career together, producing hits for artists as diverse as Ken Dodd, the Bay City Rollers, Elvis Presley, the 1970 England World Cup squad, and two legendary Eurovision entries ('Puppet on a String' for Sandie Shaw and 'Congratulations' for Cliff Richard). Via some early work for the KPM music library, Martin and Coulter's work is even featured in the cult 1967–70 *Spider-Man* television cartoon series.

Martin and Coulter's song was performed (or, as the films credits put it, 'executed') by the Michael Sammes Singers. More normally billed as the Mike Sammes Singers, the group were ubiquitous figures on the British music scene from their formation in 1957 to the mid-1970s, at which point changes in tastes and production techniques meant there was less work for vocal harmony groups. *Don't Lose Your Head* was a rare instance of the Sammes Singers being credited, the group often working anonymously on radio jingles and television adverts as well as on some very famous records including Englebert Humperdink's 'The Last Waltz' and The Beatles' 'I Am the Walrus'.

Despite moving to a more prestigious, A-Picture distributor in the shape of Rank Films, the production was not actually given any more money. *Don't Lose Your Head* is a good-looking film, but that is more to do with the clever use of locations and judicious raiding of the costume suppliers stores than the spending of any actual money. To be honest, a Carry On film with a more luxurious appearance than that presented here would have been beside the point. Audiences wanted to see those actors in those situations telling an endless stream of Talbot Rothwell's jokes and adding the production values of a David Lean epic would have added little of value. Let's face it, there was little prospect that Peter Rogers would have spent an increased budget on paying his regular cast more money.

While *Don't Lose Your Head* is filled with choice gags and well-played scenes by a strong cast, Peter Rogers' first film for Rank falls short of being an unqualified success for a number of reasons. Sid is less suited to his role as Sir Rodney Ffing than he was his parts in his previous two historical Carry Ons, *Cleo* and *Cowboy*. Despite a past that included stints as a hairdresser and a dance school proprietor, Sid was proud of his image as a tough, macho man and particularly disliked performing in drag, which was required of him here. More importantly, while his *Cleo* role of Mark Antony fit Sid like a glove, he was not born to convincingly play a lisping fop and was no threat to Errol Flynn as a swashbuckler either. This is not to say that Sid gives a bad performance, and on occasion it sparks to life. His scenes with his French co-star Dany Robin—who went on to marry Sid's manager, the aforementioned Michael Sullivan—are especially good, cleverly written by Talbot Rothwell so that they both talk directly to the audience, breaking the fourth wall in a way that became fashionable earlier in 1966 with the release of *Alfie*.

The ending of the film is also problematic, falling into a trap common among spoofs of action movie genres. At some point, they have to find a way of ending the movie, at which point the gags dry up and they become a slightly naff version of the very thing they are trying to satirise. *Don't Lose Your Head* finishes with a painfully long swordfight (in fact, it is seven or eight minutes long, depending on when you judge its beginning and ending to be), which is nothing like exciting enough, interspersed with gags which are nothing like funny enough. Talbot Rothwell was one of the few writers able to think of ways around this conundrum, having done so previously with *Carry On Cowboy*, and he would do so again, triumphantly, with *Carry On Up the Khyber*, but here the task defeats him.

Kenneth Williams has probably the most successful characterisation in the film, his Citizen Camembert ('I'm the big cheese!') being a parody of the Scarlet Pimpernel's enemy Citizen Chauvelin. This is another in the line of barely competent, self-important hypocrites that would become the standard part Talbot Rothwell would write for him. Despite being a prominent member of the revolutionary authorities, Camembert loathes the peasantry, much preferring the company of aristocrats while also chopping their heads off and revelling in the fine house and possessions taken from them—all of which are destroyed in the climax. In the Baroness Orczy's original series of novels and the subsequent films based on them, the Scarlet Pimpernel has a league of up to twenty compatriots to help carry out his daring rescues, whereas here it is just Sid and Jim Dale, who proves to be quite a convincing swordsman in a secondary role that makes it hard for the talented Dale to stand out.

Charles Hawtrey gets another of his memorable entrances, which had been a feature of his Carry On work ever since he first crashed through the barrack-room doors in *Carry On Sergeant*. This time we first come across his Duc de Pommfrit at his own execution, chuckling away at a copy of the marquis de Sade's latest work. As it happened this was a slightly ahistorical reference—de Sade was a famous and notorious sexual libertine at the time, but his literary works were not published, even unofficially, until well after the 1789 date at which the film is set. This matters, of course, not a jot, as the joke serves to establish Hawtrey's Duc as a randy old pervert, setting up his characterisation for the rest of the film. Like many of the cast members, Hawtrey was required to take part in more action scenes than was normal for a Carry On film and required the services of a stunt double. So small and bird-like was Hawtrey that the available stuntmen were unsuitably burly, thus he was doubled by Diana MacNamara, who also played the part of Princess Stephanie in the film.

It should be added that the ever-selfless Sid James suggested Hawtrey's best gag in the film, in which a messenger rushes to the duc on his way to the guillotine with an urgent letter, to which he replies, 'just leave it in the basket, I'll read it later'. Director Gerald Thomas ran a tight ship and disliked deviating from the script, but this addition was so good that he filmed it and left the sequence in the final edit.

Peter Butterworth returned to play Citizen Bidet and was once again paired with Kenneth Williams, repeating their successful double act from *Carry On Cowboy*. Giving Williams a fellow comedic presence to bounce off raised his performances, while Butterworth was a master reactor, his lugubrious presence and mobile facial features raising extra laughs that were not present on the page. Also highly effective here is Joan Sims, playing Citizen Camembert's sister Désiree Dubarry, who wants nothing more than to marry a wealthy aristocrat and live happily ever after. The period costumes particularly suited the voluptuous Miss Sims, which must have been a factor in her even more spectacular dresses (her personal favourites) in the later, Victorian-set *Carry On Up the Khyber*.

Don't Lose Your Head proved more than successful enough at the box office to please the executives at Rank, who gave the go-ahead for Peter Rogers to produce the next of his movie spoofs. Once again, there would be a Carry On without using the name, and this time efforts would be made for the series to once again conquer the American market, featuring the biggest name star yet to feature in the films.

15

Follow That Camel (1967)

Filming Dates: 1 May 1967–23 June 1967
Original Certificate: A (Classified by BBFC 10 August 1967 [cut])
Running Time: 95 minutes 21 seconds

Release Details

London Release: 14 December 1967 (Leicester Square Theatre, replacing *Billion Dollar Brain*).

In the UK, *Follow That Camel* played on the Odeon Circuit with *Sullivan's Empire* as its support feature. This was originally made in 1967 as a pilot film by Universal Pictures for an adventure series for NBC. The American TV network rejected the pilot, which was then released to cinemas with added footage. In some areas, particularly Northern Ireland, *Follow That Camel* played alongside another Universal production, *Deadly Roulette*, which starred Robert Wagner. This had originally been made under the title *How I Spent My Summer Vacation* as one of the first ever movies produced specifically for television, but was released across Europe to cinemas.

What's Carrying On?

His engagement to Lady Jane Ponsonby broken after an unjust accusation of cheating at cricket and disgraced in British society, Bertram Oliphant 'Bo' West travels to North Africa and joins the French Foreign Legion, leaving behind everything apart from his loyal valet Simpson. There he finds himself commanded by the stiff, monacled German Commandant Maximilian

Burger and the cowardly, finagling American Sergeant Nocker. Discovering Bo's innocence, Lady Jane risks fates worse than death—several times—and travels across continents to be reunited with her fiancé. Meanwhile, Bo must help defend Fort Zuassantneuf from an attack by the villainous Sheikh Abdul Abulbul.

Who's Carrying On?

A Peter Rogers Production
Director: Gerald Thomas
Screenplay by Talbot Rothwell
Music composed and conducted by Eric Rogers
Photography: Alan Hume BSC
Art Director: Vetchinsky
Editor: Alfred Roome
Phil Silvers: Sergeant Nocker, the lecherous and cowardly officer who suddenly finds he must forge his Foreign Legion troops into an efficient fighting unit.
Kenneth Williams: Commandant Maximilian Burger, in charge of Fort Zuassantneuf but with a secret past and a link to Lady Jane Ponsonby.
Jim Dale: Bertram Oliphant 'Bo' West, falsely accused of cheating at cricket, he travels to Fort Zuassantneuf as he is no longer accepted in polite British society.
Charles Hawtrey: Captain Le Pice, assistant to Commandant Burger.
Joan Sims: Zig-Zig, proprietor of Café ZigZig, where Sergeant Nocker hides out when he claims he is out on patrol acting in a heroic military manner.
Angela Douglas: Lady Jane Ponsonby, Bo's former fiancée who discovers his innocence and, several times, the perils of travelling alone while attempting to be reunited with her beau, Bo.
Peter Butterworth: Simpson, Bo's valet, so loyal to his employer that he joins the French Foreign Legion along with him.
Bernard Bresslaw: Sheikh Abdul Abulbul, villainous leader of a desert tribe that worships the prophet Mustapha Leek, who plans to massacre the inhabitants of Fort Zuassantneuf.

Carry On Critics

In *The Times*' edition of 14 December 1967, John Russell Taylor continued in print with his love of the whole idea of the Carry On films, appearing more than satisfied with this particular example:

> Habitués will know exactly what to expect, and will get it, only if anything a bit bluer than usual. Hence, no doubt, an 'A' certificate instead of the normal 'U' [in point of fact the Carry Ons had been earning an 'A' certificate for some time by this point]. Reasonable in a way, and yet all said, what could be more sublimely innocent than this joyous dip into the world of Donald McGill, that rich store of English folklore we all know and love?

No such flights of enthusiasm came from the *Monthly Film Bulletin*, whose critic greeted the film as if it were rude graffiti scrawled on a toilet wall:

> The Carry On team join the Foreign Legion in a familiar hotch-potch of all the usual ingredients—lavatory jokes in abundance, outrageous puns, and desperately strained performances from all concerned. If anything, this one is worse than ever, short on material and overworked at every level.

Variety was able to see rather more merit in the Carry On team's desert adventures: 'It all works with considerable bounce, with elements of parody of Beau-Geste-style movies for those alert to them. All the regular comics are on first-rate form.'

The Observer's film critic Penelope Mortimer loathed *Follow That Camel* beyond all reason, having in the same review column found Peter Cook and Dudley Moore's *Bedazzled* 'embarrassing': 'Embarrassment is as nothing compared with the stupefied bewilderment, the enraged incomprehension, with which I reacted to *Follow That Camel*.' This was especially puzzling as Mortimer professed to be a big fan of *Don't Lose Your Head*. 'From the titles on, everything looks hideous and sounds worse. This tatty picture deserves, in my mind, a quick death. It will probably live for years.' Well, I suppose she got one thing right.

Carry On Comments

With Sid James, by now the acknowledged leader of the Carry On cast, unavailable for the *Follow That Camel* filming dates due to the recording dates of his sitcom *George and the Dragon*, Peter Rogers and Gerald Thomas were more than aware that they needed a big name to replace him at the top of the cast list. As it transpired, just at this point a major American comedy star was in need of work and just about affordable within a Carry On budget: enter Phil Silvers.

Born in 1911 in Brooklyn, Silvers was a comic actor who had worked steadily in Hollywood throughout the 1940s in supporting roles, but did not hit the big time until he returned to the stage as the star of the 1951–2

Broadway musical *Top Banana*, which ironically saw Silvers ascend from second banana to the top of the bill. After starring in the 1954 film adaptation of the show, Silvers landed the television role that made him a comedy legend; initially titled *You'll Never Get Rich*, later renamed *The Phil Silvers Show*, the series was known to one and all by the name of its main character, Sergeant Bilko.

The adventures of a gambler/con artist who runs the motor pool at Kansas US Army base Fort Baxter, *The Phil Silvers Show* ran for 144 episodes over four seasons between 1955 and 1959. Even after TV network CBS cancelled the series, the show remained popular in repeats on rival network NBC. In 1963, Silvers began a new sitcom on CBS, playing conniving factory foreman Harry Grafton in *The New Phil Silvers Show*, but the results were nothing like as popular and the actor's career went into decline. Ironically, instead of making this show, Silvers could have been starring on Broadway in *A Funny Thing Happened On the Way to the Forum*; the lead role instead made Zero Mostel a star.

By the time casting for *Follow That Camel* was being planned in 1966, Phil Silvers' career was struggling in the USA, but in Britain, he was a fully fledged comedy legend. BBC Television began screening *The Phil Silvers Show* on 20 April 1957, showing the series weekly until August 1958, at which point it switched to twice-weekly screenings for the next year. From then until the end of the year, the BBC switched to showing Bilko three times a week. Britain clearly loved Sergeant Ernie Bilko, and the BBC screenings of his adventures continued until January 1961, before returning in a sort of lap of honour, when a series of screenings entitled *The Best of Bilko* was shown an incredible four times a week in June and July of the same year. Although Ernie left UK screens for a while, *The New Phil Silvers Show* was bought for British screenings in 1963 and 1964 by ITV region Granada (covering northern England) and ATV Midlands.

The image of Ernie Bilko was imprinted into the DNA of generations of British comedy fans thanks to periodic BBC repeats of the series, which continued into 2004, the first of which, heralded with the title *Bilko Returns* began in October 1966, just as Peter Rogers was getting its star to sign on the dotted line to star in *Follow That Camel*. As the other *Follow That Camel* cast members soon discovered however, the real Phil Silvers was by 1967 far removed from the energetic, upbeat characters he played on screen. His second marriage had broken up in 1960, and two years later, while performing in Spain, Silvers suffered a nervous breakdown, his mental health made fragile by bouts of depression and a chronic gambling habit which ensured that the earnings from his period of international fame largely found their way to various casinos and bookmakers.

While this meant that Silvers was more than willing to take up Peter Rogers' offer of £30,000 to star in *Follow That Camel*—a fortune by Carry

On standards, but hardly a huge fee by Hollywood standards—the actor's poor mental state caused problems. In short, Silvers was largely unable to memorise his dialogue, most of which had to be written on large boards off-camera, known derisively in the acting profession as 'idiot boards' or 'dummy boards'. Clearly Silvers was in a bad way and was unable to put up a good front even for the press, an interview with Peter Howell on the film's Camber Sands location for the October 1967 edition of *Photoplay* magazine being a rather sad, and definitely mirth-free, round-up of his money, divorce, and health problems.

On set, things were often no better; Kenneth Williams reported in his diary entry for 30 May 1967 that 'He blew so many takes that he got humiliated and burst into tears on the set'.[1] By 7 June, a vituperative Williams was describing Silvers as 'that incompetent fool'.[2] Especially bearing in mind the personal and professional problems Phil Silvers was suffering during the making of the film, it is a great pleasure to report that the actor's performance as Sergeant Nocker is almost miraculously good. On screen, Silvers is bursting with energy and delivers his lines with such enthusiasm and brio one would think he arrived direct from the Bilko set, rather than being a decade older and beset with problems. That his performance anchors the film so effectively is not only a tribute to an actor giving his best in difficult circumstances, but also to the skill and patience of Gerald Thomas in dealing with what must have been a testing situation.

Despite Kenneth Williams' low opinion of his co-star, he and Silvers work very well together on screen, Kenneth's Commandant Burger serving the same purpose as Bilko's hapless commanding officer Colonel Hall. Burger is a very different creation, however—Paul Ford's perennial trouble remembering his lines on *The Phil Silvers Show* produced a uniquely vague characterisation. Instead, Williams, who rarely blew a line of dialogue, is kitted out with a military-style haircut and plays the part with a Germanic accent, rather like one of his *Round the Horne* characters. It is an unusual characterisation for Williams to play on screen, however, and he rises to the challenge admirably.

Also playing rather a different character to normal is Joan Sims: dark-haired and sexy, she plays Zig-Zig, owner of the local café where Sergeant Nocker hides out when he is supposed to be on patrol. It is not the biggest part in the world, but it really is nice to see Joan get to show her range, being handed a role that required both a foreign accent and a physical transformation. Also dark-haired and attractive was Anita Harris as Cork-Tip, an exotic belly dancer in the pay of Sheikh Abdul Abulbul. The twenty-seven-year-old Harris was a newcomer not only to the Carry On films, but was largely new to dramatic acting, but proved an asset to both *Follow That Camel* and to its follow-up, *Carry On Doctor*. She was spotted by Peter Rogers and Gerald Thomas virtually by chance, as the pair had gone to see Frankie Howerd on stage at the Prince of Wales Theatre in order to discuss his appearance in *Carry On Doctor* when they saw her and realised Harris would be perfect for *Follow That Camel*.

Harris' previous experience had been largely as a singer and dancer, having been discovered by a talent scout while figure skating shortly before her sixteenth birthday. Within weeks she had been whisked off to the El Rancho Hotel, Las Vegas, as part of a dance troupe for a six-month engagement. Much of her career in the following years was spent singing, and British audiences would have heard Harris often on BBC Radio's Light Programme, where she performed on a wide variety of shows, including *Forces Jamboree*, in December 1965, on the same bill as Frankie Howerd, and as a regular performer in 1966 and 1967 on Morecambe and Wise's radio series. She also made occasional television appearances, gaining screen experience that often drew upon her singing and other performing skills. Thus she appeared on 16 January 1965 in BBC2's *Who Is Mary Morison*, a musical 'improbable story' based on the works of Robert Burns which also featured Beryl Reid, Jess Conrad, and Carry On regular Angela Douglas. From September 1966, Harris was top-billed on ITV contractor Southern Television's *The New Forest Rustlers*, a now-lost six-part children's serial that utilised her figure skating skills.

In Anita Harris, the Carry Ons gained a very attractive and talented performer on the rise, her skills (and a great deal of rehearsal) making for a memorable dance sequence. Harris, meanwhile, gained valuable acting experience and exposure via her two-film association with the Carry Ons—1967 was the year when Anita Harris hit the pop charts, giving the upcoming release of *Follow That Camel* some valuable publicity. She had been singing and recording for some years and had been a member of the popular Cliff Adams Singers but really hit the big time after talking to Dusty Springfield backstage at a recording of *Top of the Pops*. She was offered the song 'Just Loving You', written by Dusty's brother Tom Springfield, which went on to spend thirty weeks in the pop charts, five of those in the top ten, peaking at number six during the first week in September.

Aside from the presence of a high-profile Hollywood star, the *Follow That Camel* shoot was unusual anyway, involving as it did the longest location shoot of any Carry On film. This was at Camber Sands, near Rye in East Sussex, almost 100 miles and, with the 1967 road network, several hours' drive from the Carry On production base at Pinewood Studios. With such long distances involved, the production decided to get the most from the location, staying for three weeks. Camber Sands was the perfect location for any British production wanting to replicate the Sahara Desert, as it contains the country's only system of sand dunes. *Follow That Camel* was not the first production to use the Sands as a filming location—it had previously featured in Leslie Norman's 1958 production *Dunkirk* and in the 1962 classic *The Loneliness of the Long Distance Runner*—but this was the first time the area had stood in for North Africa.

The area of the sands used by Gerald Thomas' film unit was actually very small and situated right next to the car park. Gerald Thomas' skills as a director remain to this day considerably underrated: he and his director of photography, Alan Hume, expertly disguise the small size of their location, the cold weather (on some days snow had to be cleared from the dunes), and the fragile mental state of the film's star. To help the filming run smoothly, news of Sid James' heart attack, which occurred while the unit was still at Camber Sands, was kept from cast and crew to prevent distractions.

Challenges were also faced by the crew back at Pinewood. Sets constructed on the studio backlot had to be built taller than usual to disguise the presence of the scaffolding from Ken Adam's massive volcano set constructed for the James Bond film *You Only Live Twice*, which had wrapped filming some three months earlier but loomed over the Pinewood skyline for some time afterwards. Some problems were rather more self-generated: the decision to use real food in the wedding celebration scene, which took several days to shoot, had the effect of making the entire set smell as the food went bad under the hot studio lights.

Seen today, *Follow that Camel* is a more successful film comedy than its predecessor, several factors coming together to aid the film considerably: it certainly helped that the narrative of the film was carried not by the film's top-billed star but by Jim Dale who, as Bo West, finally ascends to leading man status. Dale really demonstrates his range here, proving not only a skilled physical comedian, as he had demonstrated with his much-practiced pistol gags in *Carry On Cowboy*, but also capable of being the focal point of the film.

What grounds *Follow That Camel* and helps make it ultimately a more satisfying movie than *Don't Lose Your Head* is that both its hero and villain give performances that would easily pass muster in a serious remake of *Beau Geste*. It is certainly more successful that Universal's remake of PC Wren's novel that was released in the UK in November 1966—what had originally been planned years earlier as a *Lawrence of Arabia*-style epic was eventually filmed on the cheap in Utah and on the Universal studio backlot. As mentioned earlier, despite his personal and health problems, Phil Silvers absolutely sparkles on screen with his energetic performance and constant playing to the audience—for once, a Carry On actor looks into the camera more often than does Charles Hawtrey.

It also cannot be overemphasised just what great form screenwriter Talbot Rothwell was in at this point. With *Follow That Camel*, he came up with a script that was more than merely wall-to-wall gags built around a *Beau Geste* plotline. Rothwell's work here is not only funny but clever—not a phrase often associated with the Carry On series but here entirely appropriate. He conjures up a deliberate mickey-take of the conventions of the *Boy's Own*-type adventure story, predating Michael Palin's series *Ripping Yarns* by almost a decade. Linked to this is an absurdist, and very funny, inflation of the importance of cricket to English upper-class society.

This works especially well in the early part of the film, set in Edwardian England, in which Bagshawe (Peter Gilmore) accuses Bo of deliberately running him out at cricket, as a ruse to spoil Bo's chances with Lady Jane and ruin his name in polite society. On learning of Bo's decision to join the French Foreign Legion, Lady Jane's father (the ever-excellent William Mervyn) gets one of the best gags in the film: 'Oh never mind, m'dear. It's the best thing he could do. His life wouldn't be worth living here—no other cricket club would have accepted him.'

Bagshawe, meanwhile, is so ashamed at the consequences of his deception that he both shoots and hangs himself. After Michael Nightingale (returning after a one-film absence) cuts him down to prevent him dripping all over the best carpet, Bagshawe still manages to admit his guilt before finally expiring.

At the same time as it reaches heights of invention, Rothwell's gags are also getting noticeably ruder, particularly an excellent running joke in which Angela Douglas is seduced by various men at every stage of her journey from England to North Africa once they learn she is travelling alone. While this is probably this most sexually explicit gag in the Carry Ons to this point, Douglas pulls it off (as it were) with great aplomb and Rothwell gives each stage of the running joke a great punchline. Had Universal's *Beau Geste* proved a more popular attraction, it might have given *Follow That Camel* a chance of achieving some popularity at the American and international box office. As events transpired, neither the choice of subject matter nor the presence of Phil Silvers made a lot of difference: the Americans did not take to *Follow That Camel* any more that they had other Carry On films after the success of *Carry On Nurse*.

Despite their initial reticence in using the Carry On title when they took on the series, it was clear that, for a variety of reasons, Rank still had major ambitions for Peter Rogers and Gerald Thomas' productions. Since the 1950s, Rank's most reliable source of box office hits had been its comedy series, but two of these had gone into decline. The *Doctor* series had somewhat lost direction since its star Dirk Bogarde jumped ship to appear in more serious fare outside the Rank Organisation. Meanwhile, Norman Wisdom's sentimental, sub-Chaplin style, which packed cinemas out during the 1950s, found fewer takers in the following decade. Wisdom was also in his fifties by now and getting a bit old to be playing an eternal adolescent, and his final comedy for Rank, *Press For Time*, was released on 8 December 1966. Besides the Carry

Ons—under whatever name they were being made—Rank's other great hope to revitalise its comedy output was the comedy duo Eric Morecambe and Ernie Wise. Unfortunately the comedy style that made Morecambe and Wise so enormously popular in their ATV series *Two of a Kind*, which had been running since 1961, did not translate fully to the big screen. Even shoehorned into unsatisfactory comedy thrillers, Eric and Ernie's personal popularity was so great that Rank were able to star them in three tolerably successful movies. It was clear to all concerned that their future lay on the small screen, and a 1968 move to the BBC saw Morecambe and Wise reach levels of popularity not seen since the days of Tommy Handley and *ITMA* in the 1940s.

Despite, as we shall see, talk of the Carry On series finishing the following year with *Carry On Doctor*, the ability of Peter Rogers Productions to put out highly profitable low-budget comedies, often at the rate of two a year, had become vital to the profitability of the Rank Organisation's film production and distribution arm.

16

Carry On Doctor (1967)

or Nurse Carries On Again
or Death of a Daffodil
or Life is a Four-Letter Word
or A Bedpanorama of Hospital Life

Filming Dates: 11 September 1967–20 October 1967
Original Certificate: A (Classified by BBFC 21 November 1967 [uncut])
Running Time: 93 minutes 41 seconds

Release Details

London release: 14 March 1968 (Leicester Square Theatre, replacing *Guess Who's Coming to Dinner*).

Carry On Doctor went on general release via Rank's Odeon circuit from the Sunday following the film's West End premiere, on Sunday, 17 March 1968. The support feature chosen by Rank was another Universal Pictures production made for American television. This was *The Doomsday Flight*, written by Rod Serling, famous for creating and hosting *The Twilight Zone*, and directed by William A Graham in 1966. The story concerns an altitude-sensitive bomb planted on an airliner that will explode if the plane attempts to land. This predated *Airport* and the 1970s vogue for disaster movies by some years. *The Doomsday Flight* starred Jack Lord, Edmond O'Brien, John Saxon, and Van Johnson. In some areas, *Carry On Doctor* was paired instead with Eric Sykes' short silent comedy *The Plank*, which starred Sykes and Tommy Cooper.

What's Carrying On?

When faith healer Francis Bigger falls off his own stage, he is rushed to hospital, where he finds himself sharing a ward with patents including a gag-telling layabout, a lovelorn giant, and a man suffering a sympathetic pregnancy with his wife. Francis has (as it were) bigger problems than this however, when an overheard conversation convinces him he has only a week to live. The hospital is run by the vain, self-obsessed Dr Kenneth Tinkle and the fearsome Matron, who secretly loves Tinkle. When popular Dr Kilmore discovers Tinkle took a less than professional interest in trainee Nurse Sandra when she was his patient, he and Matron plot to get both the young nurse and doctor removed. On hearing the news, the fed-up patients stage a revolt against Tinkle and Matron.

Who's Carrying On?

A Peter Rogers Production
Directed by Gerald Thomas
Screenplay by Talbot Rothwell
Music composed and conducted by Eric Rogers
Photography: Alan Hume BSC
Art Director: Cedric Dawe
Editor: Alfred Roome
Frankie Howerd: Francis Bigger, an author and public speaker attempting to spread the belief that the power of positive thought can prevent all diseases, though a visit to hospital soon reveals that he is a complete hypochondriac.
Kenneth Williams: Dr Kenneth Tinkle, vain, self-loving head of the hospital who is jealous of the popularity of the younger, more handsome Dr Kilmore.
Sidney James: Charlie Roper, a lazy malingerer who is determined to be signed off as sick so he does not have to do any work and can escape the responsibilities of being a husband and father.
Charles Hawtrey: Mr Barron, in hospital suffering from a sympathetic pregnancy while his wife is expecting their child.
Jim Dale: Dr Jim Kilmore, popular, but incredibly accident-prone doctor who Tinkle and Matron attempt to force out of the hospital when he learns damaging information about Dr Tinkle.
Hattie Jacques: Matron, an absolute dragon who makes the lives of nurses and patients a misery, but who harbours a secret passion for Dr Tinkle.
Peter Butterworth: Mr. Smith, the tent covering his nether regions hiding a mysterious and very sore operation site.

Bernard Bresslaw: Ken Biddle, a large, loveable chap who dons a series of disguises to get past Matron and see Mavis Winkle, a patient he's taken a shine to, in the ladies' ward.

Barbara Windsor: Nurse Sandra May, a trainee nurse whose arrival causes chaos in the lives of both Dr Tinkle and Dr Kilmore.

Joan Sims: Chloe Gibson, Francis Bigger's downtrodden, stone-deaf assistant and very long-term fiancée who ends up marrying Francis and showing a new side to her personality.

Anita Harris: Nurse Clarke, who carries a torch for Dr Kilmore and almost ends up being dragged off the roof of the nurse's quarters by him.

Dilys Laye: Mavis Winkle, who attempts to conduct a fledgling romance with Ken Biddle via the medium of mime, since they can't be in the same room together.

Carry On Critics

The *Monthly Film Bulletin*'s reviewer in that magazine's April 1968 edition was, as ever, dismissive and tone deaf to what was happening on screen:

> This new Carry On looks back to the Doctor series in that the farce is rather less grotesque than of late and much of the material is in light comedy vein. In all other respects, though, it is the story as before. The plot is no more than a mess of inane sketches involving the misfortunes of hospital patients and staff, punctuated by a string of tasteless jokes about castor oil, bedpans and parts of the anatomy. Frankie Howerd joins the regulars and seems quite at home.

At *The Times*, film critics John Russell Taylor was reliably more enthusiastic about *Carry On Doctor*, going to the lengths of writing an extended review of the film in the paper's Saturday 16 March edition. This fascinating artefact shows how well Taylor understood the appeal of the series, and Peter Rogers' attitude to casting:

> It all has rather the air of a family occasion, as indeed it is. Most of the regulars are there—Kenneth Williams, Charles Hawtrey, Joan Sims, Jim Dale—and a number of the occasionals, like Hattie Jacques and Sid James. (The essence of the casting has always been a team in which no member is absolutely indispensable—an arrangement, presumably, which has its advantages for the producers as well as proving generally satisfactory for a public which appreciates a measure of continuity).

How interesting that Sid and Hattie should at this stage have the status of 'occasionals'. I would venture the opinion that *Carry On Doctor* is the film that cemented Hattie Jacques' position as a mainstay of the series. This is mainly because for the first time she is given the opportunity to appear in an absolutely classic comedy sequence, in the form of her attempted seduction of Kenneth Williams' Dr Tinkle. In hindsight, it is even more fascinating that Sid James was not regarded as one of the bedrocks of the Carry On team. From this point, he would appear in every Carry On film made until 1974, during which time it became impossible to imagine the series without him.

Variety was also in positive mood regarding *Carry On Doctor*:

> Inevitably, the gags and situations waver in comic impact but the general effect is artless yocks in which audience participation carried to its fullest extent, in which that part of the fun is anticipating the verbal and physical jokes.

Even *The Observer*'s Penelope Mortimer, who had taken against *Follow That Camel* in a big way, was relatively keen on the Carry On series' return to a hospital setting: 'After the disaster of *Follow That Camel*, the Carry Ons are back on form with *Carry On Doctor*. This 'bedpanorama of hospital life' includes Frankie Howerd in the cast, for which much thanks'.

Carry On Comments

Difficult though it is to believe in retrospect, as the films had another eleven years of life left in them, there was considerable thought given to the possibility of *Carry On Doctor* being the final film in the series. With this in mind, the film carries a vein of references to *Carry On Nurse*, the key film in turning the Carry Ons from a popular comedy series into a national institution, often in quite subtle ways (and often not—this is a Carry On film, after all). This even extends to two of the alternative titles Talbot Rothwell saddled the film with, jokes having spread to the opening credits since the ninety-three minute length of the film was inadequate to contain the number of gags he had saved up for the occasion. Interestingly, *Carry On Doctor* also tips its hat to another British comedy film institution, Ralph Thomas and Betty Box's Doctor films, as the camera lingers for a second on a prominently placed portrait of James Robertson Justice.

What is also a little surprising is that Peter Rogers and Gerald Thomas had some difficulty in casting their latest Carry On production. Sidney James, who had suffered a near-fatal heart attack on 13 May 1967, was clearly in no position to take up the lead role, keen though he was to get back to work. As with *Follow That Camel*, someone special was required to lead the cast of Carry On regulars, and Frankie Howerd, who had re-established his occasional film career the previous year with *The Great St. Trinian's Train Robbery*, was more than willing to take the opportunity. Sid was also happy to return, and a smaller role than normal was written especially for him in which he could spend most of the film in bed, albeit smoking, an activity Sid's real-life doctors had strictly forbidden him from indulging in. Naturally, this being a Peter Rogers production, he was paid half his normal fee.

Somewhat less keen to appear in the film was Kenneth Williams, who initially turned down the role of Dr Tinkle in a letter to Peter Rogers: 'I hate all the physical fitness element in the role, and I've always hated stripping and showing my body'.[1] This from a notorious on-set mooner. Williams also appeared less than keen on the starring role in the film going to Frankie Howerd, expressed both in the letter to Rogers and in his own diaries: 'It's really a v.good vehicle for Frankie Howerd but the other parts are lousy.'[2]

Williams' reaction to the script was probably not helped by the fact that only the previous day he had received the news that his close friend, the playwright Joe Orton, had been the victim of a murder-suicide by his lover Kenneth Halliwell. It is also interesting to note how much Kenneth Williams underestimated his own ability to make the role of Dr Tinkle jump off the screen, as well as his chemistry with Hattie Jacques. In the end, of course, Williams took the role, grabbed it by the scruff of the neck, and dominated the film—no small feat considering the quality of the rest of the cast.

After a run of historical stories, it is nice to see the regular cast members in a contemporary setting once again. After his marvellous turn as the villainous Abdul in *Follow That Camel*, Bernard Bresslaw establishes what would become his standard Carry On screen persona of the slightly dopey, lovelorn character. This can be seen as a toned-down version of the Army Game character that originally made his name—not so outright thick as 'Popeye' Popplewell had been but maybe a quarter of a step behind the action. The contrast in physicality between the 6-foot 7-inch Bresslaw and the petite Dilys Laye, the object of his romantic affections, as well as the screen chemistry between the pair, worked so well that they were teamed up again in *Carry On Camping*.

As Kenneth Williams detected, the script in its opening stages is very much tailored to the talents of Frankie Howerd, indeed the film starts with a variation on his stage act: his character Francis Bigger gives a speech on the power of positive thinking, accompanied by a magnificently downtrodden Joan Sims as his deaf assistant/fiancée Chloe. Howerd and Sims make a marvellous comic partnership, and although Sims' part in the film is relatively small, she really makes the most of every opportunity writer Talbot Rothwell throws her way.

Bigger's message is that the mind is stronger than the body and can prevent illness: 'Look at me. I don't need doctors, I don't need medicine and nor will you if you just think "nothing, nothing can happen to me. And believe me—nothing will"'. Bigger immediately falls off the stage and is rushed into hospital at breakneck speed by ambulance drivers Peter Gilmore and Harry Locke. This is an early echo of *Carry On Nurse*, in which Terence Longden was rushed to hospital by ambulance drivers eager to catch the horse-racing results. Indeed, the whole set-up of the film is similar to *Carry On Nurse*, making the film a fascinating snapshot of what the Carry On films had become in the intervening years.

Once he arrives in the hospital's Fosdick Ward, Frankie's character takes on another role entirely: as Howerd's biographer, Graham McCann perceptively notes, he remains an outsider on screen, even though he got on well with the regulars. While he is on the general ward, he comments upon the much-loved cast members, even mocking Sid's trademark cackle, then is taken off to a private room as he cannot stand being on noisy Fosdick Ward any longer. Howerd's presence helps shake things up a bit and helps give *Carry On Doctor* its own special flavour among the films in the series.

Sid is in a reduced role here, necessitated by recuperation from his heart attack. For once, he is cast opposite an unglamorous, but age-appropriate screen wife in the form of Dandy Nichols, who was six years older than Sid, and had become a household name two years earlier as Alf Garnett's wife Else in the ground-breaking sitcom *'Till Death Us Do Part*. Sid's part as Charlie Roper mainly involves him lying in his hospital bed doling out bad jokes and doing his Sid James cackle (by this point audiences may have asked for a refund had Sid not done his trademark laugh). Much as Charlie Roper is a lazy so-and-so—he has told the Labour Exchange that he is a Hansom Cab lamp fitter—it is hard not to have a little sympathy for someone so nagged at home that he has malingered in hospital for ten weeks. It is not Sid's best role—he is at his best in the Carry Ons when he is in change—but it really is lovely to have him back.

Charles Hawtrey is both wrong and exactly right as Mr Barron in a way that makes one appreciate how such cross-casting actually makes him a more effective comic presence. It takes some swallowing that Hawtrey would be of a mind to make any woman pregnant, but when cast opposite Gwendoline Watts, some twenty-three years younger than him, the imagery is even more comedically strange. Hawtrey looks like a little old man next to Watts (who in reality was married to regular Carry On small-part actor Gertan Klauber, seen here giving an unwilling Frankie Howerd a bed wash), which is funnier than if the two performers were similarly aged. Talbot Rothwell, at the peak of his comic invention with *Carry On Doctor*, even gives Hawtrey an appropriate name: Mr Barron. Although Hawtrey carried about him a slightly feminine air, childbirth was obviously impossible to him.

We are even treated to cameos by two great British comedy characters performers who might have made interesting additions to the Carry On regular cast: Pat Combes makes a tiny appearance which does not allow her to show off her comic potential, but Julian Orchard has much more to get his teeth into as Bernard Bresslaw's visiting workmate Fred. Orchard had a wonderfully mobile face just made for comedy and would have made a wonderful Carry On regular, but such was the embarrassment of riches of comedy character performers in this era that he only made three relatively brief appearances in the series. Orchard was one of those actors who always stayed in work on stage, screen, and television, but never landed a role that cemented him in the public consciousness before his tragically young death at the age of forty-nine.

Talbot Rothwell, bursting with comedic ideas, has more up his sleeve than an update of the series' former glories, and he also incorporates a spoof of television medical dramas such as *Doctor Kildare* (Jim Dale plays Doctor Kilmore) and the home-grown *Emergency Ward 10*. He would return to this subject matter for further fun a few years later for *Carry On Matron*. There are so many gags that if one does not work, there is always another one close behind, so it does not really matter that they do not all work.

The film's credit list is of interest, as Frankie Howerd gets top billing, slightly separate on the screen from the rest of the cast (as he is during the film for much of the time), while Sid James is second-billed for once, due to his smaller than normal role. Charles Hawtrey is, for once, billed above Kenneth Williams, while Jim Dale has to be content with fifth billing. This does seem a little off, considering the major role Dale has in the film and the way he absolutely throws himself into the part, both literally and figuratively. Dale's performance here convinced Rogers and Thomas to write more material for this side of Dale's skills, and by the time of *Carry On Again Doctor* two years later, the actor was flying across the screen like a modern-day Buster Keaton.

Hattie Jacques once again plays Matron, as she had in *Carry On Nurse*. Where previously she had been a fearsome presence who kept the wards running smoothly, here she has curdled into an unwelcoming, eventually villainous figure willing to aid Dr Tinkle in covering up his past indiscretion with Nurse Sandra. Jacques undergoes various indignities in *Carry On Doctor*, her appearance being mocked by both Dilys Laye and Kenneth Williams' characters. In real life, however, Hattie was a large, attractive woman, as was well known from her tumultuous personal life, which leads us to the highlight of the film and one of the most famous scenes in Carry On history. The lovelorn Matron finally attempts to seduce Kenneth Williams' vain, self-obsessed Dr Tinkle, who not only is not interested in her attentions, but positively panic-stricken at the prospect.

The sequence is worthy of closer inspection, especially as it informs many of Jacques and Williams' future interactions, especially in *Carry On Camping*. The scene is constructed so that the characters retain their dignity: Hattie is given seductive, flattering nightwear and her hair is done very nicely. The fact that she is clearly quite attractive is part of the joke, the unwilling Williams being overwhelmed by a tidal wave of feminine sexuality. In the context of the film, it is clear that Dr Tinkle resists Matron's carnal desire because he loves only himself, but much of the audience for the film in 1968 would have been aware on some level that Williams had no sexual interest in any woman—this was, after all, when Williams was entertaining millions on the BBC Light Programme as part of the outrageously gay pairing Julian and Sandy. The joke works on multiple levels and is all the better for it. It also puts the cap on one of Kenneth Williams' most commanding Carry On performances, the script allowing him to play all the way from smooth authority figure to ranting madman (a variation on his Dr Chou-En Ginsberg voice from *Round the Horne*) with an occasional detour into his 'snide' voice.

Carry On Doctor represents the film series reaching the artistic peak of its Talbot Rothwell-scripted era, the first of a run of three films that are absolutely central to the Carry On films' special place in Britain's collective memory. The cream of British comedy actors synchronised perfectly with the joke-machine that was Talbot Rothwell, and further peaks were yet to come, starting with a return to past, as the Victorian era was mined for laughs in what would become one of the most famous Carry On films of all.

17

Carry On Up the Khyber (1968)

or The British Position in India

Filming Dates: 8 April 1968–31 May 1968
Original Certificate: A (Classified by BBFC 3 July 1968 [cut])
Running Time: 87 minutes 49 seconds

Release Details

London Release: 28 November 1968 (Metropole).

Carry On Up the Khyber played in the UK on the Odeon circuit from 8 December with *King Kong Escapes* making up the other half of a somewhat bizarre double bill. This 1967 Japanese-American co-production was something of a follow-up to 1962's *King Kong Vs Godzilla*, while also being a live-action version of the 1966–69 Rankin-Bass cartoon series *The King Kong Show*. Both the film and cartoon featured King Kong battling a villain called Doctor Who and his robot version of Kong. In some areas, *Carry On Up the Khyber* was instead paired with Walt Disney's *Greta the Misfit Greyhound*, which had originally been made for the NBC TV series *Walt Disney's Wonderful World of Color*, airing on February 3rd 1963.

What's Carrying On

Sir Sidney Ruff-Diamond has a cushy number as Her Majesty Queen Victoria's governor of the Indian state of Kalibar, on the country's north-east frontier with Afghanistan. He maintains outwardly cordial diplomatic relations with the local Raja, Randi Lal, the khasi of Kalabar, despite the fact that he is fully aware that the khasi would happily massacre every British subject in the whole of India. Unfortunately for Sir Sidney, Lady Ruff-Diamond, to whom he is unhappily married, fancies the khasi, which will have dire consequences for the British outpost. When the leader of the fearsome Burpa tribe, Bungdit Din, encounters Private Widdle of the Queen's Own 3rd Foot and Mouth Regiment at the Khyber Pass, he discovers that, contrary to legend, members of the regiment wear underpants beneath their kilts. If proof of this were to get out, the fighting reputation of the invincible 'Devils in Skirts' would be destroyed. When Lady Ruff-Diamond photographs a kit inspection revealing that most of the regiment is wearing the offending garments, she rushes to the khasi's side, hoping for a night of passion, which the Indian royal is less than willing to provide. If the khasi can get the photograph to the Burpa tribesmen, a revolt will result, threatening the whole of British rule in India.

Who's Carrying On?

A Peter Rogers Production
Director: Gerald Thomas
Screenplay by Talbot Rothwell
Music composed and conducted by Eric Rogers
Photography by Ernest Steward BSC
Art Director: Vetchinsky
Editor: Alfred Roome

Sidney James: Sir Sidney Ruff-Diamond, governor of the Kalibar province of India, one of the more far-flung outposts of Queen Victoria's empire—a right cushy number for Sir Sidney, provided he manages not to get everyone killed.

Kenneth Williams: Randi Lal, the khasi of Kalabar. The local maharaja, who maintains cordial relations with the occupying British forces, but would like nothing better than to massacre the lot of them.

Charles Hawtrey: Private Widdle, possibly the most inept soldier in the entire British army, whose choice of undergarment under his regimental kilt threatens British control of India.

Roy Castle: Captain Keene, in charge of the local British garrison. He is keen on both his duties and on the lovely Princess Jelhi.

Joan Sims: Lady Ruff-Diamond, unhappily married to the constantly straying Sir Sidney and determined to get her own back by romancing an unwilling Randi Lal.

Bernard Bresslaw: Bungdit Din, fearsome local tribal warlord who works with the khasi to foment an uprising once the terrible secret of the Devils in Skirts is revealed.

Peter Butterworth: Brother Belcher, a drunken old letch of a Christian missionary who is used as a local guide in Captain Keene's undercover mission.

Terry Scott: Sgt Major Macnutt, a hard-as-nails professional soldier who has to force some efficiency into Private Widdle and even proves impervious to spears.

Angela Douglas: Princess Jelhi, daughter of the khasi who has to choose between the love of her father and that of Captain Keene.

Carry On Critics

The Times' John Russell Taylor was reliably enthusiastic about the latest Carry On in his review of 28 November 1968, on *Up the Khyber*'s London opening at the Metropole cinema. Taylor accurately homed in on the climactic sequence as a high point of the film series to date:

> The series reaches a new height of delirium in the dramatic sequence, a terrible stiff upper-lip formal dinner at the Residency while the tribesmen demolish the place about its inhabitants' ears. Carry Ons have had their ups and downs; this is decidedly an up.

While stating that the series 'still continues to rely primarily on low-comedy visual and verbal gag situations for its yocks', *Variety*'s reviewer still found much to praise in *Carry On Up the Khyber*:

> There's a small touch of genius in the way the Pass, for instance, can be shot in North Wales to everybody's complete satisfaction. Main highlight of the film is its finale, where the tribal chiefs launch a full-scale attack on the government residence while the governor and his guests with unshaken poise nonchalantly continue dinner amid the turmoil. Performance of Sidney James as Sir Sidney Ruff-Diamond, the bluff, vulgar British governor, is a gem, impeccably timed, wily and always in character.

Even the usually disapproving reviewer of the *Monthly Film Bulletin* had for once clearly been unable to resist cracking a smile:

> The jokes run true to form, ranging from an elephant with a GB plate to the usual assortment of double entendre and ribald puns. Produced and played by experts at the game, this is the bluest—and on its level the funniest—of the series for some time.

David Rider at *Films and Filming*, writing in that magazine's February 1969 edition, had more fun at the press screening even than the *Monthly Film Bulletin*'s correspondent:

> It is useless comparing them with other comedies—they can only be judged against their predecessors. So, locking up most of my more refined critical faculties, I trotted off for a look up the Khyber. And being a truthful lad, I must confess I laughed a lot, which is to me the ultimate test of any comedy ... No gag is too old, or too vulgar or too obvious that it must be pressed into service and he [Talbot Rothwell] packs in so many laugh-lines for all tastes that scarcely a minute goes by without at least one joke inciting anything from a knowing chuckle to a full-throated guffaw liable to set the hearts of unsuspecting usherettes palpitating furiously.

Warming to his subject, Rider's enthusiasm for *Carry On Up the Khyber* seemed to grow as his article continued:

> As the series has become increasingly successful, more money has been available and ... production values in *Khyber* are easily the best yet. There's nothing worse than a tatty comedy but this film is far from that—it looks good, it sounds good and by golly it'll make a pile. If you've never seen a Carry On film, pop along to your local for this one and you may acquire the habit. You will certainly be rewarded by the final ten minutes, in which the British residents calmly sit down to dinner whilst the tribesmen, the Burpas (what else?) batter the house with cannons. Unexpected in its understatement and beautifully cut by Alfred Roome (how valuable an editor with a sense of comedy timing is to a director) this is a first-rate scene by any standards.

The Observer's Penelope Mortimer, in that paper's 1 December 1968 edition, was also enthused by a film in which 'there are a number of jokes which make one laugh suddenly, explosively, like a sneeze'. She also correctly identifies the film's climactic scene as one which might secure a place in comedy history beyond the movie as a whole, describing it as 'a triumph of insanely restrained comedy which might, by itself, find a place in the archives'.

Carry On Comments

As with previous Carry On historical films, what was being spoofed was not only actual historical events but also the Hollywood (and Pinewood) versions of those events. It is worth taking a little time to examine exactly why Hollywood fell in love with the British Empire in the 1930s, the result of a series of circumstances that fell together to form a viable genre. First, there was a large pool of suitable actors; the arrival of sound technology at the end of the 1920s attracted an influx of classically trained British actors to Tinseltown, their clear diction and ability to project their voices to the back row of theatres proving ideal for the primitive sound recording technology available. Tied to this was the happy realisation that the same locations in the Californian desert which had formed the backdrop to innumerable Westerns would just as happily double for various far-flung outposts of the British Empire. Not only that, the same situations that cropped up in Western scripts could be recycled with an added touch of exoticism, which went down well with audiences. The US Cavalry defending a fort against Indians (as Native Americans were known back them) played out in a very similar manner to the British Army defending a fort against actual Indians. Thus British Empire adventure movies offered a touch of the exotic while remaining reassuringly familiar.

The Lives of a Bengal Lancer, with Gary Cooper somewhat uncomfortably cast as a British Army officer of Scots-Canadian background, proved a major box office success for Paramount in 1935. Warner Brothers saw the opportunity to develop a vehicle for their newest star, the strapping Tasmanian-born Errol Flynn who had shot to prominence in *Captain Blood* and, to American ears, sounded like the perfect British gentleman. The result was 'The Charge of the Light Brigade', inspired by the poem by Alfred, Lord Tennyson, which immortalised the famous Crimean War military blunder and reframed it as an act of unparalleled heroism. The Warner Brothers film largely ignored the Crimean military campaign in favour of inventing an extended backstory in the fictional country of Suristan, clearly a pseudonym for Afghanistan, about Errol Flynn falling out with his brother Patric Knowles over the love of leading lady Olivia de Havilland. More importantly for our purposes, the plot also revolves around a siege and subsequent massacre based on the real-life Siege of Cawnpore, which occurred in 1857. In the film, this event is engineered by the film's villain, the wily and duplicitous Surat Khan. Thus was Talbot Rothwell supplied with not only the setting, but also the inspiration for his villain and the comedic climax for his *Carry On Up the Khyber* script.

Rothwell also has a poke at one of the sillier conventions of the British Empire adventure movie; that white soldiers could put boot polish on their faces, pretend to be mute, look down a lot and pass for natives of whichever country the film might be set in—*The Lives of a Bengal Lancer* is a pretty good early example of this tendency. In *Carry On Up the Khyber*, Talbot Rothwell sends three soldiers, Captain Keene, Sgt. Major Macnutt and Private Widdle, on a secret mission into Afghanistan along with horny Christian missionary Brother Belcher. They pass as visiting tribesmen while speaking English the entire time and wearing turbans and the absolute worst false beards imaginable, which look like they are made from black cotton wool but in the film's plot are revealed to be smelly goat-hair. Only a year earlier, a hulking Sean Connery as James Bond was passed off as Japanese with the aid of a silly wig and false eyebrows in *You Only Live Twice*, so perhaps it was time that this particular story convention was skewered.

Talbot Rothwell is also able to have some fun with that most British of obsessions—social class. This had come up before in Carry Ons when Sid was cast in a position of authority, first in *Carry On Cruising*, in which Sid was a ship's captain. In that Norman Hudis script, the unusual sight of a cockney captain of a cruise liner became the crux of the plot. Rothwell's solution to putting Sid in unlikely positions was to play the improbabilities for laughs, which was a stroke of comedy genius. In the same way that Sid's Mark Antony in *Carry On Cleo* would normally be played by a Shakespearean leading man, in *Up the Khyber*, Sid is the governor of the Indian state of Kalabar, and audiences accepted it.

One thing Rogers and Thomas calculated would be a step too far for 1968 audiences to accept was the idea of Pinewood sets and the usual Carry On locations in a 20-mile radius of the studios standing in for colonial India's north-west frontier. Thus the highly unusual step, for a Carry On picture at least, was taken of sending the cast and crew out for a ten-day location shoot, a jaunt that broke the previous Carry On location record held by *Don't Lose Your Head*'s Camber Sands shoot. Fortunately, Rank authorised a substantial increase in budget from *Carry On Doctor*, spending £46,000 more than they had on the previous film. This total was still some £28,000 less than the record holder *Follow That Camel* (which was eventually knocked off its perch, thanks to raging inflation, by the shabby and cheap-looking *Carry On Emmannuelle* in 1978), but that had its total inflated by the salary of its American star Phil Silvers. With a fully homegrown cast of Carry On regulars, receiving their usual salaries, all of the budget for this one would be seen on screen.

Packing the production off to India was clearly going to be out of the question, so Gerald Thomas and his production manager, Jack Swinburne, instead chose the mountainous North Wales area of Snowdonia. This area had for some time been popular with British-based productions whose stories took them far afield. Ten years earlier, it had stood in for China in *The Inn of the Sixth Happiness*; it had doubled for Switzerland in the ITC filmed *The Adventures of William Tell* and in *The Saint* episode 'The Queen's Ransom'. When the *Carry On Up the Khyber* production arrived, the location had recently played host to the big-budget Gregory Peck spy movie *The Chairman*, for which the slopes of Mount Snowdon had once again represented China.

Having chosen the Snowdonia region to film in, the production then drew upon the knowledge of Colonel Goodchild, who was not only a local resident but had also served with the British army in just the area of India the film was trying to reproduce. Goodchild gave Gerald Thomas and his team a choice of four different suitable locations, from which was chosen the Watkin Path. This was a donkey track originally constructed in 1882, which led from the village of Plas Gwynant to the peak of Mount Snowden, though the production kept to the lower part of a track which runs for some four miles.

In another unusual move, director of photography Ernest Steward and his camera operator, James Bawden, did not accompany the production on location. Instead, the actors and the forty-strong troupe of locally recruited extras were photographed by H. A. R. Thomson and his camera operator, Neil Binney. Thomson was a highly experienced camera operator, billed variously and confusingly as Robert Thomson, Bob Thomson, H. A. R. Thomson, and even Russel Thomson, who was at this stage just starting to gain some experience as a director of photography, including on *The Avengers* episodes 'Take Me To Your Leader' and 'The Morning After'.

It may be more than a little obvious to say so, but *Carry On Up the Khyber* represents all aspects of the Carry On team working at their very peak. A top team of Carry On regulars was assembled—only Jim Dale was missing from the then-current ensemble, with Kenneth Connor and Hattie Jacques both on extended hiatuses from the films and Barbara Windsor not yet established as a regular cast member, this was pretty much as good as it got. Jim Dale would normally have been a natural choice for the role of Captain Keene, the chipper young officer in charge of the defences of the governor's mansion. With Dale unavailable due to stage commitments, trumpeter, dancer, and occasional film actor Roy Castle was drafted in. His most notable screen acting role prior to this had been in the Amicus portmanteau horror film *Dr. Terror's House of Horrors*, and the big screen adaptation of the BBC's long-running science-fiction hit *Doctor Who, Dr. Who and the Daleks*, both films having been released in 1965.

Also at the very top of his game is screenwriter Talbot Rothwell. I realise that I may be repeating myself a little at this point, but *Carry On Up the Khyber* shows Rothwell not only filling the movie with comic situations and gags, but also constructing a tightly written story. Take as an example an early scene in which Sir Sidney and Lady Ruff-Diamond are watching a polo match along with Randi Lall, the khasi of Kalabar. In one short scene, our main characters are introduced and their relationship with each other, the motor powering the entire plot, is established. Sid knows perfectly well that the khasi would happily massacre every British person in India, while the khasi comments that Sir Sidney's 'benevolent rule and wise guidance we could well do without'.

Also hilarious in this scene is Joan Sims' faux posh accent ('Oh I say, he did not half crack that one, did he not'), which introduces another important plot strand. It is made clear during the scene that Lady Ruff-Diamond fancies the khasi—if you will excuse the expression—and Sir Sidney's reaction to his wife's failure to sound sufficiently refined tells us that all is not well in the Ruff-Diamond marriage. All we need to complete the plot that will take us through the rest of the film is the touch of bawdy comic genius that only Rothwell could have written: the strange tale of the Devils in Skirts and the missing underwear.

Up the Khyber also represents one of Charles Hawtrey's best Carry On roles, seeing him far more central to the action than he would be in many other of the films. He even appears to be having quite a bit of fun chasing a harem girl around a fountain, despite the fact that this would be the last thing he might wish to do in real life. It puts one in mind of the scene in *Carry On Abroad* where he pelts the local police with fruit. It is as if Hawtrey relished the opportunity to let the mask slip occasionally, abandoning the cheerful and delicate screen persona and revealing the more riotous personality that would emerge more fully in his alcohol-fuelled final decade. This is Hawtrey in his element, reacting to the higher quality of the role by throwing himself into his work with at times gleeful abandon. The contrast to Hawtrey here and in his most recent straight-acting role, as civil servant Joshua Yellowlees in the Amicus productions SF cheapy *The Terrornauts*, which had been released in February 1967, is all too clear. In the supposedly 'serious' film, he barks out his dialogue in a gruff monotone (well, as gruff as Hawtrey got anyway), which suggests someone speaking in a language they only partly understand.

Bernard Bresslaw returns playing another of his fierce native warriors, Bungdit Din—as well as being a pleasingly terrible pun on Rudyard Kipling's heroic Indian character Gunga Din—a variation on Bresslaw's Sheikh Abdul Abulbul from *Follow That Camel*. Bernie was so good at playing imposing villains that he even essayed a hissing, reptilian alien between these two Carry On films in the *Doctor Who* serial 'The Ice Warriors'. We are often in perilous territory when a white British actor takes on an Indian role (Spike Milligan's attempts have not dated well) but Bresslaw worked so hard on his characterisations that he was able to produce a big, comedic performance that largely avoided racial caricature. It was a shame that he got few opportunities to produce big performances like this in future Carry On roles, as there was so much more in his range than playing the likes of Bernie Lugg (*Carry On Camping*) and Bernie Hulke (*Carry On at Your Convenience*).

Peter Butterworth gets to play a slightly different role this time, many of his previous Carry Ons saw him cast as part of a double act where he gets laughs by reacting, stealing scenes with great aplomb. Here, as the lascivious religious missionary Brother Belcher, he gets to act rather more independently and is central to the legendary governor's mansion climax, acting as the increasingly panic-stricken voice of sanity as the room collapses around the assembled diners. Without Butterworth's presence, the scene simply would not have worked.

An unusual and very welcome surprise participant is Cardew Robinson, a constant presence on the British comedy scene for decades who might be almost forgotten today were it not for his casting as the Fakir in *Up the Khyber*. He was actually not first choice for the role, being contacted after the legendary comedian/magician Tommy Cooper proved unable to accept due to other commitments. One can see how the part would have fitted Cooper, who did take the occasional movie role, but the part works at least as well with Robinson. Possibly more so, as his unexpected presence, looking like a wild man and sounding like a public-school educated English comedian, remains beautifully silly, adding one of those streaks of absurdity which helps make *Carry On Up the Khyber* so cherishable.

Angela Douglas gets rather less to do this time, as was the way with Carry On casting—aside from Sid and Kenny, the size of even the most regular of cast member's roles could vary enormously from film to film. It is somewhat of a shame that the part of Princess Jehli, daughter of the khasi, was to be Douglas' last Carry On role, as she is not ideal casting as an Indian princess. In fact, Douglas would not make another film for five years, returning to feature opposite her old Carry On comrade Jim Dale in 1973's *Digby the Biggest Dog in the World*.

I leave Sid James until last because it is so easy to take him for granted, but it has to be remembered that this was sort of a comeback for Sid. His role in *Carry On Doctor* had been deliberately reduced in size as he was recuperating from a major heart attack, but *Up the Khyber* sees Sid return in triumph. Not only does the role of Sir Sidney Ruff-Diamond prove to be the quintessential Sid James Carry On part, portraying him as unhappily married, lecherous, of dubious honesty, but quick-witted. Sid makes it all look so easy. It is often said that Sid was just playing himself, but if it was that easy everyone would be doing it—it took a lot of skill and years of experience to be so natural in front of the camera.

At this point we have to address the comedic mastodon in the room: the climax of *Carry On Up the Khyber*. This is, of course, no ordinary climax, or even just a particularly satisfying ending to a Carry On picture. The siege of the governor's mansion has taken on a life of its own to become a touchstone of British film comedy. The genius of the sequence is such that it is almost as funny when watched on its own, away from the context of the film. This can be seen from the fact that the scene was lightly rewritten and performed once again by a different cast of Carry On regulars as part of the 1972 *Carry On Christmas* TV special. At the same time, it is an absolutely integral part of the film, gaining momentum as the scene becomes ever more extreme. Talbot Rothwell manages to top his achievement in creating the basic situation by actually thinking of an ending which is not only satisfying, ending the film on the biggest laugh imaginable, but is quite probably the greatest ending of an action comedy in all of cinema, and still Kenneth Williams gets the last word, which must have pleased him no end.

The BBFC required three cuts in the film, all for dialogue. One was the mysterious removal of Bernard Bresslaw's line 'He's just a travelling Fakir', which is aimed at Cardew Robinson's character and is quite plainly a mild reference to the F-word; this would be fine if they had not cleared the later, far more explicit use of the term with the line 'Fakir—off!'.[1] Happily, the footage containing the cut line was retained by Peter Rogers Productions, which tended not to keep outtakes or extraneous material, and it reinstated when the film was submitted once again to the BBFC in 1987 for home video release.

18

Carry On Camping (1969)

Filming Dates: 7 October 1968–22 November 1968
Original Certificate: A (Classified by BBFC 9 January 1969 [cut])
Running Time: 88 minutes

Release Details

London Release: 3 July 1969 (Metropole, in London's Victoria replacing *Sweet Charity*).

British moviegoers flocked to their local Odeon cinemas in unprecedented numbers to see *Carry On Camping*, which began its general release from 7 July 1969. Rank's choice of support feature was not only (as ever) seemingly random, but also dependent on where in the country you happened to see it. In many areas, audiences had the chance to see a comedy double bill, with the 1968 Universal Pictures production *Did You Hear the One About the Travelling Saleslady* providing the backup. This was a period comedy starring Phyllis Diller as a pianola saleswoman who brings chaos and disaster in her wake. Others got to see *Hell is Empty*, a British crime thriller shot in Czechoslovakia with two credited directors, John Ainsworth and Bernard Knowles, thanks to the tragic circumstances of its production. Much of the film was shot in 1965 under the direction of Knowles, but production was abandoned when leading lady Martine Carol died suddenly on location. Filming was eventually resumed in 1967, by which time another cast member, Patricia Viterbo, had also been killed in a car accident when a stunt went wrong filming another movie in Paris. If you happened to be in Wales or Northern Ireland then Camping was paired with *A Prince for Wales*, a documentary about Prince Charles, whose investiture as prince of Wales took place on 1 July 1969. In a few places, *Camping* played with the 1966 James Garner comedy spy movie *A Man Could Get Killed*, and in a few others with Eric Sykes' modern day silent comedy *The Plank*.

What's Carrying On?

Workmates Sid Boggle (Sidney James) and Bernie Lugg (Bernard Bresslaw) think that they are luring their unsuspecting girlfriends (Joan Sims and Dilys Laye) to a nudist colony. Instead, they wind up on a campsite run by greedy farmer Josh Fiddler along with a disparate group all looking for a holiday in the great outdoors. A welcome addition for Sid is a coachful of girls from Chayste Place finishing school—less welcome is a group a hippies who turn up in the next field to hold a rock concert.

Who's Carrying On?

A Peter Rogers Production
Director: Gerald Thomas
Screenplay by Talbot Rothwell
Music composed and conducted by Eric Rogers
Photography: Ernest Steward BSC
Art Director: Lionel Couch
Editor: Alfred Roome
Sidney James: Sid Boggle, the randy old man who is trying to fool his girlfriend Joan into going on a nudist holiday and instead finds himself in a muddy field in the middle of nowhere.
Charles Hawtrey: Charlie Muggins, helpless and hapless would-be camper who loses his tent and indulges his talent to eat endlessly by sponging off all and sundry.
Joan Sims: Joan Fussy, still single in her mid-thirties and trying to get from under the thumb of her harridan of a mother.
Kenneth Williams: Dr Kenneth Soaper, headmaster of the Chayste Place School for Girls, trying to keep his eyes off the girls and his body out of the clutches of fellow teacher Miss Haggard.
Terry Scott: Peter Potter, a middle-class businessman who loathes the countryside and wants nothing more than a nice, restful holiday abroad.
Barbara Windsor: Babs, ringleader of the finishing school girls who wants to get her hands on almost any feller available; also owner of the world's first flying bikini top.
Hattie Jacques: Miss Haggard, teacher at Chayste Place who attempts to chaperone the girls, and finds her dormant desires rekindled by Dr Soaper.

Bernard Bresslaw: Bernie Lugg, Sid's workmate who finds himself roped into his nudist colony scheme, who is dating Joan's friend Anthea.
Julian Holloway: Jim Tanner, laddish coach driver.
Dilys Laye: Anthea Meeks, Joan's friend, dwarfed by, but very attracted to Bernie Lugg. Also very, very carsick.
Peter Butterworth: Joshua Fiddler, the greedy farmer who owns the campsite, always armed with excuses to charge his customers extra.
Betty Marsden: Harriet Potter, Peter Potter's wife, who never listens to a word he says and has a laugh like an asthmatic goose.

Carry On Critics

The Times had a new film reviewer by 1969 in the form of Michael Billington, now a distinguished theatre critic. Although at this stage he seems generally supportive of the Carry Ons, *Camping* seems to have insufficiently tickled his funny bone: 'The jokes, however, don't pour out in their customary profusion and one gets the impression that camping (in a field that is) isn't quite as funny a subject as it sounds.'

The *Monthly Film Bulletin* were as damning as ever, while acknowledging that there actually were a group of people among the general film audience that actually enjoyed these films:

> Only really recommended for *aficionados* of the Carry On series. Full of the usual smutty jokes... *Camping* suffers from an excess of over-acting from almost everyone involved, and most of the gags are either telegraphed or mistimed. Perhaps the series now needs a rest, or at least an injection of new script talent.

Both the box office returns and the subsequent raising of the status of *Carry On Camping* to one of the classics of the series suggests that the *Monthly Film Bulletin* reviewer may be mistaken. I cannot imagine that Gerald Thomas or the cast of the film would have been too pleased at being accused of mistiming gags, either.

The general critical consensus among the glossy magazines and broadsheet newspapers was no better, with John Coleman in *The New Statesman*, Margaret Hinxman in *The Sunday Telegraph*, David Robinson in *The Financial Times*, and Derek Malcolm in *The Guardian* queuing up to heap opprobrium on poor little *Carry On Camping*. Malcolm did come up with the following amusing exchange, however:

> As a communist friend of mine said to me afterwards: 'Don't you like ordinary down-to-earth working-class humour?' 'Well, er ... no, actually.'

> I replied defensively, adding with more defiance: 'But surely the young working class of today have too much of the real thing to bother about this ersatz sexual snidery?' Wrong again, apparently. Her daughter thought it was great. Okay, I quit.

In *The Daily Mirror*, the verdict from Dick Richards was at least a qualified thumbs-up: 'It does its job well, but what this one lacks compared with Carry On Up the Khyber is even the hint of a plot.'

Penelope Mortimer's *Observer* review of Sunday, 6 July 1969 makes for grim reading:

> How nice it would be, this week, to be a complete philistine, able to say that I enjoyed *Carry On Camping* more than Jancsó (whose grim Hungarian drama *Silence and Cry* was reviewed by Mortimer in the same edition). But I didn't. After 'Khyber', which had at least 10 hilarious minutes, 'Camping' is very damp indeed.

She was, however, one of the few to identify the oddly sour note on which the film ended: 'an unpleasant sequence in which The Gang brutally destroy a harmless hippie rave-up. If this is *vox populi*, we are in worse shape than we know.'

All of the above quite neatly acts as a demonstration of the power (or lack of same) of film critics, and their ability to lag behind popular taste, as the latest Carry On movie absolutely cleaned up at the UK box office.

Variety gave an American perspective on the film that was also less than positive: 'While sticking to its well-tried, profitable formula, latest Carry On suffers somewhat on comparison to some of its predecessors in that it lacks a storyline, however slim.'

Carry On Comments

Carry On Camping is perhaps the ultimate in contemporary-set films in the Carry On series. With all the main cast members of this era present and correct with the exception of Kenneth Connor, and each given a role tailor-made for their abilities. Sid James, Bernard Bresslaw, Charles Hawtrey, Joan Sims, Barbara Windsor, and Kenneth Williams even get to keep their own forenames on screen, which demonstrates that they were very much playing the roles the Carry On audience expected of them and loved them for.

Talbot Rothwell's script is perhaps his most episodic, containing a very basic plotline in which Sid, Bernie, and Terry Scott's characters go through all manner of physical indignities until they prove their manhood by direct physical action. Only at this point do the three finally gain the physical affection of their wives and girlfriends, who have for the rest of the film either disapproved of or totally ignored them.

All this shameful overanalysing aside, another interesting part of *Carry On Camping* is its opening scene, which references a now-forgotten byway of British cinema history—the nudist movie. Younger audiences watching *Camping* might have their doubts that a suburban cinema would show such a film as *Nudist Paradise* that Sid and Bernie take the girls to see—and that they managed to convince them to go see a film with that title in the first place. In fact the nudist documentary was a genuine phenomenon, a wheeze by which exploitation producers managed to squeeze previously undreamt of amounts of nudity past the heavy censorship restrictions of the late 1950s and early '60s, when this phenomenon was at its height. Even more amazingly, some quite respected filmmakers directed some of these films (Michael Winner directed one as well), one of whom was Charles Saunders, an experienced film and television director who in 1958 was roped in to direct the first ever British nudist documentary, which was entitled—you guessed it—*Nudist Paradise*.

Made in colour and CinemaScope for an amazingly frugal £15,000, the film went into profit in a matter of weeks and spawned hundreds of imitators. Ten years later, the memory of *Nudist Paradise*, reshot for the purposes of *Carry On Camping*, allowed Rogers and Thomas to introduce the first nudity into a Carry On film since we were treated to the sight of Leslie Philips, Kenneth Connor, and Kenneth Williams' bare bottoms in *Carry On Constable*.

While Sid and Bernie are, truth be told, a tad old for the roles of bachelors struggling to attract the interest of their own girlfriends, this adds a touch of comedic poignancy to their characters not dissimilar to the fiftysomething Reg Varney as Stan Butler in television's *On the Buses* still living with his mother. *On the Buses* coincidentally started its wildly successful television run some five months before *Carry On Camping* opened in the nation's cinemas. The idea of the pair lusting after the party of schoolgirls that turns up is perhaps not the most acceptable of notions to modern audiences, but most of them do not look a day under thirty. Barbara Windsor was aged thirty-one at the time of filming and the sight of her in hot pants represents a very un-schoolgirlish symphony in cellulite.

As the adults nominally in charge of the schoolgirls of Chayste Place, Kenneth Williams and Hattie Jacques are at their peak in an acknowledged repeat of their roles in *Carry On Doctor*. When Kenneth's Dr Soaper inadvertently reignites the long-formant passions of Hattie's Mrs Haggard, the results are another hilarious bout of Williams trying to avoid the full force of Jacques' attentions. The climax to this scene is a clever acknowledgement that we have been here before, which is both incredibly self-referential and one of Talbot Rothwell's best pieces of writing.

Peter Butterworth has a smaller role than normal as Farmer Fiddler, but absolutely makes the most of his every moment on screen as the money-grabbing campsite owner. Joan Sims and Dilys Laye have somewhat thankless parts as Sid and Bernie's girlfriends. In many ways, they are straight-women acting as feeds to the men's laughter lines, but they are also the fixed points around which the film revolves. It is believable that the boys want to be with them, and that they have to truly earn a place in the girls' affections.

Terry Scott gives possibly his best Carry On performance here as Peter Potter, desperate for a comfortable foreign holiday but instead once again stuck in rainy Britain where everything possible chases, stings, bites, shoots, at or poops on him. Scott really earns his place at the top rank of Carry On actors here, his mounting humiliation expressed via an array of dead-eyed, utterly humiliated and fed up stares as he is landed not only with his own wife (the marvellous Betty Marsden) but also Charles Hawtrey as Charlie Muggins. Hawtrey reached the unheard of heights of second billing here, which partially goes to show how random the billing on Carry On movies was. This is not really his best Carry On role, but full comedic value is extracted from the sight of the spindly Hawtrey legs in baggy shorts. He also gets the best individual gag in the film, so good that it was used in full in the film's trailer—I will not spoil it here; you will have to see the film.

The trouble with films that are episodic in nature is that they are hard to write endings for, and in this respect, *Carry On Camping* drops the ball a little with one of the most bizarre endings in the series history. In the sort of story development that had previously featured in Norman Hudis' Carry On scripts, the disparate group of campers have to work together in a common cause that bonds them together. A group of noisy hippies turns up in the next field for a rock concert (composer Eric Rogers appears to have never heard a rock tune in his life), and in revenge, the campers blow up their equipment, tie the harmless hippies up, and spray them with poo—a starker example of the generation gap and on which side of it the Carry On team found itself could not be imagined.

It is a strange fact that there is so much going on in *Carry On Camping* that the film's most famous sequence, in which Barbara Windsor's bra flies off into Kenneth Williams' face during the schoolgirls' morning exercises, comes across as something of an afterthought. The scene has been used so frequently in Carry On retrospectives, shorn of its context, that it has really become an entity in its own right. Although the bra-flying scene is a bit of a blink-and-you'll-miss-it moment for audiences watching *Carry On Camping*, it has become symbolic of an entire Carry On era. In one short sequence, the established characters of Kenneth Williams, Hattie Jacques, and Barbara Windsor are summed up in the broadest of strokes.

A final word should go to *Carry On Camping*'s cinematographer Ernest Steward, who performed absolute miracles to make a freezing cold British October look like August.

The BBFC insisted on several cuts before passing Carry On Camping for an 'A' certificate, Talbot Rothwell's ever bawdier jokes were now outside the context of a historical setting, or the hermetically sealed environment of a hospital. Perhaps *Camping* being set in a contemporary environment made the film seem ruder than before. Double entendres about putting tents up (or, to use a technical term used in comedy circles, knob gags) were rather stronger stuff than silly puns about 'the duc de Pomfritte' that Rothwell was writing three years earlier. Lines such as 'Erection is fairly simple; it's getting it to stay up' had to go of the film was going to be passed with a 'A' certificate. Some lines were saved by changing the shots in which some dialogue was heard, so we see a visual demonstration to go along with the line 'How about those two things sticking out in front', reducing the innuendo to a level acceptable to 1969 censors.[1]

19

Carry On Again Doctor (1969)

or Where There's a Pill There's a Way
or The Bowels are Ringing
or If You Say That's Your Thermometer I'll Have to Believe You, But It's a Funny Place to Put It.

Filming Dates: 17 March 1969–2 May 1969
Original Certificate: A (Classified by BBFC 10 June 1969 [cut])
Running Time: 90 minutes 1 second

Release Details

London Release: 3 December 1969 (Metropole, in London's Victoria).

Although *Carry On Again Doctor* premiered in London at the beginning of December, it did not find a slot in Rank's general release schedule until the very end of the month, with the first screenings happening on 28 December. The Rank Organisation, through its Odeon cinema chain, sent *Carry On Again Doctor* out with precisely the same B-pictures that had accompanied *Carry On Camping*, simply swapping the areas around so audiences generally got to see something new. In some areas, *The Plank* was rolled out once again, while in a few spots entirely different films were chosen as support. Belfast tended to get unusual support features, in this case the comedy *Don't Just Stand There*, starring Robert Wagner and Mary Tyler Moore, while in Coventry, Jack Lord starred in *The Counterfeit Killer*. As was by now normal for Rank releases since the demise of the British support feature, all of these (with the exception of *The Plank*) were low–medium-budget productions from Universal Studios. On its re-release, *Carry On Again Doctor* was paired with *Don't Lose Your Head*, and in some places, it was seen with the compilation film *The World of Abbott and Costello*.

What's Carrying On?

The hapless and accident-prone Dr Jim Nookey is forced to leave Long Hampton Hospital and loses his girlfriend Goldie Locks after his drinks are spiked at a hospital dance. Chief Surgeon Dr Carver needs a sucker to take over running the Moore Medical Mission on Azure Bay in the Beatific Islands, and the lovesick, unemployed Nookey takes the job. He winds up at the Mission, a rotting shack where nobody ever goes for treatment, run by Medical Orderly Gladstone Screwer. Screwer has invented a miracle slimming drug, and Nookey heads for home, realising he can make a fortune from this. Carver turns up at Nookey's new clinic wanting to know his secret, while Screwer turns up wanting a bigger slice of the action.

Who's Carrying On?

A Peter Rogers Production
Director: Gerald Thomas
Screenplay by Talbot Rothwell
Music composed and conducted by Eric Rogers
Photography: Ernest Steward BSC
Art Director: John Blezard
Editor: Alfred Roome

Sidney James: Gladstone Screwer, born on the Beatific Islands and works as the orderly there at the Moore Medical Mission. Horny, boozy, and inventor of a miraculously successful slimming serum.

Kenneth Williams: Dr Frederick Carver, chief surgeon at Long Hampton Hospital. Very pleased with himself and his terrible jokes and desperate to part wealthy widow Mrs Moore from her money to set up a posh medical institution.

Charles Hawtrey: Dr Ernest Stoppidge, deputy to Dr Carver who wants to get rid of Dr Nookey and is not above a bit of cross-dressing and alcohol poisoning to get his way.

Jim Dale: Dr James Nookey, accident-prone doctor who finds himself rejected by his girlfriend and posted to a tatty Medical Mission on the Beatific Islands, only to return in triumph with a cure for obesity.

Joan Sims: Mrs Ellen Moore, wealthy widow with an interest in funding medical charities, and an even bigger interest in Dr Nookey.

Barbara Windsor: Goldie Locks (aka Maude Boggins, aka Melody Madders), model and actress whose appearance at Long Hampton Hospital in an incredible brief costume raises the temperature of Dr Nookey.

Hattie Jacques: Matron, the fearsome matron of Long Hampton Hospital who jumps ship to join Dr Nookey's slimming clinic and catches the eye of Gladstone Screwer (they like 'em big where he comes from)

Patsy Rowlands: Miss Fosdick, Frederick Carver's secretary who displays unexpected depths of passion and becomes Gladstone Screwer's latest, and probably last, wife.

Carry On Critics

John Russell Taylor was back at *The Times* to review *Carry On Again Doctor* for the paper's Thursday 4 December edition, but even this most staunch of Carry On supporters saw the latest example as falling short of classic status:

> This time it is very much the mixture as before: too much so, really, since by now the supply of bedpan jokes is getting noticeably short… What then happens provides fun which is fast enough, if scarcely furious, and the talents of Charles Hawtrey (in drag again) Kenneth Williams, Joan Sims, Hattie Jacques and the rest are exercised if not noticeably stretched. Just the thing to keep the series ticking over, if hardly likely to make any fresh converts. But then, by now who is left to convert?

Richard Roud, in *The Guardian*'s 5 December edition, was forced into all kinds of literary gymnastics in order to excuse himself from the heinous crime of having actually quite enjoyed parts of *Carry On Again Doctor*: 'From time to time my boredom was succeeded by detached peals of hysterical laughter, as if the noise weren't coming from my lungs but from someone else's. Regression, no doubt.'

The *Monthly Film Bulletin* began their review with what read suspiciously like a compliment, before returning to their usual slag-off mode:

> Something of a departure for the Carry On series in that this one has the semblance of a plot. In all other respects, though, it is the old familiar routine ... Lavatory jokes and excruciating puns proliferate, and if anything the level of humour is even lower than usual.

The mixed reception to the new film was added to by *Variety*'s verdict, which was unusually harsh: 'In this film much of the patter is flat and vulgar without being over-funny. Some situations (such as when Dale 'blows' an electric contraption and turns the hospital into chaos) are very funny. But there aren't enough.'

Readers of *Films and Filming* had to wait until February 1970 for the magazine's verdict on *Carry On Again Doctor*, which was delivered by Richard Davis. By now, the Carry Ons were so established in the entertainment world that David compared them to that anarchic band of a previous generation and favourite of the house of Windsor, the Crazy Gang:

> There's no stopping these perennial comics: they occupy the same niche in the cinema that the Crazy Gang had in the theatre, without, of course, the pseudo-Establishment respectability that was sponsored by Royalty. It would be interesting to ask Prince Philip, perhaps, never unforthcoming in his opinions, what he thinks of the Carry Ons. Then perhaps we might reserve a Royal Premiere for the next one—*Jungle Boy* I believe.

While repeating the perennial complaint of the professional film critic that nothing said in print about the film will have any effects whatsoever, Davis slipped in an admission that he was not immune to the charms of the Carry Ons:

> What on *Earth* can one say that is new about these works? Either you love 'em or loathe 'em, and nothing a critic says will matter one jot. Their devotees can recognise with delighted anticipation a gag coming half a reel away, and they're not disappointed at any predictability. Personally I adore the names. Charles Hawtrey seems exactly right as Dr Stoppidge. The new permissive aura naturally adds fuel to the Carry On fire, and perhaps the team go that much further than before. Their fans will be delighted; those who aren't won't care.

The recorded views of one critic were not revealed to the public at the time: those of Kenneth Williams, whose hilariously blinkered review of *Carry On Again Doctor* appeared in his diaries, which were edited by Russell Davies and published in 1993:

> My performance as Carver, the surgeon, is remarkably authoritative and the incredibly banal lines which I have to say are made acceptable by the sort of style and panache I bring to the role. I was surprised and pleased, save for the fact that the greying hair was quite noticeable at times. Alas! my youth has left me. This should be the last film I do.[1]

It was not, of course, but he would miss the next film due to other work commitments.

Carry On Comments

So unexpected was the roaring success of *Carry On Doctor* that a follow-up medical comedy was called for in double-quick time. Fortunately, Talbot Rothwell had just the thing in his bottom drawer in the shape of a script he had been commissioned to write a couple of years earlier. This had been a projected instalment in the Betty Box/Ralph Thomas Doctor series of films, which was ultimately passed over—one can see how Rothwell's style might have been a little broad for the Doctor films, which even by the mid-1960s still harked back in their manner to their 1950s origins.

Even the trailer for the new film promised audiences more of the same, as a rather posh Rank announcer (replacing the British-based American actor David Healey, who had been voicing the trailers in recent years) announced somewhat unenthusiastically: 'If you enjoyed *Carry On Doctor*, don't miss the most comical of the crazy Carry On Comedies with all your favourite characters in *Carry On Again Doctor*'.

With the addition of an even larger helping of broad humour than ever, what was, in effect, a direct sequel to *Carry On Doctor* was delivered. The basic idea of a miracle slimming drug was re-tooled for Rogers and Thomas' requirements with even more innuendo than previous films in the series, starting with the name of the institution in which the action was largely set—Long Hampton Hospital. The Carry Ons were approaching their peak as a box-office attraction and sex was clearly selling. The increasingly middle-aged Carry On crew may have been shut out of the sweetshop that was the 1960s sexual revolution (as the ending of *Carry On Camping* had demonstrated) but they made sure that their noses were pressed up against the window.

Jim Dale, unavailable for *Camping*, returned for what turned out to be his final appearance in the original film series, giving a full-throttle performance around which the entire film revolves. Demonstrating more than ever that, apart from Sid's place at the top, the order of billing in a Carry On movie was pretty much random, Dale was rewarded for his physically very demanding role with fourth place in the cast list.

After the almost free-form series of comedic situations that made up *Carry On Camping*, the origins of *Carry On Again Doctor* meant that the script for the new film, by Carry On standards, had a superabundance of plot. The first half hour of the film runs upon similar lines to *Carry On Doctor*, with the important difference that the focus was far more on the medical staff than the patients this time. Kenneth Williams as the preening Chief Surgeon Dr Frederick Carver and Hattie Jacques as Matron in particular play virtually the same roles as before. Charles Hawtrey this time features as one of the medics, Dr Stoppidge, deputy to Carver and determined to rid the hospital of the hapless and accident-prone Dr Nookey. The latter is played, of course, by Jim Dale, whose physical abilities and background as a trained tumbler were by now recognised and encouraged by Gerald Thomas.

So central is Dr Nookey to the film that he is given two major physical action sequences in this opening section alone. In the first, while trying to impress his new patient and potential new girlfriend Goldie Locks (Barbara Windsor), his use of the X-ray machine throws the hospital's electrical system into chaos.

Actually, the peerless Bob Todd gets the biggest laugh here with only his eyes visible as a patient wearing an oxygen mask who is literally blown up! In the second sequence, his fruit punch spiked with medical alcohol by Dr Stoppidge, Nookey runs amok through the hospital looking for Goldie. This climaxes in a genuinely dangerous stunt in which Dale hurtles down a flight of stairs on a runaway trolley, suffering quite a serious real-life arm injury in the process. Even more impressive is another stunt earlier in the scene in which Jim Dale achieves the not inconsiderable feat of bouncing across a hospital ward from one bed to the next.

It would have been nigh-on impossible for *Carry On Doctor* to top this sequence, and to its credit, it does not try. The story instead takes a sharp left-turn as the suddenly unemployed and girlfriendless Dr Nookey, at the urging of Dr Carver, accepts a job at Joan Sims' crumbling medical mission at Azure Bay on the tropical Beatific Islands. There he meets Medical Orderly Gladstone Screwer, played by Sid James, making an uncommonly late entrance to a Carry On. As the mission is ignored by the locals and the weather on the islands is anything but beatific, Screwer has little to do all day but live up to his name. Eventually, the film's second major plot strand is introduced, when Nookey discovers that Screwer has invented a miracle slimming drug. Screwer thinks little of this development, since the men of the islands like their women on the large side, but Nookey sees the commercial possibilities and heads back to England with a supply of the drug.

Things get more than a little overcomplicated at this point, as Carver heads for the islands to rescue Nookey at the urging of Mrs Moore and her cheque book, but is shipwrecked for three months. In the meantime, Nookey arrives in England and sets up a series of wildly successful slimming clinics with Mrs Moore. Carver arrives back to find Dr Stoppidge doing his old job at the hospital and ropes him in to help find the secret of Nookey's success. In the meantime, Gladstone Screwer learns how much money Nookey is making and turns up to demand a bigger slice of the action. The last twenty minutes or so actually work very well, as all the cast members are finally in the same place at the same time. The unusually complex nature of the plot, which at some points in the narrative gets in the way of Talbot Rothwell's usual flow of gags, finally allows *Carry On Again Doctor* to ascend (rather than descend) to the level of farce.

Two performers especially shine towards the end of the film: Charles Hawtrey goes undercover at the slimming clinic as Lady Puddleton, giving the actor his first opportunity in some time to appear in drag for a Carry On. Hawtrey pitches his performance perfectly—if he were any more or any less convincing, the joke would not have worked nearly so well. Later Carry On films had a tendency to attempt easy laughs by putting Bernard Bresslaw into female clothing, but this was never as effective as when Hawtrey did drag.

The tiny, bird-like Hawtrey had made a career of female roles in his early stage days and was able to give such roles an added touch of verisimilitude compared to the hulking, 6-foot 7-inch Bresslaw.

Sidney James, meanwhile, gives a lovely, relaxed, unforced performance as Gladstone Screwer. Born and raised on the Beatific Islands, he is literally an innocent abroad when in Britain, interested in little else but whisky and sex. Completely unfamiliar with Western standards of attractiveness, Screwer is an equal opportunities letch as keen on the idea of falling into bed with Hattie Jacques' Matron as he is with Lady Puddleton—at least until he realises the lady is a man.

Finally, while this was to be the final Carry On of the series' original run for Jim Dale, the series did gain a valuable new addition here in the shape of Patsy Rowlands, who gives an excellent comic turn as Carver's secretary Miss Fosdick and would return in a further eight films in the series. In *Again Doctor*, she fits in so naturally to the team that it is like she has been there forever.

Carry On Again Doctor represents something of the end of an era for the Carry On films. Jim Dale was offered the role of Cecil the Jungle Boy in the next film in the series, *Carry On Up the Jungle*, but upon seeing that the role had no dialogue turned it down flat. Dale was not approached about another Carry On role until the 1992 revival of the series with *Carry On Columbus*, but regardless of this, the actor had outgrown the series and needed a larger stage for his talents. The loss of Dale was palpable. The actor was thirty-four years old by 1969, a younger actor able to stand toe-to-toe with the likes of Kenneth Williams and Sid James and match them on screen. Although younger male actors were hired for future Carry Ons, most notably Julian Holloway, Richard O'Callaghan, and Kenneth Cope, Peter Rogers and Gerald Thomas never found a replacement who could carry the weight of a film's narrative in the way that Dale could.

20

Carry On Up the Jungle (1970)

or The African Queens
or Stop Beating About the Bush
or Show Me Your Waterhole and I'll Show You Mine

Filming Dates: 13 October 1969–21 November 1969
Original Certificate: A (Classified by BBFC 21 January 1970 [cut])
Running Time: 89 minutes

Release Details

London Release: 20 March 1970 (Metropole).

Carry On Up the Jungle appears to have had something of a staggered release, with some areas outside London getting the film from Sunday 12 April, some three weeks after the film's West End release. In other areas, it did not open until May or even June. Despite this, *Carry On Up the Jungle* proved a big hit for Rank, and the audiences that flocked to see it were in most places treated to *Mister Jerico* as the support film. This was a pilot for a prospective television series starring Patrick Macnee, star of the recently ended *The Avengers*. Made for Lew Grade's Incorporated Television Company at some expense on location in the South of France, this starred Macnee and Connie Stevens as a pair of rival con artists both trying to steal a valuable diamond from corrupt millionaire Herbert Lom. This featured many former *Avengers* crew, including producer Julian Wintle, writer Philip Levene, director Sidney Hayers and composer Laurie Johnson. After all that effort, the end result was somewhat uninspiring and no series resulted. In a few places, *Carry On Up the Jungle* was paired with the documentary *Under the Table You Must Go*, which was more widely seen with the next film in the Carry On series.

What's Carrying On?

Professor Inigo Tinkle presents an illustrated lecture telling of his recent expedition to a previously unexplored area of Africa in search of the legendary Oozalum Bird. Accompanying him are his assistant Claude Chumley and Lady Evelyn Bagly, who is in search of her son who went missing in the area when he was a small child. Guiding them on their quest are safari guide Bill Boosey and Upsidasi, head of the native bearers. During their quest they happen upon a white man who has grown up in the jungle and a tribe of Amazon-like women from Afrodisia who capture the men on befalf of their king, Tonka the Great.

Who's Carrying On?

A Peter Rogers Production
Director: Gerald Thomas
Screenplay by Talbot Rothwell
Music composed and conducted by Eric Rogers
Photography: Ernest Steward BSC
Art Director: Vetchinsky
Editor: Alfred Roome
Frankie Howerd: Professor Inigo Tinkle, renowned ornithologist who travels to Africa in pursuit of both the Oozalum Bird and Lady Evelyn Bagly.
Sidney James: Bill Boosey, the world's worst jungle guide who misses absolutely everything he aims his gun at.
Charles Hawtrey: King Tonka the Great, King of Lovers, Father of Countless ... and long-lost husband of Lady Evelyn Bagley.
Joan Sims: Lady Evelyn Bagley, searching the jungle for her son Cecil, missing in Africa since he was a baby.
Terry Scott: Cecil of the Jungle, a young(ish) white man who has grown up in the wilds of Africa, but remains unable to do anything right.
Kenneth Connor: Claude Chumley, Professor Tinkle's assistant, madly in lust with Lady Evelyn, who wants nothing to do with his advances.
Bernard Bresslaw: Upsidasi, leader of the safari's team of native bearers.
Jacki Piper: June, Lady Evelyn's personal maid, who gets parted from the main group and tries to teach Cecil some basic English. She teaches him rather more about biology.

Carry On Critics

Monthly Film Bulletin was predictably, wearily unimpressed: 'Short on plot, the script relies more than ever on blue jokes and corny puns to tide over the large gaps in between bits of knockabout farce, but it looks as though the series is beginning to run out of steam'.

Penelope Mortimer, in *The Observer*'s 12 April edition, gave a similar verdict, describing *Carry On Up the Jungle* as 'inexcusably dreadful … Perhaps this particular barrel, now thoroughly scraped, should be thrown on the junk heap'.

Variety was less enthusiastic than usual, mainly due to cast changes from the standard on-screen team:

> The usual core of the Carry On cast is on parade but notable absentees are the supercilious Kenneth Williams, Hattie Jacques, Peter Butterworth and Jim Dale, and they are missed. Instead, producer Peter Rogers has brought in another notable favourite, Frankie Howerd. Latter, a fine comedian with characteristics of his own, does not jell as well in situation comedy as when he is a standup comedian.

Derek Malcolm in *The Guardian* on 9 April also noted that Howerd was less effective than usual this time around:

> What I want to know is why Frankie Howerd is not so good in this (script by Talbot Rothwell) as he is in television's *Up Pompeii*! (script by Talbot Rothwell). I can only surmise that on telly he ogles an audience, whereas on film he does not. And without us Mr Howerd is as lost as we should be without him.

Malcolm was less than impressed with the rest of the picture, despite the best efforts of the rest of the cast: 'Pretty terrible even by the series' own standards—no Kenneth Williams either, Sidney James, Joan Sims, Terry Scott, and Kenneth Connor do their best. Gerald Thomas directs as from memory.'

Films and Filming sent Christopher Cook to see *Carry On Up the Jungle*, his review appearing in the magazine's July 1970 edition. Cook was rather more positive than some of his colleagues about how the Carry On brand was bearing up in the new decade: 'the faintly blue *double entendres* about bed, bottoms and bosoms is as traditionally English as the music hall, and still as funny. None of the slightly fly-blown trappings of the swinging society here'. Cook describes the plot as 'thinner than the paper it was written on':

> But the story's thinness is amply filled out by the broadness of Talbot Rothwell's script … The old team, almost friends by now, haven't lost an

> ounce of their zest for the excruciating, which is a backhanded way of complimenting producer Peter Rogers and director Gerald Thomas. A sad omission from the usual cast is Kenneth Williams, but Frankie Howerd more than compensates for the loss. Howerd, who weekly turns Rothwell's television scripts for *Up Pompeii* into sheer gold, as a delight. Outrage blended with innocence and that rubber face work wonders.

Cook's final comments demonstrate how the Carry On series, which at this point were at their peak at the British box office, were in 1970 seen as an indestructible force:

> The film is an assured success. The Great British Public, as indefinable as the Silent Majority, know what they like and respond generously and uncritically when they get it. The Carry On habit is becoming increasingly hard to kick—that's if you want to kick it.

Carry On Comments

Carry On Up the Jungle saw some enforced reshuffling of the onscreen Carry On team. The role of Professor Inigo Tinkle was specifically written for Kenneth Williams, but for the first time since 1963's *Carry On Cabby*, the actor was unavailable due to other work. Williams was offered the smaller role of King Tonka in order that he could at least maintain a presence in the film, but turned the part down, so Charles Hawtrey was assigned the role instead.

Performers who could be called upon to take a leading role in a Carry On picture were few in number, as was proved when Rogers and Thomas had to recruit Hollywood star Phil Silvers to replace Sid James in *Follow That Camel*. They did not have to look quite so far this time, finding a willing participant in the form of Frankie Howerd, who had previously joined the team for *Carry On Doctor* three years earlier. Having made a triumphant comeback in the early 1960s, subsequently conquering the worlds of stage and television, Howerd retained a long-held ambition to become a film star. If Frankie was never destined to become Oscar material, he did rack up no less than four starring vehicles in the wake of both *Carry On Up the Jungle*, which performed strongly at the UK box office on its release in March 1970, and his hit BBC sitcom *Up Pompeii*. The latter ran for two series in 1969 and 1970 with a movie version being released the following year, as was the norm in the early 1970s for any British sitcom that was even tolerated by the general public.

Ned Sherrin, the producer of the *Up Pompeii* film, saw possibilities in the format for a historical comedy film series to rival the Carry Ons, each of which would feature Frankie Howerd as a variation on his *Up Pompeii* character Lurcio. Thus he appeared in January 1972's *Up the Chastity Belt*, with a script by occasional Carry On scribe Sid Colin along with Ray Galton and Alan Simpson. A third film went straight into production, *Up the Front*, featuring Frankie in the trenches during the First World War and made it to cinemas by July 1972, in time for the summer holidays. Ned Sherrin certainly knew his writers, and this one was largely written by Sid Colin in partnership with Morecambe and Wise's main scriptwriter Eddie Braben. *Up the Front* managed to avoid a clash with Rogers and Thomas' 1972 production *Carry On Abroad*, which didn't reach cinemas until December of that year.

The public's interest in the 'Up The' series was not great enough to warrant the series continuing, but Frankie did manage one further movie starring role, in the 1973 mystery horror comedy *The House in Nightmare Park*. Howerd starred opposite that Welsh-born star of Hollywood's golden era, Ray Milland. This was a British twist on such Bob Hope vehicles as *The Cat and the Canary* and *The Ghost Breakers*, with Frankie taking the Hope role of the cowardly comedic hero around which murder and menace revolve. *The House in Nightmare Park* was the Frankie Howerd's favourite of his own films, but was to prove his swansong as a movie leading man—British film production was in dire straits by this time and the sad fact was that the type of comedy Frankie was best at was no longer being made for the big screen.

Meanwhile, the major role of Ug the Jungle Boy remained up for grabs after the first casting choice, Jim Dale, turned the dialogue-free part down. Fortunately, Terry Scott was on hand to give a very different take on the part than Dale would have provided. Despite having been in the very first Carry On film, Scott had only become a core cast member after his memorable turn as Sergeant Macnutt in *Carry On Up the Khyber*. Besides being a different physical type to slim Jim Dale, one of Scott's signature roles for most of his career was as an overgrown schoolboy and he brought just that sense of clumsy boyish enthusiasm to his tubby Tarzan. His casting should not really have worked, as Scott was in fact almost exactly three years older than Joan Sims, who plays his mother, but in fact it was one of the best parts of the film.

Barbara Windsor was also missing from the cast, and to be honest, there was no part really suitable for her in the film. With Joan Sims taking the main female role of Lady Evelyn, the part of June, her personal maid, needed someone with the same appeal as Angela Douglas. Rogers and Thomas had the great good fortune to discover Jacki Piper, who at the age of twenty-four was making her film debut. They were clearly impressed by her abilities as Peter Rogers Productions subsequently signed her up to a three-year contract.

Bernard Bresslaw returned as Upsidasi, leader of the safari's native bearers, his blackface performance representing, one supposes, the logical conclusion to the different ethnicities the actor had played to great effect in *Follow That*

Camel and *Carry On Up The Khyber*. The actor took his role so seriously that he went to the trouble of learning the correct African dialect, pains that were lost on the actors playing the other bearers, who were all of Caribbean heritage.

This was still a cast somewhat lacking in Carry On regulars. Luckily, Kenneth Connor was available for the first time since 1964's *Carry On Cleo* to fill the role of Inigo Tinkle's assistant Claude Chumley. In the intervening years, Connor had concentrated on stage and TV work, which left him time for only three movie roles. One of these was in *Cuckoo Patrol*, a vehicle for the Liverpudlian pop/comedy act Freddie and the Dreamers, which did not find a release until 1967, by which time Freddie Garrity and his band were no longer troubling the pop charts. Connor's other film role was in Eric Sykes' 1969 dialogue-free short *Rhubarb*. In the same year, Connor landed a role in a rather larger production, MGM's *Captain Nemo and the Underwater City*, featuring Hollywood stars Robert Ryan and Chuck Connors and shot in Malta and at MGM-British Borehamwood. His movie career from this point, however, would be tied inextricably to the Carry On series.

As for *Carry On Up the Jungle* itself, this is perhaps half a step down from the heights of comedy the Carry On series had generally maintained from *Carry On Cleo* in 1964 to *Carry On Again Doctor* six years later. Part of this is the fault of the plot's construction, which throws us into the main part of the action far too quickly. After a rather perfunctory opening scene in which Frankie Howerd's Professor Inigo Tinkle presents a magic lantern show, we are straight into the jungle setting with almost every main cast member introduced all at once. It is interesting that the film starts in precisely the same manner as *Carry On Doctor* with Howerd giving a lecture since this was a cornerstone of Frankie's stage act. It is also possible that, with the actor playing a much more central role than in *Carry On Doctor*, Rogers and Thomas worried that Howerd might overly dominate the proceedings and stepped back from giving him too much of the spotlight at such an early stage of the film.

As *Carry On Up the Jungle* is almost entirely set in a studio jungle, the proceedings have something of an enclosed and visually samey feel which is rather unavoidable, though the art director, Alex Vetchinsky, did produce a terrific group of sets. Once the film starts, the pacing of the film is off as the safari makes camp and stays in the same spot for a seemingly endless period, the plot not really getting going until most of the party are kidnapped and forced into sexual slavery by the Amazonian Lubbie Dubbie tribe. At this point, Sid gets some of his best dialogue, suggesting that the men go on strike, or as he helpfully explains 'down tools'. Sid's character of Bill Boosey, the world's worst jungle guide, is not really at the centre of the plot until this point, acting for most of the film as a sort of one-man Greek chorus, giving ribald commentary on the action going on around him.

The film also suffers a little from the series' inability to find a younger male performer. For the first time, one looks at the cast of a Carry On picture and, with the exception of Jacki Piper, sees a main cast which is starting to get on a little. On the plus side, it is really nice to see Joan Sims at this stage in her career playing a role in which her attractiveness is acknowledged, though it is a little odd to see her expressing a romantic interest in Frankie Howerd and Frankie to return the interest. This somehow does not fit in with the Howerd screen persona and is perhaps evidence of the last-minute nature of his casting.

Charles Hawtrey doesn't turn up until somewhat later in the film, which may possibly be the start of the process in the actor's last few Carry On appearances where the actor was somewhat sidelined. In this case however, I prefer to think that Peter Rogers and Gerald Thomas were keeping their powder dry and holding back one of the film's main comedic weapons until it could have maximum impact. As King Tonka the Great, aka Lady Evelyn's errant and presumed deceased husband Walter, Hawtrey gives his absolutely standard Carry On performance, which is absolutely perfect for the film. His bag of tricks may not have been deep, but he certainly knew how to use its contents.

Somewhat appropriately for a film which Peter Rogers had originally hoped to call *Carry On Tarzan*, there is an elephant in the room. As Upsidasi, Bresslaw plays the part in blackface, which is widely seen as somewhat problematic to a modern audience. In defence of both the actor and the film, the part is not written as a racial caricature and always maintains his dignity. Ultimately, *Carry On Up the Jungle*, like all of the historical Carry Ons, is not really about events of the time in which they are set, but instead is a parody of a movie genre, in this case Tarzan films.

Terry Scott and Jacki Piper, as the film's substitute Tarzan and Jane, are both excellent. Scott gets the biggest laughs with his incompetent attempts at swinging from tree to tree carrying a cartoonish edge not dissimilar to the *George of the Jungle* animated series, which had its original American run from September to December 1967. The series of jokes is also somewhat reminiscent of the Road Runner cartoons. Another pleasingly off the wall addition is Rueben Martin's spectacularly unconvincing gorilla, who is liable to turn up at any time. This series of gags can be traced back to Laurel and Hardy's 1938 feature *Swiss Miss*—at least the Carry Ons has the gorilla turn up in the depths of the Pinewood jungle instead of halfway up a Swiss Alp. Jacki Piper's character June has an unusually sophisticated character arc for a female Carry On character, developing from downtrodden personal maid to Lady Evelyn to lover/teacher/mother figure to the jungle boy.

21

Carry On Loving (1970)

or It's Not What You Feel, It's The Way That You Feel It
or Two's Company, But Three's Quite Good Fun Too
or Love Is A Four Letter Word
or It's Just One This On Top Of Another

Filming Dates: 6 April 1970–15 May 1970
Original Certificate: A (Classified by BBFC 2 July 1970 [cut])
Running Time: 86 minutes

Release Details

London Release Date: 8 November 1970.

There was an unusually long gap between the London premiere of *Carry On Loving* on 8 November 1970, at which point the reviews for the film began to appear, and its general release. Carry On fans outside the capital were not treated to the film until the very end of the month, with screenings beginning on Sunday, 29 November 1970.

Cinemagoers had a dizzying choice of supporting feature, depending on where in the United Kingdom they happened to be. In some areas, they had another chance to see Patrick Macnee capering about in the South of France in *Mister Jerico*, which had previously seen service as the B-picture to *Carry On Up the Jungle*. Elsewhere, they could have seen the fifty-two-minute documentary film *Under the Table You Must Go*, a documentary about the pubs, clubs, and discotheques in what remained of Swinging London. This was directed and produced by Arnold Louis Miller, previously responsible for such epics as *Nudes of All Nations* (1962) *Secrets of a Windmill Girl* (1966), and *London in the Raw* (1965). While *Mister Jerico* and *Under the Table You Must Go* were the most commonly occurring support features, some cinemas instead paired *Carry On Loving* with the last and least of Morecambe and Wise's three comedy vehicles made for Rank, *The Magnificent Two*. Elsewhere two different thrillers starring Gene Barry popped up in support; *Instanbul Express* and *Maroc 7*, while some places showed *Death of a Gunfighter*, a Western that achieved a footnote in movie history by being the first movie credited to the pseudonymous director Allan Smithee, the name used by directors who no longer wished to be associated with their film.

What's Carrying On?

Sidney and Sophie Bliss (Sid and Hattie) run the Wedded Bliss Agency, a marital agency that promises guaranteed results thanks to its cutting-edge computer system. The trouble is, the seemingly adoring Bliss couple can't stand each other and the computer is a fake. Sid tries to get their motley band of customers paired-up while making sure nobody gets too close to his own bit on the side, corset-maker Esme Crowfoot (Joan Sims). The trouble is, she has a huge and violent boyfriend in the shape of all-in wrestler Gripper Burke (Bernard Bresslaw) and Sophie is on to him, hiring private detective James Bedsop to find out what he is up to.

Who's Carrying On?

A Peter Rogers Production
Director: Gerald Thomas
Screenplay by Talbot Rothwell
Music composed and conducted by Eric Rogers
Photography: Ernest Steward BSC
Art Director: Lionel Couch
Editor: Alfred Roome
Sidney James: Sidney Bliss, joint proprietor of the Wedded Bliss Agency, who has been stringing his fiancée Sophie along for years with promises of their own marriage.
Kenneth Williams: Percival Snooper, the worst marriage guidance councillor in the world. He is a 'confirmed bachelor' with no knowledge of married life whatsoever forced to find a wife or lose his job.
Charles Hawtrey: James Bedsop, a private investigator hired by Sophie Bliss to find out what Sid is up to, his skills in disguise and discreet surveillance leave rather a lot to be desired.

Joan Sims: Esme Crowfoot, designer of lingerie and corsetry who Sid has designs on himself. She seems rather too nice both for him and her huge wrestler boyfriend Gripper.

Hattie Jacques: Sophie Bliss, at least she uses that as a professional name as she cannot get Sid to marry her. In desperation, she turns her attention to Percy Snooper, who might get more than he bargained for.

Terry Scott: Terence Philpot, man about town and would-be sexual adventurer sent on a series of disastrous dates by Wedded Bliss.

Richard O'Callaghan: Bertie Muffet, a non-combatant in the sexual revolution who has until now spent his spare time making aeroplanes out of milk bottle tops.

Bernard Bresslaw: Gripper Burke, boyfriend of Esme Crowfoot just back from a world all-in wrestling tour and determined to kill or main any man who even looks at her.

Jacki Piper: Sally Martin, struggling actress and model who accidentally goes on a date with Bertie Muffet and helps ruin flatmate Jenny Grubb's hot date.

Imogen Hassall: Jenny Grubb, a dull wallflower who blossoms spectacularly into a busty photographic model and the girl of Terry Philpot's dreams.

Patsy Rowlands: Miss Dempsey, Percy Snooper's loyal housekeeper, behind whose incredibly plain exterior lurks hidden passions, and in whose wardrobe lurks a lot of glittery purple clothes.

Carry On Critics

John Russell Taylor in *The Times*, always a supporter of the Carry Ons, gave a vote of confidence for the new film in *The Times*' Friday, 6 November 1970 edition:

> *Carry On Loving* is the mixture as before—how would it dare to be otherwise?—but one of the better recent examples of the series ... Perhaps in answer to recent criticisms of the Carry Ons, pays a lot more attention to reasonable farcical plotting. It also benefits from the work of one newcomer, Richard O'Callaghan, who plays the obligatory innocent with absolutely the right single-minded seriousness and apparent unconsciousness of the humour of his own situation.

The *Monthly Film Bulletin* was more antediluvian than ever in their verdict:

> Scrapings from the bottom of Talbot Rothwell's barrel of well-worn *double entendres*, delivered with mechanical efficiency by an equally well-worn

> cast of Carry On regulars. The subject is sex, but needless to say it remains a subject, since the characters shy away like startled geldings from any practical manifestation of their ceaseless preoccupation with copulation.

Amazingly, this reviewer manages to get the point while missing it entirely. The whole point of the Carry Ons is that the characters are like kids with their noses pressed against the sweetshop window, eyes wide with wonder at the delights within but lacking the price of a gobstopper. They are aware of the sexual revolution but can never be a part of it, except Sid, who is allowed to pull on memorable occasions (Sir Sidney Ruff-Diamond does very well indeed on this score, while his Mark Antony has a relationship with Cleopatra which is definitely more than platonic). Even Barbara Windsor *represents* sex in her Carry On persona more than she is an active participant.

Tom Milne in *The Observer*, on Sunday 8 November, similarly mentioned the lack of actual sex in *Carry On Loving*, partly to reassure his readers that the series regulars were not about to suddenly shed all their clothes in the cause of their art:

> So far distant is the permissive society that although the dialogue trots out every tired old sexual *double entendre* known to man, a mild cleavage is enough to see the characters twittering with excitement, while a bed is a signal for everyone to run for home.

Three days earlier, *The Guardian* printed Derek Malcolm's unenthusiastic review, which described *Loving* as 'this dizzily mirthless farrago'.

Variety described the plot as 'nondescript' and the climactic custard pie-fight as 'rather too deliberately planned and directed to achieve full comedy effect'. It was not all negative, however: 'The string of situations, heavily garnished with indigo jokes, are often crazily irrelevant yet somehow manage to fit in with a kind of crazy mad logic.'

Late to the party as ever, *Films and Filming*'s review of *Carry On Loving* did not appear until that magazine's January 1971 edition. That publication's correspondent, Peter Buckley, gave the film very fair-minded consideration indeed:

> Only a mean and angry soul could fail to derive some measure of enjoyment from the Carry On series, and while *Carry On Loving*, the 20th in this unending saga, may not be vintage foolery, it does have its predictably bright moments ... With the exception of Richard O'Callaghan, there is absolutely nothing new to be found in *Loving*: full of tired jokes, obvious situations and ludicrous performances, we have all been here at least three times before, but the crew have a way of working over the old material.

Carry On Comments

Carry On Loving is as different to its predecessor as it is possible for two films of the same series to be. In place of the studio-bound, middle-aged *Carry On Up the Jungle*, we have a film with extensive outdoor photography, giving us some lovely views of 1970s Windsor. Coupled with this is a cast that blends a set of Carry On regulars at the very top of their game with a set of younger actors who take to Carry On life like ducks to water. Clearly, this approach worked very well as *Carry On Loving* was the fourth most popular film at the British box office in 1970.

Made with traditional Carry On efficiency on a budget of £215,000, which was not a great deal of money even in 1970, this latest film showed that even in its twelfth year, the series was more profitable than ever. Despite the low budget, Art Director Lionel Couch and Cinematographer Ernest Steward conspired with Gerald Thomas to make a very good-looking film. Extensive location filming in Windsor gives *Carry On Loving* a pleasantly outdoors look while the sets constructed at Pinewood are varied and visually interesting. Especially worthy of note are the delightfully tatty offices of the Wedded Bliss agency, which are blessed with what looks like a high-tech supercomputer. This is quickly revealed to be a complete fake, but in reality the production didn't have to go too far to find this convincing prop. Gerry and Sylvia Anderson's live-action science fiction series *UFO* had recently completed production at Pinewood and had constructed such a large number of superb high-tech-looking items that a company was set up to preserve them and hire them out to other filmmakers. While Peter Rogers Productions was an early customer, barely a single science fiction production was made in England in the 1970s without a *UFO* prop being present.

Carry On Loving benefits enormously from having its central plot anchored by Sid and Hattie, two actors who work together wonderfully. In contrast to his secondary role in the previous film, here Sid really helps drive the plot (such as it is) forwards, which is only proper for a Carry On film. Hattie, in one of her best Carry On roles, shows that she was a supremely good comedic reactor. In other hands, her role as Sophie Bliss could have been a simple 'feed' to Sid James and Kenneth Williams, with whom Hattie shares most of her scenes. As it transpires, Hattie's reactions are every bit as funny as the more obviously comedic material her male counterparts are given.

Kenneth Williams is not only a very welcome sight after his break, but he is absolutely at his over-the-top best. The role written for him by Talbot Rothwell is so tailor-made for the actor as to be slightly uncomfortable viewing for anyone with even a passing knowledge of the actor's real life. His character Percival Snooper is a marriage guidance councillor who is hilariously unfamiliar with the facts of married life, as proved when he completely misses the point of Bill Maynard and Patricia Franklin's marital difficulties. When informed that he has to find a wife or lose his job, Snooper's reaction is a very telling 'but I'm a confirmed bachelor!' For the benefit of younger readers, this phrase is a holdover from the era when homosexuality was still a criminal offense and was a subtle way of informing newspaper readers that a person was gay without attracting legal action. When we see Snooper's home, it is rather large and well-appointed, in contrast to Williams' real home, which was an ascetically bare apartment. Snooper's potential new wife Hattie soon discovers that cold showers and separate bedrooms are the order of the day.

This scene also acts as a showcase for Patsy Rowlands, returning after her highly effective turn in *Carry On Again Doctor*. The actress was rewarded for her efforts there with a scene that allows her to transform from dowdy housekeeper, scrubbed of make-up, to over the top vamp, determined not to allow Hattie to take her place as the woman in the Snooper household.

Imogen Hassall is an absolute revelation as Jenny Grubb, who transforms from blank-faced wallflower in Joan Hickson's bizarre, *Addams Family*-style Victorian household to an almost absurdly glamorous, busty model. She not only looks wonderful but proves to be a very adept comedy actor, giving a wonderfully vacant stare as she fits in with the rest of the Grubb household's array of physical oddities. When Terry Scott arrives for a date he is not surprisingly terrified and runs for the hills, only to receive a very nice surprise the next time the two meet. Scott, a comedy actor who became rather taken for granted thanks to the extended run of his rather bland BBC sitcom *Terry and June*, where he appeared alongside occasional Carry On star June Whitfield, is at his absolute peak in *Carry On Loving*.

He and Hassall mesh together perfectly as a comedy pairing, particularly in their second major scene together, when he and the transformed Jenny finally try to have a night of passion together in her shared apartment. In a wonderful scene of pure farce by Talbot Rothwell, the pair endure a constant series of increasingly frustrating interruptions, punctuated by the sound of the zip on Jenny's dress going up and down (a nice touch—had it been Terry Scott's zip, the effect would have been slightly too crude). These build from mild annoyance to a dead halt to proceedings when Richard O'Callaghan's Bertie turns up early for a date with Sally—the two having got together after a disastrous start—to a riot of slamming doors and a suicide attempt by photographer Julian Holloway. It is an admirably well-written scene excellently played by all concerned but anchored by Hassall and Scott who work together as if they have been a comedy team for years. As ever, the casting is dead on—Scott and Hassall's pairing works comedically because she is clearly well out of his league.

Carry On Loving is probably the best sustained movie performance Imogen Hassall ever gave. So good is she, showing range and confidence, that it is a

Above: A pre-*Doctor Who* William Hartnell was front and centre in the poster art for *Carry On Sergeant*, emphasising the film's status as an unofficial *The Army Game* movie.

Right: A younger Kenneth Williams, from the days when he was an unlikely romantic leading man of the Carry On series.

Before he became a beloved comedy star, Sid James was a busy film character actor. Here he is about to meet a heroic end in Hammer's 1957 film *Quatermass 2*.

Future Carry On star Bernard Bresslaw was the break-out star of ITV sitcom *The Army Game*, the 1958 film adaptation *I Only Arsked!* taking its title from his catchphrase in the series, which would still turn up in his Carry On dialogue over ten years later.

Leslie Phillips left the Carry Ons early, unwilling to be typecast by a long-running series. He immediately began getting lead roles in comedies such as 1961's *In The Doghouse*, opposite Hattie Jacques.

Too Hot to Handle (1960) failed to revive Jayne Mansfield's career, but proved a springboard to success for Barbara Windsor. The film was released in the USA under the title *Playgirl After Dark*.

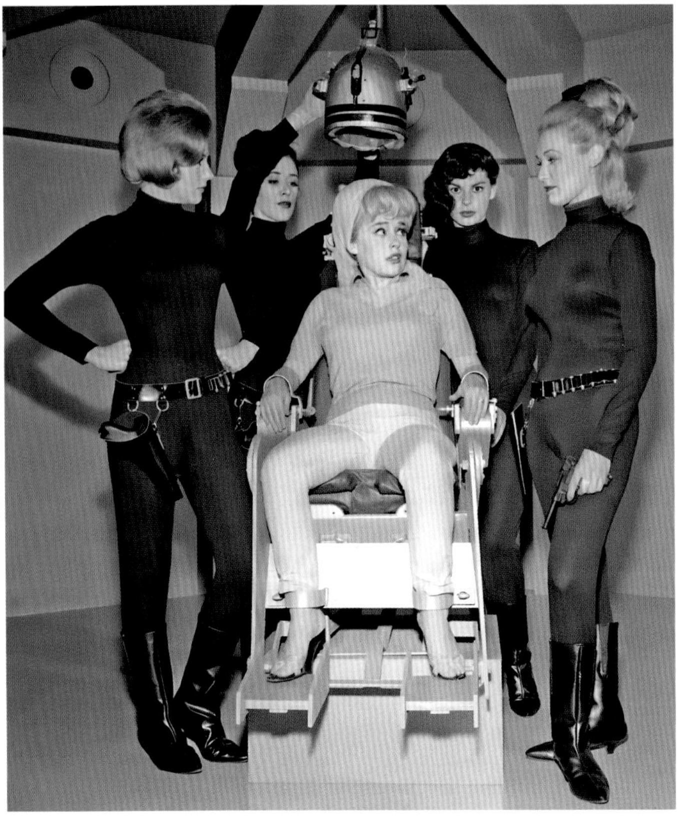

Above: Internal politics at Associated British Picture Corporation saw Ted Ray dropped from the Rogers and Thomas pictures, but not before terrific performances in *Carry On Teacher* and *Please Turn Over*.

Left: 1964's *Carry On Spying* saw Barbara Windsor join the Carry On cast, though it would be three years later before she would become a series regular in *Carry On Doctor*.

Above left: The one that got away: Liz Fraser offered glamour and comedy skills, but was dropped from the Carry Ons after upsetting Anglo Amalgamated's management.

Above right: The lovely young Joan Sims, though comedy turned out to be more her forte than glamour.

Right: A cottage industry sprang up of comedy movies featuring an array of early Carry On stars: 1961's *Dentist on the Job* starred a manic Bob Monkhouse opposite Kenneth Connor, Eric Barker, and Shirley Eaton.

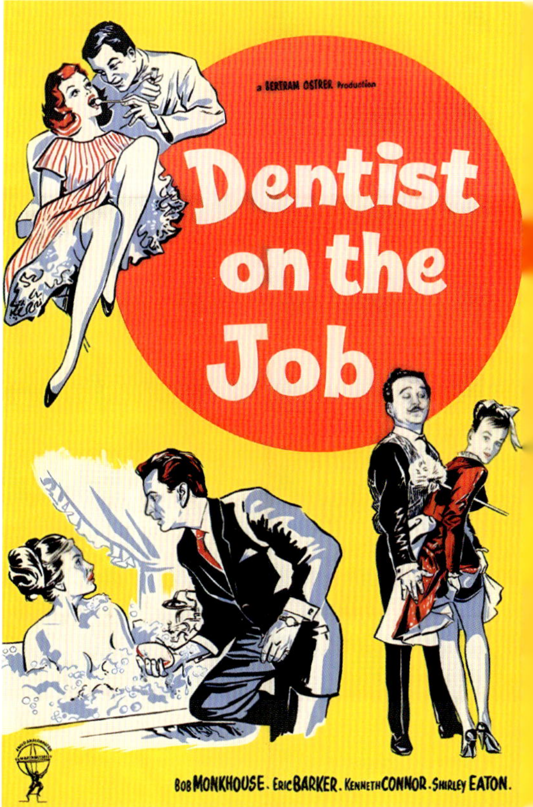

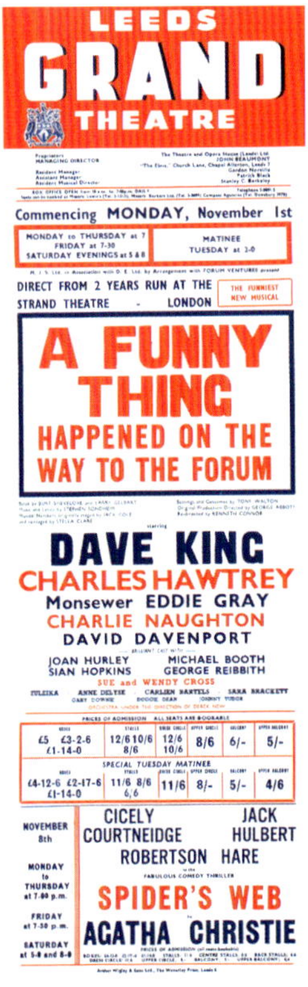

Above: Carry On Screaming continued the series' run of hits, but a change of policy at Anglo Amalgamated soon found Peter Rogers looking for a new distributor.

Left: Charles Hawtrey and Kenneth Connor did not get on well, but Connor still directed Hawtrey in the touring version of *A Funny Thing Happened On the Way to the Forum*, which fetched up at the Grand Theatre, Leeds, on 1 November 1965.

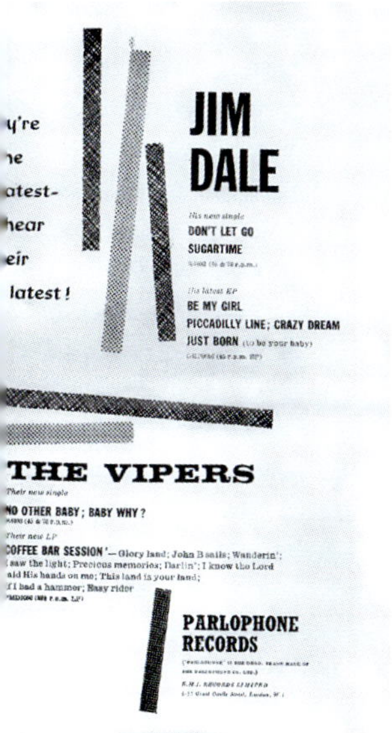

Above left: Peter Rogers and Gerald Thomas helped transform Jim Dale from a comedian and pop star (advertised here by his label Parlophone) into a genuine leading man.

Above right: Carry On Cruising took the Carry Ons into a new era of filmmaking, with Eastmancolor photography by Alan Hume rather more impressive than this hand-tinted lobby card might suggest.

Carry On Cleo was a huge success for the Carry On team, with this memorable poster artwork put together at the last minute when legal action stopped their original design being used.

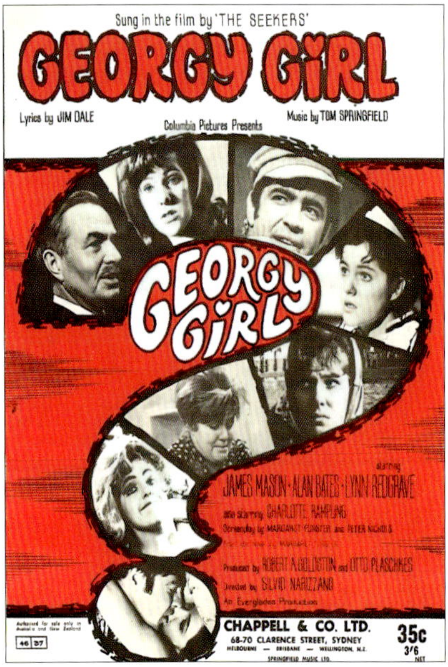

Above left: Jim Dale was a huge asset for the Carry Ons, but his talents were too large to be contained by the series. He was nominated for an Oscar in 1967 for his lyrics to the theme song for *Georgy Girl*.

Above right: Charles Hawtrey's hard-won stardom evaporated outside the Carry Ons as his personal problems overwhelmed his professionalism. His film roles reflected this, with *The Terrornauts* (1967) being almost comically bad. Even worse was to come.

The bizarre softcore sex/science fiction/spy movie mashup *Zeta One* (1969) proved a low point for Hawtrey and his co-stars, including a visibly ill James Robertson Justice.

Above left: Carry On around the world—*Carry On Nurse* was a big export success as well as a smash hit in the home market. This is the Belgian poster art, where the film had been retitled *40 Degrees of Love*.

Above right: Carry On Regardless was publicised in the USA with the bizarre slogan 'The Wackybirds is Here!'

Above left: Carry On Cleo was very popular in Italy under the title *Ehi Cesare, da cleopatra? Hai chiuso...* ('Hey Caesar, are you going to Cleopatra? You're finished...').

Above right: Carry On Up the Khyber sold as far afield as Argentina, where the film was seen as *Arriba las faldas* ('Up the Skirts').

Above left: Carry On Again Doctor was shown to Turkish audiences as *Çilginlar Doktor* ('Crazy Doctor').

Above right: Carry On at Your Convenience was seen in English-speaking countries outside the UK as *Carry On Round the Bend*—a much more appropriate title.

Left: Carry On Abroad proved a seventies highlight of the Carry Ons and was widely distributed across Europe. This typically high-quality Italian poster art features that country's retitling of the film as *Ragazze in Camera* ('Girls in the Room').

By the time of *Carry On Abroad* in 1972, it was clear that new blood was needed in the Carry On cast. Jimmy Logan was introduced with great promotional fanfare and seemed to enjoy the view.

Robin Askwith was a sort of Sid James for the seventies and could have provided the Carry Ons with a much-needed young leading man, but he achieved instant stardom in *Confessions of a Window Cleaner* instead.

Left: So many of the Carry On cast had second careers as occasional singers that this unofficial Carry On spin-off LP was issued, with excellent (though oddly coloured) cover art.

Below left: Peter Rogers branched out into producing dramas once again in the early seventies. *All Coppers Are…* proved an only partially successful attempt at gritty crime drama.

Below right: *Quest for Love*, produced by Peter Rogers and directed by Gerald Thomas' brother Ralph, was a unique and charming piece of romantic science fiction.

Above: By the 1970s, the Carry Ons were being challenged at the box office by comedies with even lower budgets, more nudity, and casts sprinkled with old comedy names. *What's Up Nurse* even featured Jack Douglas and Peter Butterworth.

Right: Probably the worst of the seventies smutty film comedies was *The Ups and Downs of a Handyman*, which even the legendary Bob Todd could not save.

Sid James worked at a furious pace, his Carry On and television stardom supplemented by constant touring in theatrical farces.

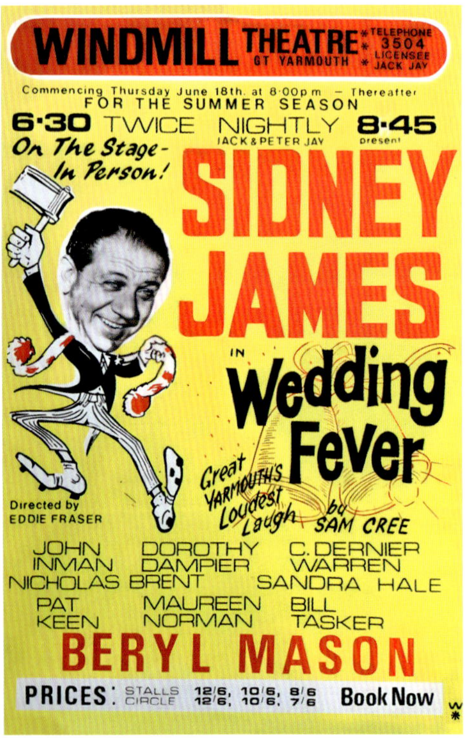

Above left and right: By the mid-1970s, Sid's personal popularity was so great that he regularly graced the covers not only of the listings magazine *TV Times*, but also its children's equivalent *Look-In*.

The last stand: As the film series began to decline, the Carry On team managed one final triumph with the huge success of the theatrical revue *Carry On London*, which ran for a year and a half.

The *Carry On London* cast celebrates the show's opening outside its West End home of the Victoria Palace Theatre.

mystery why she was never cast in another Carry On film. Worse still, her film career was almost at an end after what had been a very busy couple of years with roles in such high-profile films as the British-financed Spaghetti Western *El Condor*, *The Virgin and the Gypsy*, opposite Franco Nero and Hammer's prehistoric epic *When Dinosaurs Ruled the Earth*. *Incense for the Damned*, which she had filmed in 1969, finally limped into British cinemas after a troubled production process and much re-editing in September 1972 (director Robert Hartford-Davis had his name removed from the credits of the film, which turned up under at least three titles). She had roles in two of ITCs filmed adventure series shot in 1971, as Maria in *Overture*, the pilot episode of *The Persuaders!* opposite Tony Curtis and Roger Moore, and as Gina in the 'Stones of Venice' episode of *Jason King*. The latter was a rather less than serious spin-off of the 1969 series *Department S* starring Peter Wyngarde as the camp, bouffant-haired novelist-detective.

The ITC shows, a huge number of which had been produced since the mid-1950s, were reaching the end of their run and the British film industry was entering one of its periodic states of collapse, this one being rather worse than normal as the film business had become almost totally dependent on American funding, which was in the process of being withdrawn. For reasons unknown, the talented and beautiful Miss Hassall failed to find regular stage and television employment and made only two other movie appearances: the first was in *White Cargo*, a 1973 comedy starring David Jason almost a decade before he became a national hero as Del Boy in *Only Fools and Horses*. The second was a small role in director Lindsay Shonteff's *Licenced to Love and Kill*, a perfectly awful spy spoof starring former *New Avengers* star Gareth Hunt that received a very limited release, skulking into a few British cinemas in August 1979. Tragically, this was to be Hassall's last work to be seen by even a small audience. She was sinking into depression thanks to a combination of failed relationships, the death of her daughter after only four days of life, and the seemingly irreversible decline of her acting career. She was found dead in her London home on 16 November 1980, having taken an overdose of sedatives. One of the most beautiful and talented actresses of her generation, Imogen Hassall was aged only thirty-eight.

22

Carry On Henry (1971)

or Mind My Chopper

Filming Dates: 12 October 1970–27 November 1970
Original Certificate: A (Classified by BBFC 22 December 1970 [uncut])
Running time: 89 minutes 24 seconds

Release Details

Carry On Henry was Rank's big summer movie attraction of 1971, with special preview screenings taking place from Friday 27 May. The film then set off on a staggered release throughout Britain from Sunday 31 May, making its debut around the country throughout June and July.

In most locations, Rank paired *Carry On Henry* up on its initial release on the Odeon circuit with another feature-length pilot film from Lew Grade's ITC production and distribution empire. This time, writer Philip Levene and director Sidney Hayers, previously responsible for *Mister Jerico*, produced *The Firechasers*, in which American import Chad Everett played an insurance investigator trying to track down a prolific arsonist while modelling the flashiest male attire London tailors of the day could provide. In a few places, a couple of older Rank features were dug out to act as support: the 1968 thriller *Nobody Runs Forever* and the 1969 Bulldog Drummond spy movie *Some Girls Do*.

What's Carrying On?

Henry VIII, king of England, is a notorious womaniser and much married. In the days before divorce, this usually meant that he had to find an excuse to have his old wife executed. Henry's latest matrimonial partner is Marie of Normandy, who has the unfortunate habit of eating raw garlic before bedtime. Unable to stand the smell, Henry quickly plans to replace her, but Cardinal Wolsey warns that he will struggle to get the Vatican to agree to another annulment. Meanwhile, his chief advisor Thomas Cromwell says having Marie executed will cause war with France. The frustrated Henry has a new queen lined up, the busty Bettina, but Marie proves to be tougher and more resourceful than previous queens and is determined that her neck will not be the next one on the chopping block.

Who's Carrying On?

A Peter Rogers Production
Director: Gerald Thomas
Screenplay by Talbot Rothwell
Music composed and conducted by Eric Rogers
Photography: Alan Hume BSC
Art Director: Lionel Couch
Editor: Alfred Roome

Sidney James: King Henry VIII, a randy old tyrant only interested in chasing girls and keeping the royal coffers stocked with money.

Kenneth Williams: Thomas Cromwell, chief minister to Henry who must help put the king's whims into action, often involving creating ridiculous new taxes to pay for them.

Charles Hawtrey: Sir Roger de Logerley, who must try everything before the king does, including Queen Marie. He finds himself in the torture chamber for much of the film for his trouble.

Joan Sims: Queen Marie of Normandy, the busty, lusty new queen whose love of raw garlic means Henry advises her not to make any hairdressing appointments.

Terry Scott: Cardinal Wolsey, the spectacularly dim head of the church who must work with Cromwell to get the king out of his new marriage.

Barbara Windsor: Bettina, Henry's choice for his next queen, who refuses to let the horny Henry to come near her until the pair are married.

Kenneth Connor: Lord Hampton of Wick, an anti-royalist fanatic who, along with Guy Fawkes (Bill Maynard), gets roped into an unlikely plan to kidnap Henry to get the king out of his marriage to Marie.

Carry On Critics

I may be putting words into his mouth, but *Monthly Film Bulletin* writer John Pidgeon (that august publication having recently reversed its longstanding policy of anonymous reviewers) gave the impression that he liked *Carry On Henry* rather more than he was prepared to let on:

> The alternative title, Mind My Chopper, sets the familiarly smutty tone of the double entendres that prop up the plot of the latest, surely the most salacious, addition to the Carry On ... series, which cheerfully plunders the current popularity of Henry VIII. The cast is the familiar stock company at full force; the script is from Talbot Rothwell at his most characteristic. And the film is at any rate better to look at than most of its shoe-string predecessors.

It took until October 1971 for *Films and Filming* to carry a review of *Henry*, but it was certainly worth waiting for, Peter Buckley finding much to enjoy alongside what he describes as 'wince-making double entendres':

> But along with all of this predictable middle aged grooving there is a delicious send up of that most boring and perennial line of cinematic yawns, the historical romance.
>
> This mockery is not only very funny, but delicate and subtle, two qualities that would never expect from a Carry On, and the key is Joan Sims brilliant performance as Marie of Normandy. Her mincing, pouting, lisping Queen is a winging take-off on Genevieve Bujold's much heralded Anne and on Sarah Miles' Mary of Scotland, and bosomy Miss Sims puts them both to shame deliberately shot after shot. For unexpected joy, Terry Scott's Wolsey is not far behind, and Sid James gives a much more believable Henry than either of those highly praised ponderous pieces of impersonation that so recently glowered from our movie and television screens.

In one of the highest pieces of praise a Carry On film would receive from a critic representing the more intellectual end of film journalism, Buckley concluded his review thus:

> In fact, *Carry On Henry* is not only a delightful parody of *Anne of a Thousand Days*, it is a much better film. It looks better, it sounds better (they even seem to have lifted half of the lines straight from Anne, only this time they really are funny), it works better, and it is a much more honest piece of cinema. And thankfully, it is about fourteen hours shorter. *Henry* is by far the most successful and enjoyable Carry On I have seen.

Over at *The Times* for its Friday 28 May 1971 edition, the film reviewer's chair was being filled by none other than Melvyn Bragg, future host of long-running arts programme *The South Bank Show*, who took a very different view to *Carry On Henry*:

> A taste for the Carry Ons is rather like a taste for garlic. I have neither, but connoisseurs told me that while *Carry On Henry* ... was not one of the best it was definitely up to scratch. Addicts gurgled helplessly in the largest preview theatre of the week—like bath water, I thought, going out.

While one understands that critics cannot be expected to like all types of film, it has always mystified me why publications have always generally insisted on sending a single writer to all types of film, even ones he or she will clearly detest. Bragg ends his review with a reference to Lord Longford's privately constituted committee into pornography and its influence, which seems a bit much, to say the least: 'I think Lord Longford's committee ought to be forced to see these films as an antidote or as a stimulant or as a complete mystery'.

Derek Malcolm at *The Guardian* reviewed *Henry* the following week, on 4 June, and was in rather more forgiving mood: 'If this sceptered isle does sink giggling into the sea, Mr Peter Rogers will be on the bridge saluting with Mr Talbot Rothwell Standing to attention at his side.' The critic was less impressed by the direction of Gerald Thomas: 'What one feels like complaining about is the terrible flatness of Gerald Thomas' direction—a general feeling that anything is good enough if it gets you from point A to point B in the shortest possible time.'

Carry On Comments

Although no one could have realised at the time, *Carry On Henry* was to be something of a last hurrah for the Carry On crew, being the last time the team produced an undisputed hit that also, both at the time of its release and in the years since, has met with a high degree of critical praise. Talbot Rothwell had wanted to write a comedy about Henry VIII for some time, and the opportunity finally arose thanks to a rash of movies appearing from the mid-1960s and into the '70s centring on the tumultuous reign of King Henry.

Henry VIII had been regarded as a plum role since Charles Laughton played the part in Alexander Korda's 1933 production *The Private Life of Henry VIII*. By the early 1970s, the subject presented a marvellous opportunity to Peter Rogers, Gerald Thomas, and Talbot Rothwell unseen since *Carry On Cleo*. Since the mid-1960s, a string of popular film and television productions had presented the story of Henry's turbulent reign and his string of wives. The meant that a large audience was familiar with the period and the historical figures involved and the subject was almost desperate to have the right royal mickey taken out of it.

Robert Shaw had played Henry in *A Man for All Seasons* in 1966 opposite Paul Schofield as Thomas Moore, while three years later, Richard Burton picked up an Oscar nomination as Henry in *Anne of the Thousand Days*. Even more importantly, in January 1970, the BBC had a major success with its six part mini-series *The Six Wives of Henry VIII*, starring Keith Michell. This was exported with great success to America as part of the PBS channel's *Masterpiece Theatre* series. So acclaimed was Michell's portrayal that the story was later reshot for release to cinemas, at a much shortened 125 minutes, as *Henry VIII and His Six Wives*, released some months after *Carry On Henry* in July 1972.

Sid James was, naturally, cast as Henry and, as Joan Sims later recalled, was very keen to take the role: 'He was very much taken with the idea of playing the role of Henry VIII. I remember he said it was like going back to the serious stuff he enjoyed playing in South Africa'.[1] Ironically, considering how note-perfect he was to prove in the role, James almost did not get to play the part and was not necessarily the first choice anyway. The idea of writing a Carry On movie around the character of Henry VIII had been in the air for some time and one idea floated was to make the film as a semi-musical, with bawdy songs in period style sung by a Henry played by renowned comedy actor, *Goon Show* leading man and operatic singer Harry Seacombe.

By the end of the 1960s, Seacombe was developing his screen acting career, which was boosted considerably by a short but eye-(and ear-)catching role as Bumble in the 1968 mega-hit *Oliver!* He well and truly found himself on Peter Rogers' radar when he appeared in a major role in the last of the Doctor film series, *Doctor in Trouble*. This was produced at Pinewood by Rogers' wife, Betty Box, wrapping production in January 1970 before a June release on a double bill with the French spy movie *OSS 117: Murder for Sale*.

The idea of a musical was abandoned in favour of a more conventional narrative in the shape of a ribald take-off of the events portrayed in the film *Anne of the Thousand Days* written with Sid James in mind. An unexpected problem presented itself however in the form of Sid's ever-increasing popularity. It had not always been possible in the past to cast James in the Carry Ons, for instance when taping episodes of the sitcom *George and the Dragon* prevented him from appearing in *Follow That Camel*. This was known about well in advance, however, while in the case of *Carry On Henry*, a stage commitment meant that Sid's availability was right down to the wire.

With Sid having proved a popular favourite on radio, film, and television, it would appear that audiences' appetite for James' rough-edged charm was insatiable, for he was also spending his summers on the stage. The lucky holidaymakers of Torquay had the opportunity in the summer of 1968 to see Sid at the Pavilion Theatre in a production of Sam Cree's farce *Wedding Fever*, which also featured future television comedy star John Inman. So tailored to the James personality was Cree's play that his character was named Sidney Jones. This proved such a success that James and many of the same cast members, including Inman, reunited for the summer season of 1970 to perform *Wedding Fever* at the Windmill Theatre, Great Yarmouth. Performing two shows a night, at 6.30 and 8.45 p.m. (which must have been quite a strain for Sid, who was theoretically taking it easy after his near-fatal heart attack), the Great Yarmouth shows were a huge success.

Wedding Fever was such an effective stage vehicle for Sid that an arrangement was made to take the production to his native South Africa after the Great Yarmouth run ended. This put Sid's leading role in *Carry On Henry* in serious doubt, as the film was locked in to a start date of 12 October 1970. If Sid could not make it back to England in time for costume fittings prior to filming, Peter Rogers and Gerald Thomas would have to recast. The obvious choice in these circumstances was the actor they had thought of in the first place, Harry Seacombe, who would have been a good fit for the popular image of the older, obese Henry VIII.

'Harry would have been fine. Sidney could have survived without the film and the film would have survived without Sidney'.[2] These were brave words from Peter Rogers, but *Carry On Henry* just would not have been the same without James; King Sidney turned out to be a right royal triumph.

The film that eventually emerged was in large part a burlesque of Hal Wallis' 1969 production *Anne of the Thousand Days*, which, as mentioned above, featured an Oscar-nominated Richard Burton in a lustrous big-budget production with art direction by none other than Lionel Couch, a regular part of the Carry On team who also designed the sets for *Carry On Henry*. With *Anne of the Thousand Days* having wrapped production only a matter of months before *Henry*, some of that film's expensively made costumes were also available via theatrical costumiers L & H Nathan Limited, and Sid James got to wear some of Richard Burton's costumes as Henry. This all added together to make what is certainly the best-looking Carry On film made during the 1970s. So fleet of foot were the Carry On production team, in fact, that *Anne of the Thousand Days* was still playing in various cinemas, due to its roadshow release schedule, when *Carry On Henry* made its debut in February 1971.

Talbot Rothwell took the basic idea of *Anne of the Thousand Days*, in which Henry grows increasingly dissatisfied with his new French wife, and reworked it to Carry On requirements. This involved removing the historical motivation for his wanting to change wives—that Henry was desperate to sire a son in order to continue his royal lineage. There were not a lot of laughs to be had in this idea and Rothwell replaced it with something rather simpler and in keeping with Sid's screen image: Henry is simply a lecherous old goat.

Rothwell did not quite have the cheek to rewrite history without offering at least a tongue-in-cheek explanation to the audience, which was presented with the following on-screen introduction:

> This film is based on a recently discovered manuscript by one William Cobbler which reveals the fact that Henry VIII did in fact have two more wives. Although it was at first thought that Cromwell originated the story, it is now known to be definitely all Cobblers—from beginning to end.

With his artistic license thus endorsed, Rothwell was free to present no fewer than three queens whom the history books had not previously recorded. The first unnamed queen is only seen briefly in a striking cameo by Patsy Rowlands on her way to the scaffold. Scrubbed of make-up and looking most uncomedically like a woman facing death, Rowlands brings a slightly uncomfortable reality to the scene and makes it far more memorable than it would otherwise have been. She is replaced with great haste by Queen Marie of Normandy, after the world's fastest marriage ceremony overseen by Cardinal Wolsey:

Wolsey: 'Do you, Henry, take this woman to…'

Henry: 'I do and so does she. Right love, that's it through there'

With that, Marie is hustled to the king's bedchamber. The new queen is a lusty and busty French noblewoman played by Joan Sims, who is more that keen to consummate an *entente cordiale*, but has the unfortunate habit of eating raw garlic before bedtime. Henry is repelled by the garlicy odour and the prospects for a happy union are suddenly bleak. This queen, however, is not about to face the chop without a fight and is also not about to go short in the bedroom either.

Much of the comedic heavy-lifting is done by Kenneth Williams and Terry Scott as Thomas Cromwell and Cardinal Wolsey, who play many of their scenes together as a sort of sixteenth-century Laurel and Hardy. The pair are a total joy together, bouncing off each other to great effect as equal parts bumbling idiots, fawning sycophants and corrupt politicians. In Terry Scott, Kenneth Williams finally got a male comedy partner for the Carry Ons with whom he worked as well as he did with Hattie Jacques, and it is a shame that the two did not appear together more often.

Charles Hawtrey gets some particularly strong comic material as Sir Roger de Logerley, his character's name, of course, playing on the cuckoo-in-the-nest comedic archetype of 'Roger the Lodger'. This is quite a clever reference to his character's job as the king's taster, trying everything before the king does, including, much to the sex-starved Marie's delight, the queen. This sees the

Carry On saga reach new levels of permissiveness, as it is made extremely clear that Sir Roger has had his way with the queen (an unlikely pairing if ever there was one). Strangely, a visual joke pertaining to this appears to have been cut from *Henry*'s finale at a late stage. Queen Marie, having fallen pregnant despite Henry's lack of involvement in the process, gives the king what the real Henry VIII had always longed for in the form of a male heir. When Henry gets to finally see the child, it is clear that a shot of the child's face has been cut, but we see Sid's (now out of context) puzzled reaction to the child's face. The obvious gag is that the child looks like Charles Hawtrey, but why would the vital shot that acts as the punchline to the scene be cut? The BBFC granted the film an 'A' certificate with no cuts, so the blame appears not to lie at their door.

Hawtrey gets another, very effective sequence of visual jokes in which he is repeatedly tortured, first to confess to adultery with Queen Marie, then to retract his confession, only for the whole process to be repeated. A comedic variation of a plotline from *Anne of the Thousand Days*, this is much funnier on the screen than it reads on the page and resolves itself into a series of visual gags in which, for instance, the rack gives Sir Roger freakishly long legs. The finale to this series of jokes, in which Sir Roger appears perfectly happy to be tortured and wants to have a go on all the different machines, repeats a gag from *Follow That Camel*: Hawtrey is given a drink but the water spurts out of his perforated front.

A small storm cloud could be seen on the Carry On horizon however, as Henry saw what was perhaps a slightly unwise detour into party political humour with the following exchange:

'The Queen is in labour.'

'Don't worry, they'll never get back in.'

This was a topical gag, referencing the British general election of June 1970, four months before *Carry On Henry* went onto the studio floor at Pinewood, in which Harold Wilson's governing Labour Party was unexpectedly defeated by Edward Heath's Conservatives. Considering the large working-class audience for Carry On films, this was veering into dangerous territory. They got away with it for a single, throwaway joke, but as Peter Rogers, Gerald Thomas, and Talbot Rothwell would soon find, an entire movie filled with such references was more than the audience would stand.

23

Carry On At Your Convenience (1971)

or Down the Spout
or Ladies Please be Seated
or Up the Workers
or Labour Relations Are The People Who Come To See You When You're Having A Baby

Filming Dates: 22 March 1971–7 May 1971
Original Certificate: A (Classified by BBFC 15 June 1971 [cut])
Running time: 88 minutes

Release Details

London Release: 19 December 1971 (Metropole, Victoria).

The support features chosen by Rank to appear alongside *Carry On at Your Convenience* were perhaps the strangest and most random to date. Some areas were 'treated' to yet another failed pilot film, this time from the Warner-Seven Arts vaults. *Kona Coast* was originally released to the American market in 1968 and featured former *Have Gun Will Travel* star Richard Boone as a Hawaii-based charter boat captain investigating the murder of his daughter. In other places Peter Rogers' tale of industrial relations and indoor plumbing was supported by, of all things, the 1967 Spanish-made Western *White Comanche*. This now somewhat notorious Euro-Western (there was no Italian involvement, so the term Spaghetti Western is redundant here) starred William Shatner, between seasons on *Star Trek*, in a dual role as half white-half Comanche twin brothers, one of whom lives as a white man, the other becoming a dope-addicted mystic who plans to lead the Comanche nation into a war against the white man. Probably due to Shatner's name value, *White Comanche* would be dusted off regularly over the years whenever a support feature was needed. In other areas, various Euro-thrillers were paired with *Carry On at Your Convenience*, including the West German spy thriller *Code Name Kill*, The Alain Delon picture *The Last Adventurer*, and the French–Italian spy movie *OSS 117: Murder for Sale.*

What's Carrying On?

W. C. Boggs and Son has been making fine toiletware for 100 years but now faces an array of problems. Head of the company William C. Boggs is behind the times and refuses to allow the company to produce such modern items as the bidet, they are in debt to the bank, and industrial relations are terrible. Union shop steward Vic Spanner is behind a wave of strikes, calling the workers out for the slightest reason. When heir to the company Lewis Boggs secures a contract for 1,000 bidets from an Arab king, it seems that the company's future has been secured, but a strike is called almost immediately production begins. It appears that W. C. Boggs and Son is doomed, but absolutely nothing is allowed to get in the way of the boozy annual works outing to Brighton.

Who's Carrying On?

A Peter Rogers Production
Director: Gerald Thomas
Screenplay by Talbot Rothwell
Music composed and conducted by Eric Rogers
Photography: Ernest Steward BSC
Art Director: Lionel Couch
Editor: Alfred Roome
Sidney James: Sidney Plummer, a randy old works foreman only interested in keeping the factory running smoothly, chasing Chloe Moore and putting his next horse-racing bet on.
Kenneth Williams: W. C. Boggs, stuffy chairman of the family toiletware manufacturing company which is behind the times and in the red.
Charles Hawtrey: Charles Coote, flamboyant chief designer of Boggs and Sons products who is disturbingly fond of a game of strip poker.
Joan Sims: Chloe Moore, busty, lusty factory worker who enjoys life and flirting with Sid Plummer, but is stuck in a marriage with the dull, jealous Fred, Boggs' head salesman.

Hattie Jacques: Beattie Plummer, married to Sid and possibly the world's worst housewife. Absurdly devoted to Joey the Budgie and, like Joey, not as dumb as she might appear.

Bernard Bresslaw: Bernie Hulke, owner of Britain's loudest motorbike (a 1968 Triumph TR6 Trophy) and best mate/enforcer for union shop steward Vic Spanner.

Kenneth Cope: Vic Spanner, the factory's organiser for trade union NUCIE (National Union of Chinaware Industrial Employees), constantly taking the workforce out on strike for the slightest reason.

Patsy Rowlands: Miss Withering, put-upon secretary to W. C. Boggs who has two big secrets: that she is in love with her boss, and that she is 'blessed' with the first name Hortence.

Jacki Piper: Myrtle Plummer, daughter of Sid and Beattie and glamourpuss canteen girl at the Boggs factory. Subjected to the amorous attentions of both Vic Spanner and boss's son Lewis Boggs.

Richard O'Callaghan: Lewis Boggs, son of W. C. Boggs, who spends his time trying to modernise the company's methods and trying to get Myrtle to date him.

Renée Houston: Agatha Spanner, the mother from hell and Charles Coote's opponent in games of strip poker.

Carry On Critics

David McGillivray, later to become screenwriter of a series of a series of confrontational and highly entertaining horror movies with director Pete Walker, was in 1971 reviewing films for *Monthly Film Bulletin*:

> Talbot Rothwell tends generally to neglect his WC factory (a thinly disguised Pinewood Studios) for a series of irrelevant sketches ranging from farce (the works outing) to domestic comedy (Sid and the budgie). The result seems even more scrappily assembled than usual and, with the exception of a fairly amusing parody of sex education films, the level of humour, though noticeably cleaner than of late, is still rock bottom.

British film comedy, as it turned out, still had a while to go before it found rock bottom and in 1976 McGillivray himself was the scriptwriter of *I'm Not Feeling Myself Tonight*—not the worst British comedy ever made by any means but certainly an indicator of the direction of travel.

Over at *The Times*, John Russell Taylor had surprisingly little to say about *Carry On at Your Convenience* in that paper's 17 December 1971 edition, lumping in a few lines about the film in a paragraph about the Frankie Howerd comedy *Up the Chastity Belt*. Could it be that even this arch-fan of the Carry Ons was tiring of the films? He was certainly careful to be non-committal:

> At least you know where you are with English smut, all scatological and none of that nasty sexual stuff. The same goes, of course, for *Carrry On at Your Convenience*, in spades. Though even here the rot has set in—it is not quite the 90-minute lavatory joke you might imagine, but contains a fair amount of sexual innuendo as well among the hijinks at W.C. Bogg's sanitary ware factory.

Reading this, I still have no idea if Taylor found the film funny or not.

The previous day had seen *The Guardian*'s Derek Malcolm give his similarly brief verdict on the new Carry On, and he rather preferred *Up the Chastity Belt*, which he reviewed in the same article and found 'comfortably outshines *Carry On at Your Convenience*, which I can only describe as a particularly ghastly flash in the pan'. When the critics start delivering puns of the same standard as those in the actual film, we are in trouble.

The March 1972 edition of *Films and Filming* finally got around to printing a review of the film, Eric Braun producing what amounted to an extended tribute to one particular cast member:

> Renee Houston has not had a worthwhile film role in a small age, until this, the 22nd of the Carry On Films ... She's an unconscionable time appearing, but from the moment she is discovered ... the film perks up considerably, after a tedious opening which suffers from the disadvantage of assuming that lavatory puns are, in themselves, objects of irresistible humour, as are cocky shop stewards who call strikes for the pettiest possible reasons.

Less than keen on Talbot Rothwell's writing on *Carry On at Your Convenience*, Braun also had sharp words for some of the main cast members:

> The original comedy talent of Kenneth Williams ... has congealed into a caricature of a caricature, and although Joan Sims' natural warmth is proof against the most predictable characters and lines, few of the others seem able to inject any spontaneity into their parts—a stricture that does not apply to the splendid Renee Houston, whom one extremely eminent critic mistook for Diana Dors for the first few minutes of her appearance.

A potted history of Miss Houston's life and career follows before Braun reaches his closing remarks: 'The makers of *Carry On at Your Convenience* should be grateful for the sparks of genuine fun she has been able to strike from the dry tinder of one of the least funny of this staggeringly successful series.'

Carry On Comments

Carry On at Your Convenience was the first Carry On film to lose money during its initial cinema run, a considerable shock to all concerned at the time, especially considering that the end of the 1960s had seen the series at their box office peak. This golden run, during which it seemed that the Carry On series could not fail with its audience, came to a juddering halt with this film, and a look at *Carry On at Your Convenience* and its production history gives us a few clues as to why.

The film was initially announced in trade advertisements under the title *Carry On Comrade*, which even Peter Rogers and Gerald Thomas must eventually have agreed was a touch too confrontational for a comedy about worker–management relations. Besides, the first impression such a title may have given was that the next Carry On film was going to be set in the Russian Revolution. The alternative eventually chosen was perhaps a little unwieldy, and the term 'convenience' for a public toilet was unknown outside of Britain. This rendered the title *Carry On at Your Convenience* meaningless outside of the United Kingdom, and in other English-speaking countries, the title *Carry On Round the Bend* was used instead, which you may be excused for regarding as a rather more successful toilet gag than the one British audiences were landed with.

The popularly accepted explanation for the financial failure of *Carry On at Your Convenience* was that the series' largely working class audience rejected the film's clear bias against its trade unionist characters. This is certainly a possibility and hardly a new development for British films of the postwar era; one would search in vain for a positive portrayal of trade unionism or Labour politicians in any British films of the 1950s and '60s. The obvious example is the Boulting brothers 1959 comedy *I'm Alright Jack*, in which Peter Sellers played union shop steward Fred Kite, a militant communist with an absurdly romanticised idea of life in the Soviet Union. Other films of the time took a similar line but were deadly serious: *The Angry Silence*, released in 1960, featured Richard Attenborough as a factory worker shunned by his friends and colleagues after refusing to join an unofficial strike. This film made no bones about seeing unions as an oppressive force acting against the interests of the individual.

Perhaps in some ways the apparent antipathy by British film producers towards trade unions was understandable. The hard line taken towards such matters as demarcation disputes (a term which by the 1970s had become common knowledge in Britain) by the film and broadcasting unions were notorious and could easily have coloured the attitudes of producers towards unions in general. Still, it would have been wiser had Peter Rogers, producer of a highly successful series of films with a largely working-class audience, many of whom would have been trade union members, had steered well clear of the subject.

What is especially tragic is that crucial misjudgements caused audiences to reject a film that contained some of the strongest and most amusing material of any 1970s Carry On. The key mistake Talbot Rothwell's script makes is that it is not really about a strike in a toilet factory at all. Instead, at its heart, *Carry On at Your Convenience* is a film about a love triangle between minor union official Vic Spanner (played by Kenneth Cope, a decent comedy actor), Myrtle from the staff canteen, and the boss's son Lewis Boggs. The latter two characters were played by Jacki Piper and Richard O'Callaghan, who had worked together so well as an unlikely romantic pairing in *Carry On Loving*. Here, however, their courtship does not work anything like as well as the Boggs character is written so unsympathetically.

The first we see of Lewis Boggs is when we learn that he has caused a strike by unilaterally cancelling the worker's shop-floor tea trolley. Vic calls the strike and subsequently gets the male workers to agree so they can all go to see a football match, but the initial cause is a high-handed action by Lewis. The next we see of the pair is when they both, separately, ask Myrtle out. Vic's idea of showing Myrtle a good time is offering to take her to the football match, while Lewis breezes in, acting in an incredibly entitled manner, with absolute confidence that Myrtle, despite her turning him down, will eventually say yes. Therein lies one of the major problems with the film: between the buffoonish Vic, who subsequently stalks Myrtle during her date, and entitled rich-boy jerk Lewis, the audience is left with nobody to root for.

In the course of the film, Lewis does virtually nothing to earn the affections of Myrtle, who still agrees to marry him at the first sight of a special marriage certificate. Here the film makes its worst mistake of all. In a previous era, the male romantic lead in a Carry On movie would be played by Kenneth Connor as a nervous, downtrodden romantic failure with barely a penny to his name who succeeds against the odds. Instead, Vic spends the film being totally humiliated and defeated, his attempts to date a girl he likes resulting in his being beaten up by his rival—Rothwell gives us no reason to believe that Vic deserves this fate—and his attempts to stand up for his fellow workers' rights result in the ritual humiliation of his being spanked in front of the whole factory workforce by his own mother. Is there any wonder that the traditionally working-class Carry On audience rejected the film?

This is a genuine pity since alongside the misjudgements, there is a wealth of great comedy material in this film—*Carry On at Your Convenience* is actually one of the funniest Carry On movies of the seventies. The main subplot of the film is the quite touching story of Sid James' works foreman Sid Plummer and Joan Sims' factory worker Chloe Moore each being trapped in an unsuitable marriage and being attracted to each other. They are clearly right for each other, but a relationship can never happen as Joan is hitched to the miserable, tight-suited Boggs' chief salesman Bill Maynard (who does have a lovely red Ford Capri Mark 1, however, so cannot be all bad).

Sid is married to Beattie, played in a masterful display of housewifely incompetence by Hattie Jacques. Beattie makes almost no attempt to keep the Plummer house in any kind of order, instead gaining pleasure by lavishing her attention on the couple's surrogate child, Joey the budgerigar. In fact, the Plummers have a fully grown child in the shape of Myrtle, but as we almost never see them interact, this is easily forgotten. As we later learn, however, the trouble with Beattie is that she gains no satisfaction from housework and by the end of the film has returned enthusiastically to the world of work, at least in part to keep watch on the wandering eyes (and hands) of Sid.

Even better, our insight into the home life of the Plummers leads to the strange tale of Joey the budgie, who is able to pick horseracing winners with unerring accuracy. This not only allows the Plummers to finally decorate their house and replace their filthy, peeling wallpaper (and hang a print of Vladimir Tretchikoff's iconic green-faced woman portrait), but means Sid can replace his crumbling 1958 Ford Prefect with a brand new Morris Marina—in 1971, a symbol of British modernity, having replaced the much-loved but anachronistic Morris Minor that same year. No explanation is given for Joey's supernatural abilities, but they do allow Sid to raise enough money to save the company before his bookmaker (the ever entertaining Davy Kaye) puts a strict limit on Sid's betting—a feat attempted by many in real life, with limited success.

A special mention should also go to what is, to me at least, the funniest scene in the whole film, during Lewis Boggs' disastrous date with Myrtle when he takes her to the local cinema. Besides the genuine wit in this scene, a few well-aimed barbs are taken at what passed for entertainment in many British cinemas in the early 1970s, as increasingly disinterested theatre owners tried to find increasingly cheap and desperate ways to attract paying customers. The traditional British-produced B-movie had become extinct, but audiences still expected more than just the main feature for the price of their cinema ticket. An array of very cheaply produced documentaries of, at best, marginal interest were instead inflicted on the public. Here this is represented by a look at the allegedly fascinating habits of the Koo Koo islanders as they chop carrots for their evening meal, along with a bored-sounding American narrator who informs us that this is 'a spectacle few white people have been privileged to witness'.

This is followed by the main feature, a sex documentary entitled *The Sweet Glory of Love*, introduced by Harry Towb, giving a performance of comic genius as 'A well-known and practicing doctor' who grows increasingly wide-eyed and sweaty as he describes in a broad New York accent the in-depth examination of the male and female anatomies the film promises to present:

'Let us look at the number of ways in which we can bring da two tagedda'. In the space of barely a minute's screentime, Towb gives the funniest performance in a film that is not short of top comedy actors at the top of their game.

New boy Kenneth Cope is paired with Bernard Bresslaw as Bernie Hulke, and the pair make for an effective comic team as the huge but soft-hearted Bernie is dragged semi-unwillingly into Vic's schemes. Typically, however, this is pushed just a little too far as Bernie proves willing to go along with Vic in resorting to keeping the workers on strike by threats of violence. Despite attempting to make a weak joke about it, this is another terrible miscalculation by the filmmakers, turning characters we should like, or at least have some sympathy with, into violent thugs.

Vic actually does elicit a certain amount of sympathy when we are introduced to his harridan of a mother, played by Renée Houston. Mrs Spanner seems to blame her son for all her errant former husband's faults, including the fact that she is forced to take in lodgers. Perhaps the dog's life Vic leads at the hands of his mother explains his need to feel important at work. Mrs Spanner's main lodger is none other than Charles Hawtrey, as W. C. Boggs' designer Charles Coote. Despite the fact that Coote represents possibly the most camp performance Hawtrey had given to date in a Carry On film (in the later scenes in Brighton, he appears to be dressed as Quentin Crisp), not only do the pair plan to marry, but they are also fond of a game a strip poker in the living room.

The film takes a welcome turn away from its own strike plot when the whole cast decamps to Brighton by coach for the annual works outing. This gives us a welcome opportunity to see the regular cast members being funny in an environment that takes us away from the enclosed setting of the factory. Kenneth Williams especially shines in these scenes, his character having decided that as the strike seems about to force him to close down the company, he is going to let his hair down and have a damned good booze-up. In another replay of a plotline from *Carry On Loving*, this results in him becoming much closer to his secretary Patsy Rowlands, who has secretly loved him for thirty years and is very upset that in all that time, Boggs has not so much as pinched her bottom.

In the end, the strike is broken by the women, who are unwilling to see the company close down for the sake of a pointless dispute. Vic's militancy is beaten out of him by his own mother and even he returns to work, a changed man. His final line of dialogue even echoes one of the rejected titles for this misjudged, but at its best quite hilarious film: 'Carry On Working'. Indeed, the Carry On team would do just that, steering well clear of controversy next time and returning to the familiar territory of a hospital setting.

24

Carry On Matron (1972)

or From Here to Maternity
or Familiarity Breeds
or Womb at the Top
or The Preggers Opera

Filming Dates: 11 October 1971–26 November 1971
Original Certificate: A (Classified by BBFC 24 January 1972 [uncut])
Running time: 87 minutes 27 seconds

Release Details

London Release: 9 June 1972 (Metropole, Victoria).

The future direction of support features as a part of British cinema distribution was illustrated by the choice of *Top Gear* as B-picture to *Carry On Matron*. Like *Under the Table You Must Go*, which had played in many places on the Odeon circuit with *Carry On Loving*, this was a documentary from Arnold Louis Miller, this time on the subject of transportation and driving, narrated by Formula One champion Graham Hill. These documentaries, which has been spoofed in *Carry On at Your Convenience*, were cheap to make, attracting government money via the Eady Fund, a levy placed on each cinema ticket sold in Britain, and boosted the number of British productions screened in the nation's ever-declining number of cinemas. A number of producers were attracted to this trade at the bottom end of the British film industry, including Harold Baim (who was the leading producer of this kind of thing) and even television personality Nicholas Parsons. In a few locations, lucky patrons had yet another chance to see Patrick Macnee wearing unsuitably mod fashions in *Mister Jerico*.

What's Carrying On?

Criminal mastermind Sid Carter leads his gang of hopeless crooks (Bernard Bresslaw and Bill Maynard) in a plan to steal thousands of birth control pills, worth a huge amount to foreign buyers, from Finisham Hospital. His plan is to get his unwilling son Cyril into the hospital disguised as a female nurse to find where the pills are kept, but Cyril gets stuck in the hospital as part of a group of trainee nurses and finds himself as roommate of the gorgeous Nurse Ball. Meanwhile, hospital chief Sir Bernard Cutting has the wildest case of hypochondria known to medical science, and a chance remark has him thinking he is transforming into a woman, then desperately trying to prove his manhood by romancing Matron. Over in the maternity ward, Mrs Tidey is three weeks overdue and may at some point stop eating for long enough to actually have her baby.

Who's Carrying On?

A Peter Rogers Production
Director: Gerald Thomas
Screenplay by Talbot Rothwell
Music composed and conducted by Eric Rogers
Photography: Ernest Steward BSC
Art Director: Lionel Couch
Editor: Alfred Roome

Sidney James: Sid Carter, low-rent criminal mastermind who leads his gang of dopey crooks and unwilling son to steal birth control pills for the export market.

Kenneth Williams: Sir Bernard Cutting, the raging hypochondriac who is supposedly in charge at Finisham Hospital.

Charles Hawtrey: Dr Francis A. Goode, chief psychiatrist who spends half his time dealing with the neuroses of Sir Bernard, the other half watching a cheesy hospital soap opera with Matron.

Joan Sims: Mrs Tidey, pregnant after many years trying, her baby is three weeks late and she cannot stop eating.

Hattie Jacques: Matron, trying to keep order in the chaotic Finisham Hospital while fighting off the unexpected attentions of Sir Bernard and trying to find time to enjoy her favourite TV soap opera with Dr Goode.

Bernard Bresslaw: Ernie Bragg, long-haired, almost supernaturally thick-headed member of Sid's gang of crooks.

Kenneth Cope: Cyril Carter, the white sheep of Sid's family, unwillingly talked into dressing as a female nurse to find where in the hospital the birth control pills are kept.

Terry Scott: Dr Prodd, terror of the Finisham nursing staff who has his eye and wandering hands on the hospital's latest nurse, Cyril.

Barbara Windsor: Nurse Susan Ball, Cyril's unsuspecting roommate at the nurses' accommodation whose new girlfriend becomes her new boyfriend.

Kenneth Connor: Mr Tidey, railwayman husband of Mrs Tidey who finds that the constant delays of his work-life are repeated when his long awaited baby refuses to make its first appearance.

Carry On Critics

Kenneth Thompson at *Monthly Film Bulletin* was cautiously positive about the new Carry On offering: 'Within its anticipated terms of reference, *Carry On Matron* must be regarded as a largely successful if slightly patchy addition to the series'. *The Guardian*'s Derek Malcolm complained that this hospital-based film seemed a little under the weather itself: '*Carry On Matron* ... seems a bit flat and dispirited, like an animated McGill postcard without the courage to be properly vulgar.'

John Russell Taylor at *The Times* seemed to find the film at least some light relief from the ultra-violent Westerns that were coming from Hollywood in this period. Two of these, *The Revengers* and *Chato's Land* (the latter from the British writer and director combination of Gerald Wilson and Michael Winner), were wearily reviewed by Taylor in the paper's Friday 2 June edition, followed by the notable Carry On fan's verdict on *Matron*:

> As for *Carry On Matron*, what more is there left for anyone to say? In this one the familiar team is on home ground, with high-jinks [*sic.*] around the bedpans and sauciness in the dispensary. On the other hand there have already been three medical episodes and some of the gags are getting a little shop-worn to pass muster even as good not-too-clean corn. Still, Hattie Jacques, Joan Sims and Barbara Windsor are in fine form, and the menfolk remain fresh and undaunted, so there seems no reason why the series should not go on forever.

That turned out to be a rather optimistic assessment, but there was some life left in the series yet.

Carry On Comments

Carry On at Your Convenience failed to turn a profit during its original cinema run. I know I mentioned this fact before, several times, during my comments about that film, but the scale of that event makes it worth reiterating—a film in a popular genre, part of a legendarily popular series with a cast filled with famous, even beloved performers, costing a mere £220,000 to make, lost money. *Carry On at Your Convenience* was rejected by British cinemagoers in a big way, and the reaction of Peter Rogers and Gerald Thomas was to retreat to a familiar setting.

Thus, the autumn of 1971 saw the Carry On Crew fetch up at Heatherwood Hospital in Ascot, Berkshire, for a fourth time around at medical comedy. The cast for the new film was very strong, with Terry Scott, whose scenes had been cut from *Carry On at Your Convenience*, returning for what would turn out to be his final appearance in the series. Also making welcome returns were Barbara Windsor and Kenneth Connor, while new boy Kenneth Cope was brought back in a more sympathetic role than before.

While the idea of yet another hospital-set Carry On may (with some justification) be seen as indicating a lack of imagination and an understandably conservative approach, Talbot Rothwell's script still has points of interest. Especially interesting is Sid James' character: Sid's sitcom *Bless This House* had debuted to great success in February 1971 and had repositioned the actor's image from ageing bird-chaser to family man. Whether by coincidence or design, Rothwell wrote for Sid a character that reflected the fact that the actor was fifty-eight years of age and looked older. Not only is Sid Carter given no romantic entanglements, he is a widower with a grown up son. That son, Cyril, was played by Kenneth Cope, himself aged forty in 1971, made younger-looking by the same type of Beatle wig he wore in his 1969 TV series *Randall and Hopkirk (Deceased)*. By this point, it was clear to all concerned that it would have seemed a little distasteful to have the ageing Sid lusting after younger women, as was seen in the previous film in the series, when Sid's romantic interest was split between the more appropriately aged Hattie Jacques and Joan Sims, two actresses with whom Sid also had an excellent on-screen rapport.

The basic plotline that holds together the narrative of *Carry On Matron* is also very promising, the idea of Sid as the boss of an inept gang of criminals harking back to another production from the Rogers/Thomas/Rothwell triumvirate, 1965's *The Big Job*. Unfortunately, nothing like enough time is devoted to this part of the film's plot due to the necessity of giving the rest of the cast, based in the hospital, enough to do. Poor old Bernard Bresslaw is given particularly short shrift, reduced for the most part to standing about in a silly wig looking dopey and trotting out his old *Army Game* catchphrase 'I only arsked' yet again. We gain a glimpse into the possibilities of the byplay between James, Bresslaw, and Bill Maynard during a small scene in which the gang plan their robbery, only to be completely sidetracked into a ridiculous argument about bus routes. This silly little sequence raises a smile and makes one regret that *The Big Job* was as close as Rogers and Thomas ever got to making a full-on Carry On crime caper movie.

As it is, the focus of *Carry On Matron* is firmly on events at Finisham Hospital's maternity ward, and thereby lies the film's major problem. In setting a fourth movie in a hospital, even Talbot Rothwell's seemingly inexhaustible supply of jokes and situations is tested beyond its limits. The result is a film that seems rather tired, despite a cast that absolutely throws itself into the material in an effort to bring some life to the proceedings. It is no coincidence that *Carry On Matron* has one of the largest casts of series regulars in Carry On history. Each of these cast members has to be given enough to do in order to make their appearance worthwhile, and the result is a film which is unfocussed, with many talented performers stuck in underwritten parts.

Besides the aforementioned Bernard Bresslaw, this also affects Joan Sims, who sits about in bed eating sausages (weirdly, she does not share any scenes with Kenneth Connor, who plays her husband), and Patsy Rowlands, once again playing secretary to Kenneth Williams but this time in a tiny role—thankfully, a better Carry On part would soon follow for her. Instead, much of the film is given over to a secondary plotline that showcases Kenneth Williams' Sir Bernard, in which he is written as a raging hypochondriac. This is not Talbot Rothwell's finest work and encourages all Williams' worst instincts to go over the top and stay there for as long as possible. Eventually, this evolves into a plotline in which, after a chance remark by fellow doctor Michael Nightingale, Cutting becomes convinced that he is physically changing gender—the swapping of gender roles being a repeated theme of this film. After consulting the hospital's psychiatrist Dr Goode (Charles Hawtrey in possibly his most bouffant toupee yet), Cutting is given the rather more reasonable notion that he subconsciously needs to prove his manhood.

This allows the script to reunite the unwilling romantic partnership of Kenneth Williams and Hattie Jacques, but this time with the roles reversed—before, Hattie's character was chasing an unwilling Williams capable only of loving himself; now Williams was the sexually aggressive one forcing his attentions on an uncertain Hattie. While this represents a valiant effort to breathe life into an old situation, the trouble is precisely that it is an old situation—we have been here twice before and there is a real sense that the films have gone to this particular well once too often.

Both Jacques and Williams work very well with Charles Hawtrey. The former has an especially good joke in which the audience is led to think that the pair are arranging a romantic tryst when in fact they are indulging in their love of a Dr Kildare-style soap opera. Interestingly, British television did not have such a series when *Carry On Matron* was filming in late 1971, with the legendary *Emergency Ward 10* having been cancelled by ATV boss Lew Grade back in 1967. Grade expressed his own regret at this decision and by October 1972 had in effect brought the show back under the new title *General Hospital*.

Hawtrey's scenes with Kenneth Williams also work well, this pair of old pros working in pleasurable sync together as their relationship changes from psychiatrist and patient to sort-of love rivals and then instantly to friendship when they discover they are both members of the Newts secret society. Barbara Windsor returns, once again playing a nurse, and is good value despite the script not really showcasing the actress at her best. It is a pity as she gives a bright performance that fairly lights up the screen, whether fighting off the advances of Terry Scott's tubby lothario or in the rather desultory and unbelievable romantic subplot with Kenneth Cope.

Cope is very good as Sid's offspring Cyril, unwillingly forced into his father's contraceptive robbery scheme. He was a very sympathetic actor, skilled at comedy and here seen in a role a little more suited to his persona than *Carry On at Your Convenience*'s Vic Spanner had been. Continuing the theme of gender reversal, he spends much of the film in the female role of Cyrille, which turns out to be one of the Carry On series' better forays into the field of drag. Cope in female garb is just feminine enough for the deception to be believable within the narrative of the film, while still retaining enough incongruity for comedic effect when horny Doctor Prodd (Terry Scott with an unflattering mid-1960s-style Beatles haircut) moves in on him.

While there are some bright spots to the film it's all a bit tired and forced, as if one can see on screen the blow to the series confidence it suffered with the unexpected failure of its previous film. It is also notable that *Carry On Matron* sees the level of nudity somewhat raised; following on from the extremely sheer nightgown Barbara Windsor wore in *Carry On Henry*, this time Kenneth Cope, in nurse disguise, walks in on Gilly Grant taking a bath and, naturally, falls into the bath himself. If the level of nudity is not quite full-frontal, we see a great deal of Miss Grant and Cope's flailing hands make their way suspiciously close to bust-level.

What this helps to illustrate was that while little had changed in the world of Carry On, the outside world of popular filmmaking was altering considerably. Peter Rogers and Gerald Thomas were having to add modern elements of nudity to what was essentially a 1950s film formula, and if the comedy market wanted girls, the Carry On films that followed would certainly supply them.

25

Carry On Abroad (1972)

or What a Package
or It's All In
or Swiss Hols in the Snow

Filming Dates: 17 April 1972–26 May 1972
Original Certificate: A (Classified by BBFC 5 July 1972 [cut])
Running time: 88 minutes 5 seconds

Release Details

London Release: 1 December 1972 (Metropole, Victoria).

Carry On Abroad went on general release on 31 December 1972, though interestingly, the film opened a week earlier at the Odeon Belfast, on 23 December. At least British audiences in the early months of 1973 were given a chance to see some sun and an exotic location, albeit reproduced on a chilly-looking Pinewood lot. Rank paired the film with another Arnold Louis Miller documentary for its journey round the Odeon circuit, this time *East Side, West Side*, about New York, narrated by actor Daniel Massey. At least this meant that *Carry On Abroad*'s audiences genuinely got to see something of a foreign country. For once, it appears that this Carry On was graced by the presence of the same support feature throughout Britain, though the Belfast newspapers mistyped it as 'Low Side, West Side'.

What's Carrying On?

A disparate group of holidaymakers take up Wundatours' offer of a cheap package holiday to the Mediterranean island of Elsbels. Once there, the group meets a series of disasters as the hotel is only half finished, the sunny weather is soon replaced by torrential rain, and the entire group winds up in jail. Despite everything, the group finds they form a bond and start to solve some of their marriage problems before a flood threatens to sweep away the hotel.

Who's Carrying On?

A Peter Rogers Production
Director: Gerald Thomas
Screenplay by Talbot Rothwell
Music composed and conducted by Eric Rogers
Photography: Alan Hume BSC
Art Director: Lionel Couch
Editor: Alfred Roome
Technical Advisor: Sun Tan Lo Tion

Sidney James: Vic Flange, pub landlord, desperately fancying local widow Sadie who he has secretly arranged to go on holiday to Elsbels with.

Kenneth Williams: Stuart Farquhar, holiday representative for tour firm Wundatours, assailed on all sides by problems and desperately trying to make the holiday go well.

Charles Hawtrey: Eustace Tuttle, ageing mother-dominated office worker who wants to really let his hair down and have the best time possible. This mainly involves getting really, really drunk.

Joan Sims: Cora Flange, Vic's wife who gets over her fear of flying out of sheer determination to prevent her husband from straying with Sadie.

Bernard Bresslaw: Brother Bernard, a novice monk who questions his vows and finds himself falling for pretty young holidaymaker Marge (Carol Hawkins).

Barbara Windsor: Sadie Tomkins, twice widowed and much pursued, first by Vic Flange and then by fellow holidaymaker Bert, but tiring of men who are only after one thing.

Kenneth Connor: Stanley Blunt, henpecked and sex-starved husband of Evelyn, who finds himself drawn to Cora.

Peter Butterworth: Pepe, owner of the Palace Hotel, struggling to cope with an influx of holidaymakers in a half-built hotel with all the staff on strike.

Jimmy Logan: Bert Conway, out for a dirty weekend in the sun who sets his sights on Sadie Tomkins—with Vic suddenly out of the running, the coast is clear.

June Whitfield: Evelyn Blunt, Stanley's wife, who refers to sex as 'unpleasantness' but finds her long-buried romantic instincts unexpectedly revealed by Pepe's son Georgio.

Hattie Jacques: Floella, Pepe's wife, stuck in the kitchen all day disapproving of her husband's attempts to operate a half-finished hotel with no staff.

Carry On Critics

Barry Norman was on the cusp of becoming Britain's most famous movie critic as one of the team of critics on the BBC's *Film 1972* programme, becoming the sole presenter the following year and for most of the following twenty-five years. In December 1972, Norman was still contributing film reviews to *The Times*, though he proved in dyspeptic mood regarding the standard of films he had been forced to watch that week: 'basically a week when you feel that if the cinema really cannot do better than this it deserves to expire, or at least to fade away decently like an elderly warrior'. Norman was clearly not overly enamoured with *Carry On Abroad*, but writes in such a charming, slightly self-deprecating manner that it doesn't really matter:

> The Carry On ... films either make you laugh or not and to my eternal shame (for I like to think of myself as a sophisticated person) this actually made me laugh three times—mostly, I hasten to add in my own defence, through amazement at the sheer effrontery of the script.

Carry On Abroad, it should be said, was one of the better releases of a week in which the notorious musical flop *The Great Waltz*, about the Strauss family, and the Philippines-shot cheapie *Daughters of Satan*, the first starring role of a young Tom Selleck, were offered to the public.

Daughters of Satan also roused the ire of *The Guardian*'s Derek Malcolm, but this critic, often quite supportive of the Carry Ons, instead of bemoaning the standard of films on general release, viewed *Carry On Abroad* as something of a return to sanity: 'After this it is almost a relief to reach the familiar sanctuary of *Carry On Abroad*, the 24th of the series still going strong on sexual innuendo.'

Nigel Andrews' *Monthly Film Bulletin* review serves more to describe the film then to offer anything much by way of an opinion. This is perhaps indicative that it was becoming clear that the films were visibly declining,

> The Carry On series has reached a status where it was somehow beyond, above or possibly beneath criticism: 'Please, Miss Plunkett, you're squashing my itinerary', squeals Kenneth Williams' camp courier early on in this latest,

and thoroughly representative addition to Peter Rogers unflagging Carry On ... series. Travelling well-trodden paths of slapstick, double entendre and nudging innuendo.

Carry On Comments

After the lively but divisive and loss-making *Carry On at Your Convenience* and the water-treading exercise that was *Carry On Matron*, one could be excused for thinking that the series was entering a downward spiral. While one can see from the distance of time that this was generally true, there were certainly some pleasures still to be had, especially in *Carry On Abroad*. If *Carry On Matron* revisited the past glories of the hospital comedies, which had brought the series its greatest American success in the form of *Carry On Nurse*, this time Rogers and Thomas went back for inspiration to *Carry On Camping*, the biggest domestic box office success they had yet achieved. Thus we once again see the British on holiday, but instead of roughing it in a tent, the cast followed the example of many holidaymakers in the early 1970s and went abroad in search of the sun—or at least as far abroad as Pinewood Studios car park.

In his diaries, Kenneth Williams describes on the first day of filming 'an air of staleness over everything. A feeling of "I have been here before"'.[1] *Carry On Abroad* is, indeed, a film that really should not work. It is puerile and sex-obsessed, cheap-looking, and nothing like as funny as it either should be or imagines that it is. This should be the death knell for any comedy, but *Carry On Abroad* is sweet-natured in a way that the series had not been for quite some time and well-constructed by writer Talbot Rothwell. This means that a large cast of regulars almost all have satisfying roles with what would now be termed proper story arcs.

It is especially gratifying to be able to report that the film works so well, as *Carry On Abroad* was to prove the point at which the core cast of the series began to break up. This would be the final movie in the series (though not the final appearance under the Carry On banner) for Charles Hawtrey. For his own reasons, the actor walked away from the series. Much has been made of how his character of Eustace Tuttle represents an unflattering portrait of the actor's real life, dominated by his mother and awash with alcohol, as if the role was written as a way of ejecting a troublesome actor from the series. This does not fit in with the facts, as besides Hawtrey's subsequent stage and television Carry On appearances, the television producer character played somewhat uncomfortably by Jimmy Logan in *Carry On Girls* was clearly written with Hawtrey in mind and suffers grievously from his refusal to return to the Carry On fold.

Perhaps too many inferences have been read into the boozy life of Eustace Tuttle, especially considering how close the character is to one from the last holiday-set Carry On. Albeit written by Norman Hudis instead of Talbot Rothwell, 1962's *Carry On Cruising* featured Ronnie Stevens as a permanently drunk passenger who spent the entire voyage in the bar. While this was a rather sad portrait in the context of that film, there is real *joie de vivre* in Hawtrey's performance here. Amelia Bayntun, the Carry On's favourite battleaxe mother/mother-in-law, plays Eustace's mum in a short cameo that works despite Hawtrey being visibly older than her (in reality, she was four and a half years younger than her screen son).

This was to be the last but one Carry On film role for Hattie Jacques, who was beginning to suffer from health problems that made her difficult to insure. For this appearance, all her scenes took place in the kitchen set opposite Peter Butterworth separate from the main action. Hattie gives a big performance, constantly cooking and nagging her husband as he attempts to prevent his new hotel from collapsing around his ears, at first figuratively, then literally. If Hattie's Carry On days were numbered, at least she was still able to surprise with a performance far removed from the starchy Matron role she was best known for under the Carry On banner.

One reason *Carry On Abroad* works so well is that it is has a connecting theme to link its disparate elements as Talbot Rothwell wrote a film that is, at heart, a bawdy comedy of relationships. Sid and Joan were a natural screen couple, but are in danger here of parting because they are unable to holiday together due to the pressures of running their pub (in a nice 1970s touch, they seem to exclusively serve the notorious keg beer Watney's Red Barrel) and because Joan hates flying. Sid is tempted to stray in the direction of sexy widow Sadie Tomkins—Babs' character presumably named after Sadie Thompson, the cinema *femme fatale* played on the big screen by Gloria Swanson, Joan Crawford, and Rita Hayworth.

Babs is initially handed her standard bubbly sexpot role, lusted over by Sid and apparently happy to go on a foreign holiday with a married man, then subject to the attentions of Bert (Jimmy Logan), who is openly after a dirty weekend. As the film develops however, Sadie bridles against the idea of getting close to yet another man who is only after one thing. Bert then surprises us by demonstrating that he has genuine feelings for Sadie, and by the end of the film, we feel they have the chance of a future together. Jimmy Logan was a star of considerable magnitude in his native Scotland and a newcomer to the Carry On series. Indeed, the trailer for *Carry On Abroad* particularly emphasised Logan's contribution, beginning with the actor's opening scene with Kenneth Williams: 'That's right, it's the same hilarious Carry On team, the same hilarious faces, and a few new ones like Jimmy Logan and June Whitfield'.

Logan is given plenty to do in what would prove to be, by some considerable margin, the best of his two Carry On roles. Not only does he get to romance Barbara Windsor but he also gets a running gag in which he falls out of his hotel balcony and gets covered in wet cement. As the aforementioned trailer announced, this was also June Whitfield's return to the Carry On cast—one presumes the writers of the trailer thought nobody would remember her previous appearance in 1959's *Carry On Nurse*. Of course Whitfield, a mainstay of British radio and television comedy for decades, had been very busy in the intervening years, and in 1969, she had been a regular in the BBC television series *The Jimmy Logan Show*.

Whitfield makes a glorious return to the Carry On series as Evelyn Blunt, a role which allows the actress to demonstrate her range and uncanny ability to play everything from glacial conservatism to steaming sexuality, always with an appropriate comedic spin. She is paired with Kenneth Connor as Evelyn's husband Stanley, a cheerful soul who is constantly henpecked by a wife who has apparently no ability to gain enjoyment in any circumstances and refers to sexual relations as 'unpleasantness'. While Sid and Joan's characters rediscover the spark in their relationship by spending time together on holiday, the Blunts are brought together by spending time apart. Stanley finally takes an independent stand by allowing the coach to an excursion on the island to go without his wife. Stranded on her own in the hotel, Evelyn strikes up a May to September romance with Georgio (Ray Brooks), son of hotel owner Pepe. While Ray Brooks does not represent the most convincing casting in a Mediterranean role, he plays the part in a lovely, gentle manner which suits the material very well. Had Georgio been played as more sexually aggressive, we might well have lost sympathy for both him and Evelyn. As it transpires, it is just an enjoyable fling for both parties and lights a fire under Evelyn's long extinguished ardour. This happens not a moment too soon, as Stanley has already begun to look elsewhere, namely in the direction of Cora.

Bernard Bresslaw gets his best Carry On role in ages, albeit in a part he is a little too old for, as Brother Bernard, a naïve young novice monk who begins to doubt his calling when he starts to fall for young holidaymaker Marge. Marge is played by Carol Hawkins, who had previously had a small role in the 1970 *Carry On Christmas* TV show and here began a short career as a Carry On regular, turning up later in 1972 in the *Bless This House* TV spin-off film made by the Carry On team. She then went on to appear in two episodes of the *Carry On Laughing* television series and in 1975's *Carry On Behind* before turning down *Carry On England* due to the amount of nudity involved.

Somewhat less impressed with Brother Bernard is Marge's friend Lily, played by Sally Geeson. Geeson was, of course, an old co-star of Sid James, having played his daughter Sally in the TV sitcom *Bless This House* since

1969. She was specifically recommended for her role in *Carry On Abroad* by Sid James and would go on to appear in both the *Bless This House* movie in 1972 and in the next film in the Carry On series, *Carry On Girls*. This was a far better fate than Sid's sitcom son Robin Stewart, who did not even get a recommendation to appear in the *Bless This House* film.

As the film's trailer indicated, *Carry On Abroad* acted in part as a testing ground for potential new series regulars, and after a short cameo in *Carry On Matron* (for which the actor was paid with a crate of champagne), Jack Douglas returned for a slightly more substantial part, though still away from the main action, this time featured in the opening and closing scenes in Vic and Cora's pub.

Peter Rogers and Gerald Thomas clearly thought Jack Douglas had potential, but his comic persona was difficult to write for. The actor had what at this distance in time looks like a very strange act indeed, with a 'catchphrase' comprised of extreme physical tics which today would be regarded as straining the bounds of acceptability. By the next film in the series, he would be fully integrated into the cast, the last of the established regulars to be recruited to the Carry Ons.

For reasons that are hard to fathom, the introduction of John Clive to the Carry Ons did not result in a regular berth for the actor. Wiry-haired and with a screen persona that was suitably vague and camp enough for Carry On duties, Clive was an experienced comedy character actor and a natural to be added to the team. He had already gone before the cameras at Pinewood once before, during the filming of *Carry On Henry*, but his role found its way to the cutting room floor. As events transpired he only appeared in one further Carry On role, in 1974's *Carry On Dick*, and even in *Carry On Abroad*, he is given a story that is very interesting but curiously underdeveloped.

Several scenes were cut to keep the film down to its required sub-ninety minute length, including the entire roles of Bill Maynard and Terry Scott, and it is tempting to think that the story of John Clive's Robin and his 'friend' Nicholas (David Kernan) suffered some trimming. Their half-developed storyline is especially interesting as, for the first time in a Carry On film, major characters are revealed to be gay or bisexual. Not only this, but their sexuality is not the butt of a joke but just a part of their characters—Nicholas has a roving eye for the girls on their holiday and Robin makes it perfectly clear that he is jealous. We do not get to see how their relationship resolves itself, but it is an interesting new facet in Talbot Rothwell's writing, and one that he would explore further in the next film in the series.

26

Carry On Girls (1973)

Filming Dates: 16 April 1973–26 May 1973
Original Certificate: A (Classified by BBFC 20 July 1973 [cut])
Running time: 88 minutes

Release Details

London Release: 9 November 1973 (Metropole, Victoria).

Rank paired *Carry On Girls* with a pair of quite interesting films when it sent the latest in the series on its way around the Odeon cinema chain from 23 December 1973. In some areas, it was paired with *Go For A Take*, a 1972 comedy featuring Reg Varney and Norman Rossington (the erstwhile co-star of the earliest Carry On movies) as a pair of waiters on the run from loan shark gangster Patrick Newell who hide out in Starwood Film Studios and are mistaken for stuntmen. Hilarity ensues, in theory at least. In practice, despite being packed with reliable performers including Denis Price, David Lodge, and Bob Todd in cameo roles, the film is oddly joyless and almost entirely laughter-free. In other areas, *Carry On Girls* was seen with *Nickel Queen*, an Australian production from 1971 featuring British star of the 1940s and '50s Googie Withers and directed by her husband John McCallum. This was a comedy co-starring former Carry On performer Ed Devereaux about a pub owner in the Outback who stakes a claim for nickel on her land and becomes an instant millionaire.

Depending on where you were in Britain, *Carry On Girls* could instead be seen with alternate support features including old favourites *Kona Coast, White Comanche*, and *OSS 117: Murder for Sale* or the 1968 Lee Van Cleef Spaghetti Western *Beyond the Law*.

What's Carrying On?

Desperate to bring some business to the seaside resort of Fircombe, amusement arcade owner and local councillor Sid Fidler sets up a beauty contest, despite the opposition of his fellow councillor, prudish feminist campaigner Augusta Prodworthy. Sid and his publicist friend Peter Potter drum up schemes to attract press interest to the contest, but the best ideas come from one of the contestants, the diminutive motorcyclist Hope Springs. This tests Sid's relationship with local hotelier Connie to the limit, while pompous Mayor Bumble becomes the victim of a feminist campaign to halt the contest.

Who's Carrying On?

A Peter Rogers Production
Director: Gerald Thomas
Screenplay by Talbot Rothwell
Music composed and conducted by Eric Rogers
Photography: Alan Hume BSC
Art Director: Lionel Couch
Editor: Alfred Roome
Sidney James: Councillor Sid Fidler, amusement arcade owner at Fircombe, were there is nothing to do when it rains and it is almost always raining.
Joan Sims: Connie, owner of the biggest hotel in Fircombe, which her on/off boyfriend Sid co-opts as a base of operations for the Miss Fircombe beauty contest.
Kenneth Connor: Mr Bumble, the pompous mayor of Fircombe who is subjected to a series of humiliations (usually involving the loss of his trousers) at the hands of Miss Prodworthy's women's liberation campaigners.
Bernard Bresslaw: Peter Potter, hired by Sid to publicise the Miss Fircombe competition and unexpectedly finds himself becoming an entrant.
June Whitfield: Augusta Prodworthy, Fircombe council member and leader of the local women's liberation movement who organises the resistance to Mayor Bumble and the Miss Fircombe contest.
Barbara Windsor: Hope Springs, formerly Muriel Bogg, the reigning Miss Easy Rider and a late entrant to the Miss Fircombe contest, filled with ideas to publicise the competition and strangely attracted to Sid.
Peter Butterworth: The Admiral, a horny old bottom-pinching letch.
Jack Douglas: William, Connie's hotel receptionist and porter who causes chaos with his wild physical ticks and jerks.
Patsy Rowland: Mrs Bumble, lady mayoress of Fircombe, constantly in need of a toilet and unhappily married to Mayor Bumble.

Carry On Critics

In what was perhaps an ominous sign, especially for the landmark twenty-fifth film of the series, that reliable broadsheet defender of the Carry Ons, *The Times*, failed to run a review of *Carry On Girls*. Gareth Jones in *Monthly Film Bulletin* seemed weary of the whole thing:

> Thriving as ever on the sexual repressions of its audience, Talbot Rothwell's windy, radio-style script for the twenty-fifth Carry On turns out the usual quota of puns on such words as bang, boob, bed, bust, Bristol and bash, and makes such weary labour of it that every joke can be heard creaking into place long before the arrival of the punch-line. Sid James and Barbara Windsor's bar-room style of *savoir faire*—coupled with what seems at times to be some genuine gusto and enjoyment in the proceedings—are the only remotely vital qualities in the film.

Films and Filming covered *Carry On Girls* in its December 1973 edition, with a disapproving Eric Braun coming up with an interesting update on the old line that the Carry Ons were the filmic equivalent of the seaside postcard:

> And yet they, surely, when the jokes and illustrations on them strike the holidaymaker as pointless and feeble, are left yellowing on the rack until no longer suitable for purchase to send to friends and relations. One day the public will tumble the fact that they are not laughing so much anymore, and will act as the most effective critics of all by staying away.

These comments would soon prove remarkably prescient, but Braun did have some positive comments:

> One or two of the team do achieve laughs through establishing recognisable human beings among the frantic muggings (acting type) and cavortings, notably June Whitfield as Councillor Mrs Augusta Prodworthy, Patsy Rowlands as the slatternly, sardonical and usually incontinent wife of the mayor and Peter Butterworth as a lecherous old peeping tom of an admiral.

Thankfully, the legendary writer, social commentator, and sometime Jazz singer George Melly was covering the cinema review column in *The Observer* for its 13 November edition and set about singing the praises of *Carry On Girls*. He described the film:

> One of the best Carry On films in a long while, peppered with splendidly groan-making *doubles entendres* from the fertile imagination of Talbot

> Rothwell and set within a tightly constructed framework completely faithful to its own conventions.
>
> ... the real joy comes from the teamwork and individual brilliance of the performers, all of them rounded in that school of closely observed caricature which was the strength of the music hall tradition.

I am also happy to report that Mr Melly was appreciative in print of Patsy Rowlands:

> There's a splendid performance from Patsy Rowlands as the dressing-gowned, fag-ash-dropping, incontinent lady mayoress, whose boredom is eased only by the discomfiture of her pompous trouser-losing little spouse.

Carry On Comments

Although filming on *Carry On Girls* began on 16 April 1973, almost a year to the day after the commencement of production of *Carry On Abroad*, the genesis of the film began on 20 November 1970. On that date, at the Royal Albert Hall, took place the Miss World beauty contest, an annual event the public popularity of which is difficult to imagine today. Every year since 1956, the pageant had been broadcast live to Britain, then later a huge international audience, via the BBC. The 1970 event was keenly anticipated, especially since the comedy legend Bob Hope was comparing the proceedings—in fact, a huge audience of almost 24 million watched that year's Miss World contest in Britain alone.

Despite the enormous popularity of the contest, there was an increasing resistance in feminist and other circles to the whole idea of a competition in which women were judged by their physical attractiveness. A plot was hatched by a group of around fifty women's liberation activists, who were primed to invade the stage and backstage areas and pelt the stage with flour bombs, stink bombs, and leaflets at the pre-arranged signal of a football rattle. On the night, Hope's comedy act was, even by the standards of the day, sexist and out of keeping with the atmosphere of the occasion, so much so that the signal was given early and the stage invasion took place during his act.

Hope was a comedian who relied on a battery of writers and was completely nonplussed by this turn of events. Attempting to leave the stage as the event descended into chaos, Hope was prevented from leaving when his ankle was grabbed by Julia Morley, wife of Miss World owner Eric Morley and in charge of the night's production. Eventually, order was restored and a somewhat unwilling Hope was convinced to return to the stage so that the event could be completed. The women's liberation movement gained a huge amount of publicity from the protest—the whole world took notice, including Peter Rogers and Gerald Thomas. If the budget of a Carry On film might not stretch to a competition the size of Miss World, they could certainly manage to mount a Miss Fircombe contest.

As mentioned above, an entire year had passed since the filming of the last Carry On, the production team having been busy making the *Bless This House* in the meantime. This broke the run of two Carry On films per year that had lasted since 1966. With Rank, the film's distributors, in a process of reducing its reliance on its film production and distribution arm, the release of a Carry On film would from now on become an annual event.

Carry On Girls saw the films in a state of transition, with two of the most established cast members, Charles Hawtrey and Kenneth Williams, absent. While the latter was unavailable, busy performing in a West End stage production, Hawtrey had walked away from the 1972 *Carry On Christmas* television special in a dispute over billing and refused all offers to return to the series. Watching *Carry On Girls*, it is clear that Rogers and Thomas harboured hopes for the actor's return, the role of camp television producer Cecil Gaybody clearly having been written with Hawtrey in mind.

The part would certainly have worked better with Hawtrey present instead of Jimmy Logan, who was landed with the role. Logan looks visibly embarrassed to be playing a part he was entirely unsuited for—one presumes he was the only actor with previous Carry On experience available at short notice. The Carry Ons had a long history of presenting camp characters dating back to Charles Hawtrey's crashing entrance into *Carry On Sergeant* in 1958, but here, for the first time, there was the distinct feeling that the film was laughing at a gay stereotype, rather than participating in a long and honourable tradition of camp humour. After the fairly sympathetic portrayal of a same-sex couple in *Carry on Abroad*, this was a very odd step backwards.

This film does see a significant addition to the Carry On cast, with the promotion of Jack Douglas from the cameo roles of *Matron* and *Abroad* to main cast member, a position he would retain until the end of the series. As William the hotel porter, we see Douglas' signature 'Alf Ippititimus' in its purest form, his every line larded with nervous ticks and bizarre mannerisms that the rest of the cast do a sterling job of playing against. Douglas was the last new cast member to really stick and become associated with the series and it is easy to see why—children in particular loved his outrageous comedy schtick and it was good to have at least one comedy element that did not rely on ever increasing sexual content.

As well as being presented with a ready-made story idea by the Miss World protest, *Carry On Girls* also gave Rogers and Thomas the opportunity to present more bare flesh than ever before. Although there is less actual nudity than in some of the last few films in the series, most of the female cast members spend much of the film in skimpy swimsuits—most notably the incredibly pneumatic Margaret Nolan, who constantly struggles not to fall out of her costumes, and in two scenes has her top torn off. It was difficult for Rogers and Thomas to compete with the increasing number of outright sex comedies coming from British producers, as they were determined to hold on to their 'A' certificate. The Carry Ons were nothing if they were not wholehearted in what they were trying to achieve, and in going down the route of adding ever more sex, they could only go so far before endangering the appeal of the series to a family audience.

As it transpired, the most successful material in *Carry On Girls* was the more traditional comedy that could have been performed ten years earlier with no difficulties. Kenneth Connor and Patsy Rowlands make a superb comedic pairing: Connor's Mayor Bumble is a classic study of vanity, a puffed-up little man in a minor position of power trying desperately to hold on to both his dignity and his trousers. Rowlands, as Mrs Bumble, takes what was to prove her largest role in a Carry On film—her part in *Carry On Abroad* was almost completely cut out—and runs away with any scene she is in. Sarcastically miserable in her marriage and just plain miserable in her role as lady mayoress, she becomes the worm that turns, joining enthusiastically with Augusta Prodworthy's women's liberation group.

Bernard Bresslaw, as Peter Potter (the same character name Terry Scott was given in Carry On Camping), is paired with Valerie Leon as his severely dressed fiancée Patricia. As soon as she appears on screen with tied-back hair and unflattering glasses, you just know she is in for a serious makeover, and the film does not disappoint. Her impact is unfortunately rather lessened by a last-minute decision to have her lines dubbed by June Whitfield. The voice provided for her is perfectly adequate, but dubbing like this rarely aids an actor's performance. Bresslaw gets an even bigger makeover when he has to enter the beauty contest in drag, a situation which works better than one might expect thanks to the actor's willingness to throw himself fully into every role he was presented with.

June Whitfield is excellent as Prodworthy, leader of the Fircombe branch of the women's liberation movement—they even have an office with a plaque on the door, which I found an amusing detail. Her characterisation, all northern bluster and stiff-arsed prudery, is clearly based on Mary Whitehouse, the notorious religious zealot and head of the National Viewers and Listeners Association, who achieved huge fame and influence in her attempts to prevent the broadcasting of any televisual entertainment that was not suitable for ten-year-olds.

By Prodworthy's side at all times is Patricia Franklin, who had appeared to quite glamorous effect in *Camping*, *Loving*, and the *Bless This House* movie, but here plays the short(ish)-haired Rosemary. The character is clearly meant to be not only a lesbian, but one who is not afraid of letting the world know. The real Mary Whitehouse would certainly not have approved, but Augusta Prodworthy has no such problems with her sexuality. We are clearly supposed to find Rosemary's mode of dress mannish, but in contrast to the garish '70s' fashions seen all around her, she actually looks very stylish and well-dressed.

The funniest scene in the feminist protestors' campaign against Mayor Bumble is not the climactic assault with water and Fuller's Earth on the Miss Fircombe contest (an important and unwise change from the real Miss World protests—here the women taking part in the contest are attacked and humiliated along with the men organising the contest and the leering audience members), but instead the opening of a new hospital maternity unit. With all the babies fast asleep, the opening ceremony has to take place as quietly as possible, a task made impossible first by a cascade of pill containers from Mrs Bumble's handbag, then by the discovery that the ceremonial plaque has been covered by a picture of a trouserless Bumble. It is a short scene, but reminiscent of the best 1930s classic comedies.

There is also an interesting change in the Sid and Joan relationship, the pair having been established as the bedrock Carry On couple since at least 1969's *Carry On Camping*. While in *Carry On Abroad* Sid is tempted away from Joan by Babs, but the events of the film bring them back together, here Sid and Joan begin the film as a mismatched couple and the events of the film drive them apart. Sid's constant flirtation with the contestants, his taking Joan for granted (he constantly gives away free rooms of her hotel), and his instant attraction to Babs' character Hope Springs is more than the relationship can stand. After being chased out of the chaos of the beauty contest by angry audience members—goodness knows why, as it is hardly his fault—Sid races off in a go-kart to meet Babs, the pair disappearing into the sunset (or as near to a sunset as rainy old Fircombe can provide) on the back of Babs' motorcycle. This is quite an event in the moral universe of the Carry On films as Sid, playing the last of his laddish bird-chasing screen roles, leaves his established relationship with Joan in favour of the much-lusted after Babs.

27

Carry On Dick (1974)

Filming Dates: 4 March 1974–11 April 1974
Original Certificate: A (Classified by BBFC 10 June 1974 [uncut])
Running time: 91 minutes 7 seconds

Release Details

London Release: New Victoria, 4 August 1974.

Curiously, *Carry On Dick* went out on general release via the Odeon cinema circuit from 12 July, some weeks before its London release. In many places, this was part of a comedy double bill with *That's Your Funeral*, a 1972 comedy produced by horror specialists Hammer Films which was a spin-off of a short-lived BBC television sitcom about a firm of Northern undertakers. The stars were Bill Fraser, Raymond Huntley, and the magnificently lugubrious David Battley, alongside an array of comedy names as guest stars including Frank Thornton, Michael Ripper and, in one of his final movie appearances, Dennis Price. It also contains a rather sad cameo by former Carry On star Eric Barker, who had suffered a stroke in 1967 that severely curtailed his career. It is not even clear if we are supposed to recognise Barker in his tiny role as a man pushing his wheelchair-bound uncle—a sad fate for a man who only a few years previously had been a major comedy star. For what it is worth, *That's Your Funeral* is actually pretty good—*Carry On Dick*'s audiences got a good deal for the price of their cinema ticket. In a few places alternate support features were seen, in the form of the 1972 American thriller *The Doberman Gang*, or our old friends *Go For A Take*, *White Comanche*, and *The Intelligence Men*.

What's Carrying On?

In the year 1750, the rich folk of the English countryside are being terrorised by the notorious highwayman Big Dick Turpin and his gang. He steals not only their money and jewellery, but also their clothes, the latter being sold at church jumble sales for clerical funds. Sir Roger Daley, in charge of the local forces of the newly formed Bow Street Runners, orders Captain Desmond Fancey to apprehend Big Dick. Turpin, however, is operating under the secret identity of Reverend Flasher, vicar of Upper Dencher. Fancey and his sergeant, Jock Strapp, go undercover to the local criminal haunt, the Old Cock Inn, where they gain important information about how to identify Turpin. Big Dick manages to outwit his pursuers, but it is only a matter of time before the secret life of Reverend Flasher is uncovered.

Who's Carrying On?

A Peter Rogers Production
Director: Gerald Thomas
Screenplay by Talbot Rothwell, based on a treatment by Lawrie Wyman and George Evans
Music composed and conducted by Eric Rogers
Photography: Ernest Steward BSC
Art Director: Lionel Couch
Editor: Alfred Roome
Sidney James: The Reverend Flasher, vicar of Upper Dencher, keen to get his hands on the money of any passing rich folk in his guise as Big Dick Turpin. As both Dick and Flasher, he is also keen to get his hands on his assistant Harriet.
Barbara Windsor: Harriet, Reverend Flasher's assistant and also a completely convincing male impersonator as part of Big Dick's gang.
Kenneth Williams: Captain Desmond Fancey of the Bow Street Runners, whose attempts to catch Big Dick are constantly frustrated, despite his cunning disguise as the wanted robber 'Dandy Desmond'.
Hattie Jacques: Martha Hoggett, Reverend Flasher's housekeeper and organist, who would like a much closer relationship with her employer.
Bernard Bresslaw: Sir Roger Daley, in charge of the local Bow Street Runners and determined to catch Turpin, who keeps robbing him and stealing his clothes.
Joan Sims: Madame Desiree, the French proprietor of a group of glamourous ladies performing at the Old Cock Inn, her real identity being somewhat less exotic.

Kenneth Connor: The lecherous old constable of Upper Dencher.

Peter Butterworth: Tom, the third member of the Turpin gang and assistant to Reverend Flasher.

Jack Douglas: Sergeant Jock Strapp of the Bow Street Runners, who often proves cleverer than his superior, Captain Fancey. Known for his strange physical ticks and for hanging around the gents' toilets of the Old Cock Inn.

Carry On Critics

These were worrying times for the Carry Ons, at least as far as the film series was going. Despite the audience interest the name could still attract to the stage and television versions of Carry On, it is quite indicative of the waning interest in the film series that the Carry Ons were being critically ignored, even in this last stand of the old guard of Sid and Babs. If anything, no reviews were even worse than bad reviews, as at least a slating in a national newspaper might alert potential audiences that a new Carry On movie was being released.

Thus the main sources of reviews used in the research for this book—*The Times*, *Films and Filming*, and *Variety*—all failed to run a review of *Carry On Dick*. Thankfully, *The Guardian*'s Derek Malcolm was on hand in that paper's 25 July edition to give his verdict. 'The comic invention of *Carry On Dick* sags to a virtual standstill halfway through,' he wrote, though generally he remained indulgent towards the Carry Ons, even at this late stage of their existence: 'one has to admit that each new chapter has its cherishable moments. And there's something basically endearing about a police sergeant by the name of Jock Strapp and a gulled underling who explains: "I am a silly old constable."'

Kenneth Baily in the 14 July 1974 Sunday newspaper *The People* was enthusiastic enough to write an entire review in cod old-English:

> So I do verily commend it to ye; but with a nudge and a wink, mind—for ye must not be squeamish toward tap-room jests and privy innuendos if you would relish it all. My Lord Censor has endowed it with certificate 'A' for instant release in various cities.

One has to admire Baily's effort.

Monthly Film Bulletin, charged by its parent organisation, the British Film Institute, with reviewing every commercial film released in Britain, was one of the few publications to acknowledge the existence of the film beyond running paid advertising for its release. New rivals to the Carry Ons earned coverage not only due to the novelty value of the nudity they often featured, but also due to their sheer popularity with certain sections of the public. *The Times*' regular reviewer, David Robinson, penned an interesting piece in the 30 August 1974 edition on the release of *Percy's Progress* and *Confessions of a Window Cleaner*. The former was the sequel to 1971's *Percy*, directed as before by Gerald Thomas' brother Ralph, about the recipient of the world's first penis transplant. The latter was a phenomenal success, the most popular British film of 1974. Although neither film has aged anything like so well as even the Carry On films from the declining years of the series, they were certainly popular at the time.

For the record, *Monthly Film Bulletin*'s Nigel Gearing betrayed, to say the very least, signs of weariness, though interestingly he spotted similarities with Tony Richardson's 1963 hit *Tom Jones*:

> Perhaps only Kenneth Williams struggles manfully [*sic.*] against diminishing returns, although in his case superb facial gymnastics still fail to erase happier memories of the Hancock radio shows. Maybe their continuing appeal is beyond criticism—or, according to taste, beneath it.

The Carry Ons were still making money but were withering away from over-familiarity. Older and better Carry On films could be seen for free from the comfort of one's armchair on television. Comedy films more in touch with the times and the new standards of permissiveness could be seen at the local fleapit.

Carry On Comments

So we reach the film which is regarded by many as the last of the classic Carry On pictures. Others might think that that truly vintage Carry On period ended came earlier than this, but *Carry On Dick* certainly represents the last time the classic Carry On cast—with the exception of the already departed Charles Hawtrey—appeared together on film. Sid James, Barbara Windsor, and Hattie Jacques, for differing reasons, each made their Carry On exits here, though at the time of production no one realised. Not only was it fully expected that the series would continue for some time to come with its core cast in place, but Talbot Rothwell had signed a new six-film contract with Peter Rogers Productions. As it transpired, *Carry On Dick* would be the last film he would ever write as Rothwell suffered a breakdown while writing the script, which had to be completed by his daughter Jane from her father's notes and his dictation.

Although Jane was not credited for her contribution to the script, two other writers were. Lawrie Wyman and George Evans were initially asked to provide a storyline for a Carry On picture based around the notorious highwayman Dick Turpin, and although none of their material was used, they retained a credit in the finished film. Wyman was a highly experienced sitcom writer, best known for being the chief writer on the very long-running radio series *The Navy Lark*, which featured such past Carry On luminaries as Leslie Phillips and Jon Pertwee. Between series of *The Navy Lark*, Wyman was free to take on other work, and with George Evans, he wrote sitcom episodes for *And Mother Makes Three, Bless This House*, and *Love Thy Neighbour*. Evans was a similarly experienced comedy writer, most of his work being for television, where he wrote for performers such as Dick Emery, Harry Worth, and Terry Scott. Later in the 1970s, Evans wrote far more explicit sex comedies than the Carry On producers ever attempted for producer David Sullivan. Perhaps wisely, he wrote *The Playbirds, Confessions from the David Galaxy Affair*, and *Queen of the Blues* under the pen names Bud Tobin and Joe Ireland.

Under the circumstances, it is surprising that *Carry On Dick* hangs together as well as it does, and as it turned out, the film serves as a monument to just how much the Carry On series had grown to rely on Talbot Rothwell's contribution. Without him, the series quickly ran into trouble.

Rothwell was often a rather more sophisticated screenwriter than his constant barrage of secondhand jokes might suggest. It was no mean feat, for example, juggling the multiple plotlines required of a series of films with such a large regular cast. Also, he would often have a theme running through his scripts, such as *Carry On Matron*'s recurring motif of gender-swapping. Here, a theme of dual identities is established: Sid's Dick Turpin has his secret identity as Reverend Flasher, along with his confederates Tom and Harriet. Rothwell uses Barbara Windsor's Harriet to reverse a gag he used in films such as *Matron* and *Girls* in which male characters don absurdly unconvincing female disguises, which somehow manage to fool everyone else in the film. Here the short and extravagantly curved Babs fools everyone into thinking she is a man until the moment she strips down to her see-through vest.

Our trio of loveable villains is joined by Joan Sims' Madame Desiree, performing at landlord Bill Maynard's Old Cock Inn (splendidly unsubtle stuff from Rothwell, there) along with her *Oiseaux des Paradis*. As well as providing yet another dual identity, as Desiree turns out to be more Peckham than Paris, her act is rather interesting as it transposes the erotic tableau of the old Windmill Theatre (where many a comedian got their start trying in vain to entertain audiences who had most certainly not paid their money to be see a fully clothed man telling jokes) to the eighteenth century. Also seen at the Old Cock Inn are Jock Strapp and his boss Desmond Fancey, who go undercover as a pair of hardened villains—allowing Kenneth Williams to adopt his Rambling Sid Rumpo voice from the *Round the Horne* radio series.

Besides script and performances, the rest of the production holds up surprisingly well, despite the effects of the high 1970s inflation rate on a Carry On production budget that had barely altered in ten years. Eric Rogers' music was well up to standard, producer Peter Rogers still running to a decent-sized orchestra for his composer, which helps lend the film a whiff of the larger scale adventure films it emulates. Cinematographer Alan Hume also does wonders for the film, achieving some very attractive lighting effects, particularly in the scenes at the Old Cock Inn that form the centrepiece of the production. These scenes have a soft, smoky look which gives the impression of natural lighting, and it's interesting to note that Stanley Kubrick had been trying to achieve a similarly natural look on a much, much bigger budget during his epic 300-day shoot on *Barry Lyndon*, from spring 1973 to early 1974—not long before the cameras started rolling on *Dick*. When Kubrick's film was finally released to public view in December 1975, after an extended post-production process, the director and his cinematographer Joan Alcott received great praise for their groundbreaking use of available light photography. It is interesting to see the Carry On crew working on similar lines at a time when *Barry Lyndon* would not have been available for them to view and achieving such high-quality results.

The development of faster fine-grain films had opened up possibilities for filmmakers of all budgets, and *Carry On Dick* was able to make use of real indoor locations for many scenes, lending the film a less studio-bound look than previous historical Carry Ons. Although the production did not venture far from its home base of Pinewood Studios—St. Mary's Church, Burnham, the location of Reverend Flasher's church at the fictional Upper Dencher is only 8 miles from the studios—the film benefits greatly from its outdoor look.

As ever, *Carry On Dick* also benefits from full-blooded performances from its cast. While Sid is, as ever, the undoubted lead of the film and indeed gets to play what amounts to a dual role as the subdued Reverend Flasher and more traditionally 'Sid'-like Dick Turpin (as well as a turn in drag, which the actor always hated doing), others also get to shine. The pairing of Kenneth Williams and Jack Douglas as a comedy duo works surprisingly well, with the latter having toned down his performance from previous films while retaining his trademark twitches from the 'Alf' character. Kenneth Williams seems to have aged all of a sudden, possibly an effect of the thick brown wig he sports here. Barbara Windsor not only gives her all, giving a performance full of enthusiasm and vitality, but shows most of it, mild nudity now becoming a regular part of her appearances in the Carry On films. As Windsor was approaching the age of thirty-seven at the time of the film's release, this was not sustainable for very much longer, and it is perhaps understandable that the actress declined to appear in future films in the series. Bernard Bresslaw had shown in films such as *Follow That Camel* and *Carry On Loving* that he was very effective at playing more aggressive roles than the loveable dopes he was somewhat typecast as. Here he is on great form as the punningly named Sir Roger Daley, a role he plays completely straight, boiling with anger over his humiliations at the hands of Turpin and the incompetence of his underlings.

Even those regulars assigned smaller roles this time around are clearly having a great time, particularly Kenneth Connor as the village constable, playing his comedy old geezer role to the absolute hilt and raising the quality of any scene he appears in. Patsy Rowlands gets a single scene as Mrs Giles at the church jumble sale, but she puts such genuine fun and vivacity into the part that one remembers her well after the film has finished. Marianne Stone made a career out of playing small roles in literally hundreds of post-war British films, but here she plays the part she is probably best remembered for as Maggie the midwife. Her old crone is the centrepiece of the best gag in the film, as she reveals the existence of an identifying birthmark on Turpin's 'Diddler'. For those who have never diddled, the film attempts to explain exactly that this is, to the confusion of Kenneth Williams' Captain Fancey.

While *Carry On Dick* might not be on many people's list of top five Carry On films, it is a film that has more going for it than you might think, and it is a shame it had the misfortune to be released to a great deal of apathy. It deserved better and is about as good as mid-1970s Carry On gets.

28

Carry On Behind (1975)

Filming Dates: 10 March 1975–18 April 1975
Original Certificate: A (Classified by BBFC 10 June 1975 [cut])
Running time: 87 minutes

Release Details

Carry On Behind had an unusual premiere, eschewing the bright lights of London's West End for a charity preview held at the Dreamland amusement park in the Kent coastal resort of Margate, held for the benefit of the Langthorne House League of Friends on Thursday, 28 October 1975. This was almost two months before the film had its general release, for which Rank decided to pair *Carry On Behind* with *Fraud*, a low-budget import from South Africa—goodness knows the company had little enough of its own product to make up the bottom half of the bill, so little was Rank producing by this point. This was a Johannesburg-shot thriller directed and co-written by Donald Monat, described as 'a revealing document of cross and double cross in the financial jungle of stocks and shares.' Donald Monat was a South African-based English writer and actor who is best known to a small cadre of British classic television fans for playing John Steed in the South African radio adaptation of *The Avengers* for two years from December 1971 to December 1973. At the time, South Africa did not have a television service, being one of the last countries in Africa to set up a service, so it was the only chance for most South Africans (outside the network of 16-mm pirate copies) to be exposed to the series. Rank appears to have held on to the rights to *Fraud* for a while, at least, as the film was one of Rank's first home video releases on Betamax and VHS—formats that would soon take away the cinema audiences the Carry On films relied on.

Although *Fraud* was the most commonly seen co-feature with *Carry On Behind*, in some places, the Carry On was instead seen with previously seen co-features *The Doberman Gang, Nickel Queen*, and *That's Your Funeral*, or even Eric Sykes' silent short *The Plank*.

What's Carrying On?

A varied group descend upon the Riverside Camp Site for a caravanning holiday, including a middle-aged butcher and his dim friend trying to have some extra-marital fun, a married man whose attempts at a happy holiday are frustrated by the presence of his mother-in-law and her mynah bird, and a group of archaeologists digging Roman remains, who are led by the accident-prone Professor Crump and a Russian expert on Ancient Rome, Anna Vrooska.

Who's Carrying On?

A Peter Rogers Production
Director: Gerald Thomas
Screenplay by Dave Freeman
Music composed and conducted by Eric Rogers
Photography: Ernest Steward BSC
Art Director: Lionel Couch
Editor: Alfred Roome
Elke Sommer: Anna Vrooska, highly attractive Russian expert on the subject of ancient Rome who travels to England to help Professor Crump's dig.
Kenneth Williams: Professor Roland Crump, a distinguished archaeologist who finds himself sharing the world's worst caravan with Miss Vrooska.
Bernard Bresslaw: Arthur Upmore, whose hope for a relaxing caravan holiday are wrecked by the presence of his prudish mother-in-law and her foul-beaked mynah bird.
Kenneth Connor: Major Leep, pompous owner of the Riverside Camp Site, who has eyes for Mrs Barnes.
Jack Douglas: Ernie Bragg, twichy and dimwitted friend of Fred Ramsden who just wants to go fishing, but his pal has eyes on birds, rather than fish.
Joan Sims: Daphne Barnes, whose husband has long disappeared, acts as a cuckoo in the nest of her daughter and her husband's holiday caravan—as does her Minah Bird.
Windsor Davies: Fred Ramsden, horny butcher who hopes to take full advantage of a holiday away from his wife, but finds that when he's away from work, nobody wants his sausage.

Peter Butterworth: Henry Barnes, odd job man at the caravan site, who finds that one of the holidaymakers reveals a secret from his past.

Carry On Critics

Carry On Behind did well to garner as much critical attention as it did in the week that *Jaws*—a summer blockbuster in America—was finally released in British cinemas. The film attracted better notices than one might expect, with faint, but detectable praise from David Robinson in *The Times*' edition of Wednesday 24 December 1975:

> For *Carry On Behind* the perennial series is somewhat revitalised by the acquisition of a new writer, Dave Freeman, though he loyally observes the old rules of the game ... The sexual innuendo is about as dainty as a sledge hammer; and the double and triple meanings found in every word leave you for quite a while afterwards reeling and nervous of using even the simplest prepositions like 'down', 'in' or 'up'.

Derek Malcolm, not the most consistent of flag-wavers for the Carry On style of humour, proved even more forgiving and even enthusiastic in *The Guardian* on Saturday 27 December:

> Personally, I find the Carry Ons funnier as I, and they, get older. It's something to do with the entirely unique way they illuminate the barely-masked lechery, coarseness, greed and sentimentality behind the ducks-on-the-wall respectability they parody. This particular caravanning romp is admittedly grossly uneven but there's a patch in the middle that's really very good, thanks largely to Kenneth Connor's marvellous approximation of the seedy Major Leep who runs the site in the faint hope that it will one day become his personal brothel. His attempted seduction of the mountainously disapproving Joan Sims ... is as funny as anything in *The Pink Panther* [Malcolm having reviewed *The Return of the Pink Panther* in the same edition].

Veriner Glaessner in the *Monthly Film Bulletin* was equally enthused at the injection of new blood into the body of the Carry Ons:

> The advent of a new scriptwriter, Dave Freeman, seems to have worked a small wonder, and the film emerges as the most consistently funny Carry On in many years. Not that the script exactly strikes out into new pastures, although Freeman does keep in check the usual sniggering innuendo and the

comedy of middle-aged sexual frustration, while leaning just as heavily on double entendres and traditional sex-farce situations.

Carry On Comments

If *Carry On Dick* contained elements of *Don't Lose Your Head*, it was followed up by a film that was a direct (if unacknowledged) remake of a film popularly regarded as the highpoint, at least in financial terms, of the modern-dress Carry Ons. Despite its December 1975 release being advertised as being 'with the '76 touch', the latest in the Carry On line could just as easily have been titled 'Son of *Carry On Camping*'.

Change was still in the air, however, as the retirement through illness of Talbot Rothwell after his breakdown during the scripting of *Carry On Dick* meant that the series was in urgent need of a new writer. Dave Freeman was recruited to fill the gap, a hugely experienced comedy writer who had contributed to the *Carry On Christmas* TV specials made for Thames and for the *Carry On Laughing* TV series for ATV. Ironically, Freeman was also very experienced in writing for Sid James, being one of the key writers for his sitcom *Bless This House*, but Sid was not available for the *Carry On Behind* filming dates due to theatrical commitments. He was touring Australia with Sam Cree's farce *The Mating Season*—the very play Sid was appearing in when he died in Sunderland the following April.

With Barbara Windsor also unavailable, touring New Zealand with her variety show, cast changes were inevitable. The traditional Sid James role was this time taken by Windsor Davies, a London-born Welsh actor who had been around for years playing character parts before becoming an instant comedy star as Battery Sergeant Major Williams when the Second World War sitcom *It Ain't Half Hot Mum* debuted in January 1974. He was joined here by the German actress Elke Sommer, a German actress who first achieved popularity in the late 1950s in German and Italian films after being discovered by director Vittorio De Sica. She broke into English-language films from 1963 in films such as *A Shot in the Dark* (1964) alongside Peter Sellers' Inspector Clouseau and the 1968 Matt Helm spy movie *The Wrecking Crew* with Dean Martin.

By 1975, however, her Hollywood career was over and Sommer was largely appearing in movies by filmmakers in Britain and mainland Europe. Her asking price was high by Carry On standards—the highest by some distance since Phil Silvers has starred in *Follow That Camel*—but at £30,000, she was just about affordable. In theory, Sommer's marquee value not only gave *Carry On Behind*, missing the series' star name Sid James, a much needed publicity boost at home, but also a fighting chance of accessing European markets. It also helped that Sommer has worked for Rogers' wife Betty Box on two films—*Deadlier than the Male* (1967), which attempted to reboot the moribund Bulldog Drummond character as a James Bond-style spy, and *Percy's Progress* (1974), both of which had been directed by Gerald Thomas' brother Ralph.

Looked at from this distance in time, the most remarkable thing about *Carry On Behind* is how well the film fits in with the rest of the series. Even bearing in mind its strong structural and thematic similarity to *Carry On Camping*, it is surprising just how well Dave Freeman managed to catch the spirit of the Talbot Rothwell-scripted Carry Ons. That is not to say that the film works in all aspects, but it is a lot livelier and smile-inducing (even if it does not provoke much actual laughter) than we have any right to expect at this stage of the Carry On series.

The look of the film does not help, shooting having taken place in March and April 1975 and it is perfectly visible on camera—even more so than in *Carry On Camping*—that it was absolutely freezing. This could not be helped, but some of the problems with the film's casting were more foreseeable: Bernard Bresslaw and Patsy Rowlands work well together as a married couple whose holiday is ruined by the presence of Patsy's mum and her sweary mynah bird, but Joan Sims is rather miscast as the mother-in-law. She could play forceful, and even elderly woman with great skill, but here simply does not look old enough to be convincing as Patsy Rowland's mother—in reality, there was less than a year's difference in their ages.

Windsor Davies is an excellent actor and his characterisation is a lot of fun, but the effectiveness of his performance is harmed by the fact that he is playing a role that really looks written for Sid James. It is not Davies' fault, but the greatest thing his performance achieves is to demonstrate some of the unique things Sid brought to the Carry Ons. With the roguish, twinkling-eyed Sid in the role of Fred Ramsden (in which case they would surely have changed the character's name—Sid was not a natural Fred), you might not have wanted him to cheat on Liz Fraser, but even at the age of sixty-two, there remained a lingering feeling he could still pull if he really wanted to. Windsor Davies in the role comes across as delusional that he thinks he is in with a chance with Sherrie Hewson and Carol Hawkins.

While *Carry On Behind* is a film with an absence at its centre, one that would become even more starkly apparent when Sid James died suddenly four months after the film's release, it is still packed with series regulars giving good value. Kenneth Williams is given a high-profile role opposite guest star Elke Sommer and the pair work well together. Sommer plays her role as a Russian academic relatively straight, with much humour coming from the character's mangling of the English language. This works well against Williams' performance, which is typically over-the-top for this stage of his Carry On career and results in another feature of later Carry Ons, Williams being featured nearly nude. Nudity had become a box office draw, but this was possibly not the sort of nudity that brought in audiences in 1975. Rogers and Thomas continue to push the edges of acceptability allowed under an 'A' certificate in 1975, giving us two opportunities to see Jenny Cox's strip act, once thanks to Larry Dann showing the wrong film at Professor Crump's opening lecture and once when she is accidentally hired as the Riverside Caravan Site's evening entertainment. Kenneth Williams also gets to perform one of his much-hated scenes where he gets covered in gunk, the Williams dignity being lost when Professor Crump falls into a cesspit.

Jack Douglas returns to his twitchy 'Alf' mode here after having a slightly straighter role on *Carry On Dick*, and while one could never describe his performance as subtle, it is certainly effective. Kenneth Connor as Major Leep, owner of the campsite, gives an enthusiastic rendition one of his later-career specialities, that of the minor military officer bringing the same attitudes to civilian life.

The best role of the lot, however, is given to Peter Butterworth as Henry, the camp's odd-job man who has a secret former life. Butterworth gives a charming performance in a role which is not entirely unlike his grasping farmer in *Carry On Camping*, but here his part has slightly more depth and he also gets some of the best jokes. Butterworth had other Carry On roles to come, but this is up there with his best, which is quite an achievement this late in the day.

Also among the new recruits to Carry On are Ian Lavender, then as now famous for his role as Private Pike in *Dad's Army*, and Adrienne Posta as a married couple whose enormous dog roams the camp causing chaos. Lavender plays his role perhaps a little too straight, failing to make a strong impression as a result, whereas Posta's outsized personality is just perfect for Carry On. Lavender had the potential to be a new, younger presence in the films in the mould of Jim Dale, and it is a shame it did not work out for him. Sherrie Hewson and Carol Hawkins are a well-matched pair as cyclists Sandra and Carol, working really well together in a similar manner to Hawkins and Sally Geeson in *Carry On Abroad*, adding glamour to *Behind* in roles that avoid the dumb-blonde stereotype.

A surprising return to the Carry On fold was made here by Larry Dann, who had previously appeared as one of the saboteur schoolboys in *Carry On Teacher* back in 1959. Dann had maintained an acting career since his days as a child actor in the 1940s and 50s and would go on to national fame in the 1980s and '90s as Sergeant Alec Peters in ITV's long-running crime drama *The Bill*. In 1975 he was largely appearing on stage and on television commercials and it was here that he unexpectedly met Gerald Thomas. Thomas happened to be directing the commercial Dann was auditioning for and remembered the actor—Dann did not get the commercial job, but instead appeared in the next three Carry On pictures, which effectively relaunched his film and television career.

Perhaps even more surprising was the return of Liz Fraser as Fred Ramsden's wife Sylvia, making her first appearance in a Carry On since 1963's *Carry On Cabby*. One of the central members of the Carry On cast in that period, she left the series after getting into the bad graces of the management of distributors Anglo-Amalgamated. With that company's involvement in the films having ended some ten years previously, it is surprising that Fraser was not asked back sooner and she quickly became a regular in British smut-com movies of the seventies such as *Adventures of a Taxi Driver* and *Confessions of a Driving Instructor* (both released in 1976). The only shame here is that a bigger role was not found for the highly talented comedy actress, but it was lovely to see her back under the Carry On banner for one more time.

As the Riverside Caravan Site is swallowed up by the Earth, local publican David Lodge (providing a marvellous cameo role) having sold Major Leep a field riddled with Roman mine workings, another Carry On film ended. With the end of *Carry On Behind* came the end of the Carry On careers of Bernard Bresslaw, Patsy Rowlands, and Marianne Stone, three actors who had in various ways long been vital parts of the Carry On comedy machine. The film saw a drop-off in box office takings that did not escape the attention of the management of Rank's increasingly beleaguered film division. By now, it appeared, in the public view it was not really a Carry On film if it didn't have Sid James in it, and it soon became shockingly clear that he was not coming back.

From here on, Gerald Thomas and Peter Rogers had to become increasingly experimental in their attempts to keep the Carry On flag flying, which means that in many ways *Carry On Behind* is the last in the line of Carry Ons that had begun with Talbot Rothwell's arrival as the series writer. If the series had ended here, then it would have been a respectable send-off, but the final chapters in the Carry On story were still to come.

29

Carry On England (1976)

Filming Dates: 3 May 1976–4 June 1976
Original Certificate: AA (Classified by BBFC 29 June 1976 [later reedited to receive an 'A' certificate])
Running time: 87 minutes

Release Details

Release Date: 31 October 1976.

On its brief tour around the Odeon circuit, *Carry On England* was accompanied by one of two rather obscure films, depending on where you happened to be. One of these was at least a comedy, or a comedy-thriller to be more exact. This was *The Stoolie*, which had been shot in New Jersey and Miami Beach in 1971 and was first released in the USA in December 1972. Co-directed by future Oscar-winner John G. Avildsen, this was the feature film debut of the legendary Jewish-American stand-up comedian Jackie Mason. In other areas, an even more random film was on the bottom half of the bill: the independently made American drama *The Wrestler*, featuring Ad Asner as a wrestling promoter and an array of genuine professional wrestlers, including Harold Sakata, famous for playing Oddjob in the 1964 James Bond film *Goldfinger*.

What's Carrying On?

1940: Somewhere in England. Captain S. Melly is ordered to lead an experimental mixed-gender anti-aircraft unit which is notorious for poor discipline and rampant fraternisation between the male and female troops. Despite the resistance of his 'men' to military discipline, Melly and his sergeant-major, 'Tiger' Bloomer, turn this unit of lazy malingerers into an almost accidental group of heroes.

Who's Carrying On?

A Peter Rogers Production
Director: Gerald Thomas
Screenplay by David Pursall and Jack Seddon
Music composed and conducted by Max Harris
Photography: Ernest Steward BSC
Art Director: Lionel Couch
Editor: Richard Marden
Kenneth Connor: Captain S. Melly, possibly the most accident-prone officer in the British army, but absolutely determined to turn Experimental Battery 1313 into an effective fighting unit.
Windsor Davies: Sgt-Major 'Tiger' Bloomer, who is delighted to have a keen new commanding officer but doesn't reckon much for his chances.
Judy Geeson: Sergeant Tilly Willing, who most certainly is willing, especially if her boyfriend, Len Able, is around.
Patrick Mower: Sergeant Len Able, leader of the male troops despite being one of the least able soldiers ever to be called up for active duty.
Jack Douglas: Bombardier Ready, nervous and twitchy and as likely to bring down a British plane as an enemy aircraft.
Joan Sims: Private Jennifer Ffoukes-Sharpe, a terribly, terribly posh private who has the hots for 'Tiger' Bloomer.
Melvyn Hayes: Gunner Shorthouse—Britain was in really in dire straits if he was the country's last line of defence.
Peter Butterworth: Major Carstairs, whose overriding military purpose seems to be keeping his superior officer, the Brigadier, happy.
Peter Jones: The Brigadier, convinced he is the wittiest man alive, is under orders direct from WC to sort out the troublesome experimental battery.
Diane Langton: Private Alice Easy—short and busty, she oddly reminds one of another famous actress.

Carry On Critics

Variety's critic was less than impressed:

> *Carry On England* suffers from a particularly unfortunate hangup. It's not funny! Peter Rogers and Gerald Thomas ... have worked over what must be

> the dullest script of the series ... The cast, especially Connor, Windsor Davies and Jack Douglas, word hard to induce some excitement into the flagging dialog, but labor for a lost cause.

This being a trade newspaper, *Variety* was at least impressed by the economical nature of the production: 'Rogers still manages to bring the pix in for £200,000 ($330,000), a considerable achievement'—considerable indeed, though other estimates put the cost at closer to £250,000.

The Observer, on Sunday 31 October, presented Russell Davies' view of *Carry On England*, which was despairing of the prospects, not only of the film, but the continuing existence of the series: 'The death has surely occurred of the Carry On series,' he wrote, with some justification, going on to describe the general reaction of the press corps to the preview screening:

> To judge by the low, hooting sighs that filled the viewing theatre, it was not only over me that waves of embarrassment, impatience, boredom and despair broke relentlessly during the 90 minutes it took *Carry On England* to give up the ghost. A sense of disbelieving helplessness pervaded the stalls. This was a catastrophe.

Over at *The Times* in its Friday, 29 October 1976 edition, David Robinson expressed surprise that any filmmaking activity was actually taking place in a British film scene that had almost completely withered away: 'There is still a British film scene, though it is an odd one, rather in the nature of a devastated woodland with rare and exotic new growth endeavouring to shove its way through the tangle of dead and decaying vegetation'. Robinson actually saw some hope in the country's independent film scene, while claiming that 'the commercial cinema has never looked more dispirited'. It is not hard to guess which film released that week was flying the increasingly tattered flag of British popular cinema:

> The British establishment cinema is represented this week by *Carry On England*, the latest of the series, set in a mixed-sex Ack-Ack camp somewhere in England in 1940. It will delight all those who think that knickers, diarrhoea, overweight breasts and falling into pools of excrement are wellsprings of comedy.

With a list like that, it is almost surprising *Carry On England* did not find an audience.

Carry On Comments

Dave Freeman's work on *Carry On Behind* may have represented a logical progression from Talbot Rothwell's previous screenplays, attracting some quite positive reviews along the way, but the film took less money at the box office than previous films in the series. A new scriptwriting team was drafted in to push the next Carry On film in a new direction to arrest the decline in the series popularity, a vital step to take as Sid James was once again going to be unavailable for the new film, his globetrotting tour of Sam Cree's stage farce *The Mating Season* having now reached British theatres.

In theory, Sid's absence mattered less to the smooth running of *Carry On England* than it did for *Carry On Behind*, in which a role tailor-made for Sid needed to be recast. Sid's unavailability was known about far enough in advance that an interesting idea was hatched to create a sort of young Sid in the form of the character Sgt Len Able. This was quite a sound idea, and one which the Carry Ons might have pursued earlier had not Robin Asquith found fame in the rival Confessions comedy series. As events transpired, Sid died on stage at the Sunderland Empire theatre on 28 April 1976, only a week before *Carry On England* was due to start filming. Sid was the nation's roguish best mate and Britain went into mourning, making the prospects of a Sid-less Carry On movie achieving popular acceptance even more unlikely than they already had been.

The role of a substitute Sid had become a poisoned chalice, but at least Rogers and Thomas had managed to attract a big name to play the part in the form of Patrick Mower. This represented quite a coup for the series, especially at a stage when the Carry Ons' reputation and box office allure were looking very shaky indeed. Actually, Mower was a personal friend of Gerald Thomas and was extremely keen to try his hand at comedy. This was, in fact, quite a change of pace for the actor, who rose to prominence in 1970 when he was cast as the arrogant young government assassin James Cross in the television spy series *Callan*. There Mower was very much the second lead against Edward Woodward's title character, but he quickly moved on to co-lead in the crime series *Special Branch* alongside George Sewell. That series ended in 1974 and the actor was keen to try new things, including comedy. Before *Carry On England*, Mower made steps in the direction of comedy in two 1975 episodes of the extremely popular crime drama *The Sweeney*—'Golden Fleece' and 'Trojan Bus'. These pushed the generally tough and gritty series in a much more comedic direction than usual with Patrick Mower and George Layton playing smart-alec Australian villains Colin and Ray.

Carry On England's writers Dave Pursall and Jack Seddon had been writers of thrillers and crime movies during the 1960s, racking up some major credits, including a string of Agatha Christie adaptations: three of the famous Miss

Marple films starring Margaret Rutherford in the title role and the 1965 Hercule Poirot movie *The Alphabet Murders*, featuring Tony Randall as the Belgian sleuth. They also worked on major Hollywood features such as *The Longest Day* (1962), *The Blue Max* (1966), and *The Southern Star* (1969). The 1970s saw Pursall and Seddon move to television and eventually to comedy, initially via the halfway house of the 1972 mystery-comedy *It's Murder But Is It Art?*, which starred Arthur Lowe taking a break from his signature role as Captain Mainwaring in *Dad's Army*. Further comedy assignments followed, including half a dozen episodes of *The Liver Birds* alongside more dramatic fare such as the adventure series *Arthur of the Britons*.

In 1974, the pair contributed a script to the *Carry On Laughing* television series, which Peter Rogers liked but was viewed by the series' makers, Associated Television, as being too expensive to make within the show's budget. It was suggested instead that the script be adapted to feature length under the new title *Carry On England*, which Rogers had registered some fifteen years earlier. Rank, which had been financing and distributing the Carry Ons since *Don't Lose Your Head* eight years earlier, were producing fewer films by the mid-1970s, and the disappointing box-office returns for *Carry On Behind* caused the company to lose confidence in the series. As a result, Rank were only willing to provide half the estimated £250,000 production cost of the film. The search for alternate funding eventually reaching the unexpected destination of Prog Rock band Pink Floyd. The band's representatives agreed to put up the remainder of the budget, then pulled out due to having attracted a large tax demand. This was a potential disaster for Rogers and Thomas, who were now forced to provide the extra finance themselves.

One can imagine Pursall and Seddon's plotline for *Carry On England* appealing to Peter Rogers as a kind of ribald remake of *Carry On Sergeant*, taking the series back to its roots while also recalibrating its style of comedy to appeal to a new generation of cinemagoers accustomed to a more sexually frank style than the Carry Ons had provided thus far. Peter Rogers and Gerald Thomas even took a trip to the cinema to see one of the Confessions films in order to judge the competition. As a result, the new Carry On film would replace the occasional flashes of boob or bum, which had been seen in Carry Ons thus far with an entire screen-full of bare breasts.

Carry On England had various sets of problems to overcome; first, they had to get people to come out to see the film in the first place, and in this, the film almost completely failed. There are a number of potential reasons for this: the average age of cinemagoers had been getting younger since the arrival of commercial television to Britain in 1955. Not only were few of the people who turned out to see early hits such as *Carry On Sergeant* and *Carry On Nurse* in the late 1950s still regular cinemagoers, a fair chunk of the audience for *Carry On Camping* a decade later had also lost the regular cinemagoing habit by

1976. At this point in time, it is not too much of a stretch of the imagination to suggest that no matter how good *Carry On England* had turned out to be, to the filmgoers of 1975 the Carry Ons were a holdover from a previous generation which they would be unlikely to turn out for.

In this context, the fact that *Carry On England* was objectively terrible, the worst film in the series to that date by some considerable distance, was almost beside the point. But terrible the film was, and some time has to be taken examining just why it was so outlandishly poor. Sad to say a good proportion of the blame has to be laid at the door of Pursall and Seddon's script, and by extension, Peter Rogers for deciding that this screenplay was good enough to go before the cameras. It is painfully obvious that this ninety-minute film has been expanded from a twenty-five-minute sitcom script as there is nothing like enough plot to sustain a feature-length production. All that happens for almost the entire film is that the platoon makes increasingly outlandish and absurd attempts to defy authority, do no work, and get their hands on members of the opposite sex. Then, with literally five minutes of the film's running time to go, they almost accidentally manage to bring down an enemy aircraft, then the film ends with a very weak Winston Churchill gag.

Crucially, unlike *Carry On Sergeant*, *England* makes no attempt to garner the audience's sympathy for the ordinary soldiers it features. The former film takes pains to show us that the National Service conscripts are ordinary people taken out of their lives and set down in a situation that they were often completely unsuited to. In contrast, *Carry On England* presents us with a bunch of lazy and incompetent soldiers defying authority at a time when Britain was in a desperate fight for survival. Besides the fact that the entire bunch of them would quickly have found themselves in the glasshouse for a whole range of offences, the audience is given no reason whatever to lend its support to them. Carry On films had always been the comedy of the people, based in a reality the audience could recognise from the own lives, or at least through school history lessons. This ongoing legacy had in part been protected by the astonishing continuity of writers the series had maintained, with twenty-seven films being written largely by two people. *Carry On England* was so divorced from reality that it broke the thread connecting it to what remained of the Carry On audience.

It is interesting that such a comedy should come from a producer-director combination who were both of an age that the Second World War was a major formative influence. Peter Rogers and Gerald Thomas cannot be accused of disrespecting the wartime generation because it was their generation, therefore it was theirs to subvert and satirise. The worst that can be said is that they simply took a period about which they were intimately familiar and made a bad film about it.

Also, it is impossible for a Carry On film, with its gallery of highly experienced comedy performers, to not have a few bright spots and one would be remiss to not mention them. Shot in the early part of the blazing hot summer of 1976, *Carry On England* at least has an advantage over *Carry On Behind* that all that sunny weather makes the film look nice. Beyond that, one has to strain to find positives, but there are a few.

Kenneth Connor has much of the comedic heavy lifting to do and Captain S. Melly fits in well with the gallery of military types he played in his later career. Also, Connor finally gets top billing and it would be churlish indeed to deny him his moment in the spotlight. He and Windsor Davies make a decent comic partnership, but Connor is able to put rather more light and shade into his performance; Davies is playing a copy of his yelling Sergeant Major Williams from *It Ain't Half Hot Mum*, but what was acceptable in a half-hour sitcom format becomes rather wearing on the ears for ninety minutes—in one scene, Davies appears to have yelled himself hoarse.

Davies' *It Ain't Half Hot Mum* castmate Melvyn Hayes proves to be a Carry On natural, and it is a shame he was not given a bigger role in what would be his only Carry On film part, though he had turned up in the *Carry On Laughing* TV episode 'The Case of the Screaming Winkles' the previous year. Similarly, David Lodge, who appeared in almost every episode of *Carry On Laughing*, really grabs his brief role of Melly's predecessor Captain Bull by the throat—Lodge was hilarious in his single scene in *Carry On Behind* the previous year and showed once again what a great comic performer he was, given the chance.

Joan Sims has a relatively small role as the frightfully posh Private Jennifer Ffolkes-Sharpe, a role initially earmarked for Penelope Keith. Although one is used to seeing Sims in larger roles than this, the actress attacks the role with such gusto that she really stands out from the rest of the cast. Similarly, Peter Jones took on a role originally written for another performer, in this case Kenneth Williams. With Williams unavailable for the filming dates, comedy veteran Jones was drafted in, having last graced the series in 1967's *Carry On Doctor*, and he is absolutely marvellous in the usual understated Peter Jones manner. Despite the fact that, whatever the rest of the shortcomings of the script, Dave Pursall and Jack Seddon created a role that would have been perfect for Kenneth Williams in self-satisfied managerial mode, Jones makes the part work for him.

They also had the good idea of giving his character of the Brigadier a comic foil of Major Carstairs, in which part Peter Butterworth was cast. Their scenes together are the highlight of the film, Jones coming out with an endless stream of dreadful jokes, puns, and epigrams, which the ever-lugubrious, mobile-featured Butterworth forces both himself and everyone around him to find absolutely hilarious. If ever there was an example of Peter Butterworth's ability to steal a scene, it was his contribution to *Carry On England*.

Sadly, *Carry On England*'s high-spots are nothing like enough to save the film. The central romantic pairing of Patrick Mower and Judy Geeson are miscast, neither possessing the comedic experience to bring any life to the thin material they are given to work with. It says a lot about the pulling power of the Carry On name, even in the dog days of 1976, that Rogers and Thomas could still attract star names of their magnitude, but it says even more that they could be so completely wasted as they are here. Even Jack Douglas is given very little to do here and his presence barely registers, beyond a very laboured joke that Douglas, Geeson and Mower's characters have the surnames Ready, Willing and Able.

Star names apart, the other potential audience-draw here is the considerably increased amount of nudity, this being the point at which the Carry Ons finally abandoned their long-cherished, family-friendly 'A' certificate rating. The original cut of *Carry On England* attracted an 'AA' rating from the BBFC, meaning that under fourteens were not allowed to see the film. The trouble is that the female nudity that attracted this rating feels absolutely shoe-horned in, failing to arise naturally from the film's narrative. The most notorious scene comes when Captain Melly, in an attempt to make his charges wear proper uniform, orders the female soldiers to wear only skirts, so a group of them take Melly at his word and appear on parade topless. The scene is an embarrassment and one feels sorry for the performers. If nudity was required for box-office reasons then surely there were ways of writing this into the story in a vaguely natural, realistic manner. The idea of women in 1940 exposing themselves in public in this manner is just too silly for words.

Worse still, *Carry On England* performed disastrously on its initial release, taken off in some cinemas after only three days. The only advantage of the film presenting most of its nudity in one set-piece sequence was that it was relatively easy to re-edit and reshoot the scene as Rogers, Thomas, and the management of Rank scrambled to protect their investment and create a version of the film the BBFC would give an 'A' certificate to.

Despite plans being in an advanced stage for the *That's Carry On* compilation film involving the cooperation of Rank and Anglo-EMI, it really was already too late. Ask not for whom the Rank gong tolled, for it was about to toll for the final time for Peter Rogers.

30

That's Carry On (1977)

Filming Dates: 18 April 1977–20 April 1977
Release Date: February 1978
Original Certificate: A (Classified by BBFC 15 September 1977)
Running time: 95 minutes

What's Carrying On?

Barbara Windsor and Kenneth Williams review a series of clips from the Carry On films in one of the Pinewood Studios screening rooms, armed only with a hamper of food and a bottle of champagne.

Who's Carrying On?

A Peter Rogers Production
Director: Gerald Thomas
Screenplay by Tony Church
Compiled by Gerald Thomas
Music composed and conducted by Eric Rogers
Photography: Tony Imi
Editor: Jack Gardner

Carry On Critics

With the writing seemingly on the wall for the Carry Ons in the wake of disappointing financial returns for *Carry On Behind* and *Carry On England*, those critics who noted its existence at all used the release of *That's Carry On* to give their opinions on a much-loved series on which the sun was setting. John Pym in the *Monthly Film Bulletin* wrote a perceptive valedictory for the series:

> On the whole, the series ... wisely avoided malice and cultivated a tone of jovial decorousness: there were no full-frontals and, until the very end, only flashes of naked bosom. With the recent death of Sidney James and the withdrawal of financing by Rank, it seems unlikely that the series will continue for many more films. That the market it so successfully tapped still exists, however, is proved by the profitability of a film like *Come Play With Me* and the Confessions series—movies which, if anything, rely on an even more minimal formula. One wonders if, in twenty years, the mannerisms of the players in these later films will be regarded with the national affection now reserved for Sid James' colonial growl of sexual anticipation, Kenneth Connor's creepingly ineffective servility, Charles Hawtrey's spindly indomitability, Joan Sims' whale-boned sexual exuberance and Kenneth Williams' pursed lips and spiky ripostes.

Carry On Comments

The difficult and frustrating task of raising funds for *Carry On England* at least had one positive outcome. Rogers and Thomas knew they could no longer rely on the total (if limited) financial support of Rank and had to get themselves out into the wider world of 1970s film finance to hustle for funds. Despite the massive changes that had shaken the British film industry in the early 1970s, some familiar figures remained in situ, including erstwhile former Anglo-Amalgamated chief and Carry On distributor Nat Cohen.

Following the sudden death of Stuart Levy, his partner in Anglo-Amalgamated, on 3 June 1966 at the early age of fifty-nine, Cohen had taken the company in a new direction. Up until this point, beyond the unexpected source of regular profits that came from the Carry On films, Anglo's bread and butter were B-picture crime series *Scotland Yard*, a half-hour series that ran for thirty-nine episodes between 1953 and 1961. This was replaced by *The Scales of Justice*, which ran for thirteen episodes between 1961 and 1967, but the company was most famous for its five-year run of Edgar Wallace films, which ran as one-hour B-pictures on the ABC circuit (with occasional trips across town to Rank's cinemas) for five years and forty-seven films. By 1965, the series had reached its end as patterns of film distribution changed and the traditional B-picture became a thing of the past.

Cohen's background was in distribution and he saw which way the wind was blowing. Anglo-Amalgamated already had some major industry backing, thanks to Associated British Picture Corporation having bought 50 per cent of the company in April 1962 for an investment of £600,000. In 1967, this was raised to a 74 per cent controlling interest, which proved to be a smart move by ABPC. A change was seen in the type of film Anglo-Amalgamated backed: instead of investing £200,000 in a Carry On picture, Cohen spent the same money backing *Poor Cow*, Ken Loach's semi-documentary feature film debut. Bolstered by the star power of Terence Stamp and Carol White, this proved to be an unexpected hit in both Britain and the USA.

Formerly one of Britain's two major film producing factories alongside Rank, Associated British declined as a filmmaking force for much of the 1960s, remaining profitable thanks to Anglo-Amalgamated, as well as the company's successful ABC Television subsidiary and the worldwide success of its television spy series *The Avengers*. ABPC's largest shareholder, Warner Brothers, gave up in 1968, selling its holdings to EMI. The new owners had big plans for the company, which by this point was near-moribund as a filmmaking force.

Bernard Delfont, brother of the Lew and Leslie Grade, and himself a major showbusiness agent, was brought in to head the filmmaking division and Nat Cohan was appointed to the board. With much fanfare the actor, writer and director Bryan Forbes was installed as head of production, but Cohen retained his own slate of production within the new EMI Films organisation. Complete with a spiffy new whirling logo that announced 'Nat Cohen Presents for Anglo-EMI Film Distributors Ltd', the crafty old pro had managed to protect his Anglo-Amalgamated empire within the enormous EMI combine.

By 1970, Nat Cohen was chairman and chief executive of EMI Films—in a mere four years, he had reinvented himself from a B-picture producer to the most powerful figure in British film production. Cohen retained these positions until his retirement at the end of 1977, and was perhaps in a reflective mood when he was approached by Gerald Thomas the previous year for advice about financing *Carry On England*. He was not about to put EMI's money into that film (a wise decision), but with lines of communication opened, Cohan proved receptive to the idea of a retrospective Carry On film containing scenes from both the Anglo-Amalgamated and Rank eras of the series.

Rank was also keen on the idea, presumably seeing the possibility of an easy profit while investing a mere £30,000 in actually making the film. The shooting of the linking scenes in one of the Pinewood projection rooms took a mere two days, though was highly profitable for the two Carry On stars recruited for the occasion, Barbara Windsor and Kenneth Williams, who received more than their usual fees for a full Carry On shoot for the occasion. Both Rogers, Thomas, and Rank also had an eye on the huge profits made by the MGM's *That's Entertainment*, released in America in June 1974. This would normally have been a curio aimed at the nostalgia market but a quirk of timing meant that the film was released in the depths of an economic recession. *That's Entertainment* presented a compilation of clips from MGM's huge library of musicals and dance movies and rode a wave of longing for the certainties of a previous age. A film which would ordinarily have spent a couple of weeks in a few downtown cinemas instead became the hit of the year and was released to cinemas around the world, reaching Britain, to rapturous reviews, in October 1974.

With longstanding Carry On editor Alfred Roome having retired after *Carry On Behind*, Gerald Thomas ensconced himself in the screening room alongside Roome's assistant Jack Gardner with the difficult task of representing all the eras of the Carry On phenomenon in a mere ninety-five minutes. This included linking sequences filmed in one of Pinewood's screening rooms featuring Barbara Windsor and Kenneth Williams, in effect beginning what would be their post Carry On roles as the keepers of the series' flame. This pair of old pros work together excellently, playing to their Carry On stereotypes, the former being bubbly and sexy, the latter incredibly camp, even by Williams' standards. Problems with the film set in, though, with what turned out to be a major difference in the expectations Rank, the distributors of the finished film, and Peter Rogers had of the project.

The parsimonious Rank had a very cheap ninety-five-minute attraction on its hands and proceeded to treat the film like a cheap B-movie, to the horror of Peter Rogers, who had not made a B-picture for twenty years. *That's Carry On*, where it was released at all, was often seen as the support to the notorious Alistair MacLean adaptation *Golden Rendezvous*, a South African production, the shooting of which had spiralled out of control, leaving the tattered reputation of its star, Richard Harris, at its lowest point.

This pairing certainly did *That's Carry On* no favours, but the film was bedevilled with more basic problems—the desire to make *That's Carry On* as cheaply as possible was at the heart of the miscalculations involved in the film. Metro-Goldwyn-Mayer spent over $3 million making *That's Entertainment*, presenting its film sequences in a quality far higher than they could ever be seen on television. Audiences were thus presented with old-school musical spectacle in colour and widescreen for the first time in many years. The Carry On films, on the other hand, were already becoming television staples, and the low budgets of the original films meant that apart from lacking the communal pleasure of shared laughter, the films lost very little in their transfer to the small screen. Frankly, there was very little here that would tempt people to leave their homes and take one of their increasingly rare trips to the cinema—by 1977, that took James Bond, giant sharks, or *Star Wars*, the latter of which was on general release in the UK at precisely the same time as *That's Carry On*.

Peter Rogers was outraged at the insult he perceived to the Carry On name when *That's Carry On* was released in such a low-key manner, but perhaps Rank had a point. The first rule of showbusiness is to leave your audience wanting more, and cinema audiences clearly did not want more Carry On. Neither, it transpired, did Rank.

31

Carry On Emmannuelle (1978)

Filming Dates: 10 April 1978–15 May 1978
Original Certificate: AA (Classified by BBFC 27 June 1978 [uncut])
Running time: 87 minutes 44 seconds

Release Details

Release Date: 24 November 1978.

On seeing *Carry On Emmannuelle*, the management at Rank's Odeon cinema arm, which had agreed to show the film (even if the company had passed up the chance to finance its production), perhaps thought that anyone who had actually paid to watch it deserved a bit of excitement. Thus *Emmannuelle* was seen in the UK as half of a double-bill with *Speedtrap*, a 1977 car chase thriller starring Joe Don Baker, future *Cagney and Lacey* star Tyne Daly, and about 100 cars flying off ramps and getting wrecked. To be fair, despite the almost total obscurity into which it has fallen, *Speedtrap* has some pretty amazing stunt sequences and was probably a better reason for spending a few hours at the local fleapit than *Carry On Emmannuelle*.

What's Carrying On?

Emmannuelle Prevert, wife of the French ambassador to the United Kingdom, returns to her husband Emile's side after a long absence. Emile is unable to satisfy his highly sexed wife after a nasty skydiving accident with a church spire, so she proceeds to sleep with half of London. After initially causing chaos among the household staff, she becomes popular but a spurned boyfriend takes drastic measures that make her nationally infamous.

Who's Carrying On?

A Peter Rogers Production
Director: Gerald Thomas
Screenplay by Lance Peters (with uncredited additional material by Vince Powell, Peter Rogers and Willie Rushton)
Music composed and conducted by Eric Rogers
Photography: Alan Hume BSC
Art Director: Jack Shampan
Editor: Peter Boita
Kenneth Williams: Emile Prevert, the French ambassador to the court of King James. A former sexual adventurer whose ardour has been considerably reduced by a close encounter with a church spire while nude skydiving with his wife
Kenneth Connor: Leyland, the chauffeur—a randy old sod who has lived in London all his life, and even before. Drives a Daimler Pervertable: the roof does not go down but the driver does.
Joan Sims: Mrs Dangle, the ambassador's housekeeper, whose formidable exterior hides an unexpectedly passionate nature.
Jack Douglas: Lyons, the Butler, who runs the ambassador's household and manages to keep his hands, if not his eyes, away from Emmannuelle.
Peter Butterworth: Richmond, the footman. Ancient retainer of the ambassador's household, who had an interesting war trapped in a church with a young French maiden—he stayed until 1953.
Larry Dann: Theodore Valentine, a thirty-four-year-old mother's boy whose life is altered by an encounter with Emmannuelle in a Concorde toilet cubicle. When she later rejects him, he resorts to drastic measures.
Introducing: Suzanne Danielle: Emmannuelle Prevert, wife of the French ambassador whose habit of sleeping with almost every man she meets (apart from her own husband) makes her the most notorious woman in Britain.
With: Beryl Reid as Mrs Valentine, Theodore's over-protective mother.

Carry On Critics

Variety summed up *Emmannuelle* very neatly in its trademark mixture of American spelling and the magazine's own slang terminology:

> Carry On series now has 30 releases over 20 years. Formula is low budgets, low laughs. Which sums up *Carry On Emmannuelle* ... Rude, rollicking fun, at a breathless pace, was the order of earlier Carry On days. This

> one is rude, certainly, but the relentless phallic innuendo is as labored as makers' determination to show nothing to worry the censor. Leaden comic timing compares poorly with TV sitcoms which pic otherwise resembles in production values.

Derek Malcolm at *The Guardian*, who had over the years been generally quite positive about the Carry Ons, described *Emmannuelle* as 'misspelt as well as misconceived, being not only totally unfunny but about as genuinely saucy as a wet kipper'. John Pym at the *Monthly Film Bulletin* was something of a voice in the critical wilderness in finding several positive aspects to the film. The general tone of the review seemed to recognise, however, that the Carry On series was reaching the end of the line:

> Despite the overall and fairly predictable feebleness of the latest episode in this refuse-to-say-die comedy series—and the below-stairs flashbacks are exceptionally lacklustre—long-term addicts may derive a certain satisfaction from seeing many of the old troupers at long last achieving their hearts' desire: namely, unlimited sexual intercourse with a handsome and eager young woman. It seems unlikely at this late hour the series' scriptwriters will ever temper their outdated jibes against homosexuals, or ever present an Indian as someone other than a grinning fellow with a turban and a funny voice. This said, however, the spectacle of performers like Kenneth Connor, Jack Douglas and Peter Butterworth blandly ignoring the narrative discontinuity and rehearsing their character tics and mannerisms (Butterworth's chattering teeth are particularly relishable) provides a number of isolated pleasures.

Carry On Comments

While *Carry On Emmannuelle* might be the low point of the original run of Carry On films—in fact, you will have a hard time finding anyone to argue otherwise—the circumstances of its production and the issues both the film and its failures and successes (it does have some) raise are worthy of discussion.

After the failure of *Carry On England* to revitalise the series, followed a year later by *That's Carry On*, a film whose closing speech by Kenneth Williams carries with it a very real sense of closure, it is very tempting to wonder why Peter Rogers and Gerald Thomas felt the urge to carry on.

One has to remember how quickly events had moved: *Carry On England* had been released (albeit briefly) in October 1976, its attempt to bring new life to the Carry On name by bringing in a raft of new cast members rejected by audiences. It had only been three years since *Carry On Girls* had opened, making a healthy profit for Rank. The difficulties presented by an ageing cast and the death of Sidney James were considerable, but the Carry On brand had remained popular on television and stage, so perhaps a belief that Carry On still had a life on the big screen was not so unbelievable. We are blessed with the benefit of hindsight and should excuse Rogers and Thomas for perhaps not grasping fully the seismic changes that occurred in the British film sector during the 1970s, and that the Carry On movie audience no longer existed.

It also needs to be remembered that by 1977, Peter Rogers was aged sixty-three and Gerald Thomas fifty-seven—not young men, but by the standards of the movie business hardly ready to retire yet. Rank, however, were ready to retire the Carry Ons, rejecting not only the two scripts Peter Rogers offered them—*Carry On Again Nurse*, written by Jonathan Lynn and George Layton, and *Carry On Emmannuelle*, by Lance Peters—but also any further involvement in the Carry On film series. Not ready to give up the fight, Peter Rogers began to search for new backers.

This meant that 1978 was the first year since *Carry On Sergeant* was released twenty years previously that there would be no new Carry On film released in British cinemas. Backing was eventually found from a company called Cleves Investments, who backed the film for a quite impressive-sounding £320,000, almost a third more than Rank had been putting into the films, and had an option for a further five films. One needs to factor the high rate of inflation in to Cleves' apparent largess. *Carry On Behind* had cost an estimated £250,000 in 1976, an amount which two years later would have needed £313,653 to match, so the two films in effect had the same amount of money spent on them.

The film also found a willing distributor in the form of Hemdale, a British production and distribution company that had recently employed Kenneth Williams in a ramshackle, stunningly unfunny spoof version of *The Hound of the Baskervilles* written by and starring Peter Cook and Dudley Moore. Rank still retained an involvement in the distribution, as prints of *Carry On Emmannuelle* available for viewing still retain the famous Rank gong at the very beginning. Hemdale itself had an interesting and varied history. The company had been set up in 1967 by producer John Daly and the actor David Hemmings, soon after the latter had been propelled to stardom in Michelangelo Antonioni's *Blow-Up* (1966). Hemdale considerably reduced Hemmings' tax burden while allowing him to put money back into the film industry and pursue his interest in directing. Despite going on to both produce and direct—he reduced his focus on acting at the end of the seventies and spent most of the 1980s and '90s directing American television series—Hemmings left the company in 1971. The scope of Hemdale expanded to include managing major rock bands such as Black Sabbath and Yes, stage productions, promoting the famous 'Rumble in the Jungle' boxing match between Mohammed Ali and George Foreman, and cable television distribution. At the time Hemdale invested in *Carry On Emmannuelle*, the company's interests in filmmaking were on a relatively modest scale and centred on British productions, but soon after, in 1980, John Daly relocated the company to Hollywood.

To the surprise of many, Daly and his partner Derek Gibson turned Hemdale into a Hollywood powerhouse. Daly took a chance and backed James Cameron's SF action thriller *The Terminator*, the huge success of which changed the careers of everyone involved. Having launched the career of James Cameron, Daly then found Oliver Stone. After backing and distributing Stone's critically acclaimed but money-losing *Salvador*, the company stuck with Stone and struck gold with the multi-Oscar winning Vietnam War drama *Platoon*, both films being released in 1986. Daly's policy of backing challenging, adult films had turned Hemdale into a major Hollywood player, but cracks were beginning to show. Daly had seriously antagonised most of the talent he had worked with, very few of whom had actually been paid. Hemdale filed for bankruptcy in 1991, struggling along in different forms until 1995.

Back in 1978, however, John Daly was a medium-sized fish in the leaky pond that was the British movie business, and Hemdale released *Carry On Emmannuelle* with very little publicity. One might say that the film was not so much released as paroled, the lack of publicity, and damning nature of the few reviews the film garnered were the final nail in the Carry On coffin. After four flops in a row, there was no coming back—at least not for fourteen years.

Carry On Emmannuelle not only sank without trace in British cinemas in 1978, it disappeared from view for many years, the unloved relation of the Carry On family that nobody talked about. Myths built up around the film as it remained unavailable for viewing: that it was a soft porn film; or that Barbara Windsor walked off the set, shocked at the scenes she was being asked to perform. Neither was true, but when the film finally did re-enter public view, released by Video Collection International as a 15 Certificate VHS cassette tape in 1992, *Carry On Emmannuelle*'s reputation hardly improved.

But is *Carry On Emmannuelle* a film worthy of re-evaluation? It certainly has a go at keeping up with modern trends, as can be heard from the very beginning of the film, when instead of a breezy theme from composer Eric Rogers—returning to the series after absenting himself from *Carry On England*—we are 'treated' to 'Love Crazy', a disco song performed by a group calling themselves Masterplan and written by none other than musician and comedy actor Kenny Lynch, who we last saw playing a bus conductor in *Carry On Loving* eight years previously.

Familiarity was vital in attracting investors, however, and the experiment in updating the Carry On cast initiated in *Carry On England* was abandoned. As many regular cast members as possible were rounded up, with great difficulty encountered in getting Kenneth Williams to appear. Lance Peters' original script was considerably raunchier than that which eventually reached the screen, and the actor outright rejected any possibility of his appearing in such a project: 'It isn't a question of what can be cut, or what scenes can be modified or re-written. The very essence of it is offensive'.[1] Williams was the most senior surviving Carry On cast member and great efforts were made to rewrite the script to his satisfaction, with writer and satirist Willie Rushton and old comedy hand Vince Powell being drafted in to make changes. So different and toned down was the final shooting script from what Lance Peters had originally presented that Peter Rogers refused to allow the film's poster art to be used on Peters' published novelisation of his script.

Barbara Windsor was initially agreeable to the idea of making a series of guest appearances in the film, as the object of various characters' desires in a series of flashbacks. Unfortunately, the actress had strong objections to the draft of the script she was presented with and went public with her refusal to appear in the film: 'I'm definitely not having anything to do with it,' she fumed in the *Daily Mirror*'s 19 April 1978 edition. 'I think it's soft porn … I have read the script and it seems that the whole thing is one long nude scene.'[2] In a perfect example of having their cake and eating it, the *Mirror* printed the story next to a nude picture of Barbara from *Carry On Abroad*. By the following day, the *Mirror* was claiming that Babs had walked off the set, and a somewhat ungallant Peter Rogers was quoted as saying, 'Barbara was not originally cast in the film but she wanted to be in it and was given a small part. The film was just going to include the odd appearance by her. Now it's the odd disappearance.'[3]

Happily, several other Carry On regulars did agree to appear, with Joan Sims, Kenneth Connnor, Peter Butterworth, and Jack Douglas all playing major roles as the members of the French ambassador's household. Even with the deficiencies in the script, this meant that *Emmannuelle* retained a very pleasant core of old pros able to bounce off each other and extract whatever laughs there might be from even unpromising material. Also returning was Larry Dann, who at this point was close to being regarded as a core cast member, rising here from the small roles he had played in in *Behind* and *England* to being the young-ish male lead—the last in the line of potential replacements for Jim Dale. Even in smaller roles, there was a gallery of familiar faces, with the likes of Gertan Klauber and Michael Nightingale making their traditional appearances. Even Eric Barker, who had not worked in some time due to ill-health, returned to the series for the first time since 1964's *Carry On Spying* for a wordless extended cameo in the film's banquet sequence as a general, which was to prove his last film role. Even the film's editor was a returning old face, Peter Boita, who managed the remarkable feat of editing only two Carry On pictures, the first and the last in the original series.

Despite Peter Rogers and Gerald Thomas' efforts to create an air of familiarity, this was a Carry On film for a new era, and although the film had some serious issues, the performance of Suzanne Danielle was not one of them. She was not an experienced actress at this point, having become familiar to the producers through her relationship with Patrick Mower, which led to her being on the set of *Carry On England*. Besides having the physical attributes for the role, and bearing a passing resemblance to Sylvia Kristel, star of the *Emmanuelle* films, Danielle proves not only perfect for the role, but also a very capable actress indeed. It was a lot to ask of any young actress (Danielle was aged twenty-one at the time) in her first leading role not only to act opposite some of the most experienced comedic actors in Britain, but to stand toe-to-toe with Kenneth Williams and hold her place on the screen. If there is one thing that *Carry On Emmannuelle* gets right, it is the casting of its leading lady.

Unfortunately, the film gets plenty of things wrong, some of the gags striking wrong notes in ways unimaginable from anything Talbot Rothwell or Norman Hudis might have supplied. An early sequence in which Emmannuelle arrives at Heathrow Airport to be confronted by a Sikh immigration officer—played by Dino Shafeek, a very familiar face to British television viewers at the time thanks to his regular roles in the sitcoms *It Ain't Half Hot Mum* and *Mind Your Language*—comes across today as unpleasantly racist in tone, and it is hard to imagine the scene playing any differently in 1978. The entire subtext of the scene is 'What is this foreigner doing deciding who gets to enter Britain?'—Emmannuelle as much as says so, which was treading on some very dodgy ground.

A later scene in which Emmannuelle flashes a guardsman and gets no reaction, only for him to wink at a very camp gay man who passes by, is hardly any better and illustrates the problem the Carry Ons had dealing with camp and gay characters once Charles Hawtrey left the series. Hawtrey was playing an aspect of himself and was in on the joke, constantly breaking the fourth wall and playing direct to the audience. In later films such as *Carry On Girls* and *Carry On Emmannuelle*, gay characters were being laughed at, and the distinction is important.

When Kenneth Williams wrote to Gerald Thomas to complain that the very essence of the film was offensive, to be honest, he had a point. Emmannuelle's nymphomania is a very difficult subject to construct a comedy film around, and some scenes fail utterly in terms of taste. The film reaches perhaps its nadir when Emmannuelle visits a football match and sleeps with both sets of players and the referee. As this sequence uses clips from the 1977 FA Cup final between Manchester United and Liverpool, and most of the players we see with Emmannuelle are clearly wearing Manchester United shirts, the producers were treading dangerous waters legally. In that sense, at least, it was possibly a good thing that hardly anyone saw the film.

Despite the nature of its story, the process of deemphasising the explicit content in order that the regular cast members would agree to appear in the film meant that Carry On Emmannuelle fell between a whole bar full of stools. This was supposed to be part of Rogers and Thomas' ongoing attempts to attract the large audiences that had been flocking to see the Confessions films (though the appeal of even that series had tailed off by 1978), but those films contained more than enough nudity to gain 'X' certificates from the BBFC. *Carry On Emmannuelle*, in which Kenneth Williams spends more time naked than the title character, was actually less explicit than the original cut of *Carry On England* had been, and barely scraped a 'AA' rating.

The most annoying aspect of the whole *Carry On Emmannuelle* debacle is that it contains one very good sequence in its central section. Emmannuelle breaks with custom in the ambassador's household by going downstairs to spend time with the domestic staff. This gives us a chance to see Danielle interact with the Carry On regulars in more relaxed circumstances than the rather forced clothes-dropping situations we have seen thus far. Emmannuelle encourages the staff to share their most erotic memories with the group, and from this unpromising premise, we are treated to the final scenes worthy of the Carry On name in the original series of films. Kenneth Connor tells a tale of him meeting a stunning blonde in a pub and being taken to her palatial apartment for a night of lust. In a clever piece of storytelling, however, what we see is rather closer to the truth—the beautiful blonde is the handsome but rather large Lancashire hotpot that was Claire Davenport, a staple of the British comic scene incredibly making her only Carry On appearance, and her luxury apartment is a cramped hovel. Gerald Thomas, perhaps knowing that he was handling the best material in the film, pulls out all the stops to make the sequence work. Besides undercranking the camera to speed up some of the action, the sequence even looks a lot nicer than the rest of the film, the image being imbued with a lovely, warm glow. Even the punchline is a good one: her drunken sailor husband Norman Mitchell (back after a twelve-year gap since his last series appearance, in *Carry On Screaming*) returns home and collapses on the bed, allowing Davenport to join Connor to indulge in her favourite activity: sex in the wardrobe. What the tiny Barbara Windsor thought about a role that had originally been earmarked for her being played by the much larger Clare Davenport remains unrecorded, but Davenport is marvellous—what a shame this was her only Carry On contribution.

Peter Butterworth's Richmond tells an amusing wartime tale in which he is stranded from the rest of his military unit in wartime France. Donning female garb, he is given sanctuary by a parson and his buxom daughter, staying until 1953. It is sad to report that this sequence was the last film work to be performed by Butterworth, who died suddenly on 19 January 1979, while *Carry On Emmannuelle* was still on general release in a few places. At least his final on-screen gag was a good one.

Jack Douglas gets a sequence in London Zoo which is the weakest part of this group of scenes, but this should not distract from his strong performance throughout the film as Lyons the butler, for once shorn of his comedic fallbacks of scruffy haircut, flat cap, and twitch. Joan Sims, on the other hand, gets to play in a little comic gem as she meets Victor Maddern at a launderette and the two form an immediate attraction. The pair perform a sort of strip-tease routine, revealing to each other the contents of their laundry bags. It is a simple idea which does not sound like much on the page but works fabulously well on screen.

Emmannuelle tells the story of her own husband, and how his galloping ardour was ruined when the pair went nude skydiving and he had a nasty accident involving a church spire. This helps to introduce the latter half of the plot as Williams seeks a cure for his impotence by seeing a doctor—another unwelcome racial stereotype, this time played by *Mind Your Language* regular Albert Moses. Kenneth Williams, despite having to adopt a dodgy French accent, plays his role with a gusto which belies his reluctance to appear in the film at all. A notorious on-set flasher, one imagines that Williams, still in good trim at the age of fifty-two, had no problems with the copious amounts of nudity the film demanded of him.

Emblematic of the failures and confused nature of *Carry On Emmannuelle* is the role of Larry Dann as the (comparatively) youthful male lead of the film. It is great to see Dann finally get a Carry On role he can sink his teeth into and he has some good scenes. He is great in the opening sequence on Concorde, a satire on the famous scene in *Emmanuelle* in which she has sex in an aeroplane toilet, and pairing him up with Beryl Reid as his overprotective mother was an excellent idea. Reid filmed her scripted scenes in a single day, but was so good that she was called back and extra scenes written for her character. Unfortunately, the Reid/Dann subplot heads off in far too many directions, some of them unwise in the extreme. Surely somebody could have stopped and considered the wisdom of having Dann, the last in a long line of potential Jim Dale replacements, kidnap the heroine of the film at gunpoint and later attempt suicide. These scenes leave a nasty taste in the mouth and are horrendously unfunny, wasting two good performances and a nice character relationship between Larry Dann and Beryl Reid.

If *Carry On Emmannuelle* had been a worse film, it would be easier to watch, but it remains a film which is better than its reputation, albeit only just. It is simply impossible to completely dislike a film with this cast, still able to operate at their peak despite a script which is at times drops well beneath the dignity of the Carry On name and an extremely rushed four-week shooting schedule. The fact remains that in making the film at all Peter Rogers and Gerald Thomas ignored the first rule of showbusiness: always leave them wanting more.

32

Carry On Columbus (1992)

Filming Dates: 21 April–27 May 1992
Release Date: 2 October 1992
Original Certificate: PG (Classified by BBFC 13 August 1992 [uncut])
Running time: 90 minutes 51 seconds

What's Carrying On?

Christopher Columbus, a dodgy Italian mapmaker, believes he can find a new sea route to India from Europe that will save traders a huge amount of time. He convinces the king and queen of Spain to finance an exploratory voyage and supply a ship, the *Santa Maria*. Columbus quickly assembles a crew of crooks and misfits to set sail. The sultan of Turkey hears of these plans and will be ruined if a new route is established, as currently he taxes all trade that takes the land route to India through Turkey. He sends his best spies, Fatima and Achmed, to sabotage the mission, but Fatima, disguised as a boy, starts to fall in love with Columbus. On landing in what they think is India, Columbus and his crew are greeted by a tribe and their chief who are considerably less gullible than Christopher thinks.

Who's Carrying On?

Island World presents a Comedy House production in association with Peter Rogers Productions
Executive Producer: Peter Rogers
Producer: John Goldstone
Director: Gerald Thomas

Screenplay by Dave Freeman with additional material by John Antrobus
Music composed by John Du Prez
Song 'Carry On Columbus' written and produced by Malcolm McLaren and Lee Gorman
Performed by Jayne Collins and Debbie Holmes
Photography: Alan Hume BSC
Production Designer: Harry Pottle
Editor: Chris Blunden
Jim Dale: Christopher Columbus, a slightly crooked mapmaker who sees the chance of a big profit if he can find a new sea route to the Indies.
Bernard Cribbins: Mordecai Mendoza, Columbus' Jewish–Christian friend and assistant who comes along on the voyage as he is the only person able to read the map, which is written in Hebrew.
Maureen Lipman: Countess Esmerelda, mother of Maria (Holly Aird), who she wants to marry off to the ancient duke of Costa Brava (Jon Pertwee).
Peter Richardson: Bart Columbus, Christopher's rather dopey and innocent brother, who hopes to make his fortune on the voyage so that he can marry Maria.
Alexei Sayle: Achmed, Turkish spy working under his superior, Fatima.
Rik Mayall: The sultan of Turkey, whose finances will be ruined if Columbus finds a new route to the Indies.
Charles Fleischer: Pontiac, second-in-command of the tribe that greets Columbus and his crew when they arrive in what they think is India.
Larry Miller: Chief of the tribe that is suddenly confronted with Columbus, and is not about to give up their gold in return for a few beads.
Leslie Phillips: King Ferdinand, henpecked ruler of Castile, to whom Columbus appeals to fund his voyage.
June Whitfield: Queen Isabella of Castile, who convinces her husband to fund Columbus as they need the money from the potential riches the voyage may bring.
Julian Clary: Don Juan Diego, governor of the hell-hole prison from where Columbus is forced to find much of his crew, who comes along for the trip.
Sara Crowe: Fatima, undercover agent for the Sultan of Turkey, who dons a beard and male clothes in order to join the Santa Maria's crew and somehow convince everyone she's a man.

Carry On Comments

On paper, not only should *Carry On Columbus* have worked, but it could have been something really special. Not only did this represent the return of the beloved Carry On series after fourteen years and several false starts, but the film also saw the joining forces of three generations of British comedy royalty. Peter Rogers, now taking the position of executive producer, and Gerald Thomas were joined by an impressive array of performers from the postwar generation of British comedy actors. The film was produced by John Goldstone, producer of the Monty Python films, while the project attracted the cream of the new wave of comedians that emerged in the nineteen eighties. Sadly, the high hopes generated for the project were to be dashed.

Carry On Columbus featured fewer of the original core cast members than might have been wished, despite being made at a point in time there were more of them available than would be the case just a few short years later. John Goldstone angered some fans by stating on an interview on the TV programme *Film 92* that beloved now departed Carry On stars of the past would have been too old to appear in major roles in the new film, which may well have been true but caused some bad feeling among a section of the Carry On fanbase. As it transpired, several of the surviving cast members, including Joan Sims, Kenneth Connor, and Barbara Windsor, chose not to take up the relatively minor supporting roles they were offered.

Not all of the younger breed of comic actors took up the offer of a role in the film, either: Robbie Coltrane was offered the lead role of Christopher Columbus but turned the project down. Fortunately, Jim Dale agreed to take on the part; the Carry Ons had given Dale his acting break and helped him develop his comedic and acting talents to become a genuine leading man. By now a star of the Broadway stage, Dale felt enormous affection for both the series and his old producer and director and was happy to bring his star power to the production. Similarly, Harry Enfield was offered the key role of Christopher's dopey younger brother Bart but, as a major Carry On fan, did not want to take part in a Carry On film with so few of the key cast member present. This was a real shame as Enfield could have added a wide-eyed enthusiasm to the part that would have been perfect. Peter Richardson, who took on the role, was a talented writer and director associated with the Comic Strip troupe but the best thing that can be said about his performance was that he remembered his lines and did not bump into the furniture.

Frankie Howerd, in the middle of a major career revival in the early 1990s, was happy to return to the big screen to take up the role of the king of Spain. In March 1992, it was leaked to the press that Frankie was to appear in *Carry On Columbus*, but by 3 April, he was in intensive care and it was clear he was too ill to take up his film role. The legendary comedian died at the age of seventy-five on 19 April, just a few days before *Carry On Columbus* began shooting at Pinewood Studios. In his place was attracted at very short notice Leslie Phillips, who had walked away from the Carry On series back in 1960 after *Carry On Constable*. In the middle of tragedy, this had the rather pleasant side-effect of effecting a reunion with his *Carry On Nurse* girlfriend

June Whitfield as the queen of Spain, a role which had originally been offered to Joan Sims.

Another name long-missing from the Carry On cast, Bernard Cribbins signed up for the major part of Mordecai Mendoza, Columbus' Jewish–Christian convert business partner. Jack Douglas was back in a fairly minor part of Marco the Cereal Killer, which to be fair was no smaller than his part in *Carry On England*. Douglas actually got some of the better lines in the film and was the subject of an agreeably silly gag worthy of Talbot Rothwell ('He beats his victims to death with a sack of Rice Krispies').

Even Jon Pertwee was back, having become a television legend as Doctor Who in the years following his Carry On appearances, and now the right age to play the doddery old man role he often played in Carry Ons of the 1960s. Way down the cast list was Peter Gilmore as the governor of the Canaries. Gilmore's reputation as a dramatic actor had soared after he left the Carry Ons for the lead role in the BBC's long-running costume drama *The Onedin Line*. By 1992, he was not so often seen on screen so it was nice to see him again in any role, and his Carry On parts always ranged all the way from main villain to a virtual walk-on.

With Peter Rogers having failed to get various attempts to revive the Carry On name off the ground, despite close calls with *Carry On Dallas*, *Carry On Down Under* and *Carry On Again Nurse*, it fell to Gerald Thomas and John Goldstone to finally get a new film off the ground. John Goldstone brought the impetus to make a Christopher Columbus comedy to mark the 500 anniversary of the discovery of America by Columbus. Two major dramatic productions were being made: Ridley Scott's *1492: Conquest of Paradise*, which used Pinewood for its studio scenes with Gérard Depardieu as Columbus, and the notorious *Christopher Columbus: The Discovery*. Despite being helmed by James Bond director John Glen and produced by *The Three Musketeers* and *Superman: The Movie*'s team of Ilya and Alexander Salkind, this latter film was a notorious flop, not helped by some terrible miscasting. Both Marlon Brando as Tomás de Torquemada and Tom Selleck as Ferdinand, king of Spain, were absurd and somewhat out-acted by their Carry On counterparts James Faulkner and Leslie Phillips. Production chaos including a last minute change of director and leading man, plus funding problems, dogged the filming and the result was arguably funnier than *Carry On Columbus*.

Both of these dramas were massive productions, each one costing more than $40 million and boasting long production schedules. If there was one director who could shoot a send-up of these quickly it was Gerald Thomas, the former editor who shot absolutely nothing he did not need. The Salkinds proved distinctly unamused at the prospect of their film being sent up by a little British production, and there was a somewhat ludicrous threat to sue the Carry On team to force them to remove the word 'Columbus' from their title.[1] Naturally, all this did was give some welcome extra publicity to *Carry On Columbus*, which made it to cinemas two months after *Christopher Columbus: The Discovery* and a week before the American release of *1492: Conquest of Paradise*.

Recruiting the film's cast was also relatively straightforward, as a new breed of 'alternative comedians' had come to prominence in the 1980s, bringing a much-needed breath of fresh air into the British comic scene. As it turned out, many of these young performers were big fans of classic British comedy and were only too happy to take up what might have been their only chance to star in a Carry On film. So far, so good, but then the film's problems began, as the production had a shooting date but no script. Veteran Carry On writer Dave Freeman was called in only a month before shooting began, and despite the best efforts of both he and an uncredited John Antrobus, it was simply impossible to produce a really satisfactory script under these circumstances.

It was all such a terrible shame and a great missed opportunity, which can be summed up by the film's opening scene, featuring Rik Mayall and Nigel Planer from legendary 1980s sitcom *The Young Ones*. Mayall is absolutely note perfect as the sultan of Turkey, his unrestrained style bringing just the touch of an updated Kenneth Williams and Charles Hawtrey the film needed. Unfortunately, the scene falls flat, the dialogue being considerably less amusing than the performances. It does not help that it is Mayall's only scene and his presence really is missed from the rest of the film. To be fair to the film, most of the cast are great, with Jim Dale working really well opposite Sarah Crowe (soon to be his real-life daughter-in-law), while experienced performers such as Maureen Lipman and Richard Wilson also provide great comedic turns. Julian Clary was simply born to be a Carry On actor, his ultra-camp stage persona being exactly what the film needed, but at this point, he was an inexperienced actor and perhaps a few years later he would have brought an extra touch of self-assurance. Ultimately, he was the right actor at the wrong time.

The proceedings do perk up rather once Columbus and the crew of the *Santa Maria* make landfall and encounter the local tribe, headed by Larry Miller and his assistants Pontiac (Charles Fleischer) and Hubba (Chris Langham). In a stroke of comedic near-genius, all three are played as New York wiseguys who run rings around the hapless Columbus and company. Even the music (actually rather good, composed by John Du Prez, another Python associate) takes an entertaining new turn with the introduction of a catchy dance song written for the film by Malcolm McLaren, punk guru and former manager of the Sex Pistols, and Lee Gorman. Even this was too little, too late, and one is left with the impression of a film which is likeable, without ever for a single moment being laugh-out-loud funny.

This proved rather an impediment for the success of *Carry On Columbus,* and the reviews were predictably terrible: London's popular listings magazine *Time Out* lavished ordure on the entire cast and director, with one exception: 'In fact, the only comedian worth a fart is Larry Miller, playing a Brooklynite Red Indian chief, though the routines in the New World resemble outtakes from Abbott and Costello'. Barry Norman, host of BBC Television's *Film 92* and by far the most influential movie critic in the land, described the film as having 'a script carved out of lead'. His final comments echoed the feelings of many: 'Most of the time as the movie plodded along I found myself yearning for the old Carry On hands ... people who knew how to invest hackneyed material with vulgar energy and comic timing.'

Carry On Columbus was a very high-profile production, in Britain at least, and *Film 92* had previously devoted a ten-minute segment to an on-set report on the making of the film. Even the England football squad came to visit the Pinewood set during filming. The sense of disappointment felt by cinema audiences was keen, not helped by the fact that many old-school Carry On fans actively disliked the new breed of comedians that formed the bedrock of the *Columbus* cast. This was rather unfair, as the faults of the film are hardly their fault. Besides the shortcomings of the script, which was a couple of rewrites away from being quite serviceable, many of the new cast members were used to being able to ad-lib and improvise rather more than Gerald Thomas allowed. Despite the fact that *Carry On Columbus* made more at the UK box office than either of the two more serious takes on the subject, the death of Gerald Thomas in November 1993, just over a year after the release of *Columbus*, killed off any chances of further Carry Ons from John Goldstone, even if Peter Rogers was minded to grant him permission.

33

Carry On Trying: The Lost Carry On Projects

The Carry On franchise seemed to be dead, yet it was being seen more widely than ever thanks to television screenings of the films from their classic era, which were viewed on the small screen by far more people than the later films in the series managed to attract to cinemas. Somewhat ironically, twenty-year-old reruns did a far better job of introducing the pleasures of Carry On to new generations than had Peter Rogers and Gerald Thomas' increasingly desperate 1970s attempts to give the public what they appeared to want.

Peter Rogers was therefore convinced that there remained a market for new Carry On productions, a market which he helped to stoke by repackaging the films into new formats especially for television. Although *That's Carry On* was not a success in cinemas, this was at least in part due to Rank's seeming indifference to the film. The idea was built upon by Peter Rogers and Gerald Thomas, who were contracted in 1981 by Thames Television, then ITV's contractor for the London region, to produce *Carry On Laughing*. This was a series of thirteen half-hour programmes presenting clips from the Carry On films, along with scenes from a few other British comedies.

Thames clearly liked the results, as two years later, they called upon Kenneth Williams and Barbara Windsor to present *Carry On Laughing's Christmas Classics*. Broadcast on Thursday 22 December, Williams and Windsor introduced a selection of Christmas clips, hardly any of which, as *The Times*' television guide helpfully pointed out, have anything to do with Christmas. At least it represented home-grown entertainment on an evening in which every other primetime offering from Thames aside from the news was an American import. It is also rather interesting that on the very same evening, BBC1 presented *The Crazy Gang: A Celebration*, a nostalgic look at the Carry On team's 1930s and '40s predecessors. There was clearly a dearth of British entertainment and an enduring nostalgia for the days when the variety theatre acted as a production line producing quirky popular entertainers.

A second series of thirteen half-hour Carry On clip shows was commissioned, but this time by the BBC, for whom Rogers and Thomas made *What A Carry On*. This was virtually identical in format to *Carry On Laughing*, but this time the sequences chosen were exclusively from Carry On pictures. The episodes were screened between 1983 and 1986 and subsequently were repackaged under the *Carry On Laughing* title. The twenty-six episodes thus produced have been screened ever since, proving ideal half-hour filler material for various TV channels, while helping keep the Carry On flag flying for several generations of viewers. The success of the enterprise became something of a bone of contention between Peter Rogers and the surviving Carry On actors. Not only were they not being paid for the continued television repeats of the films, but now their contributions were being turned into an entirely new product and they still were not seeing any more money.

Peter Rogers, meanwhile, was not content for the Carry On brand to become merely a source of nostalgic laughter. Efforts were made throughout the 1980s to get a new Carry On film off the ground, with three scripts getting to various stages of pre-production without the cameras actually rolling.

Carry On Dallas

The American TV series *Dallas* was a huge worldwide success, running from 1978 to 1991 and in the process moving the soap opera format from the backwaters of American afternoon television to primetime viewing and the top of the ratings. The travails of the oil-rich Ewing family were ripe for satire, and as *Dallas*-mania swept Britain, peaking in 1980 with the 'Who Shot JR?' plotline, Peter Rogers and Gerald Thomas hit upon the idea of *Carry On Dallas*. A script was penned by Dick Vosburgh and Dave Freeman about the Screwing family, who strike not oil, but fertiliser, with Kenneth Williams planned to lead the cast—one can imagine him playing the role with the same broad accent he used as Judge Burke in *Carry On Cowboy*.

Proposed cast members Barbara Windsor, Terry Scott, Bernard Bresslaw, and Jack Douglas even appeared on ITV's breakfast television programme TV-AM to promote the proposed film, riding the wave of publicity (and utilising some of the publicity budget) produced by the release of the films on VHS. A spanner was thrown into the works by Lorimar Productions, the production company that made *Dallas*. Lorimar were most certainly not about to allow some low-budget English film producer to take the mickey out of their cash cow without substantial monetary reward coming their way. Some attempts were made to change the scripts to stave off these legal attentions, changing the title to *Carry On Texas* and the family name from Screwing to Ramming (thus spoiling one of the better jokes), but the writing was on the wall for the project.

Carry On Down Under

As unambiguously British as the Carry Ons were, it made a lot of sense for the idea of a revival of the series to take place in Australia. The country has strong links to Britain dating back to the arrival of Captain James Cook on the continent in 1770 and had always attracted migrants from the UK who remained happy to see cultural reminders from the old country. The Carry On brand of humour had always tickled the Australian funny bone, and by the late 1970s, a curious comedic phenomenon made the notion of a *Carry On Down Under* seem a very real possibility. As the 1970s wore on, it became more common not only for British comedies to be exported to Australia, but for the performers themselves to take the 9,400-mile trip to the Southern Hemisphere to make new series especially for Australian audiences.

Peter Cook and Dudley Moore were early adopters of this approach, filming two special episodes of their sketch show *Not Only ... But Also*. Irish comedian Dave Allen became a huge star with his BBC stand-up comedy and sketch series *Dave Allen at Large*, but he got his first major break on Australia's Channel 9 in 1963 with a talk show that was ahead of its time and he returned to the network in 1975 to make further comedy series. In 1977, Dick Emery, at the height of his British fame, made three Australian shows for 7 Network, while in 1979 and 1986, the Two Ronnies made series especially for the Australian Broadcasting Corporation, reworking their British material for antipodean audiences. The comedians found an appreciative audience, good pay, and a break from British taxation.

A stranger aspect of this phenomenon was a run of British sitcoms that, having outlasted either their inspiration or the interest of British audiences, suddenly fetched up, complete with at least one of their original stars, in Australia for a new run of episodes. Occasional Carry On star Frankie Howerd revived his *Up Pompeii!* concept (which had subsequently changed time frames and returned in 1973 as *Whoops Baghdad*) in 1976 on Australia's 7 Network as *Up the Convicts*. The peripatetic Howerd also made a sitcom in Canada during the same year.

Further sitcom transplants followed, Patrick Cargill and Noël Dyson reviving their *Father Dear Father* roles in 1978, five years after the series was cancelled by Thames Television following a seven-season run. *Doctor in the House* ran under various titles in the UK for eight years from 1969 to 1977, its stars Robin Nedwell and Geoffrey Davies travelling to Australia two years later for a further two series under the title *Doctor Down Under*. Probably the strangest of these transplanted sitcoms was *Are You Being Served?* in which John Inman's Mr Humphries was posted to a department store belonging to Mr Grace's Australian cousin. Although Inman was the only member of the British cast to make the trip down under, most of the other characters were carbon copies of the UK originals. Most bizarrely of all, this series was made in 1980, while the BBC original was still being produced.

At this point, the possibility of a Carry On film not only set in Australia, but shot there (quite a move for a series, which had never previously ventured any further from Berkshire than North Wales) became more than just a possibility. A good chunk of Australian finance, up to £500,000, was apparently available, and plans for the film reached such an advanced stage that Gerald Thomas flew there to scout possible locations. Writer Vince Powell, last seen performing uncredited rewrites on *Carry On Emmannuelle*, was engaged to work on the script. As it happened, Powell was flying out to Australia to write the scripts for another transplanted British sitcom, a revival of the 1972–76 Thames Television sitcom *Love Thy Neighbour*, a series which had effectively been ITV's answer to the BBC's *Till Death Us Do Part*. The idea of an Australian remake was actually quite sound, as here the show's racist antihero Eddie Booth has emigrated to Australia ahead of his family and eventually realises that he is the foreigner now.

Powell had created *Love Thy Neighbour* along with his writing partner Harry Driver and the pair had written the first three seasons and eight episodes of the fourth season when Driver died at the age of forty-two. Powell, who wrote many of the later episodes alone, was called upon by 7 Network to write the seven episodes of the Australian sequel. As he was travelling to Australia anyway to work on this project, he took the opportunity to research *Carry On Down Under* and was well advanced on the script when the project took an unfortunate turn. Basically, the Australian money disappeared in circumstances best described as 'murky' and the whole project collapsed.[1]

Carry On Again Nurse

The ignominious commercial demise of *Carry On Emmannuelle* at Britain's cinemas had put paid to the multi-film deal between Peter Rogers and his new backers Cleves Investments. Rogers and Thomas already had the script to *Emmannuelle*'s follow-up in hand, in the form of the George Layton and Jonathan Lynn-written *Carry On Again Nurse*. This was the second attempt to make a film by this title, as this had been the working title of what eventually became *Carry On Doctor* back in 1967.

The title, with its deliberate echo of the Carry On series' biggest American success, remained an obvious choice for what today would be termed a Carry On reboot. Fast forward to 1988 and none other a figure than Norman Hudis, who had long-since decamped to Hollywood for a successful screenwriting career, was tempted back to provide a new script some ten years after the release of *Carry On Emmannuelle* and twenty six years after his last produced Carry On script, *Carry on Cruising*.

The prospect of the series returning with a sequel to *Carry On Nurse* penned by the same writer is certainly lip-smacking to any Carry On fan. This would have seen something of a return to the early 1960s era of the series, with the story set in a hospital threatened with closure. This is a typical Hudis Carry On touch, with the characters putting their differences aside to unite in a common cause—also an interestingly contemporary plotline for the era of Margaret Thatcher. The proposed cast included Kenneth Williams as the chief surgeon, Joan Sims as Matron, Kenneth Connor as a hospital porter, and Charles Hawtrey as a patient. How close *Carry On Again Nurse*, also known at various points as *Carry On Nursing*, came to actually being made is somewhat unclear, with some sources claiming sets were being constructed before the plug was pulled, others that the projected budget of £1.5 million was unable to be raised.

It is also unclear how many of the Carry On cast had definitely signed on for the film, especially Charles Hawtrey, who was in poor health by 1988 and would not live the year out. Kenneth Williams had remained on good terms with the Carry On producers and was far more likely to appear in any new Carry On picture, but his death at the age of only sixty-two robbed the film of what would have been by far its biggest star. Any hope *Carry On Again Nurse* had of getting off the ground died in Williams' lonely Camden Town flat.

34

Beyond the Carry Ons: The Other Rogers and Thomas Films

Please Turn Over (1959)

Muriel Box's *The Passionate Stranger* had turned out to be something of a mess back in 1957, but that film's producer, Peter Rogers, and associate producer, Gerald Thomas, obviously saw something in the idea of a set of actors playing alternate characters in a film within a film. This notion was crying out for a broader comedy treatment and when they returned to it with *Please Turn Over* two years later, the result was of the most inventive Rogers/Thomas comedies outside of the Carry On series. Norman Hudis, as ever in this period of the Rogers and Thomas partnership, wrote the screenplay, based on different source material to *The Passionate Stranger*—the 1955 two-act play *Book of the Month*. This had been written by Basil Thomas, who would in the following year co-author the screenplay to the Arthur Askey comedy Western *Ramsbottom Rides Again*, which featured Sid James as a villain.

Julia Lockwood, so effective in Rogers and Thomas' *The Solitary Child*, stars as Jo Halliday who, like many teenagers, spends most of her time in her bedroom. Instead of listening to pop singles, she has been spending her time there writing a novel, which not only gets published but is chosen as 'Book of the Month' and is released with a blaze of publicity. Her family is so busy and distracted that they have no idea that the book even exists, but the rest of the town are agog at the steamy events in the novel, entitled *Naked Revolt*. They realise that the characters are based on Jo's own family and think that the shocking events are true, when in fact Jo has written the characters to be the exact opposites of their real life counterparts.

Thus her strait-laced chief accountant father Edward (Ted Ray) becomes a lovelorn embezzler who lavishes jewellery and furs on his greedy sex-bomb of a secretary (in reality the super-efficient Dilys Laye) who prefers the company of the impressively quiffed Lee Patterson, returning from his appearance in *Time Lock* and about to leave the British B-picture scene to try his luck in America.

His wife (Jean Kent) and her terrified driving instructor Lionel Jeffries become an adulterous and sexily stylish pair with dialogue straight out of a Noël Coward play, while Leslie Phillips' shy, golf-playing doctor becomes a sex-mad Lothario. Perhaps funniest of all is Joan Sims as Beryl, the Halliday's magnificently common cleaner, who undergoes a startling transformation into a sexy French maid. Sims is provided with some brilliant dialogue by Norman Hudis, who single-handedly invents the 'Franglais' form of speech with such zingers as '*c'est si un* proper turn-up for the book', 'not on *votre* nelly', and '*pour l'amour de* Mike'. Among the other Carry On regulars in the cast is June Jago, given a better role here than she managed in the Carry Ons as Jo's aunt. In the 'real life' scenes, a shy woman with a liking for exercise and health foods, she is fictionalised as a drunk, crazed by unrequited love.

Charles Hawtrey is given very good billing indeed, given 'Guest Star' status for the tiny role of a jeweller serving Ted Ray and Dilys Laye in the scenes portraying the novel. It is sad to say that for various reasons, Hawtrey did not turn his hard-won Carry On stardom into a regular career outside the series and his part here cannot have taken more than a morning to film.

Ted Ray shines in the ensemble cast of a film that one can usefully regard as a pair alongside his sole Carry On part in *Carry On Teacher*. The two films even came out within months of each other, *Carry On Teacher* being released to cinemas at the end of August 1959, while *Please Turn Over* came out in January of the following year. One actually gets a better idea here of what Ray would have been like as head of the Carry On cast here than in his slightly more subdued *Carry On Teacher* performance. *Please Turn Over* sees Ted Ray in full flight, giving an enthusiastic performance which hints at what British cinema lost when his film career was effectively torpedoed by the management of Associated British. After having no less than three films on release in 1959—the other was *The Crowning Touch*, a portmanteau film from B-picture distributors Butchers Film Service with the stories being linked by a hat—Ray never made another after *Please Turn Over*. His radio, stage, and TV work would ensure that Ted Ray remained a comedy legend to the end of his days.

Please Turn Over illustrates the furious pace these seemingly effortless comedies were made at. The film was shooting at Pinewood during September 1959, wrapping a week ahead of schedule and moving to the studio's cutting rooms in October and November, then gaining its BBFC certificate on 4 November. The film was ready to show to the London cinema trade on 17 December, at which point production was well underway on *Carry On Constable*. *Please Turn Over* went on general release from 7 January, with a neat little thriller from Merton Park Studios, *The Desperate Man*, in support. In many ways, this was a precursor to Merton Park's Edgar Wallace thriller series, which would soon begin production and play in support of many Rogers and Thomas pictures.

While *Please Turn Over*'s studio work was filmed at Pinewood, most of the exteriors for the film were shot in Beaconsfield, with the ultra-modern office complex in which Edward Halliday works being in reality the Sara Lee building in Slough, which in 1969 featured in the *ESP* episode of the Gerry and Sylvia Anderson television series *UFO*.

Watch Your Stern (1960)

With the Peter Rogers/Gerald Thomas comedy factory operating at full steam, the producers were always on the lookout for promising material to convert into films. Thus they happened upon *Something About a Sailor*, a stage farce with a naval setting written by Earle Couttie. Producer Jack Waller and director Harold French had tried the play out on tour, starting in October 1957, with high hopes for both the play and a young actor, fresh from rep theatre, discovered for the leading role of Ordinary Seaman Blissworth. While the play's young star Richard Briers went on to much greater things, the production itself was not well reviewed and failed to secure a transfer to the West End.

Still, there was enough in the play to suggest that it would make good film material, particularly for the multi-talented Carry On star Kenneth Connor. As Blissworth, he had to adopt disguises as a much older Scotsman and as a female scientist, a task perfectly suited to an actor able to play older, younger, rich and poor. Besides this consideration, comedies set in the armed services were in fashion. Peter Rogers had already exploited the television success of *The Army Game* when making *Carry On Sergeant*, and now there was a popular naval comedy which was attracting a lot of attention.

This time it was a radio series which debuted on the BBC Light Programme on 25 March 1959 entitled *The Navy Lark*, initially starring Dennis Price, Jon Pertwee, and that familiar face in Peter Rogers productions Leslie Phillips. Price withdrew after the first series to appear in a Broadway production of George Bernard Shaw's *Heartbreak House*. When the play closed unexpectedly quickly after 112 performances, Price was free to return to the series, only to find his role as 'Number One' has already been recast with Stephen Murray, who stayed with *The Navy Lark* until the end of the show's run in 1977.

In an era when radio in Britain still retained some of its status as a mass-entertainment medium, such was the instant popularity of *The Navy Lark* that an official film spin-off was quickly put together by veteran British film producer Herbert Wilcox, shot at the film studios in Walton-on-Thames and released during the 1959 Christmas holidays. The film performed disappointingly however, possibly because of the popular radio cast only Leslie Phillips was retained. Jon Pertwee claimed that producer Herbert Wilcox would not employ Dennis Price because the actor was known to be gay, and when Pertwee objected to Price's omission, he, too, found himself dropped from the project.[1]

With Peter Rogers already having an established working relationship with Leslie Phillips, he could make a naval farce at Pinewood with just as much legitimacy to fans of *The Navy Lark* as Herbert Wilcox had at Walton Studios. In effect, what *Carry On Sergeant* was to *The Army Game*, *Watch Your Stern* (as Earle Couttie's stage play was renamed for the screen) would be to *The Navy Lark*. Leslie Phillips was here joined by two of his fellow Carry On colleagues, Kenneth Connor and Eric Barker. These three played roughly the same roles as Phillips, Dennis Price, and Jon Pertwee did at the time on the radio version of *The Navy Lark*. They were joined by Joan Sims and Hattie Jacques with Sid James making what was billed as a guest star appearance, making the film look more than ever like a Carry On film under another guise. With the regular Peter Rogers/Gerald Thomas crew behind the camera, including Director of Photography Ted Scaife and music composer Bruce Montgomery, it must have felt just like making a Carry On picture, too. The film actually has a quite different feel to it though, displaying its origins as a stage farce quite clearly.

With Norman Hudis busy on other projects for Peter Rogers, new writers were found in the form of Alan Hackney and Vivian Cox. Hackney was a hot comedy property at the time, having in 1954 written the novel *Private's Progress*, on which the Boulting brothers had based their famous film version two years later. The Boultings returned to adapt his novel *Private Life* into the 1959 film *I'm Alright Jack*, a scabrous look at British industrial relations which scored a major personal success for Peter Sellers as union shop steward Fred Kite. This time Hackney helped write the script and thus was launched as a screenwriter. So busy was Hackney with film work that in 1960 he had three films on release: *Two Way Stretch*, *Watch Your Stern*, and *Sword of Sherwood Forest*, and also found time to write three episodes of Lew Grade's television series *The Adventures of Robin Hood*.

Watch Your Stern reunited Hackney with co-writer Vivian Cox, who had co-written *Two Way Stretch* and would later write *The Iron Maiden* for Peter Rogers Productions. Cox had been a flag lieutenant in the Admiralty during the Second World War, working closely with Winston Churchill, and on being demobilised from the service became an associate producer at Pinewood Studios for Peter Rogers' future wife Betty Box. From 1959, he spent almost a decade as an independent producer and screenwriter for Rank before retiring from the movie business to become a schoolmaster at Cranleigh College, where in his youth Cox had been a producer. Even then, Cox, who led an eventful life, had another career in store, retiring from teaching to run the Mermaid Theatre for the actor Bernard Miles.

Watch Your Stern's plot concerns a new weapon being tested out by the Royal Navy called the Acoustic Torpedo Mk 1, aka the Creeper. On its first test, the torpedo goes wild and sinks the ship that fired it (captained by Carry On regular Michael Nightingale). The plans for the missile are kept in the safe of ship's captain David Foster (Eric Barker), but are left on view in his quarters by the captain and his first officer, Bill Fanshawe (Leslie Phillips). Blissworth (Kenneth Connor), the captain's steward, a genius at theoretical electronics but a terrible electrician, sees the plans, immediately sees the problem, but is terminally clumsy and accidentally destroys the document. The rest of the plot involves the trio's efforts to get the only other copy of the plans back from an American naval officer (Ed Devereaux, Australian but doing a creditable accent) and keep news of their destruction from their Admiral (Noel Purcell, in great form in what is probably his best role for Rogers and Thomas).

While the film works to an extent as a comic vehicle for Kenneth Connor, it is honestly a bit of a disappointment. *Watch Your Stern* aims for farce, or what in American terminology is known as screwball comedy, but never quite has the pace or mad energy the form requires. Even guest star Sid James (sporting a splendid beard for half of his role) is wasted in an ineffectual subplot involving Leslie Phillips' bicycle being thrown into the sea and rescued several times. This is not really the fault of director or cast, as even the original stage version gathered better notices for the cast than for the material they were performing.

The cast here really do keep this old tub afloat. Kenneth Connor more than earns his top billing by playing, in effect, three roles: the hapless Blissworth, who is then disguised as Potter, the scientist who is sent to inspect the plans. Having no idea what Potter looks like, Blissworth makes him an older Scotsman, only to discover that Potter's first name is Agatha. He then returns in drag as the 'real' Potter, attracting the amorous attentions of the admiral, until the genuine Potter turns up in the form of Hattie Jacques, who has been arrested at the dock gates by David Lodge, thinking she's a male spy in disguise. Connor, Phillips, and Barker work together extremely well, with the latter playing his trademark befuddled authority figure to perfection. Joan Sims has a good role as the captain's sister and is at her slimmest, her trim figure shown off by a succession of very tight outfits. Eric Sykes and Spike Milligan show up as a pair of dockside electricians, a scene that is somewhat problematic in the twenty-first century as Spike is doing his comedy Indian characterisation, which has not aged well.

Shooting on *Watch Your Stern* began on 25 April 1960, while *Please Turn Over* was still on general release and following the completion of

Carry On Constable. Pinewood's stage D was booked for the studio scenes, while location scenes were shot on board the Royal Navy's Leopard-class anti-aircraft frigate HMS *Jaguar*. By 4 July, the film has been granted a 'U' certificate by the BBFC, and *Watch Your Stern* turned out to be a popular box office attraction on its release on 24 October 1960, with Nat Cohen and Stuart Levy going all-out to publicise the film widely. A publicity tie-in was arranged with Player's Anchor cigarettes at 10,000 tobacconists across Britain, while Cohen and Levy personally stumped up £300 for incentive prizes for cinema managers who produced the best local publicity campaigns for the film. Special pre-release screenings were arranged to take place on the famous ocean liners *Queen Mary*, *Queen Elizabeth*, and *Empress of Britain*.

Watch Your Stern does have another minor place in British film history, as it was paired by distributors Angle Amalgamated with *The Clue of the Twisted Candle*, the very first of their new Edgar Wallace series of mystery B-pictures.

No Kidding (1960)

No Kidding is one of the most charming of the Rogers/Thomas comedies, making up for its lack of belly-laughs with a sweet nature and a surprising amount of depth. Verily Anderson's memoir *Beware of Children* was adapted for the screen by the ubiquitous Norman Hudis, along with suspense novelist Robin Estridge. The plot revolves around David and Catherine Robinson (Leslie Phillips and Geraldine McEwan), a married couple who inherit a rambling old house which, owing to some previous failed business ventures, they will have to sell. Instead, they hit upon the idea of opening a holiday home for the children of the wealthy, an idea that turns out to be quite a success from the off, attracting ten bookings.

It is also a very good idea in story terms, as had the film had gone down the more traditional route and filled the screen with underprivileged orphans, the danger was that it would have become mired in sentimentality (see for an example any Norman Wisdom film whenever a tow-headed nipper enters camera range). Instead, we see a group of children who have been neglected by their high-achieving parents and are stiffly formal, mutely browbeaten, or defensively arrogant. Realising that the children have lost the ability to be play and enjoy themselves, Geraldine McEwan has the idea of letting the children have complete freedom to do whatever they like. Philips soon takes against this idea when the kids start chopping down the estate trees and steal the family Morris Minor Traveller for a trip to Cyril Chamberlain's transport café.

Things are further complicated with the arrival of Julia Lockwood as a horny teenage vicar's daughter who is primed and ready to leap on any available man. The males concerned are Brian Rawlinson's Will, the terrified handyman (and it is anyone's guess what accent he is attempting), and Michael Sarne, making his first credited film appearance as French guest Henri. Sarne was a fascinating figure who achieved success, for a while at least, in almost everything he did despite little evidence of outstanding talent. Eighteen months after the release of *No Kidding*, Sarne was number one in the pop charts alongside future Carry On actress Wendy Richard with 'Come Outside'. He then went on to become a film director, achieving a degree of success in 1968 with *Joanna* before in 1970 writing and directing the incredible big-budget mess that was *Myra Breckenridge*. The latter film is truly, indescribably awful and was released to a storm of controversy in June 1970, instantly torpedoing Sarne's career as a director.

Busybody Alderman Irene Handl turns up with plans to have the house compulsorily purchased and turned into a home for underprivileged children. We are clearly not supposed to like the alderman, but this actually sounds like a fine idea, especially when we discover that Phillips and McEwan have set up their holiday home without the first idea of the legal requirements. There is another film struggling to get out in which crusading council member Irene Handl struggles against the odds to help set up a refuge for needy children. In the film we are actually presented with, the kids conspire with the owners to make the home seen like the smoothest running, most regular establishment imaginable—in effect, reversing the plot of *Carry On Teacher*.

No Kidding works rather well, with Leslie Phillips and Geraldine McEwan making for a very good screen couple indeed. It is quite unusual to see the young McEwan (she was twenty-eight years old at the time) in a screen role, and this was something of a change of pace for the Royal Shakespeare Company veteran, appearing in her first film since the 1953 low budget comedy *There Was a Young Lady*. That film had featured Sidney Tafler, who also turns up here as Mr Rockbottom, a bumptious millionaire scrap metal dealer who makes his son's life a misery. The cast is otherwise packed with familiar faces from the Rogers/Thomas comedies, with the aforementioned Brian Rawlinson joined by Joan Hickson as the permanently drunk cook and June Jago as the resort's Matron, who has a terrific scene with Esma Cannon, who plays a deaf nurse. Eric Pohlmann, soon to be seen in *Carry On Regardless* and *Carry On Spying*, turns up briefly as one of the parents, as does Brian Oulton. Oulton's career lasted for six decades and took in roles in *Carry On Nurse*, *Constable*, *Cleo*, and *Camping*. Also returning is noted Dublin character actor Noel Purcell, who was something of a regular attraction in Rogers and Thomas' non-Carry On comedies.

The house used for the film's primary location was the Grade II-listed building Drummer's Yard, situated in Beaconsfield, Buckinghamshire, which had been purchased that year by Dirk Bogarde and would later be bought by none other than Peter Rogers. The film was shot there and at Pinewood in August and September of 1960. *No Kidding* was booked for release on the entire ABC cinema circuit, and began a staggered release starting on 26 December 1960 in the South London area. An Edgar Wallace mystery, *The Man Who Was Nobody*, served as the B-picture.

The film was picked up for US distribution by American International, who retitled it *Beware of Children*, the title of the original novel on which the script was based, and released it in April 1961.

Raising the Wind (1961)

Raising the Wind was the nearest Peter Rogers came to producing a remake of his wife Betty Box's *Doctor in the House*, transposing the basic structure of a group of students studying and falling in love from St Swithin's teaching hospital to the equally fictional London Academy of Music and Art. The latter had no connection to the real-life London Academy of Music and Dramatic Art (better known as LAMDA) and was represented on screen by University College, London, located in the Bloomsbury district of London. This building, coincidentally, had been used as St Swithin's Hospital back in 1954 for the filming of *Doctor in the House*.

The film was written by Bruce Montgomery, who was at this point Peter Rogers' in-house composer of film scores. It should be remembered that Montgomery was something of a polymath, and at this point had published eight acerbically witty crime novels between 1944 and 1951 under the pen name Edmund Crispin featuring his academic detective Gervase Fenn. *Raising the Wind* would be the only fictional work Montgomery would write under his own name, and the film really gives off the strong scent of being written by a professional musician in the same way that surgeon and anaesthetist Richard Gordon assembled an array of stories in his *Doctor* novels with a ring of lightly embellished truth.

The transposition of the Doctor formula to the world of music is not entirely smooth, however. For all its breezy charm, *Doctor in the House* carries a greater emotional charge than *Raising the Wind* ever can ever hope to duplicate. There is simply more at stake in the quest to become a doctor than that of becoming a professional musician. This is best evidenced in the *Doctor in the House* scene in which Simon Sparrow, still a medical student, helps to deliver a baby and is told 'it must be wonderful to be a doctor'. 'Yes,' he replies, 'it must'. Bogarde plays the scene beautifully, giving us a real sense that Sparrow's choice to become a doctor will change many more lives than just his own.

Of course, *Raising the Wind* has another connection with the Doctor film series, as its cast is led by James Robertson Justice, here playing conducting tutor Sir Benjamin Boyd, irascible and ill-tempered but good-hearted, very much in the manner of the actor's career-defining role of Sir Lancelot Spratt. As it happened, James Robertson Justice bore a striking resemblance to the legendary conductor Sir Henry Wood, who, after his 1944 death, lent his name to Sir Henry Wood Promenade Concerts, known to one and all as The Proms. Boyd's manner, and indeed some of his dialogue, is more redolent of the notoriously caustic wit of another great conductor, Sir Thomas Beecham.

Bruce Montgomery's story revolves around a group of five music students who move into lodgings run by Esma Cannon, who is conveniently stone deaf, meaning they can make as much noise practicing as they like. The rather over-age students are Malcolm Stewart (twenty-nine-year-old Paul Massie), Jill Clemons (Jennifer Jayne, also twenty-nine at the time), Mervyn Hughes (thirty-seven-year-old Leslie Phillips), Miranda Kennaway (Liz Fraser, aged thirty-one), and Jimmy Thompson (thirty-six years of age at the time of filming). You will have noticed a fair smattering of familiar Carry On names of the period, and they are joined by Kenneth Williams, who was a well-preserved thirty-one-year-old in 1961. Here Williams plays Harold Chesney, the school sneak with a highly inflated opinion of his own abilities. Eric Barker appears to great effect (with somewhat wobbly Welsh accent) as Dr Morgan Rutherford, the academy's composition tutor who would much rather be on the golf course than teaching anything about composition.

Sid James guest stars alongside Lance Percival as a pair of music publishers and advertising jingle writers (Sid's Popsey Crisps song bears a probably intentional resemblance to the Murray Mints jingle that had been around since the dawn of British commercial television). James and Percival make a very effective comic pairing, with Sid's cheerful semi-con artist persona contrasting nicely with the lugubrious Lance. This was, in fact, a nervous Lance Percival's first major film role, and he remembered in later years advice that James gave him: 'Sid calmed me down. He was very supportive. The first thing he taught me was if you're not happy with a take, say "Jesus Christ" and they will have to stop.'[2] Percival obviously impressed Rogers and Thomas, as he subsequently appeared in *Twice Round the Daffodils* the following year before being drafted in as a replacement for Charles Hawtrey in *Carry On Cruising*.

Paul Massie is very much the straight man here among an ensemble of skilled comedic actors. Massie's appeal in general failed to transfer to the screen at this stage of his career—the previous year had seen him disastrously miscast in the lead role of Hammer's *The Two Faces of Doctor Jekyll*. By the end of the decade, he had virtually abandoned professional acting to join the performing arts faculty of the University of South Florida, where he became a much-loved guide to generations of acting students.

Leslie Phillips, at this point still part of the Carry On team, is here at his absolute peak, giving as good a performance as he ever would on the big screen. He gets to share a subplot with Sid James and Lance Percival, dodgy music publishers who get him to sign a contract to publish a pop tune he writes while blind drunk (Phillips performs an admirable drunk act, a rarer feat than you might imagine), only for Phillips to realise that if it is ever performed in public it will break the conditions of the scholarship that allows his to continue studying. Phillips proved an enthusiastic student of orchestral conducting, learning the art of conducting from Bruce Montgomery for four weeks when he wasn't required on set, much to the appreciation of the Sinfonia of London, who were drafted in for the climactic scenes of the conducting examination.[3]

This scene also provides the comedic highlight of the film, as Kenneth Williams' big-headed Harold Chesney berates the orchestra for sloppy playing before starting his examination piece, Rossini's 'William Tell Overture'. Having got thoroughly on the wrong side of the orchestra, the musicians proceed to get their own back by galloping off at a rate of several times the intended pace. This scene was to prove unexpectedly important in Carry On history, as among the orchestra is none other than Jim Dale, making his film acting debut as a trombonist. It must be said that Dale's natural comedic abilities leap from the screen right away, but the young performer inadvertently made himself stand out in another way, when he broke into a Kenneth Williams impression in front of Williams himself. When Williams began an animated conversation with director Gerald Thomas, Dale thought he had made a terrible mistake, but he later learned that the target of his impression was actually enthusiastically recommending him for future employment. Thus was launched the career of one of the key stars of the 1960s Carry On films, as Dale was almost immediately rehired for role in Rogers and Thomas' *The Iron Maiden* and *Nurse on Wheels* before making his Carry On debut in *Carry On Cabby*.

Liz Fraser has disappointingly little to do as Miranda, a part written and played largely as a dumb blonde stereotype until a pleasing end scene in which it turns out that she is the most talented of the entire group. Jennifer Jayne, whose Jill provides half of the film's central romantic couple along with Paul Massie, is a very engaging screen presence, and was actually quite a big television star at the time thanks to her thirty-nine-episode stint in ITC's 1958–9 series *The Adventures of William Tell*.

The film received its UK general release at the end of August 1961, a West End engagement at the Plaza Cinema on Piccadilly Circus, which caused the film reviewer of *The Times* to take an interest in the film. The broadly positive review was published on 25 August, describing the film as 'throughout cheerfully and unpretentiously farcical'. The anonymous critic praised the abilities of the main cast members, with particular attention paid to the contribution of James Robertson Justice: 'A roaring voice, issuing from a luxuriant beard, will do something at any rate to keep things going, and so it proves with *Raising the Wind*'. The B-picture assigned to the film was generally the Edgar Wallace movie *The Malpas Mystery*, but in some areas, it played alongside another Anglo-Amalgamated supporting feature, *Crossroads to Crime*, the cinematic directorial debut of future *Thunderbirds* producer Gerry Anderson.

A bright, cheerful, well-played film with plenty of laughs, *Raising the Wind* is a good-looking film, shot in Eastmancolor by Alan Hume, with Gerald Thomas doing his usual unpretentious, economical job of direction. It is not well remembered these days except by curious Carry On fans and a small band of classical music fans with long memories. This is something of a cinematic injustice, and if you are reading this book and have never seen it, *Raising the Wind* is certainly worthy of ninety or so minutes of your attention.

Twice Round the Daffodils (1962)

One of the most interesting of the Roger/Thomas comedies outside the Carry On series is 1962's *Twice Round the Daffodils*, which was on the studio floor at Pinewood in January and released in the UK from mid-April, just about giving the film time to dry after processing. It is probably unique that the same producer and director remade the same source material only three years after their first attempt, for this is a second version of Patrick Cargill and Jack Beale's play *Ring for Catty*, from which was adapted *Carry On Nurse*. It was paired on its trip around the ABC circuit with the Edgar Wallace thriller *Candidate for Murder*.

Despite the fact that *Twice Round the Daffodils* has subsequently been tagged with the slogan 'What a Carry On!' in order to capitalise on its Carry On connection, it has quite a different feel from those films. This is reflected on the original poster which promised, with quite a high degree of accuracy, a film 'Filled with love—laughter—and just a few tears'. *Carry On Nurse* had been a very loose adaptation indeed of *Ring for Catty*, just as its predecessor *Carry On Sergeant* had taken only the basic idea from R. F. Delderfield's screen story *The Bull Boys*. In fact, *Nurse* took from the stage version merely the idea of a group of men of different backgrounds forced to co-exist in a medical setting, and a romance between a patient and a nurse. The stage version had debuted at the Lyric Theatre, Shaftesbury Avenue, on 21 April 1956, filling a month's gap in the theatre's schedule before the opening of Noël Coward's *South Sea Bubble*. This followed an earlier try-out run under the title *Time on Their Hands* at the Q Theatre, based homophonically in Kew, in July 1954.

It had been written by Patrick Cargill, a busy character actor equally skilled in playing comedy and drama who later appeared in *Carry On Regardless* and *Carry On Jack*, along with Jack Beale, drawing on the latter's enforced stay in a tuberculosis clinic. Cargill was an occasional playwright as well as actor, contributing material to revues and writing a previous stage play with Beale, the comedy *Happy Landings*. The play retained its original leading man from the Q Theatre run, Patrick McGoohan, joined in the cast at the Lyric Theatre by his wife Joan. In retrospect, *Ring for Catty* managed to attract a very impressive cast, with McGoohan being joined by William Hartnell (six years before *Doctor Who* and at this point a well-known film actor), Terence Alexander (who also later turned up in *Carry On Regardless*), and Andrew Ray.

The latter was the son of Ted Ray, the highly popular stage and radio comedian who would later be the star of *Carry On Teacher*. Andrew had been propelled into child stardom at the age of ten when he was cast by director Jean Negulesco in *The Mudlark*, a 20th Century Fox production made in 1950. He had only been considered for the part because his older brother Robin had grown too tall, but found himself an instant star. Six years down the line, Ray was a teenager and had reached his fully grown height of 5 feet 7 inches and was perfectly cast as the shy, love-struck adolescent Chris Walker. Andrew Ray would, in fact, be the only cast member to reprise their stage role when the story finally reached the screen as *Twice Round the Daffodils*.

By this point, the two original stars of the stage production were busy elsewhere: McGoohan had scored a big personal success with *Danger Man*, which in its original half-hour form began screening in September 1960 and was starring in a run of feature films. Hartnell, always a busy film and television actor, had become more popular than ever thanks to his role as Sergeant Major Bullimore in the Granada Television sitcom *The Army Game*. This had led to his casting as Sergeant Grimshawe in *Carry On Sergeant* and he was about to start filming *This Sporting Life* before accepting the title role in *Doctor Who*, with which he would be associated for the remainder of his life.

With most of the original cast being either unavailable or unaffordable, a new ensemble had to be assembled by Peter Rogers and Gerald Thomas. Screenwriter Norman Hudis also slightly reworked Cargill and Beale's original comedy drama, softening some of the harder edges and changing certain characters. Patrick McGoohan's original leading role of Leonard White—played as cockney, something McGoohan rarely attempted—became Bob White, played by Ronald Lewis, a beefy thirty-four-year-old Welsh actor who was under contract to Hammer, who starred him in a series of psychological thrillers. William Hartnell's John Rhodes became a boisterous, antagonistic Welsh miner now played by Donald Houston, no stranger to medical comedies as he had been one of the stars of Ralph Thomas' *Doctor in the House* back in 1954. Terence Alexander's flirtatious RAF officer Donald

Gray was renamed Ian Richards and now played to the hilt by Donald Sinden. The change in character name was presumably to avoid confusion with the one-armed actor of the same name who was at that point starring on television as private detective *Mark Saber*.

Anthony Parker, later to become a successful director of television sitcoms, was replaced by none other than Kenneth Williams, the character's name changing in the process from Bill Jones to Henry Halfpenny. Screenwriter Norman Hudis turns Halfpenny into a virtual repeat of Williams' Oliver Reckitt character from *Carry On Nurse*, and the film is none the worse for it. The final member of the ill-matched set of patients, country boy George Logg, is played by Lance Percival, who had previously appeared in the Peter Rogers production *Raising the Wind* and also played ship's cook Wilfred Haines in *Carry On Cruising*, which was released just weeks after *Twice Round the Daffodils*.

Ironically, the role of Catty was in the original stage version not a major part despite being the title role. Here the role was expanded in order to attract a higher profile actress, Nurse Catty being promoted from being a trainee to the head nurse in charge of the ward. Juliet Mills was eventually cast in the part—the daughter of John Mills, she was acting royalty—and clearly impressed Peter Rogers and Gerald Thomas, as she appeared in two further Peter Rogers productions. Interestingly, these were both as last minute replacements for other performers: in *Nurse on Wheels*, she replaced Joan Sims after Joan's weight gain meant that she was no longer regarded as being suitable casting for the lead in a romantic comedy, while in *Carry On Jack* she replaced Liz Fraser, who had upset Anglo-Amalgamated's Stuart Levy and was *persona non grata*.

Twice Round the Daffodils is quite an entertaining watch, though it does pull its emotional punches slightly compared to Cargill and Beale's original. When the play first debuted in 1954, the days when tuberculosis was akin to a death sentence were still a recent memory, and not all the characters in *Ring for Catty* lived to play's end. It would be very easy for a casual viewer to miss the fact that *Twice Round the Daffodils* was set in a TB sanatorium at all, the disease being represented by little more than the occasional vigorous clearing of Donald Houston's throat. Despite Houston's character banging on that he is not really ill, then confessing tearfully to Catty of his shame that he can't provide for his family, he looks throughout like he could play a game of rugby and sink ten pints of beer with no ill-effects. In fact, the only one of the characters who looks at all ill is Andrew Ray's Chris, the actor playing the shy, poetically inclined youth to perfection, as befits an actor who had played the same role on stage for over 100 performances.

Kenneth Williams and Lance Percival work especially well together, their styles meshing perfectly, and one can see why the latter was seen as an ideal replacement when Charles Hawtrey dropped out of *Carry On Cruising*. Compounding the Carry On connections are the appearances of Joan Sims and Jill Ireland. Sims has a couple of short but very well played scenes as Henry Halfpenny's sister Harriet, who writes to her brother every day but can never think of anything to say when she actually visits. Ireland, who had played Kenneth Williams' love interest in *Carry On Nurse* and later turned up in *Raising the Wind*, here plays rather against type as a sex-bomb nurse who keeps losing her skirt to reveal stocking-clad legs. Within a couple of years, both Juliet Mills and Jill Ireland would move to the USA to pursue their careers, each finding considerable success.

While *Twice Round the Daffodils* is no classic, it is pleasingly different from the Carry Ons and makes an especially fascinating companion piece to *Carry On Nurse*. While it has dated in some respects—Donald Sinden's woman-mad character comes over at times like a potential rapist—the cast work well together and the film looks rather good, helped by it having been filmed entirely at Pinewood Studios, with outdoor scenes in the studio grounds and outside Pinewood's own country mansion, Heatherden Hall. With not much money needing to be spent on sets or expensive location shooting, the budget instead went on making a smooth, good-looking production.

The Iron Maiden (1962)

The Iron Maiden was made by much of the Carry On crew but its script came from a different source: it was written by Vivian Cox, an experienced screenwriter and producer, with Leslie Bricusse, much better known as a lyricist, from a story by Harold Brooke and Kay Bannerman. As we shall see, this gives the film a very different feel to most of the other comedies made by the Rogers and Thomas team.

It might best be described as a comedy without jokes, and it is perfectly possible to watch *The Iron Maiden* without laughing even once. The film is none the worse for this, however, as it coasts along on an ocean of charm, the trade winds of audience familiarity pushing the story to its conclusion. It is a little bit like an Ealing comedy, updated from the concerns of the immediate post-war period to portray a Britain that was, quite literally, entering the jet age. It has to be said that *The Iron Maiden* is not entirely dissimilar to *Genevieve*, Rank's smash hit romantic comedy of ten years earlier set around a veteran car rally.

Michael Craig stars as aircraft designer Jack Hopkins, whose new jet plane is nearing completion for Cecil Parker's aircraft company. Jack, however, would sooner be tinkering with his beloved traction engine, which is named The Iron Maiden. Meanwhile, American industrialist Paul Fisher (Alan Hale

Jr) has arrived in Britain with his wife and attractive, high spirited daughter Kathy (Anne Helm) in order to sign a $100 million contract to buy a fleet of planes. The other design in the running or the contract is the Polygon, from a rival company run by the sneaky Lord Upshott (Roland Culver), who is determined to impress Fisher with his aristocratic ways. When Kathy drives the family Cadillac into the back of the *Iron Maiden*, she and Jack begin a combative relationship which regular moviegoers will immediate recognise can only end with the pair getting together. This is only after Hopkins' devotion to the *Iron Maiden* and a series of associated disasters causes the company to lose the Fisher contract and Hopkins to lose his job.

Carry On fans can have fun spotting the large number of series regulars who turn up in the cast in secondary roles, including Joan Sims, Cyril Chamberlain, Brain Oulton, Judith Furse, Ian Wilson, and Brian Rawlinson. Also continuing his rise up the ranks is Jim Dale as a hapless salesman suggesting ever sillier names for Hopkins' new aircraft. Perennial British supporting player Sam Kydd is also present and correct as Hopkins' engineering mate on the Iron Maiden, Fred Trotter. Also making a guest appearance is the duke of Bedford, with the film's traction engine race climax was filmed at the duke's country house, Woburn Abbey.

The cleverest piece of casting on the film is that of Alan Hale Jr (here just billed as Alan Hale) as the American industrialist Fisher. Many producers would have gone with a stereotyped grumpily vulgar rich American portrayal, but *The Iron Maiden* is such a good-hearted film that the cheerful, garrulous personality of Hale fits perfectly. As well as adding a welcome bit of zip to the film, Hale was well-known as the star of the 1958 children's Western series *Casey Jones*, in which he played the chief engineer of the railway engine the *Cannonball Express*. The series made Alan Hale beloved by generations of children, and putting him in a film about a similar piece of engineering hardware made a lot of sense. Along with the glossy Eastmancolor photography by Alan Hume, the presence of Hale suggests that *The Iron Maiden* was produced with an eye towards the American market.

The other star of the film is the *Iron Maiden* itself, a 1920-built road locomotive that had seen service working in a quarry and then as a fairground engine until it was retired from active duty and preservation work began on the machine in 1952. Until its use in the film, the engine had always been known as Kitchener, but since 1962, it has retained the name the *Iron Maiden*. Happily, the engine is still kept in good order and is available to be seen by the public at the Scarborough Fair Collection, at Lebberston, between Scarborough and Filey in North Yorkshire.

The film began shooting in June 1962, taking advantage of the summer sun on Buckinghamshire locations including Winchmore Hill, Heatherden Hall (in the grounds of Pinewood Studios), and the Delaford Park Estate, as well as the aforementioned Woburn Abbey and the Henley Regatta across in Oxfordshire. The scenes of Jack's new design of airliner were filmed at Radlett Aerodrome, close to Pinewood Studios in Hertfordshire and, rather oddly, feature a Handley Page Victor, a military aircraft designed to deliver nuclear bombs rather than passengers. The production also took up stages at Peter Rogers Productions' traditional home of Pinewood Studios in June and July 1962, where it was filmed alongside Basil Dearden's psychological thriller *The Mind Benders*, starring Dirk Bogarde, and Robert Asher's Norman Wisdom comedy *On the Beat*.

The Iron Maiden was completed in time for the ABC cinema circuit to release it just before Christmas 1962, playing alongside the Edgar Wallace crime drama *Locker 69*. This pair of films had an unusually long run, and was rereleased in some areas in June 1963, so clearly *The Iron Maiden* was regarded as a financial success, even if it did not steamroller the opposition.

Nurse on Wheels (1963)

Peter Rogers Productions were a busy and ambitious company, and there was industry talk of Rogers hiring another producer-director team in order to double the company's output from three to six films per year. A production slate was announced, with proposed titles *Second Opinion, Whistle in the Dark, The Great Spinoza Robbery, Not in My Book, Up the Armada*, and *Call Me a Cab*. Only the last two of these scripts would actually be produced, eventually retitled as *Carry On Jack* and *Carry On Cabby*.

In the meantime, with *The Iron Maiden* in the can after being shot in the summer, Norman Hudis' script for *Nurse on Wheels* began shooting at Pinewood and Buckinghamshire locations including the village of Great Missenden. The script had been based on an original novel entitled *Nurse as a Neighbour*, ostensibly a memoir written by Joanna Jones, but this was actually a *nom de plume* for none other than John Burke. In the 1960s and '70s Burke, as well as being a screenwriter, was the king of the film and TV novelisation, either under his own name or as Robert Miall.

Joan Sims was cast in the lead role of District Nurse Joanna Jones, but lost the part after gaining weight and being judged insufficiently glamorous for the part. Sims was heartbroken. The fact remained, however, that the script revolved around a pretty young district nurse whose arrival in the village of Blandly is quickly the talk of the town, attracting romantic interest, jealousy, and a degree of doubt as to her ability to replace her highly experienced and elderly predecessor. Joan Sims was still a young, attractive woman, aged only thirty-two at the time the film was made, but she could no longer pass muster as an *ingenue* nurse.

Fortunately, Rogers and Thomas had a known quantity they were able to turn to in the form of Juliet Mills, who had recently played a not-dissimilar role in *Twice Around the Daffodils*. Mills had the air of confidence and competence the role required and was over a decade younger than Sims, turning twenty-one just after the film's 12 November 1962 start of filming. Joan Sims was instead given the choice of any other female role in the film and, in a rare move indeed for Peter Rogers, her fee was increased. Nonetheless, losing a lead role, especially under these circumstances, was a crushing blow to the actress.

Nurse on Wheels tends to be thought of as one of a pair with the previous year's *Twice Around the Daffodils*, since both feature Juliet Mills as a nurse who comes into contact with Ronald Lewis. Actually, the film is in many ways a little brother to the more colourful and expensively made *The Iron Maiden*, both in terms of the cast and crew who made it, and the general themes of the two films. While *Twice Around the Daffodils* is (like *Carry On Nurse*, which was based on the same source material) about the experiences of a group of disparate people in the closed environment of a hospital, both *Nurse on Wheels* and *The Iron Maiden* are celebrations of small-town British eccentricity.

Newly qualified District Nurse Joanna Jones (Mills) is finally able to begin her career as she passes her driving test after 106 lessons, despite almost choking sour-faced examiner Deryck Guyler to death with his own pipe. She takes up an offer to become the district nurse of the small country village of Blandly, and the villagers find Nurse Jones quite a change from her predecessor. She is taking over from the elderly Nurse Merrick, who had held the role for twenty-seven years, and the arrival of an attractive young replacement immediately makes Nurse Jones variously an object of suspicion, fascination, and desire.

Almost the first person she bumps into, literally, on her bicycle, is local farmer Henry Edwards (Ronald Lewis), and their relationship tentatively blossoms into a romance. She works alongside local GP Dr Golfrey, played by the ever-charming Ronald Howard, who was always best known throughout his career as being the son of Hollywood star Leslie Howard. Despite his physical resemblance to his famous father, Howard had a particular laid back screen personality of his own and was almost never out of work, being a fixture of British B-pictures and television series throughout the 1950s and '60s.

Joan Sims plays the daughter of local vicar Raymond Huntley, who is suffering a crisis of faith after the death of his wife. It is actually a pretty good role, enabling Sims to express a wide range of emotions, and one can see how the actress was attracted to the role once she was denied the lead part. Sims plays the different shades of the part very well, playing a cheerful soul who has a difficult relationship with her father and is carrying a torch for the apparently oblivious Dr Golfrey.

Other members of the Peter Rogers stock company of actors are thick on the ground in Blandly; Noel Purcell returns from *The Iron Maiden*, this time as nosey shopkeeper Abel Worthy, who is so desperate to catch sight of Nurse Jones that he falls through the roof and is hit on the head with a family-sized tin of corned beef. Norman Rossington returns after appearing in the *Carry On Sergeant*, *Nurse*, and *Regardless* as Worthy's lively but accident-prone nephew George. Brian Rawlinson not only returns from *The Iron Maiden*, but plays exactly the same part; a west-country Bobby who gets knocked off his bike. Joan Hickson has a small, but very funny role as the Vicar's nosey housekeeper, who feigns a sprained ankle just to get a close look at the new District Nurse. Renee Houston returns from *Twice Around the Daffodils* as Mrs Beacon, fierce wife of the ailing George Woodbridge, and would soon appear in *Carry On Cabby* and *Carry On Spying* before coming back to the Carry Ons in probably her best role, in 1971's *Carry On at Your Convenience*.

Not a part of the Rogers and Thomas unofficial troupe of actors, but making a very welcome appearance is British acting institution Athene Seyler as Miss Farthingale, initially mistrustful of Nurse Jones and her seemingly new methods, but soon won over. Seyler was aged seventy-three at the time of filming, had made her acting debut back in 1909, and had been president of the Royal Academy of Dramatic Art since 1950.

Nurse on Wheels trundles along quite nicely, its time taken up with the eccentricities of the locals, Nurse Jones' terrible driving, and her slowly developing romance with Farmer Edwards. At about the hour mark, a plot development arrives that carries *Nurse on Wheels* to its conclusion, when homeless young married couple Jim Dale (returning for his third Peter Rogers Productions film in a row) and his heavily pregnant wife Amanda Reiss pitch their caravan on Edwards' land. Edwards wants them off his land, but Jones and some of the other villagers try to ensure that they can at least stay until the birth of the baby.

The film is a lot less glossy and expensive-looking than *The Iron Maiden*, which had clearly been produced with an eye on the export market. *Nurse on Wheels* is more parochial stuff, with its cast of small-town eccentrics being won over, to the surprise of absolutely nobody, by the charm and brisk efficiency of Nurse Jones. Being written by Norman Hudis, this film is also blessed with rather more sight gags than *The Iron Maiden* had been, and it is a fun, entertaining ninety-eight minutes. The film was released on the ABC circuit as a family-friendly attraction in time for the Bank Holidays at the end of May 1963. The film's poster art attempted to pull in some of the massive audience that had been attracted to *Carry On Nurse*, not only claiming that *Nurse On Wheels* was 'Even funnier than *Carry On Nurse*', but presenting a painted image of Juliet Mills cycling in her nurse's uniform revealing stockings and suspenders.

The ABC circuit presented *Nurse On Wheels* as part of a 'U' certificate double bill, a wise move as Britain had just gotten through a brutally cold winter which had lasted from December 1962 to March 1963. It was certainly possible that the British weather might have sent holidaying families searching for indoor entertainment. The film it was presented alongside was certainly something of a contrast: *First Spaceship on Venus* was a 1960 East German-Polish science-fiction epic, which had been dubbed into English and had some fifteen minutes removed from its running time. This film had played in the American market the previous year with a rather more fitting co-feature: the Japanese monster movie *Varan the Unbelievable*.

The Big Job (1965)

With *Carry On Cleo* wrapped and ready for release, Rogers and Thomas swung back into action with *The Big Job*, an attempt to capitalise on the events of two years previously, which quickly became known to a fascinated public as The Great Train Robbery. In the early hours of 8 August 1963, a mail train travelling from Glasgow to London was halted and robbed of £2.6 million. Something about this particular robbery caught the imagination of the public and the fifteen-strong gang achieved a strange sort of folk heroism. This was partially because the raid was committed without the use of firearms—though train driver Jack Mills suffered brain damage from the beating he took by one of the gang with an iron bar.

Along with the comparative lack of violence, the film had the interesting cinematic mystery that most of the gang was caught but the money never recovered. The Great Train Robbery immediately felt like a British comedy drama script that somehow found its way into the hands of genuine criminals, who used it as a template for an actual raid. This real robbery inadvertently fitted into a rich seam of British films such as *The Lavender Hill Mob*, *The Ladykillers*, and *The League of Gentlemen*. Fortunately for Peter Rogers, he had developed a strong working relationship with the British cinema's absolute master at playing comic variations on exactly the sort of dodgy working-class criminals who committed the robbery—Sidney James.

Rogers and Thomas were quick off the mark, beating other films based in various ways on the Train Robbery such as *The Great St. Trinians' Train Robbery* (1966) and *Robbery* (1967) to the cinemas by some distance—though to be fair, ABPC's *Crooks in Cloisters*, featuring Barbara Windsor and Bernard Cribbins, made it into cinemas even sooner, in August 1964. John Antrobus, the Associated London Scripts writer who had taken a run at knocking *Carry On Sergeant* into shape before Norman Hudis, provided a story treatment which was turned into a solid eighty-five minutes of gags by Rogers and Thomas' new favourite writer Talbot Rothwell.

The whole thing was done very cheaply, but *The Big Job* fits perfectly into the Peter Rogers and Gerald Thomas Carry On formula of putting together a cast of highly talented old pros, giving them a script full of comedic situations, and filming the results in a fairly straightforward manner. The cast was, naturally, headed by Sid James as George Brain, head of the most inept band of crooks in London—played by Dick Emery and Lance Percival. The latter returned to Peter Rogers Productions after replacing Charles Hawtrey three years earlier in *Carry On Cruising* and was about to start an interesting voiceover assignment providing the voices of both Paul McCartney and Ringo Starr for the King Features cartoon series *The Beatles*.

Dick Emery was continuing his occasional career as a movie character actor, having made his name as a radio comedian on such shows as *Workers Playtime* and as an occasional substitute performer in *The Goon Show*. His big break came with a regular role in the later episodes of *The Army Game*, which led to him being headhunted by the BBC, who gave Emery his own series which lasted from 1963 to 1981 and would eventually make him a household name. This rather derailed Emery from film work, and *The Big Job*'s 'Booky' Bins represented probably his largest film role before he achieved television fame.

The film features would-be criminal mastermind George Brain—played by Sid—and his gang (the film was at one point to be titled *The Great Brain Robbery*) who pull off a bank robbery in 1950 while disguised as funeral directors despite their own bungling incompetence. They are quickly caught by the police after a car chase involving a real funeral cortège, but before being arrested Brain hides a briefcase containing the £50,000 loot in a tree. When the trio are released fifteen years later they find that the farmland that they were chased through in 1950 has been replaced by a new town and the tree now stands in the yard of the town's police station. Brain and his gang rent rooms in a boarding house opposite the police station and try various absurd schemes in order to get to the tree undetected. At this point, the film settles into an amusing, Laurel and Hardyesque group of set pieces in which the gang try to get past policemen Jim Dale and Deryck Guyler. The former is keen, but daft (Dale puts in a marvellous performance of comic grotesquery) while the latter is more interested in organising his police choir than he is in investigating crime.

The Big Job also features some notably strong female roles, particularly for Joan Sims as Mildred Gamley, widowed landlady of the boarding house in which the gang stay. Only thirty-five at the time the film was made, rather typically she is playing a character at least ten years older. Also given a central role is Sylvia Sims as George's girlfriend Myrtle, who wants nothing more than to settle down with the man she's waited fifteen years for. Sylvia Sims' performance is a highlight of the film, as we discover she has learned to stand up for herself while George has been in prison. In one very well observed sequence, she thinks of an idea that could help the gang only to be completely ignored, then George repeats the idea word for word.

Although *The Big Job* contains a fair number of Carry On regulars, and almost the entirety of the series mid-sixties behind-the-camera crew, it does feel different enough from a Carry On film for the decision not to include it in the series to feel correct. What the film does feel similar to is a film from six years earlier which featured both Sid James and Bernard Bresslaw: Mario Zampi's 1959 production *Too Many Crooks*. This had starred Terry-Thomas as a crooked, tax-dodging businessman who is targeted by George Cole's hopeless gang boss 'Fingers' and his men Bernard Bresslaw, Sid James, and Joe Melia. While the plots of the two films are quite different, a surprising number of similarities are apparent: Sid's role as the mutinous gang member 'Sid' is very similar to Dick Emery's part in *The Big Job*, while Lance Percival's absurdly credulous 'Dipper' Day is analogous to Bresslaw's *Too Many Crooks* role. A key sequence in *Too Many Crooks* sees the gang disguised as funeral directors and driving a hearse, and there is even a joke repeated in both films where the crooks encounter a safe which is already open, but then accidentally shut by the bumbling crooks. Ultimately (and we are well into spoiler territory here, so if you have not seen the films already, skip the next sentence), both the *Too Many Crooks* and *The Big Job* gangs are taken over by strong, confident women.

Although it is not the most original of films, to the extent that it can be regarded as being a partial remake of *Too Many Crooks*, it must be emphasised that *The Big Job* is very funny—possibly the highlight of Peter Rogers Productions' non-Carry On films and is well worth tracking down. It went on release from mid-August 1965, being sent on the road with a rather larger-scale running mate than the usual b-picture crime movie: the colour, widescreen Harry Alan Towers production *24 Hours to Kill*, featuring Lex Barker and Mickey Rooney in a thriller filmed on location in Lebanon.

The Second Victory (1986)

With any chances of relaunching the Carry Ons with the remaining cast members at its core apparently dashed, Gerald Thomas attempted to relaunch his own directing career outside of the orbit of Peter Rogers. While Rogers was attempting to raise interest in and money for *Carry On Again Nurse*, Thomas had formed his own production company and not only managed to get his own movie into production, he wound up producing and directing his first dramatic film in some thirty years. It should be noted that getting any sort of British film into production at this point in time represented quite an achievement. Film production in the UK dwindled to virtually nothing in the late 1970s, collapsing to a historic low in 1983 when a mere thirty-seven films were produced in the United Kingdom. By 1987, the situation had recovered slightly, with seventy-two films being made, but to place this into some sort of perspective, in 2018, there were 257 films produced in the UK. The 1980s were tough times for British filmmakers and, as Gerald Thomas was later to discover, getting your film before the cameras was only half the battle.

The Second Victory was a sort-of murder mystery set during the post-war occupation of Austria, based on a 1958 novel by the Australian author Morris West. The author's works had been adapted for the screen several times before—in fact, this was the sixth film version of his books. Some of the previous efforts had been major productions, such as 1968's *The Shoes of the Fisherman* and 1981's *The Salamander*. With this in mind, it must have seemed like quite a coup to get West to write the screenplay himself.

An international cast was assembled, headed by Anthony Andrews, who was still riding the wave of popularity generated by the huge success of his 1981 television series *Brideshead Revisited*. He was backed up by an extremely strong cast of European actors, which must have improved the chances of the film's being seen in central Europe. The legendary Max von Sydow appears as the town doctor, while Paul Verhoeven's leading lady Renée Soutendijk also has a strong role, as do two of the greats of German character acting, Mario Adorf and Wolfgang Preiss. Even Jack Douglas shows up in the small role of an anaesthetist, giving the film a small connection with the Carry Ons in front of the camera. With Gerald Thomas' regular composer Eric Rogers having died in 1981, the director turned to Stanley Myers to write the score, and he did a really fine job. A familiar face behind the camera was cinematographer Alan Hume, whose glowing, shadowy photography and visual compositions are ill-served by the blurry VHS copies which are the only format in which *The Second Victory* could be viewed at time of writing.

With a budget healthy enough to facilitate extensive location filming in the picturesque Austrian resort of Badgastein, as well as studio work in the more familiar surroundings of Pinewood, prospects for the new film must have looked pretty good. Unfortunately, the experience of watching the film demonstrates that novelists are perhaps not the best people to adapt their own works. Although West had a lot of experience writing radio dramas and stageplays, this was only the author's second screenplay and the first he had written in ten years. The result is a film that starts off strongly but loses focus as it goes along, causing the pace of the film to slow down to a crawl. It is as if West was unable to pare down his narrative to what really mattered, leaving us with too many characters and different plot threads. The film devolves into a succession of scenes in which actors in rooms talk to each other. By 1987, this approach to writing and directing seemed rather old-fashioned.

The story concerns a British major (Anthony Andrews), who arrives in an Austrian town shortly after the end of the Second World War in charge of Allied occupation forces. Almost immediately on arrival, his sergeant is shot dead by a deranged enemy soldier who appears unaware that the war is over. Andrews is convinced that the man is a local being shielded by the people of the town. From there, the plot goes off in several different directions, involving Andrews' past as a trainee priest, a war criminal hiding out under an assumed name, various black market activities by the locals, and Andrews' affair with a local woman. The message of the film is that the aftermath of war is as messy as the war itself, and in order to win the second victory, a peaceful reconstruction of Europe, compromises will have to be made. While it is undoubtedly a good thing that Thomas directed a thoughtful picture shot through with moral complexity, this was an era when the cardboard heroics of Stallone and Schwarzenegger were triumphing at the box office. The slow pace and moral ambiguities of *The Second Victory* were simply not what audiences and thus distributors were looking for. One cannot help but wonder whether *The Second Victory* might not have worked better, and been more widely seen, as a television mini-series.

The Second Victory appears to have been given a US cinema release during May 1987, and was reviewed in guardedly positive terms in *The New York Times*, though 'Mr West's theological pretentions' were criticised. It was also released on VHS in the States on the AIP label, which was more usually associated with lowbrow fare and perhaps was making a brief stab at respectability. The film was also released in Australia at around the same time, but failed to secure any UK cinematic distribution, which must have been a blow to Gerald Thomas.

Gerald Thomas was not finished as a director, however. Between Carry On films, he often kept his hand in by directing adverts—this was how he made contact with Larry Dann after many years and reintroduced him to the Carry On cast in the 1970s. Thomas' continued efforts to get a new production off the ground were eventually to lead to the next chapter in the Carry On story. While he was searching for production partners, he met a producer by the name of John Goldstone who had quite a comedic pedigree of his own. Born in 1943, Goldstone had been a young production assistant on the 1962 classic 'kitchen sink' drama *A Kind of Loving* when he was taken under the wing of the film's producer Joseph Janni. This resulted in him becoming Janni's personal assistant, working on a range of films over the next seven years from *Billy Liar*, director John Schlesinger's 1963 follow-up to *A Kind of Loving*, the wild 1966 spy spoof *Modesty Blaise*, and Ken Loach's film breakthrough *Poor Cow*.

In the 1970s, Goldstone began producing his own films, beginning a long relationship with the Monty Python team when he acted as executive producer of their 1973 film *Monty Python and the Holy Grail*. Made on a tiny shooting budget of £150,000, this proved hugely profitable thanks to the previously untapped Python fanbase in America who had seen the BBC's *Monty Python's Flying Circus* series on PBS Television. Goldstone was next involved with the 1975 musical *The Rocky Horror Picture Show*, another very low-budget film which turned in a huge profit over the years. After becoming involved with the Pythons again with the Terry Gilliam-directed *Jabberwocky*, he produced a 1978 comic version of *The Hound of the Baskervilles*. A starring vehicle for Peter Cook and Dudley Moore, playing Sherlock Holmes and Doctor Watson, this featured an array of talent from the glory days of British comedy, including Terry-Thomas, Max Wall, and, playing Sir Henry Baskerville, none other than Kenneth Williams.

Goldstone maintained his relationship with the Pythons (which has lasted to the present day), producing all the subsequent Python movies. This proved especially tricky in the case of *Monty Python's Life of Brian*, when EMI Films walked away from the film once its management saw the controversial storyline. The day was saved when former Beatle George Harrison was approached and formed a company, Handmade Films, especially to finance the project. Goldstone had largely worked outside the comedy genre for some years, but with two major films planned for release in 1992 to commemorate the 500th anniversary of Christopher Columbus' discovery of America, he felt that the subject was ripe for comedic treatment. Once Gerald Thomas was involved, the idea of a Carry On film was naturally broached. After fourteen years of raised and dashed hopes, at last a new Carry On film was really going to happen.

35

Carry On Biographies

The Carry On films would be nothing without the incredible cast assembled by Peter Rogers and Gerald Thomas. Here we present the stories of the fourteen performers who made up the core cast of the series over the years, the likes of whom we shall never see again.

Kenneth Williams

B. 22 February 1926
D. 15 April 1988
Carry On Film Appearances: 26

Kenneth Williams was his own greatest creation, born to working-class parents but rejecting both the accent and expectations of his background. He was a clever child who loved both art and English at school and inherited from his mother Louisa a talent for mimicry. He also had a talent for performing in front of any audience that would listen to him and clearly had stage ambitions. Williams was a mass of contradictions defined by a single central one: he developed from an early age a hard shell of what he described as 'affectation and play acting' to cover his inferiority complex and lack of formal education, both in intellectual matters and in performing.[1] He spent his life surrounded by people with university education and RADA training, while he had neither.

Williams' father Charlie insisted that his son learned a trade, thus the young Kenneth, on leaving school, became a trainee draughtsman, fulfilling his artistic interests by joining an amateur dramatic society. The Second World War intervened and Williams was called up to the army, his professional artistic skills meaning he was sent to an army map-reproduction unit.

Williams' nascent performing skills were clear to all and when the unit was disbanded he was transferred to the Combined Services Entertainment Unit, entertaining the troops in the Far East.

Here Williams was in his element, meeting figures who would become lifelong friends such as performer Stanley Baxter and future playwright Peter Nichols, who later wrote about his CSE experiences in the hit play and later film *Privates On Parade*. Despite almost crippling levels of self-doubt, Kenneth Williams started out his life as a professional actor soon after being released from his army service. Like many performers of his generation, Kenneth Williams learned his craft in some of the huge number of repertory companies operating the length of Britain. He started out in Newquay, Cornwall, about as far away from the London theatre scene as it was possible to get. Williams began building a professional reputation, gaining small stage roles in more prestigious productions and the occasional small movie role, starting with an uncredited bit in the 1952 film *Trent's Last Case*.

Kenneth Williams' career was transformed when he was cast in a major production of George Bernard Shaw's *Saint Joan* which opened at the Arts Theatre Club, London, on 29 September 1954. Williams brought the part of the Dauphin to life and was singled out for praise in all the play's reviews. Just as importantly, this role of a lifetime was being seen by the right people. He was quickly approached by BBC radio producer Dennis Main Wilson, who was in the process of putting together a new radio vehicle for rising comedy star Tony Hancock. This became the massively popular *Hancock's Half Hour*, and Williams' vocal versatility was exactly what the series needed. Despite having first been noticed in a drama, the future direction of his career was to lay in comedy and Williams appeared in a series of theatrical revues (a sort of stage precursor to television sketch comedies) including *Share My Lettuce* (1957), *Pieces of Eight* (1959), and that show's follow-up *One Over the Eight* (1961).

His parallel radio career made Williams a national comedy star, his 'snide' character in *Hancock's Half Hour* getting so many laughs that Hancock felt it was derailing the series. As a result, Hancock had Williams' role reduced to such an extent that Williams left the series. By this time, he was a part of the radio comedy team performing with Kenneth Horne in *Beyond Our Ken*, an extremely popular show that reached even greater heights when reformatted as *Round the Horne*. Radio had by this point been supplanted by television as the primary home entertainment medium, and *Round the Horne*'s ending after the sudden death of Kenneth Horne in 1969 is seen by many as the closing of the classic era of British radio comedy. Kenneth Williams remained a popular figure on radio, as a panellist on the BBC 4 show *Just A Minute* from its inception in 1967 until his death, dazzling listeners with his endless reserves of wit and erudition.

The course of Kenneth Williams' big-screen career was set by his role in *Carry On Sergeant* in 1959, and indeed Williams was the actor who appeared in the most films in the series, sticking with the films until the bitter end with *Carry On Emmannuelle*. The international success of the Carry On series and Williams' major role in them did not lead to a sustained career in films for the actor, however, and his other major film roles were in other Peter Rogers and Gerald Thomas films such as *Twice Around the Daffodils*. At first, Williams operated as a sort of intellectual romantic lead in the Carry Ons, but his roles, and Williams' playing of them, became increasingly broad until by 1964's *Carry On Jack*, he was able to go joyously, magnificently over the top.

Increasingly during the 1970s and beyond, Kenneth Williams became a personality rather than a performer. There simply were not the films being made any more to harness his particular talents, and radio comedy had become an endangered species. As his final two on-screen performances (as opposed to voice-overs) were 1978's *Carry On Emmannuelle* and Paul Morrissey's *The Hound of the Baskervilles*, a production of arguably even lower artistic merit than *Emmannuelle*, this may have been a blessing. Instead, Williams drew upon his lifetime of experiences and love of holding forth before an audience, writing his memoirs, entitled *Just Williams*, and becoming a popular guest on the chat show circuit. In the process, he turned his life and aspects of his own personality into a sustained piece of performance art. The best example of this is probably *An Audience With Kenneth Williams* from 1983, in which he enthrals a celebrity audience, many of whom were personal friends, for well over an hour with stories from his life and a couple of his most famous comic songs. The most amazing thing about this performance his how effortless he makes it seem, referring only once to some notes, giving every impression that he could have happily continued for another hour.

It was possibly inevitable that this would happen. The Carry Ons and the Kenneth Horne radio series encouraged Williams' most outrageous instincts until it was thought by casting directors, audiences, and possibly even Kenneth Williams himself, that there was nothing else that he could do. Williams had become a close friend of Joe Orton and his lover (and later murderer) Kenneth Halliwell, during the mid-1960s and, after his breakthrough success with *Entertaining Mr. Sloane*, Orton wrote the key role of Inspector Truscott especially for Williams in his second stage play, *Loot*. Unfortunately, Orton's blackly comedic parody of detective fiction had been somewhat rushed into production before it was ready, despite extensive rewrites, with the result that this 1965 production was largely rejected by both critics and audiences. A revised version of the play opened the following year and proved a great success, eventually transferring to Broadway. A discouraged Williams did not return for this new version, however, with the role of Truscott being played in the 1966 London run by Michael Bates. Williams did later direct two of

Orton's plays at the Lyric Theatre—*Loot* in 1980 and *Entertaining Mr. Sloane* the following year.

The memory of Kenneth Williams lighting up the West End theatre scene in *Saint Joan* became forgotten, however, and despite his talent and love of the theatre, he never became a major star of the stage. While this is sad, what Williams did instead he did brilliantly and enthralled audiences for decades. His letters and diaries, published posthumously to great acclaim, revealed a more complex personality than his public could ever have imagined

The death of Kenneth Williams is perhaps not to be dwelt upon greatly. Some close friends, including his literary collaborator Gyles Brandreth, believed that he committed suicide whereas his authorised biographer Christopher Stevens makes a very good case for Williams' death being due to an accidentally lethal combination of drugs.[2,3] Either way, audiences were robbed of a unique talent.

Joan Sims

B. 9 May 1930
D. 27 June 2001
Carry On Film Appearances: 24

The daughter of a stationmaster, the young Joan Sims would entertain travellers waiting for their trains. She was a born entertainer who would eventually, after much struggle, gain a scholarship to RADA, where she studied between 1948 and 1950. She was immediately spotted by a young agent, Peter Eade, who was already proving to be an extremely shrewd judge of comedy talent, signing up Kenneth Williams and Ronnie Barker at the very start of their careers. All three would stay with Eade for most of their careers, only forced to seek new representation after his sudden death in 1979.

With Eade's support, Joan quickly began picking up stage roles as well as broadcasting work on both the BBC's radio and television services. BBC Television returned to the airwaves in June 1946 after its wartime hiatus, and Sims first television work came in 1952. At this stage, she was often providing voices for children's programmes, her hard-won skill with accents being recognised already at this early stage. For these shows, she often found herself working alongside her future Carry On comrade Kenneth Connor, a master of the voiceover art.

By the mid-1950s, Joan Sims was an established part of the British comedy scene. She was slim and attractive, but at the same time capable of playing dowdy or older parts, and blessed with natural comedic timing and vocal skills, all of which proved huge advantages in gaining work. Joan seemed to be everywhere, her television opportunities expanded with the launch of the commercial television network ITV in September 1955. With adventure series being made on film by experienced filmmakers using the same pool of talent that populated post-war cinema, Joan was squarely on the radar of casting agents. Thus she could be seen in episodes of *Colonel March of Scotland Yard* (opposite the great Boris Karloff), *The Buccaneers*, and *The Adventures of Robin Hood*.

On stage, Joan first made a big impression in revue, a sketch show format that was often highly popular with audiences and provided great early experience for young performers. She made her West End debut in *High Spirits* in 1953, which proved a popular success and also featured future comedy stars Ian Carmichael and Patrick Cargill, as well as future Carry On star Dilys Laye. The latter became a lifelong friend, while the production also featured Joan's old RADA classmate Ronnie Stevens. *High Spirits* had initially been titled *Intimacy at Eight*, and its 1954 follow-up, *Intimacy at Eight Thirty*, proved an even greater success, really helping put Joan on the map.

At the same time, Joan was making inroads into radio, which was at this stage still the most popular mass entertainment medium. Probably her most high-profile radio work at the time was a five-week spell on *Ted Ray Time*, a vehicle for Ted Ray, probably the most popular radio comedian of the day and the future star of *Carry On Teacher*. *Ted Ray Time* was basically a temporary retitling of the immensely popular *Ray's A Laugh*, which ran from 1940 until 1961 and provided early mass exposure for talents such as Peter Sellers (who returned for Joan's five-week run) and Kenneth Connor.

Only a few years into her professional career, Joan was working with the best in the business. It was hardly surprising, then, that she was approached by Peter Rogers and Gerald Thomas when it became clear that Dora Bryan was not going to return for the second Carry On film. Joan was an instant hit in the Carry Ons, her glamour meaning that she quickly replaced not only Bryan but eventually became the main love interest in the early films, supplanting Shirley Eaton in that role. Film and broadcasting work largely replaced stage roles as the 1960s continued, with the actress becoming a part of the unofficial Rogers and Thomas stock company for their non-Carry On Films. A particular highlight was the 1959 film *Please Turn Over*; director Gerald Thomas would have been more than aware of Joan's ability to play both comedic grotesques and glamorous romantic leads, and here the script (in which all the actors play two sets of characters) pushes both of these to their extreme. Sims plays a slatternly cleaning lady, fag constantly hanging from her mouth, and her total opposite, a sexy French maid. As if this contrast was not enough, she gets many of the best lines of dialogue, in a sort of hybrid French-English. In the wake of the success of the early Carry On movies, Joan was also cast in the 1960 ITV sitcom *Our House* along with fellow Carry On alumni Hattie Jacques (another lifelong friend) Charles Hawtrey, Bernard Bresslaw, and Norman Rossington.

While Joan's propensity to weight gain meant that her glamour period was relatively short-lived, in her thirties, Joan was able to play younger and older roles with equal élan, best witnessed by her astonishing transformation into the character of Gran in the sitcom *Till Death Us Do Part*, a role she took on at the age of only thirty-seven. Perhaps the physical changes she underwent over the years enabled Joan to escape the long shadow of the Carry Ons and remain in professional demand for the rest of her life. Though she tended to stick to comedy roles, the occasional meaty dramatic role did come her way, a 1970s highlight being Joan's role in the 1975 production *Love Among the Ruins*, shot in the UK for American television, where she appeared opposite Katherine Hepburn and Laurence Olivier.

Joan stuck with the Carry Ons until the very end of the original run, her total of twenty-four films being easily the most of any of the series' female cast, and in fact only being topped by Kenneth Williams, who appeared in twenty-six, though his total includes the scenes he filmed for the compilation film *That's Carry On*. Joan remains in the Carry On record books however for her unbroken run of twenty original Carry On films from *Cleo* to *Emmannuelle*.

Joan's career continued in the post-Carry On era with little pause, save for one period in the early 1980s. She had been deeply affected by a series of bereavements in at the end of the 1970s, including the deaths of her agent Peter Eade and close friend Hattie Jacques, and spent time in hospital recovering from the effects. She remained a regular guest star on television series throughout the 1980s and '90s, including a role in the 1986 four-part *Doctor Who* story 'The Mysterious Planet'. Joan was also a main cast member of two successful sitcoms, a form she had not taken a starring role in since the 1967 ATV series *Sam and Janet* (which had been based on a BBC Light Programme sitcom she had appeared in the previous year). These were the 1986–7 series *Farrington of the FO*, where she was second-billed opposite the show's star Angela Thorne, and *On the Up*, which ran for three series on BBC1 from 1990 to 1992 and starred Dennis Waterman. In the latter series in particular, Joan was a delight, and her public profile was the highest it had been for years.

Perhaps above all, it was a pleasure to see her operating as part of an ensemble cast of old pros once again, and the actress gave every impression of having a lot of fun with the role. *On The Up* benefitted from classy scripts by Bob Larby, half of the renowned comedy writing duo of Esmonde and Larby, who would also write a recurring role for Sims in his next solo sitcom project, the long-running popular success *As Time Goes By*. Joan also remained a regular performer on radio, as late as 1999 appearing in the BBC Radio 4 sitcom *Bristow*, in which she appeared alongside her old Carry On chum Liz Fraser.

Her physical health also began to fail during the final decade of her life, and Joan Sims died at the still relatively young age of seventy-one in 2001. News of her declining health was kept from all but a very few close friends, her agent receiving offers of work for Joan even while she lay in hospital during her final illness.[4]

Charles Hawtrey

B. 30 November 1914
D. 27 October 1988
Carry On Film Appearances: 23

Charles Hawtrey was, it is generally agreed, a deeply odd man. He was also an actor who made up for what he lacked in range (straight roles were beyond him) by being absolutely brilliant at what he could do. One small example will suffice for now: Hawtrey's tiny role in the 1956 romantic comedy *The March Hare*. This featured Peggy Cummins and Terence Morgan in a dismally dull horseracing saga, packed to the gunnels with every Irish cliché under the sun and with an annoying 'diddly-dee' theme tune that hits the audience over the head at regular intervals. Charles Hawtrey, at the edge of achieving national stardom on the new ITV commercial television network, has a single scene of no more than two minutes in length. He is genuinely the best thing about the film, lighting up the screen playing a terrified bookmaker's clerk responsible for a mistake that might bankrupt his employer.

That Charles Hawtrey ever became a film and television star was nothing short of miraculous. Hawtrey spent his career afraid that he was not getting his due: that he was not getting the roles he deserved, or enough money for the ones he did get, or that other cast members were getting more screen time and better dialogue than he was. Stardom really did not happen to actors of his type, who tended to be a part of the furniture of British comedy before disappearing from stage and screen, to be remembered fondly by those of us who love old British comedy actors. Hawtrey refused to accept this fate, pushing himself and his career well beyond any supposed limits imposed on it by others.

He even refused to accept his own family background, being born with the name George Frederick Joffre Hartree to a working class family with no theatrical connections. Young George showed promise as a keen stage performer and a talented boy soprano. He gained a scholarship to be taught by the famed teacher of child actors Italia Conti, Miss Conti had previously worked for the theatrical knight Sir Charles Hawtrey, and she encouraged her pupil to adopt his name.[5] With Sir Charles being safely dead since 1923 and thus unable to raise any objections, Hartree neglected to correct anyone who assumed that he was the son of Sir Charles—he was even billed professionally as Charles Hawtrey Jr on occasion. Bizarrely, he continued the deception enthusiastically to anyone who would listen till the end of his days, many decades after any possible professional advantage could be gained by it.

The newly minted Charles Hawtrey first gained regular professional stage employment as a boy soprano, releasing records and making his first BBC radio appearances as one half of a duo with Evelyn Williams. He remained proud throughout his career of his convincing skills, especially when younger, in the field of female impersonation. This reached its widest exposure in the 1939 West End production *Counterfeit,* the dénouement of which revolved around Hawtrey, who had a relatively minor role looking like himself, being revealed as the true identity of the play's leading lady. Happily, his skills in this area were preserved in the low-budget 1940 film *Jail Birds,* which gives us an opportunity to see the younger Hawtrey in an extended sequence performing in female garb and looking entirely feminine. Seeing cross-dressing in a 1940s comedy film presented other than for the comedy value of seeing a man in an ill-fitting dress is highly unusual in itself and deserves a small place in British cinematic history.

His small but regular film appearances eventually led to Hawtrey being employed as a foil to the famous British comedy actor Will Hay. Hay's signature character was an incompetent, slightly seedy schoolmaster in charge of a class of badly behaved, visibly over-age 'children'. Hawtrey's role was as the ringleader of the class, forever pointing out the inadequacies of Hay, who appeared to be worse-educated than his class. He appeared alongside Hay between 1937 and early 1945, featuring in four extremely popular films, as well as stage productions and radio shows. The two were genuinely close colleagues for a while but, as Hawtrey would discover to his cost, there was only one star in a Will Hay production and Hawtrey's attempts to secure a larger role resulted in his expulsion from the Hay ensemble. As events transpired, Hay suffered a stroke in 1946, after which he worked little, so Hawtrey would have been professionally out in the cold in any event.

Outside of the Will Hay pictures, Hawtrey's movie roles in the 1940s and '50s were often discouragingly small, such as the tiny parts he was cast in for the George Formby comedies *Much Too Shy* and *Bell Bottom George*. There were occasionally more substantial supporting roles, each one holding out hope for a brighter professional future, such as his role as railway stationmaster Thomas Duckett in Powell and Pressburger's *A Canterbury Tale* in 1944. He slogged through minor roles between such highlights, and for extended periods gained no movie roles at all—after *A Canterbury Tale*, Hawtrey did not land another meaningful film role for the next three years. It is a testament to Hawtrey's professionalism and determination that he kept going in the meantime, his career kept afloat by semi-regular radio appearances, especially on the BBC's *Children's Hour*, and the occasional stage role. He even tried his hand at directing, both for the stage and two low-budget films.

Things actually improved somewhat as the fifties began, with two good supporting roles in the 1952 films *Brandy for the Parson* and *You're Only Young Twice*. This was followed by his break into adult radio with regular roles in the comedy series *Ray's A Laugh*, starring Ted Ray, and *Life With the Lyons,* starring Ben Lyon and Bebe Daniels. These were some of the most popular radio comedies of their day, listened to by millions; finally, Hawtrey was reaching a large audience. The days of radio's ascendancy as Britain's primary home entertainment medium were, however, numbered from the moment on 22 September 1955 when ITV first launched in the London area.

This was an event which opened up great opportunities for actors such as Charles Hawtrey who had made little headway with producers and casting directors at BBC Television. ITV's northern English contractor Granada Television cast him in the regular role of Private 'Professor' Hatchett in *The Army Game*, which ran from 1957 to 1961 and quickly became the new commercial network's first genuine sitcom hit. Hawtrey gave a finely detailed comic performance as the prissy National Serviceman, but still was regarded as dispensable by the show's producers, and was dropped as part of a cull of cast members after the show's second series.

By now, it was 1958 and the timing could not have been better for Hawtrey, who walked straight into the role of Private Golightly in *Carry On Sergeant*. From the moment he crashed through the barracks doors to join Sergeant Grimshaw's platoon, Charles Hawtrey's career was transformed. Finally, after years of hardship and struggle, he had achieved a level of stardom, but the struggle had come with costs to Hawtrey's psyche. He was beset by insecurities and increasingly dependent on alcohol, partly due to the stress of caring for his increasingly ailing mother.

A self-defeating pattern emerged in Hawtrey's career in which he would achieve a degree of success but would overestimate his bargaining position and lose roles. Will Hay dropped him when he demanded better billing, and he walked away from his long-running role in the BBC *Children's Hour* series *Norman and Henry Bones, Boy Detectives* over an absurdly minor point of principle about his Radio Times billing being above that of Patricia Hayes. Finally, he walked away from the Carry On series before shooting began on the 1972 *Carry On Christmas* television special because he would not countenance being billed below Hattie Jacques.[6] He was traditionally third-billed in the Carry Ons, and in the absence of Sid James and Kenneth Williams from the production, he thought top billing was his due. The sad fact was that by this point, Hawtrey had almost no career outside the Carry On movies and Hattie Jacques was a much bigger television name than him.

This same obsession with his star status ruined his very real chances of TV stardom in the 1960s. Hawtrey made a good impression in the 1960–2 sitcom *Our House* and was retained for the same company's follow up *Best of Friends*. This also starred Hylda Baker and the pair's working relationship was so fractious that the series was scrapped after a single series of thirteen episodes, despite gaining decent audience ratings. Baker was eventually forgiven and by 1968 had a hit sitcom once again (*Nearest and Dearest*, which ran until 1973 and was marred by a similarly poisonous relationship with her latest co-star, Jimmy Jewell). Hawtrey, in contrast, never worked meaningfully in television again outside the Carry On banner.

Charles Hawtrey's position in the industry had been so tenuous for so long that he felt the need to magnify both small triumphs and minor slights. By the time he did start achieving measurable success from the late 1950s, Hawtrey was approaching his mid-forties and the protective shell he had built up around himself to protect against failure prevented the actor from appreciating and building on his hard-won successes. As a result, time and again, he overplayed his hand with unrealistic demands about his billing and salary.

One of the tragedies of this situation is that by this point, Charles Hawtrey had developed into a truly unique, brilliant comedic talent. *The Army Game* had launched him as an adult star, and no other actor on Earth could have played that part. He did things on screen that no other performer would have even attempted, such as his signature move of saying his lines not to the actors he was playing the scene with, but staring directly at the camera (and, by extension, the audience). This goes against every rule of screen acting, but somehow it works, forcing the viewer to look only at Hawtrey. After years of neglect by much of the entertainment business, Hawtrey was absolutely determined not to be ignored.

Eventually, Hawtrey's demons overwhelmed his hard-won professionalism. His obsession with status and billing became ever more destructive, while alcohol eventually become more important than work, or indeed anything else in his life. A final decade that should have seen Charles Hawtrey become a beloved national treasure instead saw him retreat to the Kent coastal resort of Deal, where he became a notorious figure, banned from every pub in town. Perhaps, this was an inevitable fate for a difficult man unable to accept either failure or success, who was touched by genius.

Sidney James

B. 8 May 1913, Newcastle, Natal, South Africa
D. 26 April 1976, Sunderland, England
Carry On Film Appearances: 19

The man who would be Sid arrived in England a very different sort of performer to the one he would become famous as. In South Africa, Sid had been regarded as an actor of great dramatic reputation, arriving in England with a letter of recommendation from the Welsh actor and director Gwen Ffrancon-Davies. Sid had scored some notable dramatic successes with her in leading roles such as Emlyn Williams' *Wind of Heaven* and John Streinbeck's *Of Mice and Men*. Sid's roots, however, were firmly in the music hall or vaudeville tradition. The South African theatrical scene was almost completely divorced from that of Britain, and he was coming to England as a complete unknown.

Sid's father went by the stage name Lew James, but was born Lazarus (later changed to Laurie) Cohen on 29 March 1884. He and Reina Solomon were East Londoners who married and formed a comedy song and dance duo to play the music hall circuit under the name 'James and Selma'. Reina's mother Flora was also a stage performer who had emigrated to South Africa to run a theatrical boarding house, and the pair eventually took the long sea journey to join her and seek their fortune. The James and Selma act played as far afield as New Zealand, Australia, India, and Rhodesia. Lew also had a solo stand-up comedy act, plus did some stage acting and later in his career even appeared in at least one silent movie.

On 8 May 1913, the Cohens' second son, Solomon Joel Cohen, was born in Newcastle, in what is now the KwaZulu-Natal province of South Africa, some 180 miles from Johannesburg. Young Solomon was the couple's second child, joining the James and Selma act in its international touring, an experience that turned him into a natural performer. This peripatetic childhood ended when Solomon had to finally go to school, while at around the same time Lew and Raina split up, divorcing in July 1922. Lew James relocated to Australia, where he continued his career with some success.[7]

The teenage Sid, his formal education complete, returned to the stage and became a member of the Johannesburg Repertory Company. His acting career was interrupted by the outbreak of the Second World War, and in 1941, he joined the army, serving in an anti-tank regiment before being recruited into the newly formed Defence Force Entertainment Unit. There, Sid produced shows and did a near-the-knuckle stand-up routine inspired by Max Miller.[8] In retrospect, this is interesting as in later years, Sid professed to be completely unable to tell a joke or ad lib. He also showed off his skills as a soft-shoe shuffle dancer, and he retained a dancer's grace for the rest of his life. One of the performers in Sid's army shows, who became a close friend for a while and went across to England with him, was a young actor called Larry Skikne, who later renamed himself Laurence Harvey. Harvey went through a similar process of shedding the skin of his South African past and becoming completely accepted as English, though his perfectly modulated vowels made him a completely different type of Englishman to Sid.

Sid quickly gained acceptance on the British acting scene, picking up stage work and small acting roles, the first of his many film appearances coming with the 1947 film *Black Memory*. On screen, Sid specialised at this stage in roles such as barmen, gamblers, taxi drivers, and non-commissioned military officers. There was plenty of this kind of work around in the British film scene as the 1950s rolled around, and he could also approximate a reasonably convincing American accent, which came in handy occasionally. Sid was perfectly happy with this sort of work, making decent money playing small roles in a lot of different productions and taking a few stage parts. He was a much-appreciated regular in British films, but on the surface was never the type of actor who would normally become a star, or that would even seek to become one. In fact, he clearly had the potential to become a dramatic star, as can be seen from the strong roles Exclusive Films (which were soon to become much better known as Hammer Films) gave Sid in films such as *The Man in Black* (1950) and *The House Across the Lake* (1954).

This began to change on 2 November 1954, when the first episode of radio comedy *Hancock's Half Hour* was broadcast on the BBC Light Programme. Hancock was already a big name thanks to his stage and radio appearances, but *Hancock's Half Hour* became a popular sensation, making stars not only out of the already popular Tony Hancock, but also his co-stars Kenneth Williams and Sid James. This only intensified when the BBC began making the series for television as well as radio. Hancock eventually had Kenneth Williams' role eliminated from the show, frustrated that Williams was getting big laughs from his popular catchphrases, a type of comedy he was keen to move away from. It was a much bigger shock when Hancock had Sid's character dropped from the series after the 1960 run of episodes. The two had great comedic chemistry and the show's writers Ray Galton and Alan Simpson had become masters at writing for the two characters, whose interplay became the heart of the series.

It was a terrible blow to Sid, but his break-up with Hancock turned out to be a surprisingly good move professionally. The BBC, and Galton & Simpson, were extremely keen to develop a solo vehicle for Sid, and eventually came up with *Citizen James*, which ran from 1960 to 1962. This and the BBC's next series for him, the 1963–4 comedy/drama *Taxi*, kept Sid in the public eye without hitting the heights of popularity he had reached with Hancock. This mattered little to an actor with a full diary of movie assignments and who had become the acknowledged head of the Carry On troupe of actors after being introduced in 1960's *Carry On Constable*. Quite unexpectedly, Sidney James was now a leading man, though he remained happy to keep his hand in doing bit parts from time-to-time, including a tiny role as a mortuary attendant in the 1966 spy thriller *Where the Bullets Fly*.

When Sid finally did manage to land a hit television series, it was for the BBC's commercial rivals ITV, and again it was as part of a comic partnership, opposite Peggy Mount in the 1966–68 programme *George and the Dragon*.

Years of overwork, booze, and cigarettes caught up with him, however, and he had a serious heart attack while making the series. On his recovery, Sid returned to the Carry Ons, though his role in *Carry On Doctor* was reduced and his character largely confined to bed. Soon, Sid returned to a furious pace of work, taking on stage shows, Carry On movies and television work. This included the TV series that he would be remembered for in later years, the domestic situation comedy *Bless This House*. This was something of a change for Sid, his family man character replacing the old bird-chasing image that was starting to look a little undignified for a man approaching the age of sixty.

The success of *Bless This House* and his association with the Carry On films series meant that Sid James was one of Britain's biggest stars by the mid-1970s, so much so that his filming and touring schedule meant that Sid was not free to appear in *Carry On Behind*. By the time filming began on 1976's *Carry On England*, Sid was busy touring with the stage farce *The Mating Season*. Sid was performing in this at the Empire Theatre, Sunderland, when he suffered a fatal heart attack while on stage. He was a mere sixty-two years of age and Britain mourned the passing of a much-loved star.

Kenneth Connor

B. 6 June 1918
D. 28 November 1993
Carry On Film Appearances: 17

Kenneth Connor was born during the dying months of the First World War, the son of a royal naval officer. John Francis Connor was no ordinary sailor: not only was he was chief petty officer on the Royal Yacht *Victoria and Albert*, he was also a leading light of navel concert parties. On one of these theatrical occasions, the two-year-old Kenneth Connor made his stage debut, playing the role of an organ grinder's monkey. On leaving the navy, John Connor ran a pub on the Old Portsmouth Road, where Kenneth worked while also taking drama and elocution lessons.[9] The young Kenneth showed clear evidence of talent and was awarded a scholarship to study at the Central School of Drama, which was at this point based at London's Royal Albert Hall. There he studied alongside classmates such as the future Doctor Who Patrick Troughton.

Connor left Central in 1936, having been awarded the school's gold medal, but his fledgling career was interrupted by the outbreak of the Second World War, just at the point when he was starting to make an impression, including a role in the popular BBC Radio comedy *Bandwaggon*. He was drafted into the army, where he served a long, six and a half year stint, his service including being rescued from the beach at Dunkirk. Eventually, he was posted to the

15th Scottish Regiment, in order to appear in their concert parties, and there, he met his future wife Micky; the pair were married within six months.

Once the war was over in 1945 and Connor was eventually demobbed, he was invited to join the prestigious Bristol Old Vic theatre company. He stayed at Bristol for eighteen months, which was followed by a breakthrough into a London acting scene he had been absent from for over seven long years, with a nine month stint at the London Old Vic. This was followed by quite a fallow period, eventually broken by a good role in *Queen Elizabeth Slept Here*, which ran at the Strand Theatre in London's West End from 3 November 1949, starring theatrical husband and wife team Michael Denison and Dulcie Gray. The show was written by none other than Talbot Rothwell, who transposed George S. Kaufman and Moss Hart's show *George Washington Slept Here* to a British setting.

This was followed by a starring role in *Waggonload o' Monkeys*, a stage farce by none other than R. F. Delderfield, who would soon write the screen treatment *The Bull Boys*, which was eventually transformed into *Carry On Sergeant*. Two performers in Delderfield's farce got better reviews than the play itself: Kenneth Connor and another future Carry On star Esma Cannon. While this production had a shorter than anticipated run, as the Savoy Theatre had to make room for Noël Coward's play *Relative Values* and no alternate venue could be found, it pointed the way to Connor's immediate future, as the production was broadcast on BBC Radio. Kenneth Connor's skill at accents had become noted by this point, and he was recruited for the cast of the hugely popular radio comedy *Ray's A Laugh*, starring future *Carry On Teacher* star Ted Ray. He was replacing Peter Sellers who was also splitting his time between radio's *The Goon Show* and his swiftly developing film career. Connor was so skilled that he was even drafted in to fill in on *The Goon Show* on a couple of occasions when Sellers was ill. His association with the Goons also reached to television, where Connor appeared in three series in 1956 for ITV contractor Associated-Rediffusion starring Goons Peter Sellers and Spike Milligan: *The Idiot Weekly, Price 2d, A Show Called Fred* (from whence came the famous Goon Show single *The Ying Tong Song*), and its successor *Son of Fred*.

Connor's ability as a master voice artist made him perfect for a young producer of childrens' puppet series called Gerry Anderson, who would go on to great things with shows such as *Stingray* and *Thunderbirds*. It was quite a coup for such a small company to attract Kenneth Connor for the series *Torchy the Battery Boy* and *Four Feather Falls* and he proved a great choice, providing eight different regular voices for the first series and seven for the latter.

Kenneth Connor's film career was extremely sporadic before he became one of the original Carry On cast members—though he had appeared in a small role in the Harry Seacombe star vehicle *Davy*, which was released in January

1958 and represented another link with the Goons. *Carry On Sergeant* represented by far Connor's biggest movie role to that date. Although he never ascended to the status of a cinematic leading man, the film put Kenneth Connor on the map, turning him from a respected comedy actor into a star name on both big and small screens. In the wake of the success of the early Carry On films, there was a run of low-budget, high-energy British comedy films featuring Kenneth Connor and various other Carry On cast members. In 1960, Connor had a major role opposite Bob Monkhouse and Eric Barker in *Dentist In The Chair*, which was followed a year later by a sequel, *Dentist On The Job*, reuniting this trio and also featuring Charles Hawtrey in a cameo role. Also in 1960, Peter Rogers and Gerald Thomas cast Connor in *Watch Your Stern*, a naval lark featuring about half the *Carry On Nurse* cast plus Sid James, while in the very busy year of 1961, Connor featured in four films, plus the aforementioned *Dentist* sequel. This included a starring role in *Nearly A Nasty Accident*, in which he was second billed behind Jimmy Edwards, but got to sing the theme song, which was released as a single. In *What A Carve Up!*, Connor got to form a double act with Sid James in a horror comedy that has become a staple of British television and was the subject of a best-selling satirical novel of the same title in 1994 by author Jonathan Coe.

Connor also starred in two situation comedies, which happened to be the first products of the renowned writing duo of John Esmonde and Bob Larby. The first was *Spare A Copper*, which debuted on the BBC Light Programme radio network in 1965 and featured Connor as PC Albert Hereward Lamp, paired with Deryck Guyler as his desk sergeant. After making his name in radio, this was Connor's first leading role in a radio series, reflecting his new, higher profile in the twilight years of a medium which had been overtaken by television as a source of popular entertainment. Connor and Guyler returned in *Room At The Bottom*, another Esmonde and Larby sitcom. This time the production was for television, debuting on BBC 1 in March 1967, with Connor and Guyler as part of an ensemble cast including Gordon Rollings and Kenny Lynch.

Kenneth Connor also had a parallel career as a star supporting actor on the West End Stage. It was this which kept him away from the Carry Ons for six years between *Carry On Cleo* in 1964 and *Carry On Up The Jungle* in 1970. In that time, Connor had long runs in two West End musical comedies—*A Funny Thing Happened on the Way to the Forum* and a show that reunited him with Harry Seacombe, *The Four Musketeers!* The former in particular was a huge success, running at the Strand Theatre for almost three years, opening on 3 October 1963 and closing on 31 July 1965. Frankie Howerd played the lead role, while Connor took the second lead (gaining many of the best reviews) as Hysterium, slave to Senex, played by former Crazy Gang member 'Monsewer' Eddie Gray. While the show was a great success, all was not well behind the scenes, with Connor, Howerd, and Gray not getting on well at all, co-star Isla Blair reporting that they 'would sabotage each other any way they could.'[10] Despite the strain of appearing in the show, Connor certainly seemed to bear the production itself no ill-will, as he directed the touring version which began on the closure of the West End version in 1965. His role of Hysterium was taken over by none other than Charles Hawtrey, while stand-up comedian turned actor Dave King took on Frankie Howerd's lead role.

By the time Kenneth Connor was available to return to the Carry On films with *Carry On Up The Jungle*, he was fifty-one years of age and visibly older than when he had appeared in *Cleo* six years earlier. Talbot Rothwell was an intelligent writer as well as a joke machine, and the roles he created for Connor altered as a result of the actor's changed appearance. Instead of the nervous working class characters he had played from *Sergeant* to *Cleo*, he now portrayed rather posher, often military types. This reached its comedic peak in *Carry On Girls* in 1973 with his cherishable portrayal of ineffectual Mayor Frederick Bumble, for which he dusted off the voice he had previously used for the character of Sidney Mincing on the radio show *Ray's A Laugh* back in the 1950s.

Kenneth Connor was so adaptable as a performer that he avoided being stereotyped by his association with the Carry On films and never found himself out of work for very long, becoming a television regular, especially in the works of David Croft. He played the recurring character of Sammy Morris in Croft and Jimmy Perry's *Hi-de-Hi*, and the regular character of Monsieur Alfonse in Croft and David Lloyd's *'Allo 'Allo*. His contribution to British acting was recognised in 1991, when he was awarded the MBE in the Queen's Birthday Honours List. Kenneth Connor hated not working and in later years would lapse into severe depression when the gaps between roles became longer.[11] As a result, he worked right to the very end, recording an episode of the television quiz show *Telly Addicts* only two days before his death from cancer on 28 November 1993. An episode of *The Memoirs of Sherlock Holmes* was already in the can and would be screened five months after his death.

Peter Butterworth

B. 4 February 1915
D. 17 January 1979
Carry On Film Appearances: 15

Peter Butterworth died of a heart attack between performances as Widow Twankey in the pantomime *Aladdin* at the Coventry Theatre, an Art Deco edifice owned at that point by the EMI corporation. *Carry On Emmannuelle* had only opened in November 1978 and was still playing in some of the few cinemas that had agreed to book the sad, sorry fag end of the Carry On film series. Nothing illustrates more starkly how shockingly fast we began to lose members of the much-loved troupe of actors that populated the Carry On films once the series had run its course.

Peter Butterworth was a naturally funny actor with the wonderful ability to make what he did natural and effortless. He was blessed with a wonderfully mobile, hangdog face which allowed him to gain laughs by reacting to what was happening around him, even if the script gave him no dialogue. As such, Butterworth worked especially well when paired with another actor. He was not a traditional comic foil whom the 'funny' half of the partnership would bounce off—Peter Butterworth's reactions would easily bag half the laughs in any scene he was cast in. Thus in *Carry On Screaming*, he is paired with Harry H. Corbett, and in *Don't Lose Your Head*, he is particularly effective opposite Kenneth Williams' Citizen Camembert. Williams gets a lot of laughs, but the audience can always see him trying hard to get them, while Butterworth (who admittedly does not have the pressure of carrying the scene) is every bit as effective with nothing like the amount of visible effort. He even managed the quite incredible feat of coming away from *Carry On Emmannuelle* with a certain amount of credit.

Butterworth's first connection to the Carry On pictures came long before they even began, when he found himself an unwilling guest at Stalag Luft III in western Poland, later immortalised in the 1963 film *The Great Escape*. While there, he was introduced to the world of public performance as part of a double act with future Carry On scriptwriter Talbot Rothwell. Although these performances were at least in part designed to mask the sounds of their fellow inmates digging tunnels, Peter Butterworth had found his future career path. After the war, he set out on the variety circuit as a comedy act meeting his future wife Janet Brown during rehearsals for a Jack Hylton review in Scarborough in 1946. The pair were married the following year.

Butterworth and Brown quickly became a part of the new comedy scene that would dominate British radio and cinema in the 1950s and '60s. They were a part of the group of friends that met in the back room of the Grafton Arms pub in London's Victoria area for comedy sessions which the participants began to record and which eventually resulted in the creation of *The Goon Show*. Butterworth quickly began appearing in small movie roles from 1947, often uncredited. He did manage to score a good role in *Old Mother Riley's Jungle Treasure* in 1951, a low-budget comedy that saw him play opposite minor variety circuit royalty in the shape of Arthur Lucan, who had been performing his Irish washerwoman character opposite his wife Kitty McShane for the last quarter century.

As well as appearing as a film character actor, Butterworth was also a regular television performer from 1950 onwards, when he was part of the cast of the BBC sketch show *How Do You View?* This live sketch show featured his old pal Talbot Rothwell among the writing staff and starred Terry-Thomas. Peter featured in the 1950–51 season, while Janet Brown joined the cast for the following season. Further television work followed, with the BBC sitcom *Friends and Neighbours* in 1954 and *Those Kids*, which ran for two series on ABC Weekend Television in 1956. In 1960, he appeared in *Meet the Champ* as Sammy, the trainer of boxer Bernard Bresslaw in a BBC sitcom written by Sid Colin in attempt to duplicate the success he and Bresslaw had found with *The Army Game*. Butterworth also has a place in television history as the Meddling Monk, *Doctor Who*'s first recurring villain beyond the Daleks.

Like many comedy performers, Peter Butterworth found regular employment on BBC radio, which represented the earliest national exposure for the freshly demobilised performer in an October 1945 edition of *The Old Town Hall*. He first turned up as a regular character in the series *Happy-Go-Lucky*, playing Creep opposite a young Tony Hancock as Mr Ponsonby. By the mid-1950s, Butterworth was getting featured performer billing in his regular appearances on popular shows such as *Variety Fanfare* and *Workers Playtime*, the latter being a staple of BBC radio schedules until well into the sixties.

Peter Butterworth was a relatively late addition to the regular Carry On cast, joining the troupe with *Carry On Cowboy* in 1965, in effect replacing Kenneth Connor, who was unavailable due to his long stage run in *A Funny Thing Happened On the Way to the Forum*. He fitted in to the group immediately and loved appearing in the films, even popping in for a day's filming when he was unavailable for his usual, more substantial role. This explains why his appearances in *Carry On Again Doctor*, *Carry On Loving*, and *Carry On Henry* are so brief.

He remained in demand even when the Carry Ons began winding down in the mid-1970s. Johnnie Mortimer and Brian Cooke wrote a sitcom for him and Peter Jones in 1971, *Kindly Leave the Kerb,* with the pair playing impecunious street entertainers, and the following year he appeared in another sitcom, *A Class by Himself*, opposite John Le Mesurier. He also had a long run on BBC1 in the series *Scott On...*, a sketch show in which occasional Carry On star Terry Scott looked at different aspects of society from 1969 to 1972. Butterworth's final sitcom was rather less successful: John Inman's dire *Odd Man In*, made by Thames Television for a mercifully brief run of seven episodes in 1977.

Like many seasoned comedy performers, Peter Butterworth appeared in material that was beneath his talents, such as the aforementioned *Odd Man In* and the 1978 sex comedy *What's Up Nurse!* (more on which in the chapter in this section on his co-star Jack Douglas), but there is plenty of reason to believe that he would have continued on to better roles had his career not been curtailed by his early death at the age of sixty-three. He was a part of the stock company of director Richard Lester and had recently filmed a role in Michael Crichton's *The First Great Train Robbery*, starring Sean Connery and Donald Sutherland, which was released posthumously. His final role was the high profile and classy television production *Afternoon Off*, written by Alan Bennett and directed by Stephen Frears. This was screened by London Weekend Television on 3 February 1979, just over two weeks after Peter Butterworth's death.

Hattie Jacques

B. 7 February 1922
D. 6 October 1980
Carry On Film Appearances: 14

Born Josephine Edwina Jaques, Hattie gained her early professional reputation (and her stage name, borrowed from the American actress Hattie McDaniel, the family surname already having been amended) at the Players' Theatre, Covent Garden. This staged for many years Victorian-style music hall shows and was often chaired by Leonard Sachs, who helped bring the concept to television, transplanted to the City Varieties theatre in Leeds, as *The Good Old Days*. Her talent was recognised nationally and her career transformed after Hattie successfully auditioned for the most popular radio series of the era.

Hattie Jacques was to make her reputation on the medium of radio, featuring in three of the key productions of the golden age of British radio comedy: *ITMA*, *Educating Archie*, and *Hancock's Half Hour.* Landing a role on *ITMA* was a huge break for Hattie, so much so that a few words of explanation are needed. *ITMA*'s reputation has faded over the decades; full episodes have rarely been aired since the show went off the air in 1949 and it has gained a certain notoriety, even among comedy buffs, of being an impenetrable mixture of fast dialogue and endless catchphrases. This verdict is a little unfair, but understandable. A year after the series ended, its writer Ted Kavanagh claimed even he could not understand some of the jokes, so modern audiences can be excused a degree of bafflement.[12]

Nevertheless, *ITMA* was a genuine popular phenomenon, its characters and catchphrases entering the national vocabulary and its audience topping 20 million, with an estimated 10 million worldwide.[13] The show's ten-year run only ended with the sudden death of its star Tommy Handley, an event which was regarded a national tragedy. *ITMA* thrived for two main reasons:

first, it was a much-needed pressure release at a time of war for the general public, poking fun both at the Nazis (the title stood for 'It's That Man Again', which referred to Tommy Handley, but was originally taken from a popular newspaper headline about Adolf Hitler) and at the layers of petty officialdom the British public were having to negotiate at time of war. Secondly, the series was fast on its feet, dropping popular characters before they wore out their welcome and even changing the entire format of the series several times. This meant that *ITMA* was not just a wartime phenomenon, but was still operating at full steam when its eleventh series began in September 1947, at which point Hattie was drafted into the cast.

Interestingly, although radio was clearly an audio medium, Hattie was attracting roles that referred to her size, a phenomenon that continued with her later role as Grizelda Pugh in *Hancock's Half Hour*. Hattie, the last of *ITMA*'s regular cast to join, played food-obsessed schoolgirl Sophie Tuckshop (a reference to the American singer and comedian Sophie Tucker), complete with her own catchphrase, 'but I'm alright now'. Hattie stayed with *ITMA* throughout series eleven and returned for series twelve, which began on 21 September 1948. The series was truncated when Tommy Handley died after a brain haemorrhage, three days after what would be the final episode of *ITMA* was broadcast on 9 January 1949. Handley was a generous performer and *ITMA* had a large cast, but there was no way that the series could continue. Hattie had made her mark as a radio comedian, though, and her career in this medium would continue.

Eric Sykes had seen Hattie at the Players' Theatre and had been very impressed, especially by her physical performance, which famously included her leaping into the air and landing lightly on the stage, doing the splits, 'landing as softly as a snowflake in July'.[14] Like the majority of the British population, he had heard her on *ITMA* and set about creating a character especially for her in the radio comedy he was contracted to write for the BBC. This was *Educating Archie*, which used what was on the surface the bizarre idea of creating a radio series around stage ventriloquist Peter Brough and his naughty schoolboy dummy character Archie Andrews.

The series proved a huge popular success, running for ten years and proving a training ground for some of the most popular comedians in the country in its run from 1950 to 1960. Archie was taught by a series of tutors, including Tony Hancock, Benny Hill, Bruce Forsyth, and, during Hattie's tenure on *Educating Archie*, Max Bygraves. Eric Sykes wrote the character of Agatha Dinglebody for Hattie, making her the devoted, but scatty, girlfriend of Bygraves' tutor character. Hattie left *Educating Archie* in 1955, at the end of the show's fifth series, joining the cast of another radio sitcom that would prove to be an even bigger success. *Hancock's Half Hour* had been running for three series already by the time Hattie joined the cast in 1956, steadily improving as writers

Ray Galton and Alan Simpson found their feet and developed the comedic personas of regular cast members Tony Hancock, Sid James, Bill Kerr, and Kenneth Williams. The series had a problem finding a female character to fit comfortably into the format, with Moira Lister and Andrée Melly featured at various times as Hancock's girlfriend. The idea of Hancock in a steady relationship really did not work in the context of the sitcom, so Galton and Simpson had the brilliant notion of introducing a new type of female character in the form of Hattie Jacques as Hancock's harridan of a secretary, Griselda Pugh. Hattie's tenure on *Hancock's Half Hour* represented the peak years of the series as a radio entity.

Hattie had appeared in three legendary radio sitcoms right at the point when radio was at its height as an entertainment medium, giving her a massive popular profile. Television was displacing radio and Hattie's link with Eric Sykes allowed her to transfer to the small screen successfully. Not only did Sykes create a series with himself and Hattie as an onscreen partnership, but he made them brother and sister. With a sense of the absurd honed during his years writing scripts for *The Goon Show* with Spike Milligan, Sykes made them twins. The *Sykes* sitcom was produced in two iterations: From 1960 to 1965, it was produced as *Sykes and a ...*, with the subject matter of the episode added to each week's title. Along with Sykes and Hattie, two other top comedy actors featured in each episode: Deryck Guyler as PC 'Corky' Turnbull and Richard Wattis as the Sykes' busybody neighbour Mr Brown. This cast remained largely constant for the first three seasons and returned when the series was revived from 1972–79 under the title *Sykes*.

Hattie also maintained a career as a character player in films from the late 1940s onwards and was a natural to be drafted in to the Carry On ensemble when *Carry On Sergeant* was being made. In real life, Hattie was widely acknowledged as being a strikingly attractive woman, and the Carry Ons often made use of her unconventional sensuality in interesting ways without resorting to endless cheap fat references. She was often put into romantic pairings with Sid James, and the pair had genuine screen chemistry together. This was evident in *Carry On Constable*, where it was clear that their characters are close and their relationship will soon blossom into romance. By the time of *Carry On Cabby*, Sid and Hattie are playing a married couple, and as late as 1970s, in *Carry On Loving*, they are still together, though Sid's character has a roving eye and is doing everything possible to avoid marrying Hattie.

Hattie could play yearning and lovelorn to perfection, and both Norman Hudis and Talbot Rothwell wrote for this, not only in *Cabby* and *Loving*, but also most effectively in *Carry On Doctor*. Here we see the eruption of unrequited sexuality released by Hattie's Matron—who has no other name in her professional life, but in private moments, we learn is called Lavinia—crash helplessly against the ego of Kenneth Williams' Doctor Tinkle, who is only capable of loving himself. The joke is not at Hattie's expense, laughing at the fat lady, but instead satirises British attitudes to, and embarrassment about, sexual attraction.

Hattie's own love life was complicated. She married John Le Mesurier in 1949, but in 1962, she began an affair with another man, John Schofield. The following year, Schofield moved into the family home, while her husband moved into the spare room.[15] The situation was unendurable, and eventually, the pair divorced, but the affair ended in heartbreak for Hattie when Schofield left her for another woman while Hattie was on location in Italy for the 1966 Peter Sellers film *The Bobo*.[16] Hattie, who had previously lost 5 stone, responded to her unhappiness by comfort eating and her weight ballooned, which would have serious effects on her long-term health. By 1972, she was at her largest while filming her role in *Carry On Abroad*, and her high blood pressure meant that her role was considerably reduced. The film's insurers were so alarmed at Hattie's health that they told Peter Rogers they were no longer willing to cover her for further productions.[17] At the time, Hattie was only fifty years of age, and as a result, she only appeared in one other Carry On cinema release, 1975's *Carry On Dick*, in which she once again had a relatively minor role.

She did appear in the 1972 Christmas Carry On television show, *Carry On Stuffing*. This was to be a momentous production in the history of the films, as Charles Hawtrey walked away from the show rather than accept anything other than top billing in the absence of Sid James and Kenneth Williams. There was no way that Peter Rogers would bill Hawtrey above Hattie Jacques, who had maintained a consistent television presence throughout the 1960s and into the '70s, which continued with her association with Eric Sykes.

She worked less as the 1970s continued and her health began to decline, Hattie's maladies including the aforementioned high blood pressure, plus pain from kidney tumours, which thankfully turned out to be benign—arthritis and ulcerated legs. Though their personal relationship deteriorated somewhat in later years, her work with Sykes, both on television and in touring stage productions, kept her in the public eye.[18] In fact, from 1975 onwards, virtually all Hattie's television work was for Eric Sykes, the final of these being a short appearance in the silent comedy *Rhubarb, Rhubarb*, which was screened by Thames Television on 15 December 1980, just over two months after Hattie's death from a heart attack on 6 October the same year.

Bernard Bresslaw

B. 25 February 1934
D. 11 June 1993
Carry On Film Appearances: 14

Bernard Bresslaw was, for this writer's money, the best actor among the Carry On regulars. Trapped by his own 6-foot 7-inch frame into a screen career largely spent playing slow-witted oafs, he proved himself capable of so much more. He did so via a stage career which spanned everything from pantomime to the classics of theatre and, happily for us, in a surprisingly varied set of Carry On roles. Peter Rogers and Gerald Thomas were intelligent filmmakers and knew what they had in Bresslaw. In their constant quest to get value for money, they played to the strengths of their ensemble casts and were not about to waste the talents of an actor of Bernie's range. Thus, as well as playing characters such as *Carry On Camping*'s Bernie Lugg and *Carry On At Your Convenience*'s Bernie Hulke, who are perfectly described by their names, Talbot Rothwell also wrote him big, villainous roles that utilised the actor's screen presence and hard-won facility with accents. These included *Follow That Camel*'s Sheikh Adbul Abulbul and *Carry On Up The Khyber*'s Bungdit Din. A late-period highlight was Bresslaw's turn as Sir Roger Daley in *Carry On Dick*—angry, upper class and always the victim of Big Dick Turpin's highway robberies.

Bernard Bresslaw was born in Stepney, in London's East End, and first gained a taste for acting while at school, encouraged by one of his teachers. He won a scholarship to RADA, against the advice of his father, who wanted his son to join him in the tailoring trade. The young student actor quickly gained attention for his hard work and acting skills, rather than his height, though both were probably factors in Laurence Olivier's picking him to play an Irish wrestler in a production of Gerald McLarnen's *The MacRorty Whirl*. On graduating from RADA with the school's most promising actor award, Bresslaw's career plans were delayed by two years of National Service, during which he was a driver/clerk for the Royal Army Service Corps. The military life stayed with him even after Bernie was discharged from the services, as one of his first professional acting jobs was in a repertory theatre company touring army and RAF bases.

He soon began picking up stage roles and even broke into movies. His height, allied to a frame which at this stage could pass as required for either slim and athletic or comedically thin, gave Bresslaw a unique screen presence which was soon spotted by casting directors. One of these early roles was in the 1956 Norman Wisdom comedy *Up In The World*. Wisdom was a huge film star at the time, with audiences queueing around the block to see each of his films, and this one was no exception. At one point, Wisdom's window cleaner character is sent to jail for twenty-five years, a prison sentence which so impresses his cellmates that he is immediately appointed their leader. Bernard plays Williams, one of the cellmates. He was fortunate in appearing in the best sequences of what was rather a disappointing film for one made at the height of Norman Wisdom's career. While an overconfident Wisdom overplays throughout, Bresslaw draws the attention by underplaying his role with a slow-witted drawl. This proved pivotal to his future career when he was spotted by scriptwriter Sid Colin, who attended a screening of *Up in the World*.[19]

Colin was at that point in the middle of creating the sitcom *The Army Game* for Granada Television and immediately set about writing a character specifically for Bresslaw. *The Army Game* debuted on 19 June 1957 and proved to be the ITV network's first major comedy hit, with Bresslaw's Private 'Popeye' Popplewell being the breakout popular character with the wider public. Bresslaw found himself an instant star with his own ITV comedy special, a top ten hit single ('Mad Passionate Love', which reached number six in September 1958), and a catchphrase that would stick with him for years. The Popeye character was seen as so central to the popularity of the series that his catchphrase, 'I Only Arsked!', was used as the title of the show's 1958 big screen adaptation.

The Army Game may have made Bernard Bresslaw a star, but it also typecast him in the eyes of film and television casting directors. In the wake of the series ending in 1958, the actor only managed to be cast as a regular in one other sitcom; the very Carry On-adjacent 1961–2 series *Our House*, which also starred Hattie Jacques, Charles Hawtrey, Norman Rossington, and Joan Sims. Bresslaw was unwilling to spend his entire career playing variations of his *Army Game* character, and with few film and TV offers outside of the Carry On series laying outside this narrow range, he turned back to stage work.

Bernard Bresslaw was a highly intelligent man, an avid book collector who specialised in tomes on the history of London and of the theatre. He gained great satisfaction from his theatre work, which allowed him to perform some of the great works of the form from writers such as Sheridan, Chekhov, and Shaw. He never lost his love of performing in comedy and was a regular in pantomime, which he saw as being vital in attracting children to live theatre.[20] Another stage comedy turn was in the 1992 stage production *Wot A Carry On*, which played a season in Blackpool in 1992. This reunited Bresslaw with Barbara Windsor in a show written by Barry Cryer and Bernard's old RADA pal Dick Vosburgh.

The actor's health was starting to fail by this time, however. Bresslaw had one scare in the 1980s when his sight had to be saved by a pioneering operation. Thankfully, this allowed him to continue his acting career and he joined the cast of the hugely successful West End revival of the musical *Me and My Girl*, playing the part of Sir John Tremayne opposite star Gary Wilmott. He began to be plagued by heart trouble and collapsed in his dressing room waiting to go on stage in an open air production of Shakespeare's *The Taming of the Shrew* on 11 June 1993, aged only fifty-nine. The theatre world truly lost a giant of the acting profession.

Jim Dale

B. 15 August 1935
Carry On Film Appearances: 11

The Carry On films have a reasonable claim for having discovered Jim Dale and turned him into a genuine movie star. The truth is that Dale was so multi-talented and energetic that major stardom would have come his way anyway, and eventually, his talents were too many and too large to be contained by the Carry Ons. In the end, he was presented with a choice of a dialogue-free role in *Carry On Up The Jungle* or an invitation from Laurence Olivier to join the National Theatre. This was not the kind of engagement you could take the afternoons off from to shoot a few scenes at Pinewood.

Dale was born Jim Smith in Rothwell, Northamptonshire, some 80 miles north of London. Taken by his parents to see a West End stage musical, he immediately told them that he wanted to perform. Fortunately, his father had worked in theatre as a young man, even working with the great Harry Houdini, and paid for young Jim to have lessons in dance and movement to gain physical confidence for the stage. He developed a standup comedy act and performed in local talent contests, which resulted in him being discovered by Carroll Levis, a Canadian talent scout who toured the UK in hugely popular stage shows which were, in effect, a sort of forties and fifties equivalent of *Britain's Got Talent*. Levis saw in the raw young performer a talented physical comedian, and made him a permanent member of the touring show.

Jim Smith, boy comedian, was starting to go places and had even made his television debut when he got the dreaded call to complete his compulsory two years of National Service. He spent almost the entire time organising entertainment at an RAF base instead of pursuing his fledgling career. Finally free of military service, he gained an agent, Stanley Dale, and trod the boards of the theatres of Britain learning his trade as a standup comedian. As there was another Jim Smith working as a comedian, Jim Dale was born, borrowing his new surname from his agent. The newly minted Jim Dale got his big break with the emergence of rock 'n' roll as a popular phenomenon in Britain. BBC Television, in its paternalistic way, latched on to this and in early 1957 began a show to feature this new music: *Six-Five Special*. Dale was hired as a warm-up act and so impressed the producers that they made him a regular performer on the show. There was such a dearth of rock 'n' roll singers in Britain that any potential talent in this area was leapt upon, and Jim Dale found himself no longer a comedian, but instead a singer. He was noticed by a young recording manager newly hired by EMI called George Martin, and together the pair recorded a number two hit single, *Be My Girl*.

Being a pop star was not to Dale's taste, however, and he eventually announced his intention to return to comedy. By now, however, he was in the position of having appeared extensively on television and radio to promote his record releases, and immediately was offered an afternoon TV show by ITV contractor Southern Television. This was titled *Take it Easy*, running three times a week featuring Dale as compère and singer but also performing in comedy sketches written by himself and Dick Vosburgh. He had also picked up some film experience, turning up on the 1958 movie spin-off of *Six-Five Special* and playing a very small role in the 1961 Peter Rogers and Gerald Thomas production *Raising the Wind*. This proved pivotal to Dale's future career, as a quick on-set ad-lib impression of that film's co-star Kenneth Williams led Williams to enthusiastically recommend Dale be cast in the Carry Ons.

Dale was immediately put to work in the upcoming slate of Peter Rogers/ Gerald Thomas productions, with roles in *Nurse on Wheels*, *The Iron Maiden*, and *Carry On Cabby*. He was a quick study and by the time of *Carry On Cleo* in 1964, Dale had become a key member of the team. He filled a vital role in the films which allowed the Carry Ons to move into spoofs of popular adventure movies: as well as being a gifted physical comedian, Dale was also a charming and handsome leading man. The development of Jim Dale's potential completed the classic line-up of the Carry On series' glory years. His time with the films only lasted until 1969, ending with his rejecting the part of Jungle Boy in *Carry On Up The Jungle*, which was released in 1970. By this point, his talents had been recognised elsewhere; Dale had already won an Oscar nomination in 1967 for his lyrics from the theme song to the film *Georgy Girl*. This was co-written with Tom Springfield, brother of singer Dusty Springfield, and was a top five hit in both the UK and USA for the Seekers.

Dale was also gaining major success on the stage, starring in *Scapino*, for which he also wrote the music and co-wrote the script. This proved a highly important role for Dale, opening a lot of doors for him. He was invited to open the then-new Young Vic theatre company in the production, which so impressed Laurence Olivier that he was asked to join The National Theatre. There he appeared in Peter Nichols' remarkable *The National Health* (and its 1973 film adaptation), in which the cast appear in both a jet-black comedy drama set in a crumbling English hospital, and a bizarre glossy soap opera patterned after the television hit *Doctor Kildare*. *Scapino* transferred to Broadway during 1974 and 1975, establishing Jim Dale as an American star. He was signed by Walt Disney to a three-picture deal, starring as the villainous Doctor Terminous in *Pete's Dragon* (1977), a triple role in the Western comedy *Hot Lead and Cold Feet* (1978), and again as the villain, playing Sir Mordred in 1979's *The Spaceman and King Arthur*. This was a science fiction spin on Mark Twain's *A Connecticut Yankee in King Arthur's Court*, and it was a mark of the uncertainty afflicting the Disney organisation in the wake of *Star*

Wars that the film was retitled *Unidentified Flying Oddball*, which served merely to make the film less appealing.

Attempts to make Jim Dale a film star largely ended at this point, mainly because the actor simply didn't have the time. He landed a huge personal success in the title role of *Barnum*, which tested his physical and vocal skills to the full, and stayed with the role from opening night in April 1980 until October 1981. Although there was a highly successful London production of the show, Dale never performed the role in his native land, being busy with the Broadway version while Michael Crawford played P. T. Barnum on the West End stage, patterning his performance after Jim Dale's original interpretation. Dale moved permanently to New York, appearing in stage productions and becoming a renowned reader of talking books, most famously vocalising the entire Harry Potter novel series for their American releases. He returned to Britain occasionally, taking on the role of Fagin in 1995 for a revival of Lionel Bart's *Oliver!* at the London Palladium and touring in a one-man show about his own life, *Just Jim Dale*. In 2003, he was awarded the MBE in the Queen's Birthday Honours for his work in promoting children's English literature.

Barbara Windsor

B. 6 August 1937
D. 10 December 2020
Carry On Film Appearances: 10

The phrase 'national treasure' is overused, but most certainly applied to Dame Barbara Windsor. Her remarkable life and incredibly durable career made her, if anything, a bigger star in the twenty-first century than she had been at the height of her Carry On fame. She was a true East End girl, born in Shoreditch on 6 August 1937. The young Barbara Deeks was evacuated to Blackpool during the war, where she attended dance classes, and as a result on her return home was sent to drama school by her mother. At the age of fifteen, in September 1952, Barbara made her West End theatre debut in the musical *Love From Judy*. At this point, the young actress was still billed under her birth name of Deeks—she changed her name to Windsor the following year, an appropriate choice in the year of the queen's coronation.

As well as acting, Windsor sang with Ronnie Scott's jazz band and later performed at Scott's famous jazz club, experience which stood her in good stead a few years later when she successfully auditioned for Joan Littlewood's now legendary theatre company. The road to stage and screen success began, however, with some far smaller film roles, one of which proved especially important. Windsor was cast in August 1959 in *Too Hot to Handle* (aka

Playgirl After Dark). This rather uncomfortable collision between film noir and musical was made as a vehicle for Jayne Mansfield, whose career as a pound shop Marilyn Monroe had by this point begun to fade. Thus she was packed off to England to make two cheap thrillers, *Too Hot to Handle* and director John Gilling's *The Challenge*. Barbara was cast in *Too Hot to Handle*, at the age of twenty-two, as Pony Tail Swanson, an underage dancer at Leo Genn's Soho nightclub the Pink Flamingo. This was a big opportunity for Windsor, but was not a happy experience, with Mansfield unfriendly on set and the production becoming notorious for actors not being paid.[21] Despite La Mansfield not welcoming the competition, Windsor actually had the best dramatic role in the picture, in spite of her sporting a strange accent which sinks somewhere in the middle of the Atlantic.

At the end of each day's filming, Windsor would meet up with East End acting chums such as James Booth and regale them with stories from the Borehamwood set of *Too Hot to Handle*. Many of this social group were associated with Joan Littlewood, and word got back to her about the tiny actress from Shoreditch with a huge personality. Littlewood cast her in a major role in her 1960 West End musical *Fings Ain't Wot They Used T'be*, and rehired her for the successful 1963 movie *Sparrows Can't Sing*. In the same year, she performed in Littlewood's First World War musical *Oh What A Lovely War* and stayed with the production when it crossed the Atlantic and played on Broadway.

Another film role, as Bikini in the crime comedy *Crooks in Cloisters*, not only demonstrated her newly won star power, with Windsor getting second billing behind Ronald Fraser, but also put her on the radar of Peter Rogers and Gerald Thomas, who needed a replacement for the out-of-favour Liz Fraser for the upcoming *Carry On Spying*. Barbara fitted in with the team immediately, both on-screen and off, becoming especially fond of Kenneth Williams and Charles Hawtrey. Her stage career meant that Windsor would not return to the series until 1967's *Carry On Doctor*, at which point she became a true series regular, sticking with the films until 1974's *Carry On Dick* and the following year's television series *Carry On Laughing*.

Her later time in the Carry Ons was increasingly marred, by the account in her autobiography, by Sid James' increasingly obsessive love for her and their eventual affair. This was despite the fact that both parties were married, Windsor to notorious London gangland figure Ronnie Knight, a fact which could have put Sid in some considerable physical danger. Fortunately, the marriage was already in trouble and Knight appears not to have been the jealous type.[22]

Barbara's reputation with the public proved bulletproof, surviving the bad publicity of her association with Knight, their marriage surviving for twenty-one years despite affairs on both sides. Windsor's testimony was partly responsible for Knight being acquitted in 1980 of ordering the murder of Alfredo Zomparelli, who had killed his brother David Knight during a fight.[23] In his 1997 book *Memoirs and Confessions*, Knight went on to claim that the charge was actually true. By the time Windsor finally divorced Knight, he was living in Spain, on the run from the British authorities for his part in the 1983 robbery of a Security Express depot, in which almost £6 million was stolen. When his funds began to run out, Knight returned to the UK and was jailed for seven years.[24]

Barbara Windsor continued working throughout, enjoying the challenge of working with the new breed of comedians who emerged in the 1980s. Like many of the Carry On regulars, her career declined somewhat after the films ended, but she gained a huge new following, becoming more famous and feted than ever before, when in 1994 she was cast as matriarch Peggy Mitchell in the BBC's popular soap opera *EastEnders*. This role both traded on the image created by her personal life and allowed her to cast off the bubbly, giggly image of her Carry On character, proving her worth instead as a serious actress. She played the role, on and off, for twenty-two years.

Sadly, by this point, Windsor had been diagnosed with Alzheimer's disease, and she died on 10 December 2020 at the age of eighty-three. Happily, opportunities had been taken before this to make clear to Barbara just what a beloved national figure she was. She was made an MBE in the 2000 New Year Honours, and in 2016 was granted the greatest honour available to her, becoming a dame of the British Empire.

Patsy Rowlands

B. 19 January 1931
D. 22 January 2005
Carry On Film Appearances: 9

Patsy Rowlands was one of those valuable performers who made every single production on stage, cinema screen or television she appeared in better by her presence. Even in productions that attracted otherwise disappointing reviews, Patsy would almost invariably be singled out for praise. A perfect example of this phenomenon is this excerpt from a mixed (at best) review in *The Times* of the 1964 stage show *Chaganog* at the Vaudeville Theatre. The anonymous reviewer wrote: 'Miss Rowlands, with her pale moon face and enormous, melancholy eyes, has the classic clown's mask already and knows just what to do with it ... She is quite irresistable'.[25]

Her range was vast, illustrated by her huge experience in musical theatre, serious drama, and broad comedy. For example in late 1962, Rowlands opened opposite Laurence Olivier in a production of David Turner's *Semi Detached* at the Saville Theatre, London, a huge contrast to her very next West End theatre role, replacing Joan Sims in the lead role of the Brian Rix farce *Instant Marriage*.

Patricia Amy Rowlands was born in Palmers Green, North London. She was sent by her parents to an elocution teacher, a popular practice in the early and mid-twentieth century, when a working class accent could be a serious impediment to acceptance in many types of employment. The tutor saw potential in the young Patsy as advised her to take up acting. Subsequently, she won a scholarship to the Guildhall School of Music and Drama in the city of London. She proved an apt pupil and began picking up professional work in touring musical theatre productions. Patsy's West End debut came in 1958, at the bottom of the cast list in writer Sandy Wilson's musical *Valmouth*, which proved a hit with both critics and audiences and made a star of Fenella Fielding.

Patsy was establishing herself as a valuable stage performer, and in the sixties spent several years as a regular at the Players' Theatre, that purveyor of Victorian-style music hall entertainment for which Hattie Jacques was a star for many years. Patsy also began gaining roles for highly regarded art theatre companies such as the Royal Court, for whom she performed in their original production of writer N. F. Simpson's absurdist comedy *One Way Pendulum* in 1959. This adaptability to a wide range of roles would become a hallmark of the actress's long theatre career.

Her West End theatre career was interrupted for a decade from the mid-1960s when the television and film work she had been gaining since the end of the fifties became her primary focus. An actress with such great range and a formidable reputation as a comedy performer was not about to escape the attention of Peter Rogers and Gerald Thomas, and she accepted their offer to appear in 1969's *Carry On Again Doctor* in the memorable role of Miss Fosdick. Patsy quickly became a vital member of the Carry On ensemble, staying with the films until 1975's *Carry On Behind*. At the same time as appearing in Carry On movies, she was also a recurring cast member in Sid James' extremely popular ITV sitcom *Bless This House* as Betty, Sid, and Jean Abbot's neighbour. She repeated this role in the 1972 film version of the series produced by Peter Rogers and directed by Gerald Thomas, though the role of her husband Trevor was recast for the occasion, Anthony Jackson being replaced by Carry On performer Peter Butterworth.

With the decline in British film production from the mid-1970s, Patsy was able to return to the stage, and it is typical of her stature in the stage world that she was immediately signed up for a high-profile production of Chekhov's *The Seagull*, directed by famed cinema and stage director Lindsay Anderson. Patsy became a part of the furniture of the British acting scene: never getting the starring role but instead being a vital ingredient in the glue that held together innumerable productions. She won regular parts in numerous sitcoms: even while *Bless This House* was still running, she was part of the ensemble cast of ATV's popular 1974–6 office-based comedy *The Squirrels*. Patsy was also a regular in *Quatermass* writer Nigel Kneale's strange 1981 SF comedy *Kinvig* and spent two seasons opposite Thora Hird in Yorkshire Television's Salvation Army comedy *Hallelujah*.

Alongside these and other regular roles she guest starred in everything from *Supergran*, *Juliet Bravo* and *Bottom*, Roman Polanski's 1979 film *Tess* and even an occasional recurring role in children's favourite *Rainbow*. In her final decade, Patsy Rowlands' career in musical theatre blossomed; in 1990, she had been part of the cast of the first West End production of Stephen Sondheim and James Lapine's *Into the Woods,* and four years later, she appeared in Sam Mendes' lavish London Palladium revival of *Oliver!* That show had been produced by impresario Cameron Mackintosh, who also backed what would be Patsy's final theatrical production before illness prevented her from working—the Olivier Award-winning 2001 revival of *My Fair Lady* directed by Trevor Nunn at the Royal National Theatre.

It was a tragedy that Patsy Rowlands' death in 2005, just days after her seventy-fourth birthday, prevented this consummate professional, multi-talented actress, from achieving her ambition of retiring from the stage and instead teaching a new generation of actors.[26] Instead, she continues to inspire with her vast storehouse of performances in a career well spent.

Jack Douglas

B. 26 April 1927
D. 18 December 2008
Carry On Film Appearances: 9

The last of the regular cast members Carry On to join the film series, Jack Douglas was in some ways an unusual choice for Peter Rogers and Gerald Thomas. He had very little previous screen acting experience, save for a small role in director Don Chaffey's 1961 comedy *Nearly A Nasty Accident*. Although Jimmy Edwards was top billed, this was, interestingly, one of the group of comedies made in the wake of the early Carry On films reuniting various cast members, in this case Kenneth Connor, Shirley Eaton, Eric Barker, and Cyril Chamberlain.

Jack Douglas was a creature of the stage, coming from a showbusiness family, and was stage struck from an early age. He was born John Douglas Roberton, the son of a stage director and producer. He was technically a

Geordie, being born in Newcastle at the insistence of his mother, despite the family having settled in London.[27] The young Jack wanted nothing more than to work in the theatre, paying close attention to every detail of his father's work. Roberton senior tried his best to discourage such ambitions, with such spectacular lack of success that not only did Jack dedicate his life to acting, but his other son Bill became a theatre director, going on to direct the stage show *Carry On London*.

Jack was a theatre natural and accidentally fell into a double act as straight man to Joe Baker after standing in as an emergency replacement for a stage show the two were both appearing in when another performer had a heart attack. The tall, slim Douglas and the tubby Baker made a visually funny pairing and the pair stayed together for ten years, playing Butlins holiday camps in Britain and touring the world. They also spent a period as resident comedians on the BBC's long-running children's TV series *Crackerjack*. By the mid-1960s, however, Baker had broken through as a solo star, appearing in the sitcoms *Fire Crackers* (1964–5) *My Man Joe* (1967), and *Baker's Half Dozen* (1967). His popularity soon faded, and by the early 1970s, Joe was more familiar from a series of washing powder adverts, so he tried his luck in America, where he lived out his days until his death in 2002 as a busy character actor, comedy performer, and voice artist on US films and television.

Baker's erstwhile comedy partner Jack Douglas, meanwhile, was keen on becoming a solo comedian after the double act ended, but he was advised by his agent Leslie Grade against such a move.[28] This was despite the fact that by this point, Douglas had developed his signature character, the slightly dim northerner Alf Ippititimus with his huge nervous twitch. The character had its roots in an on-stage incident where Joe Baker was supposed to enter the stage to join Jack from the audience, but had accidentally been locked out of the theatre. Forced to fill in, Douglas ad-libbed a nervous twitch based on a bandleader he knew from the variety circuit. By the time Baker finally got on stage, he was surprised to see his straight man getting more laughs than their regular act normally did.[29]

Somewhat disheartened, Jack even left showbusiness for a short while, becoming a restauranteur in Blackpool. His career really took off soon after when popular singer and comedy performer Des O'Connor contacted him with an offer of work in his television series being made for Lew Grade's ATV. O'Connor, a perennially underrated performer whose career proved incredibly durable, had a variety show running on ATV from 1963 to 1973, which with Douglas on board went from strength to strength. The pair proved an instant hit, playing together after the show's first season in a lavish version of *Humpty Dumpty* at the Leeds Grand Theatre co-written by David Croft for the 1964–5 pantomime season. Even more prestigious assignments followed, with O'Connor and Douglas appearing together on the 1966 Royal

Variety Show, and they were featured on coast-to-coast American television on the enormously influential *Ed Sullivan Show*, the very same series that had catapulted The Beatles to US success. Even better, Lew Grade sold *The Des O'Connor Show* to the American NBC network to shown in the summers of 1970 and 1971 under the title *Kraft Music Hall.*

Seeing the arrival of Jack Douglas into the Carry On cast in this context is very interesting. Perhaps, if he could be successfully transplanted into the existing roster of actors, this most English and provincial-appearing of comedy performers could help Peter Rogers recapture the American market. It was certainly worth a shot, and in 1972, he was cast in what amounted to a cameo role in 1972's *Carry On Matron*. This proved successful enough for Douglas to become a regular feature of the 1970s Carry On crew, his roles in the films growing increasingly large as other cast members left the series. He also appeared in five roles in the 1973 *Carry On Christmas* TV special and was almost ever-present in the 1975 television series *Carry On Laughing*. Douglas was also in the eighteen-month run of the *Carry On London* stage review at the Victoria Palace Theatre, London from 1973 to 1975, his star appeal reflected in a very prominent spot on the publicity poster. Jack also featured in the *Carry On Laughing* stage show that played in Scarborough over the summer season of 1976, taking top billing over Kenneth Connor, Peter Butterworth, and Liz Fraser.

Oddly, it is easiest to see what Jack Douglas brought to the Carry On films through the lens of a film in which he appeared outside the series. *What's Up Nurse!* was released to the every-declining number of still operating British cinemas from May 1977, in that fallow year between the unsuccessful release of *Carry On England* in 1976 and the even more unsuccessful release of *Carry On Emmannuelle* in 1978. The cheapness of the film's production is visible in every frame and the jokes have a very familiar feel to them, to the extent that the operation scene from *Carry On Doctor* is lifted wholesale. Like many cheap British comedies of this period, *What's Up Nurse!* occupies an uneasy middle-ground between bawdy comedy and outright soft porn and managed to secure the services of an astonishing array of British comedy actors. Some are clearly there to grab the cheque and run—Cardew Robinson's role must have taken most of an afternoon to film, and he approaches the task with a distinct lack of enthusiasm.

Jack Douglas, on the other hand, turns up at a fairly late stage as a police constable, sharing some scenes with Peter Butterworth as his sergeant. Douglas absolutely throws himself into his role, bringing some old fashioned music hall vitality to all his scenes. He winds up handcuffed to the film's hero, managing in the process to raise the performance of comedically challenged leading man Nicholas Field and lifting the tone of a desperately poor film. *What's Up Nurse!* was noticeably more successful than the last two Carry On films. A sequel, *What's Up Superdoc!* (which was even worse—I watched it so you do not have to) was released in 1978 while the original was still showing up in British cinemas as late as 1985.

While the Carry Ons had by this point passed into cinematic history, perhaps the greatest contribution Jack Douglas made to British showbusiness was yet to come. Terry-Thomas had made an increasingly good living since the end of the war as the quintessential English gentleman rotter, becoming firmly established by the 1960s as an international film star. In 1971, he was diagnosed with Parkinson's disease, which by 1980 had robbed him of the ability to work and, by 1987, along with some unwise investments in film productions, had left him penniless. Mute and ravaged by illness, the comedy legend was living in an unfurnished flat on the charity of the Actors Benevolent Fund. Word quickly got out among the acting community and Jack, along with writer Richard Hope-Hawkins, organised a gala benefit concert for Terry-Thomas on 9 April 1989. This great act of charity and kindness enabled the actor to live out his remaining days in greater comfort before his death on 9 January 1990.[30]

The 1990s proved to be an important decade for Jack Douglas. In 1996, he appeared in a production of *Me and My Gal* at the Shanklin Theatre and promptly met his future partner, Vivien, who was his leading lady in the show. Jack fell in love with both Vivien and life on the Isle of Wight. He lived there for the rest of his life and worked there often at the Shanklin Theatre, though he did take a role in *Carry On Columbus* in 1992 as Marco the Cereal Killer. He carried on working until just before his seventy-fifth birthday in 2002, though was very happy to appear at Carry On tribute events and film festivals. Jack Douglas died at the age of eighty-one on his beloved Isle of Wight on 18 December 2008.

Terry Scott

B. 4 May 1927
D. 26 June 1994
Carry On Film Appearances: 7

Terry Scott's Carry On career goes right back to the very first film in the series, *Carry On Sergeant*, but so small was his role that you would be forgiven for forgetting he was in the film at all. Scott had barely broken into film acting at this point, and while he had a solid body of work on BBC television and radio under his belt, he was by no means a star. When he came back to the Carry Ons ten years later, things were very different, and Terry Scott was a central part of the late 1960s and early '70s ensemble cast, just at the point when the series was reaching its box office peak.

Terry Scott was born Owen John Scott in Watford, Hertfordshire, the youngest of three children. Abandoning his original career path of accountancy, Scott joined the acting profession after a spell serving in the Royal Navy. He was 'discovered', along with his future comedy partner Hugh Lloyd, by the husband and wife team of Ronnie Brandon and Dickie Pounds, who ran concert parties and summer reviews under the title *Out of the Blue* from the 1930s, and again after the Second World War, continuing until the mid-1950s.[31]

He performed a successful audition for BBC radio and began appearing on the service from 1949, debuting on the 23 January edition of *Variety Bandbox*, where he was on the bill with Frankie Howerd, Jon Pertwee, and Peter Butterworth's wife Janet Brown. Scott quickly became a familiar presence on the airwaves, becoming a regular on future Carry On star Eric Barker's sitcom *Waterlogged Spa*, performing stand-up comedy on the popular *Workers Playtime* and appearing regularly on Charlie Chester's show *Stand Easy*. He made his television debut in 1951, on *The Centre Show*, though it would be 1954 before he began appearing on TV regularly. In the following year, he finally landed a starring role, opposite Bill Maynard in the series *Great Scott—It's Maynard!* Although Bill Maynard was to become famous as an actor, he started out as a comedian and had formed a partnership with Scott while the pair were performing a summer season at Butlins' holiday camp in Skegness, along with Hugh Lloyd.

While Scott was a television regular, he didn't achieve true stardom until the 1960s dawned. This was alongside Hugh Lloyd in the successful sitcom *Hugh and I*, which had its origins in Scott and Lloyd's stage act in the *Out of the Blue* shows, in which they played a pair of lodgers. In the television version, the pair were lodgers with Terry's mother, Scott very much playing Oliver Hardy to Lloyd's Stan Laurel. Written by John Chapman, *Hugh and I* ran for sixty-nine episodes over seven series, lasting from 1960 until 1967. For 1968, the format was altered and the title changed to *Hugh and I Spy,* in which Hugh wins £5,000 on the Premium Bonds and the pair go on a cruise. This results in Scott and Lloyd becoming involved in espionage in a six-episode continuing plot. For 1969, Scott and Lloyd featured in an entirely new comedy series, the downright strange *The Gnomes of Dulwich,* in which they played a pair of garden gnomes commenting on the world around them.

By 1968, Terry Scott had established himself as part of the Carry On ensemble with his role as Sergeant Major Macnutt in *Carry On Up the Khyber*. Highlights of his time with the team include his wonderfully dopey Jungle Boy in *Carry On Up the Jungle*. Although Jim Dale had been first choice for the role, the part actually proved perfect for Scott, playing on his long-running act as an overgrown schoolboy and updating it to an overgrown adolescent. His schoolboy act was best known for his popular 1962 song *My Brother*, and in the 1970s a series of television commercials for Curly Wurly chocolate bars.

Terry Scott remained with the Carry On films until 1972, in which year audiences could see him in *Carry On Matron* and the Rogers and Thomas movie spin-off of Sid James' television sitcom *Bless This House*. He also filmed a cameo role that year for *Carry On Abroad*, but this was deleted from the final print, and subsequently his TV and stage career meant Scott was simply too busy to commit to future films. In fact, Terry Scott's greatest period of popular fame was still ahead of him.

Scott had maintained a presence as a solo performer during his years with Hugh Lloyd, which on television manifested itself in the *Scott On...* series. One of BBC2's earliest comedy successes, each episode of this was centred on a different subject matter, with sketches performed by a regular cast of players. This had a run in 1964–5, written by Barry Took and Marty Feldman, then a more regular run from 1968 to 1972, which employed a roster of writers including future Carry On scriptwriter Dave Freeman. Joining the cast from 1968 was June Whitfield, who would go on to become Terry Scott's most enduring and best-loved comedic foil. In 1974, the pair recorded a pilot for a new sitcom, written by John T. Chapman (who had written not only *Hugh and I* but whose association with Terry Scott went back as far as *Great Scott—It's Maynard!*) and Eric Merriman, the latter having helped establish Kenneth Williams as a radio star by creating and writing *Beyond Our Ken*.

This was entitled *Happy Ever After*, featuring Scott and Whitfield as a middle-aged married couple who get into adventures and scrapes after their adult children leave home. This proved an immediate success after the pilot, broadcast as part of the BBC's *Comedy Playhouse* strand, was developed into a full series. *Happy Ever After* ran for forty episodes over five series until 1978, when the writers called a halt. The BBC were loath to lose such a ratings winner, thus Scott and Whitfield were quickly reteamed in the almost identical *Terry and June*, *Happy Ever After*'s domestic sitcom format being so basic that it was pretty well impossible to copyright. The British public took this 'new' show to their hearts and it gained huge audiences, running from 1979 to 1987. By the time the series finally ended it was, perhaps inevitably having run in one form or another for thirteen years, regarded as being something of an anachronism, but it had certainly had a good run.

Scott's health had become an increasing concern during *Terry and June*. He had suffered a brain haemorrhage in 1979 and his mobility had become increasingly limited, and the year after *Terry and June* ended he was diagnosed with cancer. Though he was a notoriously prickly character behind the scenes, Terry Scott was certainly a trooper, and maintained both a television and stage career throughout his illnesses. He was an accomplished performer in stage farces, appearing with June Whitfield in the original production of Dave Freeman's *A Bedfull of Foreigners, The Mating Game* (the same play in which Sid James was appearing in when he died), and *Run for your Wife*. In later years, he battled through ill-health bravely, giving an energetic performance every night on stage even though his cancer was progressing to its inevitable conclusion.

Leslie Phillips

B. 20 April 1924
D. 7 November 2022
Carry On Film Appearances: 4

Although he only appeared in three of the original Carry On films, all near the beginning of the series, Leslie Phillips was forever associated with the Carry Ons throughout an incredibly long and distinguished career.

A true icon of British acting, Leslie represents a certain type of incredibly smooth, upper middle-class Englishness so perfectly that it is probably no surprise that he was from a cockney background, the Phillips family originally hailing from Tottenham before relocating to Chingford. His father having died from a heart ailment when Leslie was aged eleven, the future course of his life was set by his mother, who encouraged young Leslie's nascent acting abilities. Leslie was accepted into the Italia Conti acting school, that famous youth academy which had previously taught Charles Hawtrey. The Phillips family having little money, young Leslie's fees were taken from his earnings from stage work that Conti found for him. Actor Jack Watling, a school friend of Phillips, was another Conti student, slightly more advanced, which made the idea of a career on the stage seem not quite so strange.

Leslie was keen and a hard worker, putting a lot of effort into losing his cockney accent, and was rewarded not only with theatre work, but with his first film role, a bit part in *Lassie from Lancashire*, a 1938 romantic comedy starring musical theatre star Marjorie Browne and directed by John Paddy Carstairs at Welwyn Studios for British National Films. He picked up more film work at the much larger-scale Denham Studios, where he had a small role in American director King Vidor's *The Citadel*, where he closely observed the film's co-star Rex Harrison, whose smooth charm was a key influence on the future screen persona of Phillips.

Still below the call-up age at the outbreak of war, Leslie picked up a lot of stage work as many other young actors went off to fight, gaining valuable experience on the West End stage as an assistant stage manager and playing small roles opposite some of the biggest stars of the era. Eventually, however, his acting career was interrupted by military service, with Phillips' acquired upper-class accent being a major factor in his being selected for officer training.

Commissioned as a second lieutenant in the Royal Artillery, he was removed from active service shortly before D-Day after being diagnosed with a neurological condition that struck Phillips with partial paralysis. Thus he found himself back in civilian life in December 1944, almost a year before the end of the war and back into a British acting scene ahead of an approaching flood of new talent. As well as theatre work in repertory companies, Leslie picked up the threads of his screen career, turning up in major productions such as *The Magic Bow* (1946) and *The Red Shoes* (1948), but in uncredited bit parts. Things improved, however, and in 1952, he got a lead role in the BBC Television sitcom *My Wife Jacqueline*, opposite Joy Shelton.

Phillips' aquiline looks, splendid comic timing and a smoothly purring voice which made him sound at time like a cat contentedly licking cream off his paws made him stand out as a very distinctive figure in the British acting scene. He also had a policy of saying 'yes' to almost any offers of work that came his way, which led to an interesting and varied career. He even had a shot at a Hollywood career when called upon to play the part of Sir Gerald Wren in director George Cukor's 1957 musical *Les Girls*, opposite Gene Kelly, Mitzi Gaynor, and his old friend Kay Kendall. Despite both him and the film being successes, Phillips decided to stay in Britain to pursue his theatre career, which ironically led to him becoming a major star in British film and radio. He became one of the stars of *The Navy Lark*, which had an astonishingly long run on BBC radio from 29 March 1959 to 16 July 1977.

Meanwhile, Leslie was sent the script for *Carry On Nurse* by his agent, the perceptive John Redway, with a note attached which read, 'The money's rubbish but it's only five weeks work. I think it's very funny. Give it a read and see what you think'.[32] Phillips agreed and signed up for the film, which not only gained him the princely sum of £500 (his entire fee for the film being his daily rate for *Les Girls*), but also two catchphrases that would stay with him for the rest of his career. 'Ding dong' made sense within the context of that film, his character being named Jack Bell, but it somehow stuck with him. The second was a simple, single word drawn out in Phillips' unique manner into an expression of lusty physical admiration: 'Hello!'

Towards the end of shooting *Carry On Nurse*, Phillips was approached by Peter Rogers, the producer full of confidence that his new film would be a big success. He wanted to keep his core cast together for the next two films—*Teacher* and *Constable*—and gave Phillips the impression that a percentage deal was in the offing.[33] After appearing in the three films, the actor was growing restive, having been contracted for the same tiny fee despite the huge success of *Carry On Nurse*, and the idea of a percentage of the profits never having been mentioned again. Money, however, was a secondary factor when Leslie Phillips decided to leave the Carry On films:

> I could see what was coming and had no intention of getting locked into an interminable series with the risk of getting totally typecast across the world. Even if there'd been a respectable deal in it, I still didn't want to know.[34]

Ironically, one factor in Phillips leaving the Carry Ons was that he had received a better offer from Peter Rogers' wife, Betty Box, to join the cast of the Doctor film series for the upcoming *Doctor in Love*, the original series stars having dropped out. Michael Craig was signed to take over from Dirk Bogarde, while Leslie Phillips became a rough approximation of Kenneth More's hale and hearty character from *Doctor in the House*. He was by now established as a film actor and greatly in demand, even returning to work for Peter Rogers a few times, demonstrating that there were no hard feelings. For *Watch Your Stern* (1960) and *Raising the Wind* (1961), he was part of an ensemble, for the latter film indulging his love of orchestral music by learning to properly conduct an orchestra, while for *No Kidding* (1960), Phillips was the undoubted star.

He rode a wave of cinema popularity into the mid-1960s, by which point changing tastes meant that the types of film comedies he thrived in were no longer being produced. Phillips had stayed busy, however, and had maintained a stage career, which took over in the latter half of the decade. He also returned to television sitcoms, scoring a hit in 1963 with the BBC production *Our Man at St. Marks* as the Rev. Andrew Parker. Sadly he lost that role on the ending of his first marriage, which the Corporation thought gave the wrong image for a fictional man of the cloth. The series ran for another three seasons with Donald Sinden in the lead role.

On stage, he had a huge success with the long-running comedy *The Man Most Likely To*, while at the same time continuing with *The Navy Lark* on BBC Radio, the sitcom *The Culture Vultures* on BBC television, and nipping off to shoot the film comedy *Some Will, Some Won't*. As Leslie Phillips grew older, he somehow managed to make his louche image work on stage and screen better than ever. In 1990, at the age of sixty-five, despite having never really been away, he made a major television comeback in the role of duplicitous bank executive Jimmy Blake in the series *Chancer*. This made him a high-profile addition to the cast of *Carry On Columbus* in 1992, a film he agreed to make out of friendship for Gerald Thomas.[35] Leslie Phillips was by now finally free of the dead hand of typecasting, accepted as a serious dramatic actor, but retaining the self-confidence to appear in the occasional comedy, such as the 1994 sitcom *Honey for Tea*. Seemingly indestructible, Leslie Phillips' career continued until 2012, by which point he had been introduced to a whole new audience as the voice of the Sorting Hat in the Harry Potter films.

36

Music Maestros: The Carry On Composers

The Short Life and Mysterious Times of Bruce Montgomery

Bruce Montgomery is a fascinating, tragic, totally unique figure in British cinema, equally famous in two different, entirely unrelated fields. As an Oxford undergraduate, he was friends with future literary stars Philip Larkin and Kingsley Amis, and at first outshone both. In 1944, while still at university, he wrote a funny, clever crime novel under the pen name Edmund Crispin. *The Case of the Gilded Fly* was published by Victor Gollancz and was immediately well-received. The young novice writer, at the age of twenty-three, was launched into the orbit of the very golden-age crime novelists that he himself deeply admired.

The witty adventures of Montgomery's hero, amateur detective and Oxford professor of English Language Gervaise Fen, ran to eight novels and a collection of short stories between 1944 and 1953. Despite the huge demand for further novels, Montgomery did not produce another in the series until 1977. By the early 1950s, his primary career had become music, and he became one of the main in-house composers employed by the Rank Organisation. He could turn his hand to many styles and lent his talents to thrillers such as *Eyewitness* and *Checkpoint* (both in 1956), but he became far better known for his comedy scores. This was partially due to the enormous success of *Doctor in the House* in 1954, and the subsequent importance of comedies to Rank's production schedules.

As well as working regularly for director Ralph Thomas on both the Doctor film series and many of his other films, Montgomery became a part of the fledgling Peter Rogers/Gerald Thomas production team, working on the producer/director team's first film together, *Circus Friends* (1956). Two years later, he provided the score for *Carry On Sergeant* and was retained as an integral part of the team for the first six films in the series. Bruce Montgomery's Carry On scores were simply wonderful, topped off by the main theme he wrote for *Carry On Sergeant*, which was retained and reworked for most of the films that he scored and which remained associated with the films long after Eric Rogers took over as the films' composer and its use ceased.

Sadly, the fact was that Bruce Montgomery had another great enthusiasm that overwhelmed his creative spark—he was an alcoholic to such an extent that he became unable to sustain the concentration required to write either a film score or a novel. The fact that credit for the score of *Carry On Cruising* in 1962 was shared with Douglas Gamley tells its own story about the troubles Montgomery was having and producer Peter Rogers never hired him again. In fact, the composer only wrote one further score, for Don Sharp's 1966 thriller *The Brides of Fu Manchu*.

Montgomery lived quietly in Totnes, Devon, the wolf being kept from the door by his continued high reputation in the field of the detective novel, despite the fact that his output was reduced to a single very short story. He was still able to edit collections of both crime stories and science fiction and was active in the writers' organisations the Detection Club and the Crime Writers Association. For many years, he was also the crime fiction reviewer of *The Sunday Times*, in which role Montgomery was very highly regarded, using his position to champion the early work of writers such as Ruth Rendell and P. D. James.[1]

Despite the much-delayed appearance of a final Gervaise Fen novel, *The Glimpses of the Moon*, some twenty-six years after the previous one ('Worth waiting for!' was emblazoned on the cover of the first edition), the fact was that his health, as well as his creative urge, had been ruined by alcohol. Bruce Montgomery died on 15 September 1978, aged only fifty-six. His death was a tragedy to both the worlds of cinema and literature and a prime example of a huge talent unfulfilled.

Eric Rogers: The Ultimate Professional Musician

Although he is best known for his composing duties on twenty-two Carry On films, Eric Rogers had a much wider musical career that put him at the centre of the British musical scene as a conductor, composer, and arranger for decades.

He was born as Eric Gaukroger in Halifax, West Yorkshire, in the north of England, but the family moved to Morriston, near Swansea in South Wales, when young Eric was only three years of age. He took to music early, and when he was thirteen, he began taking lessons from the organist at his local chapel. Within three years, Eric was playing piano as part of a nine-piece band at the Park Hall, Swansea. His fledgling musical career was interrupted by the outbreak of the Second World War, during which he trained as a pilot and flew Spitfires in Burmah. During his downtime, he kept his hand in musically by playing piano in local pubs for beer.[2]

After the war, he entered the London musical scene with great success as a talented multi-instrumentalist; Eric by this point was a talented pianist and had mastered a range of woodwind and brass instruments. As well as an expanded range of instruments, Eric also had two new surnames: professionally he became Eric Rogers, much easier to pronounce than Gaukroger, while privately he hyphenated his original name to Gauk-Roger. Setting up his own orchestra, Rogers played regularly at London's Trocadero restaurant, a grand Edwardian catering establishment which in the post-war period presented cabaret in its grill room. He also began working as an arranger and accompanist for a variety of entertainers such as the character comedian Fred Emney. This brought him into contact with the wider entertainment world, and his career in film music began.[3]

Eric Rogers composed music uncredited for dozens of British films in the 1940s and '50s, often dance hall music required for the background of scenes. Into the 1950s, Rogers' musical career began to move up a level, leaving the Trocadero for the London Palladium, first arranging ballet music and eventually rising to become musical director and resident conductor for the theatre. As his career in film music began to develop, Rogers left the Palladium to concentrate all his energies in this area. Rogers entered the orbit of Peter Rogers via Bruce Montgomery. The latter had been composing the music for the early Carry On films, but the pressures of his parallel career as a novelist and his increasing dependence on alcohol meant that he began to struggle to meet his deadlines. Montgomery began employing Rogers to compose sections of his scores, which did not go unnoticed by Peter Rogers, and by the time of *Carry On Cruising*, Douglas Gamley had been drafted in as co-composer. After composing music uncredited for the 1957 film *After the Ball*, along with the similarly anonymous Ken Jones, Eric Rogers was hired by his namesake Peter for the films *Nurse on Wheels* and *The Iron Maiden*, before being handed the composer's chair on the Carry On films permanently.

Eric Rogers became great friends with Peter Rogers, staying with the Carry On pictures until the end of their original run, stepping down only for *Carry On England*, which featured music composed by Max Harris. Eric also provided music for many of Peter Rogers' dramatic productions such as *Assault*, *Revenge*, *Quest for Love*, and *All Coppers Are....* Beyond the Peter Rogers productions, Eric Rogers' skills as a conductor gained him a huge amount of film work. It was Eric, for example, who conducted the orchestra that performed Monty Norman's score for the first James Bond film

Dr. No in 1962. A friend of Lionel Bart, a brilliant theatrical songwriter who could not read music, Rogers collaborated on the smash hit stage production *Oliver!*, turning Bart's musical ideas into a written score and full orchestral arrangement. In the early 1970s, he worked in a similar capacity for Charlie Chaplin, orchestrating and conducting several of the old comedy master's scores for rereleases of his classic silent films.

He worked with the Walt Disney studio in the 1960s on several of their British-based productions for American television, some of which were released to cinemas in the United Kingdom. This helped establish Rogers with American producers, and he became the in-house conductor for Disney's rival animation studio DePatie-Freleng throughout the 1970s. He worked on nine different series for the studio, which not only included cartoon comedies such as *The Houndcats*, made for the Saturday morning television market, but also serious science fiction adventure with *Return to the Planet of the Apes*, and superhero action cartoons *The Fantastic Four* and *Spider Woman*. For this final series, Rogers also composed the music. His last work for DePatie-Freleng, which turned out to be Rogers' final screen work, was conducting the orchestra for Joe Raposo's score on the one-off cartoon *Dennis the Menace in Mayday for Mother*, this being the American version of Dennis the Menace, with no connection to the Beano comic character.

Tragically, by the time this production was screened by the NBC network on 8 May 1981, Eric Rogers had been dead for exactly a month, passing on at the relatively young age of fifty-nine.

Endnotes

Chapter 1

1 *West London Observer*, Friday 16 August 1957.
2 'Successful Film-making on a Small Budget: Mr Peter Rogers Tells How He Does It', *The Times*, Thursday 5 November 1959.
3 *Truth*, 22 November 1957.
4 *Kinematograph Weekly*, 5 December 1957.
5 *Northern Daily Mail*, 3 August 1957.

Chapter 2

1 'Successful Film-Making on a Small Budget', *The Times*, Thursday 5 November 1959.
2 Norman Hudis quoted in Stevens, C., *Born Brilliant: The Life of Kenneth Williams* (John Murray, London, 2010), p. 116.
3 Monkhouse, B., *Crying with Laughter* (Century Random House UK, London, 1993) p. 180.

Chapter 3

1 Sharpe, G., *Gambling's Strangest Moments* (Robson Books Ltd, London, 2005), pp. 139–40.

Chapter 4

1 'Anglo Success in Jersey', *Kinematograph Weekly*, 13 August 1959.

Chapter 6

1 Bright, M. and Ross, *Mr Carry On* (BBC Worldwide, London, 2000), p. 98.
2 Goodwin, *Sid James: A Biography* (Virgin Books, London, 2011), p. 138.
3 Merriman, A., *Hattie* (Aurum Press, London, 2007), p. 102.
4 Phillips, L., *Hello* (Orion Books, London, 2006), p. 215.

5 Butters, W., *Whatshiname: The Life and Death of Charles Hawtrey* (Tomahawk Press, Sheffield, 2010), p. 157.

Chapter 7

1 Ross, R., *The Carry On Companion* (Batsford, London, 1998), p. 34.
2 Ross, A., *Too Happy a Face: The Authorised Biography of Joan Sims* (Fantom Films Ltd, Coventry, 2017), p. 68.
3 Butters, W., *Whatshiname: The Life and Death of Charles Hawtrey* (Tomahawk Press, Sheffield, 2010), p. 160.

Chapter 8

1 Williams, K., *The Kenneth Williams Diaries* (HarperCollins, London, 1993), p. 207.
2 Stevens, C., *Born Brilliant: The Life of Kenneth Williams* (John Murray, London, 2010), p. 172.
3 Merriman, A., *Hattie* (Aurum Press, London, 2007), p. 128.

Chapter 9

1 Bright, M. and Ross, *Mr Carry On* (BBC Worldwide, London, 2000), p. 120.
2 Stevens, C., *Born Brilliant: The Life of Kenneth Williams* (John Murray, London, 2010), p. 171.

Chapter 11

1 Williams, K., *The Kenneth Williams Diaries* (HarperCollins, London, 1993), p. 238.
2 *Ibid.*
3 Ross, R., *Sid James: Cockney Rebel* (JR Books Ltd, London, 2009), p. 131.
4 Stevens, C., *Born Brilliant: The Life of Kenneth Williams* (John Murray, London, 2010), p. 183.

Chapter 12

1 'Still time to buy a ticket', *Kent and Sussex Courier*, Friday 25 March 1966.
2 Note: Both of Sid James' biographers, Clive Gifford and Robert Ross, despite producing very different portraits of their subject, are in agreement about James' high opinion of *Carry On Cowboy*.
3 Ross, A., *Too Happy a Face: The Authorised Biography of Joan Sims* (Fantom Films Ltd, Coventry, 2017), p. 72.
4 Williams, K., *The Kenneth Williams Diaries* (HarperCollins, London, 1993), p. 261.
5 *Ibid.*, p. 262.
6 *Ibid.*, p. 273.

Chapter 13

1 Williams, K., *The Kenneth Williams Diaries* (HarperCollins, London, 1993), p. 271.

2 Stevens, C., *Born Brilliant: The Life of Kenneth Williams* (John Murray, London, 2010), pp. 194–198.
3 Bright, M. and Ross, *Mr Carry On* (BBC Worldwide, London, 2000), p. 141.
4 Butters, W., *Whatshiname: The Life and Death of Charles Hawtrey* (Tomahawk Press, Sheffield, 2010), p. 173.
5 See gylesbrandreth.net for the full text.

Chapter 14

1 Bright, M. and Ross, *Mr Carry On* (BBC Worldwide, London, 2000), p. 142.
2 Letter to *The Guardian*, Alexander Walker, 17 March 2000.
3 Powell, M., *Million Dollar Movie* (William Heinemann, London, 1990), pp. 401–2.
4 Williams, K., *The Kenneth Williams Diaries* (HarperCollins London, 1993), p. 288.

Chapter 15

1. Williams, K., *The Kenneth Williams Diaries* (HarperCollins, London, 1993), p. 305.
2. *Ibid.*

Chapter 16

1 Williams, K., *The Kenneth Williams Letters* (HarperCollins, London, 1994), p. 65.
2 *Ibid.*, p. 309.

Chapter 17

1 bbfc.co.uk/education/case-studies/carry-on-up-the-khyber-1968

Chapter 18

1 bbfc.co.uk/education/case-studies/carry-on-camping

Chapter 19

1 Williams, K., *The Kenneth Williams Diaries* (HarperCollins, London, 1993), p. 363.

Chapter 22

1 Quoted in Ross, R., *Sid James: Cockney Rebel* (JR Books Ltd, London, 2009), p. 184.
2 Ross, R., *Sid James: Cockney Rebel* (JR Books Ltd, London, 2009), p. 187.

Chapter 25

1 Williams, K., *The Kenneth Williams Diaries* (HarperCollins, London, 1993), p. 423.

Chapter 31

1 Williams, K., *The Kenneth Williams Letters* (HarperCollins, London, 1994), p. 150.
2 Jenour, K., 'Saucy Carry On Has Babs Fuming', *Daily Mirror*, 19 April 1978.
3 Jenour, K., 'Now Showing', *Daily Mirror*, 20 April 1978.

Chapter 32

1 *Daily Record*, 16 August 1992.

Chapter 33

1 Bright, M. and Ross, *Mr Carry On* (BBC Worldwide, London, 2000), p. 199.

Chapter 34

1 Pertwee, J. and Howe, D. J., *I Am the Doctor: Jon Pertwee's Final Memoir* (Virgin Books, London, 1996), p. 20.
2 Ross, R., *The Complete Sid James* (Reynolds and Hearn, Cheltenham, 2007), pp. 121–2.
3 Phillips, L., *Hello* (Orion Books, London, 2006), p. 228.

Chapter 35

1 Williams, K., *Just Williams* (JM Dent & Sons, London, 1985), p. 13.
2 gylesbrandreth.net/blog/2018/4/14/remembering-kenneth-williams
3 Stevens, C., *Born Brilliant: The Life of Kenneth Williams* (John Murray London, 2010), p. 333.
4 Ross, A., *Too Happy a Face: The Authorised Biography of Joan Sims* (Fantom Films Ltd, Coventry, 2017), p. 177.
5 Butters, W., *Whatshiname: The Life and Death of Charles Hawtrey* (Tomahawk Press, Sheffield, 2010), p. 63.
6 *Ibid.*, p. 194.
7 esat.sun.ac.za./index.php./Lew_James for information about Sid James' parents
8 Ross, R., *Sid James: Cockney Rebel* (JR Books Ltd, London, 2009), p. 11.
9 Connor, J. and Burton, P., *Life With Kenneth Connor* (FeedaRead.com, Solihull, 2014), p. 19.
10 Cooper, B. R., *Great Britons of Stage and Screen: In Conversation* (Rowman and Littlefield, Lanham, Maryland, 2015), p. 26.
11 Connor, J. and Burton, P., *Life With Kenneth Connor* (FeedaRead.com, Solihull, 2014), pp. 85–191.
12 Foster, A. and Furst, S., *Radio Comedy* 1939–1968 (Virgin Books, London, 1996), p. 28.
13 bbc.co.uk/mediacentre/proginfo/2016/itma
14 Sykes, E., *Eric Sykes' Comedy Heroes* (Virgin Books, London, 2003), p. 100.
15 Merriman, A., *Hattie* (Aurum Press, London, 2007), pp. 122–124.
16 *Ibid.*, p. 142.
17 *Ibid.*, p. 163.
18 *Ibid.*, pp. 198–200.
19 televisionheaven.co.uk/biographies/bernard-bresslaw

20 Wetstone, D., 'Panto's Giant Carries On Regardless', *Newcastle Journal*, 31 December 1990.
21 Windsor, B., *All of Me: My Extraordinary Life* (Headline, London, 2000), pp. 68–70.
22 See Windsor, B., *All of Me: My Extraordinary Life* (Headline, London, 2000), pp. 149–150 for just one example.
23 'Old Bailey jury hears story of killing in pinball arcade', *The Guardian*, 11 November 1980, p. 4.
24 'Errant Knight jailed for 7 years over £6m robbery', *The Guardian*, 5 January 1995, p. 5.
25 'Comedienne with Classic Clown's Mask', *The Times*, Friday 4 December 1964, p. 15.
26 en.m.wikipedia.org/wiki/Patsy_Rowlands#Later_years
27 chroniclelive.co.uk/news/north-east-news/farewell-geordie-born-carry-favourite-1478917
28 en.m.wikipedia.org/wiki/Jack_Douglas_(actor)
29 carryon.org.uk/articles26.htm
30 heraldscotland.com/news/11997657.charity-performance-for-actor-terry-thomas/
31 chestercinemas.co.uk/latest-update-january-2018/
32 Phillips, L., *Hello* (Orion Books, London, 2006), p. 196.
33 *Ibid.*, p. 201.
34 *Ibid.*, p. 215.
35 *Ibid.*, p. 367.

Chapter 36

1 detecs.org/fen.html
2 morristonorpheus.com/eric-rogers
3 carryon.org.uk/ericrogers.htm

Bibliography

Books

Bright, M. and Ross, *Mr Carry On* (BBC Worldwide, London, 2000)
Butters, W., *Whatshiname: The Life and Death of Charles Hawtrey* (Tomahawk Press, Sheffield, 2010)
Connor, J. and Burton, P., *Life With Kenneth Connor* (FeedaRead.com, Solihull, 2014)
Cooper, B. R., *Great Britons of Stage and Screen: In Conversation* (Rowman and Littlefield, Lanham, Maryland, 2015)
Foster, A. and Furst, S., *Radio Comedy* 1939–1968 (Virgin Books, London, 1996)
Goodwin, *Sid James: A Biography* (Virgin Books, London, 2011)
Merriman, A., *Hattie* (Aurum Press, London, 2007)
Monkhouse, B., *Crying with Laughter* (Century Random House UK, London, 1993)
Pertwee, J. and Howe, D. J., *I Am the Doctor: Jon Pertwee's Final Memoir* (Virgin Books, London, 1996)
Phillips, L., *Hello* (Orion Books, London, 2006)
Powell, M., *Million Dollar Movie* (William Heinemann, London, 1990)
Ross, A., *Too Happy a Face: The Authorised Biography of Joan Sims* (Fantom Films Ltd, Coventry, 2017)
Ross, R., *Sid James: Cockney Rebel* (JR Books Ltd, London, 2009)
Ross, R., *The Carry On Companion* (Batsford, London, 1998)
Ross, R., *The Complete Sid James* (Reynolds and Hearn, Cheltenham, 2007)
Sharpe, G., *Gambling's Strangest Moments* (Robson Books Ltd, London, 2005)
Stevens, C., *Born Brilliant: The Life of Kenneth Williams* (John Murray, London, 2010)
Sykes, E., *Eric Sykes' Comedy Heroes* (Virgin Books, London, 2003)
Williams, K., *Just Williams* (JM Dent & Sons, London, 1985)
Williams, K., *The Kenneth Williams Diaries* (HarperCollins, London, 1993)
Williams, K., *The Kenneth Williams Letters* (HarperCollins, London, 1994)
Windsor, B., *All of Me: My Extraordinary Life* (Headline, London, 2000)

Articles/Newspapers

'Anglo Success in Jersey', *Kinematograph Weekly*, 13 August 1959
'Comedienne with Classic Clown's Mask', *The Times*, Friday, 4 December 1964, p. 15
Daily Record, 16 August 1992
'Errant Knight jailed for 7 years over £6m robbery', *The Guardian*, 5 January 1995, p. 5
Jenour, K., 'Now Showing', *Daily Mirror*, 20 April 1978
Jenour, K., 'Saucy Carry On Has Babs Fuming', *Daily Mirror*, 19 April 1978
Kinematograph Weekly, 5 December 1957
Letter to *The Guardian*, Alexander Walker, 17 March 2000
Northern Daily Mail, 3 August 1957
'Old Bailey jury hears story of killing in pinball arcade', *The Guardian*, 11 November 1980, p. 4
'Still time to buy a ticket', *Kent and Sussex Courier*, Friday, 25 March 1966
'Successful Film-making on a Small Budget: Mr Peter Rogers Tells How He Does It', *The Times*, Thursday, 5 November 1959
Truth, 22 November 1957
West London Observer, Friday 16 August 1957
Wetstone, D., 'Panto's Giant Carries On Regardless', *Newcastle Journal*, 31 December 1990

Websites

bbc.co.uk/mediacentre/proginfo/2016/itma
bbfc.co.uk/education/case-studies/carry-on-camping
bbfc.co.uk/education/case-studies/carry-on-up-the-khyber-1968
carryon.org.uk/articles26.htm
carryon.org.uk/ericrogers.htm
chestercinemas.co.uk/latest-update-january-2018/
chroniclelive.co.uk/news/north-east-news/farewell-geordie-born-carry-favourite-1478917
detecs.org/fen.html
en.m.wikipedia.org/wiki/Jack_Douglas_(actor)
en.m.wikipedia.org/wiki/Patsy_Rowlands#Later_years
esat.sun.ac.za./index.php./Lew_James
gylesbrandreth.net/blog/2018/4/14/remembering-kenneth-williams
heraldscotland.com/news/11997657.charity-performance-for-actor-terry-thomas/
morristonorpheus.com/eric-rogers
televisionheaven.co.uk/biographies/bernard-bresslaw